VEGETARIA

This is the most compre... ld, carried and relied on by ...ns, and recommended by a... nd magazines.

It's also handy for mea... will massively up your chances when dating a veggie or vegan.

Featuring...

145 vegetarian restaurants and cafes and 27 vegetarian take-aways across the capital including ...
18 vegetarian restaurants within 10 minutes walk of Oxford Street
4 vegetarian restaurants and cafes in Covent Garden
38 all-you-can-eat veggie buffets under a tenner, some under £6
238 more restaurants with big vegetarian menus
300 wholefood and green shops
Maps, features on vegetarian living, photos, accommodation

See how many restaurants, cafes and take-aways are in your area:

	Vegan	Veggie	Omni	Shops	Page
Soho & W1	8	11	32	23	49
Covent Garden	1	3	10	13	72
Bloomsbury	2	3	10	2	88
Euston	2	4	4	4	106
The City	2	7	14	10	128
South Bank	–	1	17	2	142
East End	5	15	29	51	153
North	6	24	44	62	195
South	4	23	36	71	265
Sloane Zone	1	1	15	21	320
West	2	47	37	53	332
TOTAL	33	139	244	312	

For what's new in this edition, see page 8

"For people living in or visiting the capital, this book is
more important than the A-Z."
The Vegetarian Society

Vegetarian London

6th edition

Introduction   6

What's New 8
My Favourite Veggie Table . . .11

Veggie Pages   14

Raw 28
Shoes 36
Wine 40
Vegan Festivals 44
Chain Restaurants 46

Central London   48

* Soho (MAP) 49
* Covent Garden (MAP) 72
* Bloomsbury (MAP) 88
* Tottenham Court Rd (MAP) .98
* Euston (MAP) 106
* Marylebone/Mayfair (MAP) .116
* The City (MAP) 128
* South Bank (MAP) 143

East London   153

* Brick Lane & Spitalfields . .154
* Broadway Market 162
Canary Wharf 168
* East Ham 170
* Forest Gate 172
* Globe Town (MAP) 174
Hackney 179
Hoxton & Shoreditch 185
Leyton, Stratford, Wanstead .189
Walthamstow & Chingford . .191
Essex 193

North London   195

* Camden (MAP) 196
Finchley 208
Finsbury Park & Archway . . .211
Golders Green 215
Hampstead & W.Hampstead .218
Hendon & Brent Cross 222
Highbury 224
Highgate 227
* Islington (MAP) 229
Kings Cross 238
Kentish Town 240
Muswell Hill 243
Crouch End 245
* Primrose Hill 246
* Stoke Newington & 250
  Newington Green (MAP) . . .257
Wood Green 259
Rest of North London 260
Hertfordshire 262

* indicates a VEGGIE HOTSPOT with a high concentration of dining and shopping.

(MAP) indicates a local map showing restaurants, shops and anything else we liked.

See also the inside front cover for the master map of London's veggie areas.

Contents

South & Surrey — 265

Brixton 266
Battersea & Clapham (MAP) .270
Crystal Palace 278
Greenwich 281
Kingston–upon–Thames 282
London Bridge 284
Putney 288
Richmond–on–Thames 289
Streatham 293
* Tooting & Balham 296
* Vauxhall 302
Walworth 306
Wimbledon 308
Rest of South-East 309
Rest of South-West 317

West & Middlesex — 319

Sloane Zone 320
(Victoria to Fulham)
Bayswater 332
Chiswick 336
Ealing 338
* Edgware 342
* Hammersmith, Olympia &
Shepherds Bush (MAP) . . .347
* Harrow & Kenton 356
Hounslow & Heathrow 362
Kilburn & Willesden 364
* Kingsbury 368
Notting Hill 371
Southall 375
Twickenham 376
* Wembley (MAP) 378
Rest of Middlesex 388

Hot Tips — 389

Accommodation . . . .
Guest Houses & Hotels . .390
Backpacker Hostels 398
Camping in London 399
Moving to London 401
Caterers 402
Local Groups 404
National Organisations 410

Where to Eat? — 411

Vegan 420
Organic 421
Cheap 422
Posh 423
Drink Alcohol 424
Coffee & Tea 425
Veggie Breakfast 428
With the Kids 429

Index 430

For latest openings visit
www.vegetarianguides.co.uk/updates

Credits

Design and maps by Mickaël Charbonnel, Jill Spence and Alexandra Boylan. Cover photo by Mike Bourke.

Photos by Tony Bishop Weston, Alex Bourke, Mike Bourke, Mickaël Charbonnel, Chava Eichner, Jennifer Wharton.
Vegetarian Guides logo designed by Marion Gillet.

Contributors: Ljuba Aiardo-Esposito, Carole Backler, Anna Ber, Jasmijn de Boo, Lukasz Birycki, Tony & Yvonne Bishop Weston, Kim Coussell, Alistair Currie, Peter Despard, Lesley & Paul Dove, Simon England, Paul Gaynor, Rachel George, Sean Gifford, Jonahan Grey, Dr Michael Grill, Dr Mike Hooper, Brian Jacobs, Ayda Kay, Lily Khan, Christine Klein, Laurence Klein, London Vegans, London Vegan Campaigns, Caroline McAleese, Nitin Mehta M.B.E., Åsa Melander, Dr Rima Morrell, Yasmin Patel, Sherry Nicholls, everyone at London Vegans, Lisa Preti, Claire Ranyard, Miriam Rice, Julie Rosenfield, Bani Sethi, Mahersh & Nishma Shah, Zofia Torun-Shaw, Kelly Slade, Patricia Tricker, Jennifer Wharton, Lucy Wills, Ronny Worsey and everyone else ...
THANK YOU!!!

Cataloguing in details

VEGETARIAN LONDON

(6th edition) by Alex Bourke

ISBN 1–902259–08–4
EAN 978–1–902259–08–6

Published April 2008
by Vegetarian Guides Ltd
PO Box 2284 London W1A 5UH, UK

Trade and mail order:
vegetarianguides.co.uk
Tel: 020–3239 8433 (24 hrs)
International: +44–2032398433

Updates to this guide at:
vegetarianguides.co.uk/updates

Link and earn 10% commisssion:
vegetarianguides.co.uk/affiliate

Printed by Mega Printing, www.mega.com.tr

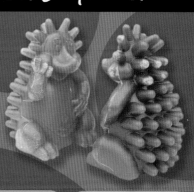

INTRODUCTION

Some people think it's hard to eat vegetarian, vegan, or just less meat and dairy and more of the good stuff.

But with this guide in your pocket or bag it's going to be really, really easy, tasty, inexpensive and heaps of fun.

Whether you care for animals, health, the environment, or relentless self-indulgence, enjoy eating and shopping your way around London's 145 veggie restaurants and 300 wholefood and cruelty-free shops.

Alex Bourke
Founder, Vegetarian Guides

Favourite cafe: **Beatroot**
Favourite restaurant: **VitaOrganic**
alex@vegetarianguides.co.uk

NEVER OUT OF DATE !

PRINTABLE UPDATES TO VEGETARIAN LONDON
www.vegetarianguides.co.uk/updates

Features about veggie travel
Extracts from Vegetarian Guides
Vegetarian Festivals Calendar
Overseas veggie travel websites

My Favourite Veggie Table

Some of London's most popular V-Listers reveal where they hang out and what keeps them veggie.

flavourphotos.com

Benjamin Zephaniah
Poet & TV Presenter

My favourite place to eat in London is **Chawalla's** in Green Street, full of Indians, the real taste of authentic south Indian, but they also have burger and chips if you want it.

I'm a vegan because I will not eat my friends, vegetables are sexy and vegans are great lovers (I've been told).

www.benjaminzephaniah.com

What's new in this edition

These are just the veggie places. There are lots more new omnivorous entries too that cater well for veggies and vegans. (V) = vegan

CENTRE

Buddha Cafe (V)
Buffet V (V)
Gi Gi Hut (V)
Greens & Beans
Saf (V)
Sagar
Tai Express (V)
Tai Piccadilly (V)
Veg Theobalds (V)
VitaOrganic (V)

EAST

Amita
Chennai
Chennai Dosa
Gossip
Hornbeam
Rainforest Creations
Rootmaster (V)
Saravana Bhavan

NORTH

Green Note
InSpiral Lounge
My Village
Straw Bale Cafe
Woodlands

SOUTH

Cafe Crema
Courtyard Cafe
Lorentson's
Pulse
Saravana Bhavan
Spirited Palace (V)
Spring Gardens Cafe
Synergy Centre

WEST

Bush Garden Cafe
Celebration
Chhappan Bhog
Chennai Dosa
Delhiwala
Dosa Junction
Mr Man
Mayura
Sagar
Sanghamam
Saravana Bhavan
Satyam
Tamu Tamu
Udupi Palace

BODYCARE

B
Helios
Lush
Neal's Yard
   Apothecary

FOOD SHOPS

Ambala
Earth Natural
The Grocery
Julian Graves
Mother Earth
My Village
Revital
Simply Natural
Total Organics
Wholefoods Market
Wholsum
Unpackaged
Zelda's Pod

HAIRDRESSER

Daniel Field

SHOE SHOPS

Birkenstock
Crocs
Equa
Natural Shoe Store
Stella McCartney

VEGGIE PAGES

Directory
Raw
Shoes
Wine
Festival Calendar
Chains

(V) vegan place

My Favourite Veggie Table

Some of London's most popular V-Listers reveal where they hang out and what keeps them veggie.

Dr Mike Hooper
General Practitioner

My favourite veggie restaurant in London changes regularly but at the moment it would have to be **Pogo** for its variation, decor and spirit of cooperation, or **Rootmaster** for its style, professional service and originality.

I went veggie about ten years ago, definitely for animal welfare reasons but as time goes on the health benefits and knock-on environmental effects (the latter more so with veganism) are becoming clearer.

Dominika Stachowska
Lead Practice Nurse

My favourite veggie restaurant is **222** in West Kensington for great food, good options, quite a large place compared to Mildred's and they have vegan wine.

I went vegetarian originally for health but now also for green reasons and as well as recycling I don't wear leather.

Andrew Knight
The Ethical Vet

For me, at the moment, it would have to be the **Tai** buffet in Greek Street, Soho – it's all you can eat!

I went vegan to impress a former girlfriend – it's the most powerful way you can do good in the world.

www.vegepets.info, see advert page 14.

Jasmijn de Boo, Chair of Animals Count political party

I like **Bonnington Cafe** and **222**. I became vegetarian when I saw trucks with screaming pigs on their way to the slaughterhouse while I cycled to school. Later I became vegan because we don't need to use animals to satisfy our needs. Plant-based diets take a lot less water and energy and do not contribute to global warming while meat production is very polluting. www.animalscount.org

Robin Lane & Alison Coe London Vegan Festival

Robin: I love **Buffet V** in New Oxford Street with a fantastic selection of Chinese food, really reasonably priced and staff are very friendly, plus I like eating with chopsticks. **Alison**: I love **Beatroot** for great food, friendly atmos-phere, right in the centre and lovely smoothies and juices. We are vegan because it's the most compassionate diet, it uses less land, and with a proper balance it's the healthiest diet you can have. www.vegan-campaigns.org.uk/festival

Johannes Bishop-Weston London's youngest environmental campaigner

Here I am aged one and three quarters handing out leaflets about World Vegan Day 2007. The UN report *Livestock's Long Shadow* revealed that cows are worse than cars when it comes to making our environmental predicament even worse. I say being vegan is "Easy!" – my favourite vegan foods are baked beans, potatoes and chocolate.

fashion victim

leather is dead skin – think about it ...

H + T Accountancy Services

H+T Bookkeeping Services provide a complete outsourced accounting service. Leaving you free to concentrate on other areas of your business'.

Accountancy Services
Computerised Sage Line 50.
Monthly management report.
Year end accounts.
Prepare cash flow and budgets.
Payroll: Weekly and monthly payslips.
Dealing with Inland Revenue affairs.
VAT: We prepare monthly and quarterly
VAT returns in-house or at your premises.
Self-employment
We can give financial advice on your new business as a sole trader, partnership or limited company. We can organise all the paperwork for you at a small fee.

Company Formation: We help you to set up a limited company at no extra charge.
Tax: We offer services and advice on self-assessment tax, corporation tax, P11ds etc.
What is our fee?
We aim to provide an affordable service for start up companies and small business. Call for a quote and we can save you hundred of pounds on your accountancy fees.
Offices
34 Marsh Green Road, Dagenham, Essex RM10 9PR.
77 Warner Place, Bethnal Green, E2 7DB.
Tel 0770 460 4159. Fax : 0208 220 8482

14

Veggie Pages

Directory of vegetarian businesses and advice

London is the best place in Europe to be veggie or vegan. There are so many great places to eat and shop. But there are stacks of other great resources too to help you and this new section lists some of the best.

Accountants

www.jacksonandjackson.co.uk
Vegan accountant specialising in small businesses and charities.

H&T Bookkeeping www.ht-as.com
Accountant to Vegetarian Guides, one of the partners is vegetarian. See page 14.

Animal Rights

Free leaflets and websites to open the eyes of non-veggie

Vegan Society 16 page booklet

friends:
www.animalaid.org.uk, p.24
www.peta.org.uk., p.13
www.viva.org.uk, p.21
www.vegansociety.com, p.14
www.vegancampaigns.org.uk
www.arcnews.org.uk Online animal rights magazine.
www.veggies.org.uk Online directory of every veggie and vegan business in the country.

Box Schemes

Too busy to shop? Some wholefood stores have box schemes that deliver to your door. As do these specialist companies:

www.farmaround.co.uk. Page 21
www.organicdelivery.co.uk
www.woodfieldorganics.com
www.growingcommunities.org
www.abelandcole.co.uk

Caterers

Many restaurants offer outside catering for your wedding, party or corporate event, and this is indicated in their entries. Specialist veggie caterers are listed on pages 403–5. Our favourite is **Shambu's Kitchen** who do amazing creamy vegan curries and crunchy chocolate sweets.

The Window in Islington is London's only corporate venue with all-veggie catering. See page 405.

Charities

Millions of people lack clean water or sufficient food in a world bursting with resources. These vegetarian run charities provide clean water, emergency vegetarian food, tools and seeds, giving life and independence to the world's most deprived:

www.amurt.org.uk
www.ffl.org
www.hippocharity.org.uk
www.vegfamcharity.org.uk

Animal sanctuaries allow abused and rescued farm animals to live out their lives free from human persecution. You can sponsor an animal, raise funds for a project, or volunteer to help out. FRIEND farmed animal rescue in Kent is supported by the London animal rights movement:

www.friendsanimalrescue.org.uk

For a comprehensive list of animal sanctuaries see the online Animal Contacts Directory published by Veggies:

www.veggies.org.uk/acd

Cosmetics & Bodycare

The following brands are entirely or mostly vegan (no animal testing or ingredients): Aveda, B, Beauty Without Cruelty, Dr Hauschka, Earth Natural, Faith In Nature, Green People, Jäson, Jurlique, Lavera, Lush, Neal's Yard, Ren, Urtekram, Weleda and Yaoh. They can be found in wholefood stores across London.

Shops in central London with bodycare and natural beauty products and trained advisors are Alara, Antimony Balance, B, Fresh & Wild, Helios, Lush, Neal's Yard Apothecary, Planet Organic and Revital.

Look for the Vegan Society sunflower, which guarantees products contain no animal ingredients and are not animal tested.

Dating

Don't like the idea of kissing someone with chicken stuck between their teeth? Then find yourself a lovely veggie or vegan at one of these three excellent businesses:

Contact Centre or VMM, see next page. Also:

www.veggieromance.com

Dentists

TLC Dental Surgery in East London offers mercury-free NHS and private treatments by vegetarian dentists Sunita and Sanjit Chaudhuri. See page 171. www.tlcdental.co.uk

Dog & Cat Food

Cats and dogs can thrive without animal products. See the website of London based vet **Andrew Knight** (page 11): www.vegepets.info (page 14)

VeggiePets sells all kinds of dog chow and moggy fodder mail order. Tel. 01243-537 641, See page 5.

VeggiePets.com

Arcnews's (page 15) cats love Redwood's fake tuna and salmon and Beanies/Fry's mince (in health food shops).

Entertainers

World famous entertainer **Rubber Ritchie** can bring a twist to any event. The vegan contortionist has performed to astonished audiences around the world in theatre, tv, film, opera and many others. www.flexinthecity.com

Mishel veggie children's party entertainer and caterer. Tel: 079623 46087.

Fitness & Bodybuilding

The following groups are for veggie and vegan cyclists, runners, athletes and body-builders:

www.vcac.vegfolk.co.uk
www.veganfitness.org
www.veganbodybuilding.org

Vegan martial arts champion James Southwood teaches French kickboxing at Waterloo:

www.londonsavate.co.uk

GNC shops specialise in bodybuilding supplements.

Gardening

Is it vegetarian to use fertiliser made from blood or bone meal, or even manure from "slave" animals? Vegan organic horticulture cuts the last link with the slaughter-house. The **Vegan Organic Network** can tell you how.

www.veganorganic.net

Squires Garden Centre in Twickenham has a wholefood store in the car park. See page 377.

Hairdressers

Daniel Field in Enfield (page 263) have their own lines of vegan products. Aveda (Covent Garden, Marylebone) have some (but not all) too.

Holidays

Holidays with vegetarian food:
www.vegiventures.com p.18
www.bicycle-beano.co.uk
www.veggiesnow.org p.18
www.yuvaholidays.com
www.vegtravel.com (USA)

Hypnotherapy

Vegan Harley Street clinical hypnotherapist **Brian Jacobs** can help you quit smoking or lose weight, overcome phobias, handle stress, and trains hypnotherapists (p.43).

www.hypnoticsolutions.co.uk

Ice-cream (dairy-free)

These fabulous treats have never seen the inside of a cow and are available from wholefood stores:

B'Nice rice-cream p.10
Booja Booja (cashew)
Swedish Glace (soya)
Tofutti (soya)

Magazines

Lifescape has features on vegetarian living. Available from Planet Organic or Fresh & Wild.
www.lifescapemag.com

The Vegan, published by the Vegan Society, available in some health food shops or by subscription.
www.vegansociety.com

Vegan Views is a quarterly UK vegan magazine. £4 for 4 issues including UK postage. Send cheques/postal orders to Vegan Views, Flat A15, 20 Dean Park Road, Bournemouth, Dorset, BH1 1JB. Also downloadable from the website for free.
www.veganviews.org.uk

Macrobiotics

A system of eating based on Japanese wholefoods, which greatly enriches the veggie

Vegan Views
A Forum for Vegan Opinion
No. 113   Winter 2007/8   £1

OI. ANGLERS' SLING YOUR HOOK!

In this Issue:

4 Books
7 Letters
7 Buddhism and Meat-Eating
9 A Look at the News
10 Feeding the World...
11 Non-Animal Experiments
12 Poetry
13 Cartoon
14 Vegan Organic Growing
15 Recipes
17 Veggies in your Area
20 Business with Ethics

"It was this big!"
(cartoon by Ruth Lewis)

culinary repertoire. **Luscious Organics** wholefood store and cafe in Kensington High Street is owned by macrobiotic teachers Simon and Dragana Brown.

www.macrobiotics.co.uk
www.chienergy.co.uk

Meat and cheese substitutes

Check the fridge in any of the food shops in this book for amazing ranges of fake "meat", burgers, sausages and "cheese" from Beanies/Fry's, Redwood and Linda McCartney. New for 2008 from Italy is Yagga who make vegan steaks, roast and strips. For eating out, the bargain Chinese vegan buffet restaurants have various fake meats that fool meat-eaters.

www.beanieshealthfoods.co.uk

www.lindamccartneyfoods.co.uk
www.redwoodfoods.co.uk
www.yagga.co.uk

Medical Herbalism

Herbalism is the indigenous healing tradition of the British Isles and indeed the whole world. Medical herbalists normally have a degree in the subject and 500 hours of clinical training. Two vegan central London practitioners: Lakshmi Shivalanka, Tel. 07944 762873, and nadiabrydon.com

Nutritionists

Feeling low on energy? Even veggies and vegans can succumb to the effects of a modern stressful lifestyle. If your GP can't help, book a consultation with a qualified veggie nutritionist such as Yvonne Bishop-Weston (page 23):

www.foodsforlife.org.uk

Vegan caterer and nutritionist Liz Cook publishes gorgeous nutrition wallcharts for your kitchen.

www.thevegancook.co.uk

The Vegan Society and the Vegetarian and Vegan Foundation (VVF, page 21) have lots of free information on nutrition on their websites and as leaflets and answer

Plant Based Nutrition
Healthy eating without
animal products

16-page Vegan Society booklet

Animal Aid gets results - please join today!

Recent successes include:

- Cambridge University has abandoned plans for a new primate research laboratory, following a campaign co-ordinated by Animal Aid.
- We persuaded the Focus DIY chain to stop selling all animals by the end of 2005.
- Our new report on livestock markets has been welcomed by DEFRA.

But there is so much more to do. With your help, we can:

- Continue to implement vital, imaginative and successful campaigns
- Produce more reports exposing the truth about animal cruelty
- Recruit and train more school speakers
- Provide all our resources free of charge

queries:

www.vegansociety.com
www.vvf.org.uk

A handy summary is the free 16-page booklet *Plant Based Nutrition and Health* available from the Vegan Society, or read it on their website.

The Vegan Society has just published a catering pack for hospitals and care homes so do help them get them out there.

Vegan Catering Guide
for hospitals and care homes

Omegas

Fish are not the optimum source of omega-3 essential fatty acids they're cracked up to be. Firstly there are not enough fish left in the world for everyone to be able to eat them. There are numerous plants sources that are both sustainable and also safer, especially hemp and flax seeds, either ground or as oil in health food shops. Unlike oily fish they do not come with added PCB's, dioxins or mercury, so you can safely eat them every day and when pregnant. Talk to the staff in your local health food store or read up on the subject on the Vegan Society website.

www.vegansociety.com/html/food/nutrition/e_fatty_acids.php

Political Parties

Which one is best for animals?

Conservatives want to bring back hunting with dogs.

Labour supports shooting, have failed to effectively ban hunting with dogs, and have ducked their 1997 manifesto commitment to an independent review of animal experiments, presumably because they receive multi-million pound donations from pro-vivisection people who fear the outcome.

Liberal Democrats have proposed an Animal Protection Commission.

The Green Party has policies on animal welfare and making vegetarian food available everywhere, and some of their elected representatives are veggie, such as Hackney Councillor vegan Mischa Borris.

25

The **Protecting Animals in Democracy** website compares the policies of the four main parties, and whether their actions once elected match their rhetoric:

www.vote4animals.org.uk

The new **Animals Count** party (page 21) is modelled on the Dutch Party for the Animals, which now has two MP's and a senator.

www.animalscount.org

Removals

The Big Van Company in London is run by vegan Graham Neale. See page 27.

Shoes & accessories

Non-leather shoes are available in Neal Street in Covent Garden at **Birkenstock, Crocs** and the **Natural Shoe Store**. High fashion women's shoes can be found at **Equa** in Islington and **Stella McCartney** in Mayfair. Many Londoners take a day trip to Brighton to visit the shop **Vegetarian Shoes** in Gardner Street (closed Sundays) or buy from mail order companies. See the shoes feature on p.37.

Soya Milk

Dropping cow's milk gives up the last connection with beef and veal. If you "hate" soya milk, try sweetened Alpro/ Provamel on cereal, or blend a glass with a banana or two for a smoothie and be surprised!

Travel

Vegetarian Guides sells guides to London, Britain, Europe and USA/Canada. The website has links to restaurant listings all over the world.

www.vegetarianguides.co.uk

TV on the internet

VeggieVision.co.uk (page 9) has mini-programmes about lifestyle, while **PetaTV**.com focuses on animal rights.

Wine and Beer

Some wholefood stores sell vegetarian wine and beer that has been fined without the use of animal products. Mail order suppliers include **Festival Wines, Vintage Roots** and **Vinceremos.** See the alcohol feature on page 40.

Going Veggie or Vegan

A funky new CD guide to everything vegan is available from the Vegan Society, or free to schools.

www.vegansociety.com

For free Go Veg packs:

Animal Aid, page 2
PETA, page 13
The Vegan Society, page 14
Viva!, page 21

Or go to a meeting of one of London's many vegetarian and vegan groups, especially **London Vegans** or **Vegan Campaigns**. See pp406-411.

www.londonvegans.org.uk
www.vegancampaigns.org.uk

Vegan Buddies is an online discussion group for new vegans:
www.veganbuddies.org.uk
See also pages 407-411.

What's On Listings

Green Events free magazine and the online **London Vegans Diary** list vegetarian events across London.

www.londonvegans.org.uk (p.407)
www.greenevents.co.uk (p.45)

Wanted for next edition

Veggie builders, carpenters, electricians, child-minders, you name it we'll list it.
updates@vegetarianguides.co.uk

*the*fresh network

The one-stop shop for all things raw

- gourmet raw ingredients
- raw seeds, nuts and nut butters
- raw crackers and bars
- raw chocolate
- natural seasonings and sweeteners
- cold-pressed oils
- sprouting seeds and equipment
- superfoods
- top-quality natural supplements
- cleansing and detox products
- raw, vegan and organic skin care, body care and hair care
- kitchen equipment
- books and dvds
- teleclasses
- seminars
- raw food preparation classes

*the*fresh network

+44 (0)845 833 7017
orders@fresh-network.com
www.fresh-network.com

Raw food, pure health

by Sarah Best

*If there's one thing better for you than being vegan, it's being a vegan who eats plenty of nutrient-rich whole foods in their natural state, says **Sarah Best**, the editor of **Get Fresh**! magazine. Here she outlines what raw food can do for you and some easy ways to incorporate more of it into your life.*

You've probably noticed that raw is *in*. It seems everyone is juicing and detoxing. Is this just another passing diet fad to separate the gullible from their hard-earned cash? Or is there something in it?

The less processed a food is, the better. Does this mean we should all give up cooked food and 'go raw'. No! Although many thrive on this diet and it is becoming an increasingly popular choice, it is not for everyone. However, we can all benefit from including more natural raw foods. More energy, easier weight loss and greater mental clarity are just a few of the benefits you can expect.

Be aware that you may initially feel worse before you feel better. Unless you're both very young *and* very healthy you may experience unpleasant detoxification symptoms when you increase the amount of raw food you eat. This doesn't mean that it's not working for you; just that it is very powerful so it's best to take it slowly and if in doubt, always seek the guidance of an experienced practitioner.

1. Expand your horizons

If your 'five a day' consists mainly of bananas, apples, carrots, potatoes and iceberg lettuce it's time to branch out. There are so many fruits and vegetables – aim to experiment with a new one every week. And while you're at it, try to make your fruit and veg intake at least ten-a-day.

...Raw food, pure health

2. Start an indoor garden

Think healthy eating has to be expensive? Growing your own sprouts takes seconds and costs pennies. They are an easy way to add more organic raw vegetables to your diet, and it's hard to find foods more filled with enzymes and vital nutrition. Lentils or mung beans are a great way to start. Soak a cup of them in water for 8 hours, rinse and leave in a glass jar to grow. They'll be ready in 2–4 days and all you need to do is remember to rinse them each day. Once ready, they'll usually keep for up to a week in an air-tight container in the fridge.

3. Buy a juicer

No multi-vitamin and mineral pill can rival the nutrient infusion you get from fresh raw juices. Think you can't afford one? You can get them for less than £40 these days, and as Tony Robbins wrote in his book Unlimited Power: "If you own a car but not a juicer, sell the car and buy a juicer. It will take you further!" It may sound crazy, but not to those who have discovered the power of juicing.

4. Learn to make to-live-for dressings

These will transform any salad into a gourmet treat. Try a plate of dark green leaves such as spinach, rocket and lamb's lettuce mixed with a big dollop of guacamole, or a bowl of seaweed salad (in small packs at health stores to rehydrate at home) with an oriental dressing made of equal parts olive oil and soya sauce, and agave nectar, fresh grated ginger and chilli to taste.

5. Discover novel uses for the avocado

Avocado is a *great* addition to fruit smoothies. giving them a wonderfully creamy texture that turns them into decadent yet guilt-free puddings. For example, blend half an avocado with half a banana and a ripe mango. Seriously...do it. You'll thank me.

...Raw food, pure health

Make raw chocolate dessert by blending two ripe avocados with two tablespoons of agave nectar, and two tablespoons of carob powder or raw chocolate powder. Taste it and add more powder or sweetener if desired, then drift off into chocolate heaven.

6. Invest in a raw recipe book

Whether you want advice on simple salads, multi-course dinner parties, raw burritos, biscuits, Mexican, Japanese or Italian – there is a book out there for you. See www.fresh-network.com for a huge selection of books on all aspects of raw food and holistic health and if you are confused as to which one is right for you, ring 0845 833 7017 for friendly advice.

7. Get surfing

You can network with thousands of raw-minded individuals around the world. Check out the forums at **rawfood.com** and **rawfoodtalk.com**. You can comment, ask questions and add your own words of wisdom; but if you'd rather just read what everyone is saying, that's fine too.

Blogs can be a great source of ideas and inspiration. You will be amazed at the number constantly updated sites which include food diaries and inspiring transformation stories. Check out the 'Big Ultimate Raw Food Blog List' at **www.rawfoodrightnow.com**. You may even be inspired to start your own!

8. Read *Get Fresh!* magazine

The world's leading magazine on the raw diet and lifestyle is a quarterly source of raw inspiration and information, full of ideas, recipes, advice and inspiring life stories. Most importantly, it makes raw food fun! Readers say how much they look forward to it and how much it has changed their lives.

9. Attend a raw food workshop

There are numerous raw food experts in and around London offering classes on anything from the psychological and social side of being more raw, to raw recipes and shopping. These can save you years of trial and error. You'll also have loads of fun and meet new friends. See the end of this section for our recommendations.

10. Become a festival-goer

London has an annual raw food **Festival of Life** in September where you can be inspired by top speakers, watch uncooking demos, taste new foods, shop and meet others into plant-based diets and ethical living.? For this and other raw events see
www.totalrawfood.com/events

Raw food is also showing up more and more at mainstream vegetarian and vegan events, including the annual London Vegan Festival. See **www.vegetarianguides.co.uk/calendar**

...Raw food, pure health

Raw-friendly restaurants

Although London has a thriving raw vegan community, it lags far behind US cities like New York which already has 10 raw restaurants. That has all changed with top raw chef Chad Sarno opening gourmet restaurant Saf in April 2008 in Shoreditch (see page 134) and others eyeing the capital.

Vita Organic, Soho   Innovative raw alongside lightly cooked. Fresh juices, a salad bar and buffet, a la carte, even raw cakes. (page 54)

Madder Rose Café, Primrose Hill New cafe in a yoga centre with lots of raw. (page 248)

Inspiral Lounge, Camden   Organic raw food, smoothies, chocolate and books in new music venue & cafe. (page 198).

222, Fulham   Bargain lunch buffet 7 days a week and great salads. (page 351)

Bonnington Café, Vauxhall   Every 2nd, 4th and 5th Sunday is hosted by raw chef Anya Ladra. (page 304)

Tony's Holistic Centre, Kings Cross   Cafe with raw mains, salads, juices, smoothies and chocolate. (page 239)

Rainforest Creations, Spitalfields and other London markets. Raw buffet and cakes. (page 161)

Shopping

The larger health stores in American cities have fridges full of gourmet raw foods from falafels and burgers to fresh cakes and puddings, and packaged goods aisles boasting raw crackers, breads, bars and cookies. In London raw chocolate and energy bars are now in most health stores and several bigger ones have dedicated raw sections where you can stock up on goji berries, maca powder, cacao butter and other store cupboard staples. Of course you'll be well catered for in any supermarket fresh produce section, greengrocer or market.

Brixton Wholefoods Raw superfoods and chocs. (page 269)

Little Miss Tree raw vegan chocolate, truffles and sweets available from Kitchen Buddy (see below) and at Inspiral Lounge, Unpackaged (Islington) and Soho Fresh & Wild.

Raw Food Courses in London

Nadia Brydon www.nadiabrydon.com Pimlico, SW1.

Andrew Davis www.therawfoodschool.com Soho, Chiswick, Richmond

Kitchen Buddy Theresa Webb kitchenbuddy@hotmail.com. Tel:020-8697 2755. Courses plus Little Miss Tree raw vegan chocolates.

Catherine Parker www.rawteacher.com/catherineparker Courses in N4. See page 33.

Peter Pure www.rawfoodparty.com Central London.

Raw Fairies www.rawfairies.com Also raw food deliveries.

Sweet Sensations www.lizbygrave.co.uk Chocolate and dessert workshops in north London or your home.

The Author

Sarah Best *is the editor of* Get Fresh! *magazine, the world's leading magazine on raw food and holistic health. Published four times a year, each issue is packed full of cutting edge nutritional information, expert advice, news, reviews, inspiring true stories and delicious recipes. Get Fresh! is published by The Fresh Network, the UK's one-stop shop for all things raw. It sells a huge range of raw ingredients, gourmet raw foods, superfoods, supplements, detox aids, books and kitchen equipment and regularly runs events and classes. For more information, or to subscribe to Get Fresh! magazine, visit* **fresh-network.com** *or ring* **0845 833 7017.**

Vegetarian Shoes

Why vegetarian shoes?

After being vegetarian for a few years, many of us are horrified to realise that we are still wearing animals on our feet as shoes and around our waists as belts. Whilst few today would wear fur, it can come as a shock to realise that leather is just fur with the hair scraped off. The skin is a large part of the value of an animal. Without it, the meat industry would not be viable. For these reasons, at Veggie Guides we don't wear leather.

What's the alternative?

Materials used to make 21st century vegetarian shoes are as good as or better than leather in every way. They breathe like leather, letting perspiration out, but don't let water in – great news if you've just stepped in a deep puddle.

Where to buy

Many vegetarians get shoes mail order from a number of specialist manufacturers and catalogues, or take a trip to the shop **Vegetarian Shoes** in Brighton, founded by veggie fashion graduate Robin Webb. Once upon a time there were no veggie shoes in Britain, so Robin started making them from lorica, a mountaineering material that breathes like leather but is waterproof. Now his shop in central Brighton sells shoes and boots, belts, jackets, bags, wallets and T-shirts. Combine a shoe shopping expedition with a day trip to the veggie cafes and cute shops nearby Just remember they are closed Sundays and bank holidays.

In London you can find a few possibilities at three stores in **Neal Street, Covent Garden** (p. 85). **The Natural Shoe Store** has a few styles of vegetarian shoe in one corner. **Birkenstock** specialises in durable sandals. And **Crocs** has just opened up selling comfortable waterproof plastic shoes in a huge range of colours, originally designed for yachting, but now popular with gardeners, chefs and waiters for their ruggedness and comfort. For high fashion women's shoes and boots, **Equa** in Islington (p.237) stocks a few of the stunning *Beyond Skin* women's range, and **Stella McCartney** is in Mayfair (p.127).

Mail Order

There are beautiful online and printed catalogues available from these excellent companies:

www.beyondskin.co.uk   www.bboheme.com

www.ethicalwares.com   www.freerangers.co.uk

www.vegetarian-shoes.com

They run stalls at vegan festivals such as Bristol and London in summer, and Christmas Without Cruelty. Keep an eye on the Vegetarian Guides festival calendar for upcoming dates at

www.vegetarianguides.co.uk/calendar

For handmade vegan shoes or repairs, contact **Vegan Cobbler** in Devon: AxeVegans@yahoo.co.uk, Tel: 01297-631133.

More information

www.cowsarecool.com   vegansociety.com/images/leather.pdf

Vegetarian Wine
by Ronny, who likes her quality booze

It's a closely guarded industry secret, but a bottle of wine can contain all kinds of nasties. Grapes are a delicate fruit, and an arsenal of toxic chemicals are employed to blast the voracious bugs and fungi which infest them. There are over 50 pesticides in use by the wine industry, which puts vineyard workers, our environment, and you the drinker at risk. However the good news is that there's an increasing demand for organic wine, and it is now very easy to find in off-licences, supermarkets and other shops.

We veggies have an additional concern. Although gelatine is less often used as a 'fining' (clarifying) agent, the fish extract isinglass is still added to many wines, regardless of whether they're organic, and it's very unlikely to be listed on the label. Many vegetarian wines are cleared with beaten egg white. Organic producers can use the eggs of free-range organic chickens.

So, if you want to be sure that your wine is both free from toxic chemicals and cleared with clay rather than animal products, it's best to get it from a health food shop. Some of the bigger shops have an entire wine aisle! Most of them, along with many vegetarian restaurants, source their wines from two companies, Vintage Roots and Vinceremos. Both have excellent catalogues listing a wide range of red, white, rosé and sparkling wines from all over the world, and they're happy to sell to the public by the bottle or the case, so why not treat yourself? There's also a new company called Festival Wines.

Jem Gardener from Vinceremos has provided us with a list of his top 5 tipples for 2008. Here they are, in no particular order:

1.) Côtes du Rhône Villages Valréas Grande Bellane. This full, spicy red from Southern France is great with strongly-flavoured food.

2.) Pinot Grigio Perlage. This soft, aromatic, dry white is lovely on its own.

3.) Sauvignon la Marouette. A crisp, dry white. There are great red (Merlot) and rosé (Syrah) Marouettes too.

4.) Nero d' Avola 'Era'. Full, fruity and smooth Sicilian red. Goes well with rich food.

5.) Cabernet Sauvignon Rosé Domaine de Clairac. Rosé wines have become very popular lately and go well with many kinds of food.

Check the **Drink & Eat Veggie index** for restaurants that have a good wine list. The exclusively vegetarian places are your best bet.

Many of the wholefood stores listed in this guide sell wine and if so we tell you. Some good places to start exploring:

As Nature Intended
Bumblebee
The Grocery
Earth Natural
Fresh & Wild
Planet Organic

Luscious Organic
OHFS Natural Foods
Revital (certain branches)
Sedlescombe @ Spitalfields (Sun)
Wholefoods Market

For mail order catalogues of vegetarian and vegan wine, beer, ale, cider, perry and spirits, or a trade price list if you run a restaurant, these are your people:

www.vinceremos.co.uk
Tel: 0800 107 3086

www.vintageroots.co.uk
Tel: 0800 980 4992

www.festivalwines.co.uk
Tel: 0800 0242 969

www.pitfieldbeershop.co.uk
Tel: 0845 833 1492

Ronny is an experienced cook and a bit of a booze fan. Her excellent vegan cookbooks *The Cake Scoffer* and *The Salad Scoffer* are published by Animal Aid and also available from the Vegetarian Guides website.

Vegan Festivals

London has two vegan festivals in late summer, the **London Vegan Festival** with 100 stalls, entertainers and lots of food, and the smaller but still excellent two-day raw food **Festival of Life**:

www.vegancampaigns.org.uk/festival
www.festivaloflife.net

You can do it all again on the closest Sunday to 1st December and get your presents in one place at **Christmas Without Cruelty**:

www.animalaid.org.uk

For UK one-day vegan festivals all over the UK, including the annual summer two-day Bristol Vegan Fayre, Viva!'s (see page 21) roving Incredible Veggie Roadshows, and week-long international festivals which make great holidays, keep an eye on the Vegetarian Guides Festival Calendar:

www.vegetarianguides.co.uk/calendar

For vegan meals, restaurant trips, walks and demos, read the **London Vegans Diary** online. **Green Events** free magazine lists events and courses and has a list of distribution points across London on its website.

www.londonvegans.org.uk

www.greenevents.co.uk

The Chains
Best non-veggie places

When your family, workmates or friends veto a veggie venue, these are the places that really do "get it" about veggie food.

New in town

1. Giraffe restaurants are lively and very child-friendly. Dishes include hummous with pine nuts, warm naan and veg, soup with garlic toast, mezze with tabouleh, Tunisian ratatouille, falafel burger and fries, green curry, tofu veg noodles stir-fry. They do breakfast/brunch till noon.

2. Hare & Tortoise are great value international restaurants with lots of vegan Asian dishes including miso soup, spring rolls, tofu and satay, even tofu "duck" pancakes.

3. Leon fast food cafes have soups, hummous, green pea curry, vegetable tagine, salads, sweet potato falafels and yumy vegan chocolate.

4. Le Pain Quotidien is a French cafe chain with vegan soups, tofu salad and blueberry muffins.

Old faithfuls

Italian and pizza restaurants can make pizzas without cheese, garlic bread with olive oil, bruschetta, grilled veg, salads, and of course pasta with tomato sauce. **Bella Italia** has 16 restaurants in central

and west London. **Cafe Uno** has cheese with most dishes but can make them vegan. **Pizza Express** guarantee their pizza bases are dairy-free. **Ask Pizza** is also good.

Wagamama Japanese noodle restaurants are noisy and great fun with huge portions of soupy noodle dishes. **Wasabi** take-aways have boxes of vegan sushi.

Lebanese and **Turkish** restaurants usually do a vegetarian platter of starters (meze). In central London try **Tas, Ev, Levant, Gaby's** and **Sofra**. Also **The Dervish** and **Clicia** in Stoke Newington, **Solché Cilician** in Hackney and **Fresco** in Bayswater.

Crussh juice bars have vegan soups and wraps. Many sandwich chains think veggies live on cheese and eggs, but **Pret-à-Manger** have a hummous salad sandwich.

Ambala Indian sweet shops are great for picking up samosas to eat on the run. Wholefood stores and **Holland & Barrett** often, though not always, have a fridge with sos rolls, bean slices and pasties, and are great for energy bars, flapjacks, dried fruit and nuts.

YOU CAN MAKE YOUR VEGGIE GUIDE EVEN BETTER!

Share your secrets and receive the next edition free!

Make the world of veggies even richer! Send us your favourite veggie and vegan friendly addresses in London, Britain or Europe and see them in the fatter next edition.

Email us at: **updates@vegetarianguides.co.uk**

Mapping the vegetarian & vegan world

For stockists, mail order, updates and veggie travel articles visit:
www.vegetarianguides.co.uk

 Vegetarian Guides  Alex Bourke

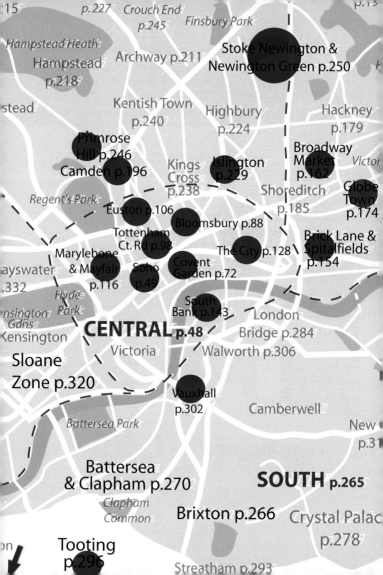

* Soho 49
* Covent Garden 72
* Bloomsbury 88
Tottenham Court Rd 98
* Euston 106
* Marylebone/Mayfair 116
* The City 128
* South Bank 143

CENTRAL LONDON

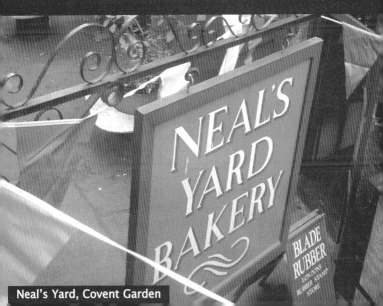

Neal's Yard, Covent Garden

SOHO Central London

Soho – the central area to the south of Oxford Street – is where you are likely to spend most of your time in central London. Here there are dozens of cinemas and theatres, fashion shops galore, cafes and sight-seeing. Our munchie map of Soho enables you to locate the closest place in seconds.

Soho now has a total of 12 vegetarian eateries, half of them vegan. There are four excellent new 100% vegan restaurants, plus stacks of new cafes with heaps of veggie food and some rather yummy new shops.

VitaOrganic has taken the place of the much missed

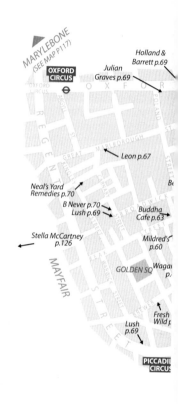

MARYLEBONE
(SEE MAP P117)

OXFORD CIRCUS

Julian Graves p.69

Holland & Barrett p.69

Leon p.67

Neal's Yard Remedies p.70

B Never p.70
Lush p.69

Buddha Cafe p.63

Stella McCartney p.126

Mildred's p.60

GOLDEN SQ Wagar p.

MAYFAIR

Fresh Wild

Lush p.69

PICCADILLY CIRCUS

Beatroot, our favourite cafe

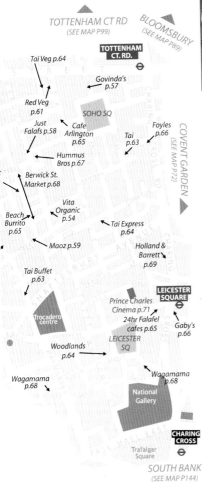

Tai Veg p.64

Govinda's p.57

Red Veg p.61

SOHO SQ

Just Falafs p.58

Cafe Arlington p.65

Foyles p.66

Tai p.63

Hummus Bros p.67

Berwick St. Market p.68

Vita Organic p.54

Beach Burrito p.65

Tai Express p.64

Maoz p.59

Holland & Barrett p.69

Tai Buffet p.63

Prince Charles Cinema p.71

24hr Falafel cafes p.65

Gaby's p.66

Trocadero centre

LEICESTER SQ

Woodlands p.64

Wagamama p.68

Wagamama p.68

National Gallery

CHARING CROSS

Trafalgar Square

TOTTENHAM CT RD (SEE MAP P99)

BLOOMSBURY (SEE MAP P89)

TOTTENHAM CT. RD.

COVENT GARDEN (SEE MAP P72)

LEICESTER SQUARE

SOUTH BANK (SEE MAP P144)

Tai Oriental vegan buffet

Country Life as the healthiest restaurant in London with a unique Malaysian and living foods buffet. There are **three new Chinese all-you-can-eat buffets** on Old Compton St, Lexington St and Great WIndmill St. Like the older branches in Greek Street (which has added a salad bar) and Great Chapel Street, they are full of meat-eaters who do not even realise that the "beef" is actually soya.

Just Falafs is a new mostly veggie cafe that offers much more than just falafels. The cafe in **Foyles** bookshop now has several vegan cakes. Also listed are new omnivorous cafes **Hummus Brothers**, **Arlington**, **Leon** and **Beach Burrito** for their veggie specialities or when your mates veto a veggie venue.

Our favourite cafe remains **Beatroot** in the fruit & veg market on Berwick Street, with a superb buffet, gorgeous smoothies and several vegan cakes. **Red Veg** has the best veggie-burgers, some unique falafels and hot dogs. **Maoz** falafel cafe and salad bar is the cheap and filling antidote to a midnight munchie craving long after all other veggie places have closed. After 2am when even Maoz is probably closed, you can still pick up falafels and coffee at the **24-hour cafes** on the north-east corner of Leicester Square before catching a night bus from Trafalgar Square.

For a proper sit down meal, party atmosphere **Mildred's** and Indians **Woodlands** and **Govinda's** have now been joined by vegan Malaysian **VitaOrganic**. Many people make the trip to the fine international restaurant **Eat & Two** Veg in Marylebone, near Baker Street station. If you're with a pack of carnivorous mates who absolutely refuse to go to any veggie place, you'll find plenty of veggie choice at **Giraffe**, **Hare & Tortoise**, **Wagamama** or **Gaby's**.

Fresh & Wild is a tremendous wholefoods supermarket on two floors with a cafe. For a quick snack on Charing Cross Rd or Oxford Street visit **Holland & Barrett, GNC** or **Julian Graves**. **Lush** and **B** in Carnaby Street are vegan soap and bodycare heaven. Just the other side of Regent Street, **Stella McCartney** (see Marylebone section) has the highest of high fashion non-leather shoes and boots. For more modest budgets there are some vegan shoes in three stores on Neal Street in Covent Garden.

If you're a student or counting the days till the next pay cheque, here's how to do a West End movie and dinner for a fiver on a weekday afternoon or a tenner any other time. **Prince Charles Cinema** is only £1.50 weekday afternoons if you invest £10 in annual membership. Add £3 for a take-out Chinese vegan buffet to eat on a park bench in Leicester Square, or a gorgeous £2.80 or £3.50 falafel from Maoz. At night films are £3.50 (£5 non-members) and a sit-down buffet is £5.95 (£3.50 after 7pm), at Govinda's, £3.50 or £4.90 at Beatroot (10% off with PCC membership), or £6.50 at the Chinese places.

Our Top 5 Best of Central London

See also the 8 "Where to?" indexes

Cosmetics

Alara, Bloomsbury
B (never too busy), Soho/CG
Fresh & Wild, Soho
Lush, Soho/Covent Garden
Planet Organic, Tott Ct Rd

Flapjacks & snacks

Ambala or **Gupta**, Euston
Health Food Ctr, Tott Ct Rd
Julian Graves, Soho
Holland & Barrett
Planet Organic, Tott Ct Rd

Food shopping

Alara, Bloomsbury
Fresh & Wild, Soho
Health Food Centre, Tott CR
Peppercorn's, Tottenham CR
Planet Organic, Tott Ct Rd

Late night

Wagamama, 11pm/midnight
Gaby's, Leic. Sq, midnight
Maoz, Soho, 1 or 2am
Levant, Marylebone, 2.30am
Leicester Square cafes, 24hr

Lunch with friends

Drummond Street, Euston
Food For Thought, Cov Gdn
Mary Ward, Bloomsbury
Sagar, Tottenham Court Rd
World Food Cafe, Cov Gdn

Picnic Spots

Golden Square, W1
Gordon Sqare, WC1
Regents Park, NW1
Soho Square, W1
St James's Park, SW1

Soho all you can eat

Buddha Cafe, Lexington St
Tai, Greek St
Tai Buffet, Great Windmill St
Tai Express, Old Compton St
Tai Veg, Great Chapel St

Vegan Cake/Dessert

Beatroot, Soho
Food For Thought, Cov Gdn
Foyles, Charing Cross Rd
Health Food Ctr, Tott Ct Rd
Neal's Yard Salad Bar, Cov G

West End Cafe

Beatroot, Soho
Just Falafs, Soho
Govinda's, Soho
Neal's Yard Salad Bar, Cov G
Red Veg, Soho

West End Dinner

Chinese buffets, all over
Eat & Two Veg, Marylebone
Mildred's, Soho
Vita Organic, Soho
Woodlands, Leicester Square

VitaOrganic

Vegan organic raw and Malaysian restaurant

Open:
Mon–Sat   12.00–22.00
Sun   13.00–21.00
No credit cards.
12.5% service charge evenings.
32 seats, groups should book.

74 Wardour Street, Soho
London W1F 0TE
Tel: 020-7734 8986
Tube: Tottenham Court Rd,
              Leicester Square
Menus at www.vitaorganic.co.uk
See map on page 51

There's nowhere like this amazing place, in our opinion the best and healthiest restaurant in Europe, which is why we give them two pages!

Phong and Mui (right) use ancient and modern cooking techniques to show that healthy food is tasty and leaves you feeling light and energised. They specialise in live juices and multi-cultural tapas-style dishes. No added sugars, nothing heated above 100°C, dishes gently cooked by steaming, blanching and other methods, and using only mono-unsaturated oils (no fried ingredients), lots of raw food and sprouts. Amongst others, they use ayurvedic principles and are great for macrobiotic, wheat/gluten-free and raw food diets.

From 12–6 you can order from the Vi-Thali bar, where you choose a small, medium or large plate (3, 5, 7 scoops of food at £5, £6, £7) or from 12 till late you can order Vi-Tapas, where you pick 1, 2, 4 or 6 tapas dishes from £2.50–£8.50. Dishes include Thai green curry, steamed moussaka, crispy stir-steamed vegetables, crème de floret and many more. You can also choose from the gourmet raw food/salad bar. There is a minimum charge of £5 per person for the food from the Vi-tapas and Vi-thali menus. Happy hour from 3–5pm.

From 6pm you can also order from the a la carte menu, offering a mouth-watering selection of raw dishes, such as sprouted buckwheat pizza, green lasagne, spicy yellow noodle laska and more.

For dessert there are raw/live enzyme cakes, around £3, that are completely wheat, sugar and dairy-free, sweetened with low GI agave syrup, though the slices are

VitaOrganic

smaller than they used to be. Try live mixed berry cheesecake, raw cocoa cake, or even a green tea tofu cheesecake!

Throughout the day you can order drinks from Vita Organic's replenishing live enzyme juice bar £2–£4.80. They say that these juices offer a wide array of healing properties. For example, if feeling a little tired, try the Green Rejuvenator, or ladies if you want to feel as beautiful on the inside as you do on the out then try the Pink Mermaid Tonic. The menu also boasts a wide variety of organic teas, coffees (and caffeine free alternatives), live milks and soft drinks £1.80–£2.80.

If you like this you'll probably join those who come back again and again as it is totally unique.

Beatroot

Open:

Mon–Fri	09.00–21.00
Sat	11.00–21.00
Sun	closed

Smoking allowed outside
No credit cards

92 Berwick Street, Soho
London W1V 3PP
Tel: 020-7437 8591
Tube: Oxford Circus
Tottenham Court Rd,
Piccadilly Circus
See map on page 51

Our favourite central London café, with almost all desserts vegan, near the south end of Berwick St by the fruit and veg market.

Couple of outside tables.

They do take–away too so it gets a bit manic at lunchtime, whereas in the afternoon you could sit quietly here and write a letter.

Point to whatever you fancy from 16 hot dishes and salads and they'll fill a box for you, small £3.90, medium £4.90 or large £5.90. Choose from, for example, pasta with basil oil, lentil dal with spinach, spicy Moroccan tagine, sausage rolls, organic rice, shepherd's pie, all kinds of salads. Soup with organic brown rolls £3.20.

Lots of cakes, all vegan, £1.20-2.20 including fabulous chocolate dream cake with custard 50p extra, carrot cake, hemp flapjacks.

Fresh juices such as Vitalizer (apple, carrot, ginger), Beatnik (beatroot, celery, spinach, carrot), Breeze (pear, ginger, lemon, apple) 8oz for £2.20 or 12oz for £2.90. Fresh orange or carrot or apple juice. Gorgeous soya or rice–milk fruit smoothies made to order £3.20, wheat-grass shot £1.20.

Teas £1.10, filter coffee £1.40, cappuccino or latte £1.70-1.80, chai £1.10.

If you like this you'll probably like Pogo Cafe in Hackney, East London, great for chilling out with vegan cakes and soya cappuccino.

Govinda's

Vegetarian
Indian restaurant

Open:

Mon–Sat 12.00–20.00
(last orders)
Sun closed

9/10 Soho Street
Soho
London W1V 5DA
Tel: 020 020-7437-4928
Tube: Tottenham Court Rd

No alcohol.
Children welcome.

See map on page 51

Popular Hare Krishna owned and staffed vegetarian, Indian restaurant and café, with some fast food, next door to their temple, just off Oxford Street and near Tottenham Court Road.

No eggs, garlic or onion.

Surplus food is given to London's homeless after hours and their Food For Life project cooks specially for them after hours.

Starters include pakoras, samosas and kachori 60p eat in (50p take-away) and spinach roll ££2 (£1). 3 pakoras for £1.60 (£1.40), 6 for £2.50 (£2.20). Salads £1.30-4.20. Beanpot or subji veg curry £1.95–2.80 (£1.75–2.50). Dahl £2 (£1.50). Add brown, yellow or white basmati rice, chapatis, (olive) bread, popadoms or wholemeal roll 30p–£1.80. Baked spuds £2.10 (£1.60).

Thali £5.95 (£3.50 after 7pm), but the best value is

their all-you-can-eat buffet for £5.95 3-7pm, £4.95 after 7pm, with rice, veg, salad, soup, bread roll and popadom.

Several desserts and cakes and more of them are now vegan: apple crumble £2.15 (£1.75) or fruitcake ££1.80 (£1.50), muffins 80p–£1.30 (60p–£1). Energy balls 90p.

Drinks 50p–£1.60, herb tea or decaf coffee 80p. Freshly squeezed juices and smoothies £1.35-2.35. Soya milk sometime available.

If you like this you may also like Indian Vegetarian Bhelpuri House in Islington for its great value buffet and vegan lassi.

Just Falafs Soho

Mostly vegetarian cafe and take-away

Open: (hours may vary)
Sun closed
Mon-Sat 09.00-22.00 summer
Mon-Fri 09.00-21.00 winter
Sat 12.00-21.00 winter
www.justfalafs.com for menus
Children welcome. MC, Visa.

155 Wardour Street (north end)
Soho W1F 8WG
Tel: 020-7734 1914
Tube: Tottenham Court Rd
Oxford Circus
See map on page 51

Very yummy new mostly veggie cafe (apart from four dishes) in Soho and Covent Garden, specialising in wraps, soups and salads made with 70%+ organic ingredients, and of course falafels made with balls of cooked organic chickpeas, herbs and spices that "satisfy more than a sandwich yet don't require a full seating experience." They also do breakfasts.

Five kinds of falafel in 1, 2 or 3-ball sizes £2.95-5.95, with any of the following: filling of the week, seasonal beans, mixed sprouts, beetroot, grated carrot, chili or garlic sauce.

Soup £3.25. Organic dhal with khobez flatbread £3.95.

Salad box with 3 salads and sauce £4.75, 4 salads £5.45, add 50p for falafel. Khobez bread 35p.

Magic breakfast oat porridge until 11am £1.99 with spice, add 50p for mixed seeds and nuts. Home-made granola from £1.49.

Bombay mix, mango slikces, chocolate, chocolate apricots, dried fruit, nuts, tortillas, kettle chips, cake and fruit. Vegan chocolate biscuit cake £1.75.

Smoothies £2.95 made to order. Fair Trade organic tea, coffees, cappuccino, hot chocolate £1.49-2.39. Bottled water, organic and other drinks 95p-£1.80. At the time of printing they do not have soya milk, just rice milk.

Alcohol available with eat-in. Wine £2.95 tumbler, £12 bottle. Organic cider £3.15, beer £2.95.

Compostable salad boxes and they recycle bottles. One long wooden table and bar seating. 17.5% discount on most take-away food.

If you like this then try their other branch in Covent Garden Piazza.

Maoz

Open every day of the year:
(including Christmas & New Year)
Sun-Thu 11.00–01.00
Fri-Sat 11.00–02.00
www.maozveg.com.
Cash only. No credit cards.

43 Old Compton St, Soho
London W1D 6HG
Tel: 020–7851 1586
Tube: Leicester Square
Piccadilly Circus
See map on page 51

Fantastic value falafel cafe, open till well after midnight, at the west end of Old Compton Street in the heart of the gay zone, opposite the pink fronted Admiral Duncan gay pub. They specialise in falafel, crunchy deep-fried chickpea balls with coriander, garlic, fresh parsley and spices, served in white or wholewheat pita. There is a help-yourself salad bar to top it off. You can also just have a box of salad, or pita with humus or aubergine. Everything is made fresh daily and nothing kept for the next day.

The basic falafel in pita costs £3.30 small, £3.80 large, and is made piping hot in front of you. Add 50p for humus or fried aubergine. Then squirt one of the sauces such as tahini (sesame sauce) or ketchup liberally all over the chickpea balls and pile on top as much as you can from the self–serve salad bar.

The salad bar includes pickled baby aubergine, carrot, couscous, tomato, olives, gherkin, red cabbage, mushrooms, fried cauliflower, coleslaw (not vegan). Sauces in the salad bar are red chili, green chili, onion and coriander. Sauces in squirty bottles include tahini and ketchup. The other sauces are not vegan: mayonnaise, yogurt and garlic sauces.

If you're less hungry, a self–serve salad box is £2.50. On the other hand if you're really hugnry, have a Salad Meal £4.50 with a salad box, fries and soft drink or freshly made juice. Small Maoz Meal with small falafel, fries and drink £4.20 (add 50p for humus and aubergine); Big Maoz Meal £4.90 with a regular falafel, aubergine, hummus, fries and drink. Belgian fries £1.70.

Freshly squeezed orange or carrot or apple juice £1.70. Soft drinks 90p.

If you like this then try their other branches in Paris, Amsterdam and Barcelona. See www.maozveg.com

Mildred's

Vegetarian restaurant

Open:
Mon–Sat 12.00–23.00
Sun closed
Cheques & debit cards, but no credit cards.
Children welcome.

45 Lexington Street,
Soho, London W1F 9AN
Tel: 020 7494 1634
Tube: Piccadilly Circus, Oxford Circus
www.mildreds.co.uk
See map on page 50

Stylish vegetarian café-restaurant and take-away with hip young clientele to match, crowded and enthusiastic. This is the top place in Soho for veggies going out for dinner and a bottle of wine. It can get quite noisy but is lots of fun.

The food is modern European with some Asian influences. Lots of healthy Mediterranean or stir-fry, but you can also have a burger and fries.

Lunchtime takeaway specials include burger of the day with salad and fries £4.90; stir-fry with rice or wheat noodles £4.20, with cashews £4.70, with tofu £5.20, with both £5.70; fried or stir-fried veg with brown rice; energizing detox salad £4.40, with tofu £4.90. Lite bites such as homebaked bread with olive oil and balsamic.

Many of the main courses £6-7.95 are vegan, such as mixed mushroom, porcini and ale pie with mushy peas and fries; stir-fried Asian veg in sesame oil and teriyaki sauce with ginger on organic brown rice, optional organic marinated tofu and/or toasted cashews; organic detox salad; fennel and chickpea tagine with date and pistachio couscous; sweet potato stew with cornbread.

Several desserts include warm chocolate and prune pudding with mocha sauce and vegan ice-cream; or tofu, banana, lemon and coconut cheesecake with maple syrup and soya cream, £4.25.

Organic smoothies and fresh organic juices £2.95. Organic house wine £3.25 glass, £12.65 bottle. Vegan wine and beer. Optional 12.5% service charge added to bill. No reservations but you can have a drink at the front while you wait.

If you like this you may also like vegetarian restaurant and bar Eat & Two Veg in Marylebone (Central London).

Red Veg

Vegetarian fast food cafe and take-away

Open:
Mon-Sat 12.00–21.30
Sun   12.00–18.30
Kids welcome
No credit cards

95 Dean Street, Soho
London W1V 5RB5
Tel: 020-7437 3109
Tube: Tottenham Court Rd
www.redveg.com
See map on page 51

Veggie burger and falafel bar with a few tables. perfect for a quick meal on the run, or sit and relax a while. They develop all their own products, everything is GM free and all items can be made vegan.

Try a RedVeg or ChilliVeg or MushroomVeg or Hickory smoked veg burger for £3.65–3.85 (very tasty and "meaty").

Falafels (regular, coriander and parsley, sesame or chilli) are £4.35 and come with lime and coriander wrap with humous, tahini, green chilli relish and sald:

Vegwurst hotdog £2.95, with caramelised red onions £3.15.

Fries £1.65. Spicy potato wedges £2.15. Spicy baby corn firesticks £2.25. Stuffed jalepeno peppers £2.45. Breaded mushrooms £2.25.

Stuffed vine leaves with mint, coriander and rice £3.75.

Fresh fusilli pasta £3.95 with one of four homemade pesto sauces: red pepper, chilli and coriander, basil or sundried tomato.

Soft drinks £1.95 to £3.35 for an organic beer. £1.50 for coffee. Soya milk available. Whole Earth organic cola, lemonade, sparkling elderflower or cranberry.

If you like this you'll probably like their other branch at 21 Gardner Street, Brighton.

Fresh & Wild Soho

Wholefood supermarket and cafe

Open:

Mon–Fri	07.30–21.00
Sat	09.00–20.00
Sun	11.30–18.30
Bank hols	12–19.00

Outside catering events & parties.

71–75 Brewer Street
London W1R 3SL
Tel: 020-7434 3179
Tube: Piccadilly Circus
www.wholefoods.com
See map on page 50

Organic wholefood super-market on two floors in the middle of Brewer Street. Downstairs are organic fruit and veg, heaps of take-aways, deli, salad bar and juice bar/cafe with seating.

Upstairs is a wholefood supermarket, bodycare and natural remedies where staff have a high level of knowledge, all either working as complementary health practitioners or well on the way to qualifying.

As you enter the store, around the tills you'll find magazines, chocolate, flapjacks and drinks. Many sandwiches £2.25–3.50, can be gluten free, with rye or multi-grain baguette. At the back is the deli hot buffet counter. £1.30 per 100 grammes, seasonal menu with daily specials, e.g. curry and brown rice with steamed veg £3.75. Get there before 1pm to avoid the rush. On the right are cafe tables, drinks, smoothies, cakes and organic bread. On the left

behind the big organic fruit and veg section, is a self-serve salad bar, £1.19 per 100g. All ingredients are clearly marked. Prepared take-aways £3.50-4.00 include pies, wraps, riceballs, slices, exotic salads, dips.

Highlights upstairs include 12 kinds of tofu, veggie ready meals, wheat-free pasta, breakfast cereals, organic juices, non-dairy cheeses and yoghurts, hemp and soya ice-cream, soya dessert, and they even have vegan haggis! New ethnic ranges include Thai and Mexican.

Health, body and skincare includes Dr Hauschka, Ren, Weleda, Faith in Nature, Jason, Urtekram, Green People. Aso aromatherapy, herbs, probiotics, flax oil, supplements, world music and books, including Veggie Guides.

If you like this you'll probably like their other stores in Clapham (South), Camden (North), Stoke Newington (North), and the Wholefoods Market that opened in Kensington summer 2007.

Buddha Cafe

Chinese vegan buffet restaurant

41 Lexington St, W1R 9AJ
(corner of Beak Street)
Tel: 020-7287 9620
Open: *Mon-Sun* 12.00-22.00
Tube: Piccadilly Circus
      Oxford Circus

New Chinese vegan all-you-can-eat buffet near Mildred's. £5 lunch 12-5pm, £6 evenings and Sunday. Menu could include Pa Tai noodles, Tai curry, rice, sweet & sour balls, black beans, soya chicken, sea-spcied aubergine, special fried rice, Singapore noodles, lemon grass pot, sesame salad, crispy spring rolls, salad. Drinks £1.50,no alcohol

Tai Buffet, Piccadilly

Vegan Chinese buffet restaurant

40 Great Windmill St, W1V 7PA
Tel: 020-7287 3730
Open: *Sun-Thu* 12.00-22.00
      Fri-Sat 12.00-23.00
Tube: Piccadilly Circus

The latest in the chain, all you can eat from 20 dishes for £5.50 until 5pm, £6.50 evening and all day Sunday plus 10% "service charge", so it's really £6.05 till 5pm and

£7.15 later. Take-away £3.50, £4 large. Dishes include fruit salad, noodles, mixed curry, fried or boiled rice, broccoli, soya prawn, spring rolls, various fake meats that fool meat-eaters, seaweed. Make your own mock duck pancakes with sauce. No alcohol. Cash only.

Tai, Greek Street

Thai Chinese vegan buffet restaurant

10 Greek Street, Soho W1D 4DJ
Tel: 020-7287 3730
Open: *every day* 12.00-23.00
Tube: Tottenham Court Rd
www.vegveg.com

The original vegan Chinese buffet restaurant, run by a Buddhist temple. Incredibly popular for its amazing value, delicious food, which features lots of fake meats which fool many carnivores.

All you can eat buffet, as many trips as you like for £5.50, or £6.50 in the evenings and all day Sunday. Allow another £1 or more for a drink and £1 for a tip. £3 or £4 for a take-away box. Rice, curry rice, chow mein, crispy soya luck, sweet & sour veef, spiced aubergine, black beans soya protein, spring rolls, tofu, stir-fry veg, salad and more.

Soft drink or unlimited Chinese tea £1. Organic juices or beer or wine £2.50. Bottle of wine £10. Cash only.

Tai Veg, Gt Chapel St
Vegan Chinese buffet restaurant

3–4 Great Chapel Street
off Oxford Street, W1V 3AG
Tel: 020–7168 9468
Open: every day 12.30–22.30
Tube: Tottenham Court Rd

Another vegan Chinese all-you-can-eat buffet restaurant, also offering amazing value at £5, or £6 after 5pm and Sunday, including fresh fruit salad. Unlimited Chinese tea £1. Soft drinks £1.50. Cash only. Next door to an internet cafe.

Tai Express, Old Compton St
Chinese vegan buffet restaurant

33 Old Compton Street, W1
Tel: 020–7734 1407
Open: Mon–Sun 12.00–23.00
Tube: Leicester Square

The newest all-you-can-eat Chinese vegan buffet for £5.50 daytime, £6.50 after 5pm and Sundays. Buffet includes chown mein, crispy aromatic veg duck, seaweed, northern style dim sum, northern Chinese stew, Chinese pizza, special fried rice, veg beef, fresh fruit salad. Take out boxes £3 and £4.

Woodlands Piccadilly
Vegetarian S. Indian restaurant & bar

37 Panton St, London SW1Y 4EA
(between Haymarket and south-west corner of Leicester Square)
Open: every day 12.00–22.30
Tel: 020–7839 7258
Tube: Piccadilly Circus,
Leicester Square
www.woodlandsrestaurant.co.uk

One of four branches in London. Lunchtime all you can eat buffet Mon–Fri 12.00–14.30 for £7.50, lunchbox £4.50. Also an a la carte menu, for more details on the dishes see the full page entry for the branch in Marylebone (page 118).

House wine bottle £13, glass £3.25. Small beer £2.75, large £4.95. Visa, MC, Amex.

Arlington Cafe

Omnivorous organic Fair Trade cafe

92 Dean St, W1D 3SY

Tel: 020-7287 0048

Open: Mon-Thu 08.00-16.00
       Fri   08.00-16.00
       Sat-Sun closed

Tube: Tottenham Court Road

They sell the Fresh! range of sandwiches, some of which are vegan/veg, Clive's pies and snacks, falafel & hummus ciabatta sandwiches which they can toast for you, various vegan soups from Knobbly Carrot Company, plus vegan chocolate cake. Cafe Direct fair trade coffee, soya milk for cappuccino. Profits go to projects to help the homeless and other disadvantaged people.

Beach Burrito Cafe

Omni CalMex cafe & take-away

Opposite Somerfield grocery, south end of Berwick Street W1

Tel: 020-7437 3010

Open: Mon-Sat 11.00-18.00
(planning to open till 22.00)
       Sun   closed

Tube: Leicester Square
       Piccadilly Circus

Californian–Mexican cafe with lots of vegetarian wraps made to order. Most are £4.20 and have cheese, but vegans can order without. Beach burrito is a flour tortilla with tomato salsa, lettuce, slow cooked pinto beans and chilli rice. White corn tacos have chipolte sauce and fresh lime. Nacho chips with filling on top. Bikini Salad Wrap has roasted vegetables rolled up with shredded lettuce, salsa and cucumber. Also quesadillas £3.70. Add vegan gaucamole to anything for 50p.

Nachos with tomato salsa and guacamole dip £2.20.

Phone orders for 3 or more people, allow 10 minutes or tell them when you're coming.

Falafel cafes Leic Square

Omnivorous cafe

North-east corner of Leicester Square, opposite Warner West End cinema and Hippodrome

Open: Every day 24 hours

Tube: Leicester Square

Fiori Corner and **Cafe Rimini** are 24-hr Mediterranean style cafes which sell a basic falafel with runny tahini sauce for £3.50. Grab one after buying a bargain cinema ticket at the nearby Prince Charles Cinema (see page 71) if you don't have time to go to Maoz. Or hang out with a coffee at 3am after the disco before taking a night bus from Trafalgar Square.

Foyles Cafe

Omnivorous cafe with vegan cakes

theCafe@Foyles, first floor
113-119 Charing Cross Rd,
WC2H 0EB
Tel: 020-7440 3207
Open: *Mon–Sat* 9–21.00
       Sun   11–18.00
Tube: Tottenham Court Road

Regular cafe on the first floor of the giant bookshop Foyles, with Monmouth fair trade coffee and soya cappuccino and several vegan cakes such as banana and orange loaf, pear and nut loaf, passion loaf, ginger loaf or triple chocolate cake, all £1.80–2.00. Vegan flapjacks and date slices. Vegan and veggie baguettes, panini and sanwiches and a vegan salad. Espresso £1.20, mocha £2.50. 40% organic ingredients. Live jazz music every Thursday evening.

Gaby's

Omnivorous Mediterranean cafe

30 Charing Cross Rd (east side) just below Leicester Square tube, London WC2H 0DB
Tel: 020-7836 4233
Open: *Mon–Sat* 09.00–24.00
       Sun   12.00–21.00
Tube: Leicester Square

Gaby's has been a veggie standby for years both for eat-in and take-away. Most dishes are vegetarian, many vegan, and prices are great too. Point to what you want in the deli style counter.

Starters and salads £2.80 or £4.80 for combo, such as hummus, stuffed vine leaves, falafel with salad, bata bean salad. Soups £3. Chips £1.80, olives £2, pita 30p.

Mains £7 include couscous, stuffed aubergine or pepper, veg fritter or aubergine with salad and pita.

Freshly squeezed orange or carrot juice £2.90–£3, sodas £1.50, teas/coffees £1.30–1.80. House retsina or Greek Rotonda wine £12.90 bottle, £6 half, £3 glass. Beer £3.50. Air conditioned. Children welcome, no high chair. No credit cards. Disabled friendly, one step to toilet.

Hummus Bros

Omnivorous cafe

88 Wardour Street W1F 0TJ

Tel: 020-7734 1311

Open: *Mon-Thu* 11.00-22.00
Fri-Sun 12.00-23.00

Tube: Leicester Square
Tottenham Court Road

www.hbros.co.uk

New cafe opened by two brothers who love hummus with pitta bread. Try it made with chickpeas or fava beans, plain or with mushrooms, guacamole (vegan) or salad, small or regular £2.70-5.20 lunch, £4.20-6.70 evenings and weekends.

Mixed veg, grilled veg, tabouleh salad or barbecued aubergine £2.50-3.50. Mixed pickles £1.20.

Desserts £1.50-2.50 but nothing vegan.

Juices, teas, coffees, Innocent smoothies, hot spiced apple juice, £1-£2. No soya milk. No alcohol.

Take-home tubs of hummus and toppings , £1-2.50. MC, Visa, Amex

Leon

Omnivorous cafe & take-away

35 Great Marlborough Street (corner of Carnaby St, W1F 7JE

Tel: 020-7437 5280
Fax: 020-7437 5281

Open: *Mon-Fri* 08.00-22.30
Sat 09.30-22.30
Sun 10.30-18.30

Tube: Oxford Circus

www.leonrestaurants.co.uk

New fast food bar with lots of veggie things and dairy free clearly marked, e.g. 3 vegan soups £2.50, hummus £1.80, green pea curry or vegetable tagine £4.90, superfood salad £3.95, roasted sweet potato falafel in flatbread £2.70 or with rice and sesame slaw £4.80. Evening prices are very good for London, same as lunchtime + 17.5%.

Lots of puddings but only fruit salad is dairy-free, £2.30.

Juices 95p-£2.40. Teas and herb teas 90p. Coffees £1.20-2.80. House wine £3.95 small carafe, £7 large. Beer £2.50, libre £6.50. Cocktails £3.90-£6.

Wagamama

Omnivorous Japanese restaurants

Leicester Square branch:
14A Irving Street, opposite
Garrick Theatre, WC1V

Tel: 020-7839 2323

Open: *Mon–Thu* 12.00–23.00
Fri–Sat 12.00–24.00
Sun 12.30–22.00

Tube: Leicester Square,
Charing Cross

Haymarket branch: 8 Norris St,
off the Haymarket, SW1Y 4RJ

Tel: 020-7321 2755

Open: *Mon–Sat* 12.00–23.00
Sun 12.30–22.00

Tube: Leicester Square

Soho branch:
10A Lexington Street W1R 3HS
Tel: 020-7292 0990

Open: Mon–Thu 12.00–23.00
Fri–Sat 12.00–24.00
Sun 12.30–22.00

Tube: Piccadilly Circus

Omnivorous fast food Japanese noodle bar with over nine veggie and vegan dishes. Very busy, totally authentic, heaps of fun.

Allow about £12–£15 for a belt-buster, less if your're only eating mains. Prices start at £1.35 for miso soup up to £6.50 for an enormous bowl of miso ramen noodles.

See Bloomsbury, WC1 branch for menu (page 93) or www.wagamama.com.

Berwick Street Market

Fruit and veg market

Pedestrianised south end of
Berwick Street, W1

Open: *Mon–Sat* 09.00–18.00

Fruit and veg market with bargains in £1 bowls. Also a flower stall and a dried fruit and nuts stall. Combine your shopping with a smoothie or cake at Beatroot cafe in the same street.

GNC, Plaza

Health food shop

The Plaza, Oxford Street,
London W1D 1LT (between Wells
Street and Berners Street)

Tel: 020-7323 1990

Open: *Mon–Sat* 10.00–19.00
Sun 12.00–18.00

Tube: Tottenham Court Road,
Oxford Circus

www.gnc.co.uk
www.plaza-oxfordst.com

In a shopping centre opposite Holland & Barrett, this shop is more for body-building and supplements.

Holland & Barrett

Health food shop

65 Charing Cross Road
just above Leciester Square
Tel: 020 7287 3193
Open: *Mon-Sat* 10.00-20.00
Sun 12.00-18.00
Tube: Leicester Square

123 Oxford St, London W1R 1TF
(corner of Berwick St)
Tel: 020 7287 3624
Open: *Mon-Fri* 08.00-20.00
Sat 10.00-20.00
Sun 12.00-18.00
Tube: Oxford Circus,
Tottenham Court Road

Great for flapjacks, dried fruit, nuts, vegan chocolate, drinks and snacks such as pastries and pies.

Julian Graves

Health food shop

141 Oxford Street W1D 2JB
(corner of Poland St)
Tel: 020-7734 7735
Open: *Mon-Sat* 10.00-20.00
Sun 12.00-18.00
Tube: Oxford Circus

Health snack heaven. All kinds of nuts, seeds, dried fruit and berries. Also flapjacks, chilled drinks, spices, herb teas, omega oils.

Lush

Cruelty-free cosmetics

40 Carnaby Street, W1V 1PD
Tel: 020-7287 5874
Open: *Mon-Sat* 10.00-19.00
(Thu -20.00)
Sun 11.30-17.30
Tube: Oxford Circus

1-3 Quadrant Arcade,
80-82 Regent St, W1R 5PA
Tel: 020-7434 3953
Open: *Mon-Wed* 10.00-19.00
Thu-Sat 10.00-20.00)
Sun 11.00-19.00
Tube: Piccadilly Circus

Lovely cosmetics, all vegetarian and most of it vegan and clearly labelled with the Vegan Society logo, and all ingredients clearly listed in both English and Latin. Worth going in just for the fantastic smells. Solid shampoo is perfect for travellers and foaming bath balls make luxurious gifts. A lot of the products are solid so no need for preservatives or excess packaging. And they're big on fair trade, organic and buying from women's cooperative.

B never too busy to be Beautiful

Cruelty-free cosmetics

39 Carnaby Street, W1V 1PD
(next door to Lush)

Tel: 020-7287 5492

Open: *Mon-Sat* 10.00-19.30
Thu-Fri 10.00-20.00
Sun1 11.30-18.00

Tube: Oxford Circus

bnevertoobusyto bebeautiful.com

Exquisite sister store next door to Lush, but more glamorous and luxurious as they wrap things in organza see-thru gold bags and do lots of gift sets. Think Harrods for vegans, and the same delightful and helpful staff. Everything is vegetarian and almost everything is vegan and labelled. Lots of Fair Trade, even the packaging. They use essential oils in perfumes, not synthetic stuff.

Prices from £3.95 for a bubble bath up to £36 for a gift set or £45 for the top perfume. Big makeup range is all vegan. Brushes, gift sets.

This shop is perfect for scared blokes who don't know what to buy their girlfriends. They say they get a lot of them, and they'll help you choose. She can always change it later if necessary if you keep the receipt.

Come in just to feel good even if you don't buy anything. Aladdin's cave downstairs with lighting and flowers, a beautiful place to be.

Neal's Yard Remedies, W1

Herbs and complementary health

12 Fouberts Place,
Carnaby Street W1F 7PG

Tel: 020-7494 9862

Open: *Mon-Sat* 10.00-19.00
Thu till 20.00
Sun 11.00-17.00

Tube: Oxford Circus

www.nealsyardremedies.com

200 herbs and spices by weight, organic toiletries, natural remedies, cotton-wool, soaps, books on homeopathy and remedies. Consultations available with multi-lingual staff. All products tested on human volunteers, not animals. Mostly organic, lots of Fair Trade, 10p for every primary item of packaging you return for recycling.

They also have therapy rooms offering massage, nutrition and herbal medicine, with express treaments starting at £12 for 15 minutes.

Prince Charles Cinema

Amazing cheap films in Soho

7 Leicester Place (corner of Lisle Street, north from the Haagen-Dazs on Leicester Square)

Tel: 020-7494 3654

Open: *Mon-Sun* 13.00-23.00

Tube: Leicester Square
      Piccadilly Circus

www.princecharlescinema.com

They don't sell veggie food, but this place really is too good to leave out. You can watch blockbuster movies here in central London for only £1.50! Now that we've got your attention....

Films at around 1pm, 4pm, 6pm, 9pm. Mon-Fri daytime £4, members £1.50. Evenings, weekends and public holidays £5, members £3.50. Special events some evenings cost more such as Singalonga Sound of Music. Membership costs £10 for a year and also gets you 10% off at some West End shops and cafes including Beatroot.

The 6pm and 9pm films sell out so arrive early, get your ticket and head off for some food nearby with all the money you've saved.

Check website for listings or pick up free flyers outside for this week's and next week's films.

"Eat food.
Not too much.
Mostly plants."

Michael Pollan
In Defense of Food

COVENT GARDEN
& Charing Cross / Embankment

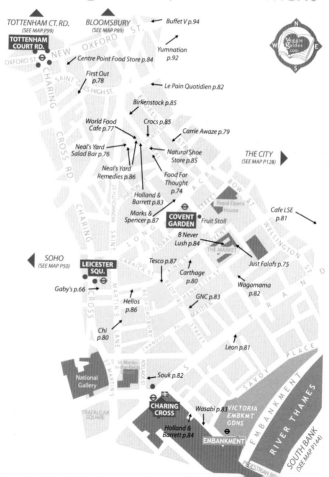

TOTTENHAM CT. RD.
(SEE MAP P99)

TOTTENHAM COURT RD.

BLOOMSBURY
(SEE MAP P89)

Buffet V p.94

Yumnation p.92

Centre Point Food Store p.84

First Out p.78

Le Pain Quotidien p.82

Birkenstock p.85

World Food Cafe p.77

Crocs p.85

Carrie Awaze p.79

Neal's Yard Salad Bar p.76

Natural Shoe Store p.85

THE CITY
(SEE MAP P128)

Neal's Yard Remedies p.86

Food For Thought p.74

Holland & Barrett p.83

Cafe LSE p.81

Marks & Spencer p.87

COVENT GARDEN

Royal Opera House

Fruit Stall

B Never Lush p.84

THE MARKET

SOHO
(SEE MAP P50)

LEICESTER SQU.

Tesco p.87

Just Falafs p.75

Gaby's p.66

Carthage p.80

Wagamama p.82

Helios p.86

GNC p.83

Chi p.80

Leon p.81

National Gallery

Souk p.82

St. Martin-in-the-Fields Church

CHARING CROSS

Wasabi p.83

VICTORIA EMBKMT GDNS

TRAFALGAR SQUARE

Holland & Barrett p.84

EMBANKMENT

RIVER THAMES

SOUTH BANK
(SEE MAP P144)

have a drink and light meal at **Neal's Yard Salad Bar**. For a fast lunch, pop around the corner to the basement **Food for Thought**, one of London's oldest vegetarian restaurants.

Neal Street now has three shops selling non-leather shoes: **Birkenstock**, **Crocs** and **Natural Shoe Store**.

South of the tube station is Covent Garden 'proper' with street theatre in the Piazza, and the **covered market** with craft stalls and a complex of trendy shops including **Lush** and **B**, gorgeous new bodycare stores with hundreds of animal-free delights and all clearly labelled. In the south-east corner is the new cafe and take-away **Just Falafs** which is great for breakfast.

Neal's Yard

A big tourist attraction for its "cute" shops, Covent Garden has two highlights for veggies: **Neal's Yard** in the north and the **covered market** in the south, linked by Neal Street.

The area around **Neal's Yard**, Long Acre and Neal Street is packed with unique and amazing shops and all sorts of designer gear. Stock up at the large **Holland & Barrett**, behind which is Neal's Yard itself, a courtyard with two superb cafe-restaurants, an apothecary, and Neal's Yard Meeting Rooms where you can find green events, personal development and alternative therapy courses. Try the **World Food Café** for a substantial lunch, or

Neal's Yard Salad Bar

Food for Thought

Vegan & veggie restaurant

Open:

Mon–Sat 12.00–20.30
Sun 12.00–17.00

No credit cards.

They do catering.

Unlicensed, BYO, free corkage.

31 Neal Street, Covent Garden
London, WC2H 9PR

Tel: 020–7836 9072 (office)
/0239 (restaurant)

Tube: Covent Garden

See map on page 72

Extremely popular veggie take-away and café on fascinating Neal Street in a vaulted basement. Pine tables and buzzy, cosmopolitan atmosphere. They offer good value and a global menu. Crowded at peak times and you'll need to queue on the stairs at lunchtime for counter service. Many dishes are vegan or vegan option.

Menu changes daily, here are some examples: vegan carrot and butterbean soup or butternut squash soup £3; two bean salad, pasta with pesto, potato salad with tofu mayo, all £3.30 to £6

Vegan main courses £4 to £6 include Ethiopian Wat; Middle Eastern mezze; Carri coco curry; Malay sambal; shepherdess pie; satay and tofu noodles; roast Mediterranean veg with polenta; mushroom stroganoff; cauliflower & peanut arial; sir-fry veg.

The evening menu from 5pm

is slightly different with many different ingredients on a big plate, for example cannelloni filled with aubergine, sundried tomatoes and basil served with polenta, broccoli and tomato frissée salad for £6.20 to £6.70.

Scrummy vegan desserts such as strawberry and vanilla scones, apple and plum crumble or fruit salad £1.30 to £3. Lots of drinks including organic fresh juices, tea, coffee, soya milk.

If you like this you'll probably like the cafes round the corner in Neal's Yard too, though to be honest there is nowhere quite like this place.

Just Falafs Covent Gdn

Mostly veggie falafel take-away and cafe

Open:

Winter Mon–Sun 09.00–19.00
Summer Mon–Sun 09.00–23.00

Patio heaters and parasols
Kids welcome. MC, Visa
£1 eat-in supplment
www.justfalafs.com for menus

27b The Piazza, Covent Garden
London WC2E 8RD (SE corner,
opposite Transport Museum)

Tel: 020–7240 3838

Tube: Covent Garden (nearest)
Temple, Charing Cross

See map on page 72

Very yummy new mostly veggie cafe at the bottom of the Piazza, specialising in wraps, soups and salads made with 70%+ organic ingredients, and of course falafels made with balls of cooked organic chickpeas, herbs and spices that "satisfy more than a sandwich yet don't require a full seating experience." There are 100 seats in the Piazza if you should however feel the need for a seating experience. And they do breakfasts!

Five kinds of falafel £2.95–5.95, with any of the following: filling of the week, grated carrot, beetroot, seasonal beans, mixed sprouts, chili or garlic sauce.

Soup £2.75. Organic winter warmer bean/pulse dhal with khobez bread £3.75.

Salad box with 3 salads and sauce £4.45, 4 salads £5.45, add 50p for falafel. Khobez bread 35p.

Magic breakfast oat porridge until 11am £1.99 with 4-spice, £2.59 large, add 50p for mixed seeds and nuts. Home-made wheat-free granola £1.85.

Snacks include Bombay mix, Green & Blacks chocolate, mango slices, nuts, tortillas, choc apricots, cake and fruit.

Fair Trade organic coffee, hot choc, latte etc from £1.79. Teas £1.49, £1.79. Water, juices, Innocent smoothies and other drinks 99p–£1.79.

Wine £2.95 tumbler, £12 bottle. Organic cider £3.15. Beer £2.95.

At the time of printing they do not yet have soya milk, just rice milk, but doubtless that will change. All wood from sustainable sources. Compostable salad boxes. and they recycle bottles.

If you like this then try their other branch at 155 Wardour Street in Soho.

Neal's Yard Salad Bar

International 98% veggie café-restaurant

Open: *Every day* 08.30–21.00
till 22.00/22.30 in summer

Children welcome, high chairs.
Lots of food kids love like pizza,
spaghetti, shakes, cakes.
Licensed. Birthday cakes. Parties.
www.nealsyardsaladbar.co.uk

2, 8–10 Neal's Yard,
Covent Garden, WC2H 9DP
Tel: 020–7836 3233
Tube: Covent Garden
Tottenham Court Rd
See map on page 70

*Brazilian vegan owned
wholefood café downstairs
with tables inside and out,
and an evening restaurant
upstairs. Vegan, wheat and
yeast-free clearly marked.
There's only one non-
veggie dish. Huge range of
drinks and desserts to
enhance your chill-out.
Look out for exotic Brazilian
juices such as açai, an
amazing fruit that tastes
like chocolate milkshake.*

Six breakfasts 08.30–12.00
£3–6.15 from toast and
peanut butter to full English
with everything.

Mon–Fri take-away large
special £4.

Soup £5.50 (£2.50–3.00
take-way). Appetizers such
as olives, stuffed aubergine,
Snacks include sundried
tomato rice bread, vegan
quiche, pumpkin polenta pie,
bruschetta £1.90–6.50. 5
salads £5.50–£6.50.

Daily specials £9–10.

Specialities £11.50 such as
Brazilian feijoada of black
beans, soya meat, rice, finger
tapioca, fried banana, farofa
and pumpkin; spaghetti
bolognese with minced soya
meat. Vegan hamburger with
finger tapioca and side salad
£7.15. Vegan soyannaise
pizza £5.50.

14 desserts, 8 vegan, £3.95
such as berries and ginger
tart with almond, apple pie,
mango truffle, banana and
cinamon cake, açai cream.
Muffins £2. Soya ice-cream
machine for take-away cones
in chocolate, mango and
sometimes others flavours
such as açai-lemon.

Juices and shakes £3.95
include Brazilian fruits.
500ml beer £3.95. Sangria
£3.95, jug £15.50. House
wine £3.95, bottle £15.50.
Brazilian cocktails £5.

Hot drinks include soyaccino
fresh mint or ginger or
lemongrass tea, tea with rum,
hot choc with ginger £2–3.

World Food Cafe

International vegetarian restaurant

Open:

Mon–Fri 11.30–16.30
Sat 11.30–17.00
Sun closed

Kids welcome
Visa, MC over £10
No alcohol.

First Floor, 14 Neal's Yard
Covent Garden WC2H 9DP
Tel: 020-7379-0298
Tube: Covent Garden
Tottenham Ct. Rd.

See map on page 70

Upstairs international wholefood vegetarian restaurant, overlooking Neal's Yard. 90% vegan. There's an open plan kitchen in the centre so you can see all the food being prepared. A sign of a good vegetarian restaurant is that 75% of the customers are not vegetarian, they just like the environment and the food.

Meals from every continent £6.50-6.85 such as Indian spicy veg masala with steamed brown rice; falafel. Small mixed salad £4.85. Soup of the day £3.85.

Big meals £7.95 could be thali; Turkish meze; West African sweet potatoes and cabbage in creamy groundnut and cayenne sauce, with fresh banana, steamed brown rice and salad; Mexican platter (salsa, refried beans, corn chips or tortillas, salad); large mixed plate of all the day's salads.

Desserts £3.45 include fruit compote, carrot cake, apple crumble, vegan flapjack £1.75.

Fresh fruit juice £2.35, fresh lime soda £2.1, herb teas (pot) or barleycup £1.75, coffee £1.95. They have soya milk.

Minimum charge £6 12.45-14.00 and all day Saturday., which may be waived if not busy. All dishes can be made vegan and take-aways are the same price.

If you like this you'll probably like 222 near Earl's Court (West London), The Gate (Hammersmith) or Manna (Primrose Hill).

First Out

Gay & lesbian vegetarian cafe

Open:
Mon–Sat 10.00–23.00
Sun 11.00–22.30
Kids ok upstairs. Visa, MC.
www.firstoutcafebar.com (events)

52 St Giles High St
London WC2H 8LH
Tel: 020-7240 8042
Tube: Tottenham Court Rd
See map on page 70

Smart, modern and very popular gay and lesbian vegetarian café since 1986 with international menu and basement bar. Music for all tastes and low enough not to be intrusive. Modern art on the walls. Can be lively or very laid back depending on time of day. Great value.

Cooked breakfast £2.60–4.50 such as muesli, juice and coffee/tea. Toast and jam/Marmite £1.25. Sunday brunch £4.95 with sausage, potato rosti, baked beans, tomatoes, garlic mushrooms on toast.

Soup of the day is vegan £3.50. Large mixed salad £5.75, small £3.50. Salads include puy lentils, mixed beans with peppers, carrot/sprout/leaves.

Main meals £5.95–6.25 such as curry, pasta, salad platter (with selection of mixed salads, houmous, baba ghanoush and warm pitta), mezze (spicy chickpeas, broad beans, dips, black olives, green salad and warm pitta), spinach and red peppter tortilla with 3 salads, felafel with houmous and salsa, spicy bean burger, soup and salad combo, soup and sandwich.

Good for vegans until you get to the many cakes and home-made flapjacks, but hooray no "vegan tax" for soya milk in your coffee or hot chocolate £1.25–2.10. Pot of tea £1.40, for 2 £2.50. Shakes £2, fruit smoothies £2.75. Soft drinks and juices £1.40–1.50.

Glass of wine £2.95, large £4.25, bottle £12. Beer £2.80–2.90. Cocktails £4.75–5.00. Pitcher of Pims or Sangria £11.95, Halimocho (retsina and cola) £9.95. Pitcher in happy hour 5–7pm £8.50. Mon–Tue 2 for 1 cocktails. Any day 4 Becks or San Miguel beers £10. Red Bull £2.60.

Friday night is 'Girl Friday' or women's night with men as guests from 8pm, or fellas you could try Just Felafs or Neal's Yard Salad Bar. See website for events.

Carrie Awaze

Omnivorous Indian and international cafe and sandwich shop

Open:

Mon–Fri	10.30–20.00 (last orders)
Sat	12.00–20.00
Sun	closed

No mobiles unless you are a doctor or nurse.
Licensed for alcohol with food.

27 Endell Street
Covent Garden, WC2H 9BA
Tel: 020-7836 0815
Tube: Covent Garden
Kids welcome. MC, Visa.
See map on page 70

An oasis from the bustle of central London for 18 years, this is nothing like the factory production line in a chain cafe. Richly decorated inside with warm deep reds, Indian tapestries, mobiles, fans, paintings, wooden tables with decorative tablecloths and wooden benches or chairs with cushions. There is classical sitar music which the vegetarian owner Guruji teaches. You'll find stacks for veggies and vegans and they use separate utensils for veggie food. It's a good place for an early evening meal too.

"Vegetarianism is an act of conquering yourself," says Guruji. "When you conquer yourself, you don't cause the destruction of anything."

Soup £3.25, take-out £2.95.

7 vegan and 21 veggie sandwiches £2.55–3.25 take-away, £3.25–4.20 eat-in or delivered, such as "Brown Bomber" onion bhajia with hummous and salad.

Filled jacket potato with salad £5.95–6.25 such as "Arne Street" with dhal and onion bhajia, or with veg curry and cashews. Main meal £7.95 such as vegetarian or vegan thali, curry and rice, or Hyderabadi korma with veg and fruit.

Seasonal fresh fruit salad is the only vegan dessert £3.25.

Beer £2.35 with food. Indian Soma wine £12.95 bottle, £3.25 glass. Soft drinks £2.25 include organic lemonade and ginger beer, Azerbaijani pomegranate juice, mango juice, coconut water. Teas, coffees, chai £1.25–2.25, they have soya milk.

If you like this you'll probably like Sabras in Willesden.

Chi

Chinese vegan buffet restaurant

56 St Martin's Lane
Covent Garden, WC2N 4EA

Tel: 020-7836 3434

Open: *Every day:* 12.00–23.00
Sun 12.00–22.00

Tube: Leicester Square,
Charing Cross

All you can eat Chinese vegan buffet restaurant, not as manically busy as the ones in Soho, one block back from Charing Cross Road in the heart of theatreland. They tell us that many customers arrive clutching a copy of *Vegetarian London*. Fill up at the West End's best value restaurant with fried and boiled rice, noodles, crispy seaweed, stir-fry vegetables, tofu, mushrooms, spring rolls, several kinds of fake meat, and fruit salad, with as many visits to the buffet as you like for just £5 before 5pm, then £6 afterwards and all day Sunday. Take-away £3 or £4 for a large box.

Soft drinks, juices, teas £1.50–2.00. No credit cards. No alcohol.

Carthage

Mediterranean omnivorous restaurant

9 King Street, Covent Garden
London WC2E 8HN

Tel: 020-7240 5178

Open: *Mon–Sun* 10.00–23.00
(last orders)

Tube: Covent Garden

A new restaurant with friendly staff and good prices for central London. The veggie/vegan mezze is great with 8 cold and one hot starters £3.25–3.95 such as hot falafel with broad beans; dolma stuffed vine leaves; kisir crushed wheat with walnuts, hazelnuts, tomato juice, herbs, peppers etc; imam bayildi aubergines and chickpeas. Two North African hot main courses are veggie, lunch £6.50, dinner £9.95, either tagine or Moroccan couscous with mixed veg and chickpeas in spiced sauce topped with sautéed raisins. Also spaghetti napolitana £7.45, penne all'arabiatta £8.45.

House wine £10.95 bottle, £3.25 glass. Children welcome, high chairs. Visa, MC.

The Cafe, LSE

Omnivorous cafe

East Buildings Basement
Houghton Street, Aldwych
London WC2 2AE

Tel: 020-7955-7164

Open: *Mon-Fri*
        9.00-18.00 term
        10.00-16.00 holidays

Tube: Temple

Student basement café in the London School of Economics, no longer completely veggie but with lots of options for veggies, sometimes vegan. These may change daily and prices are very reasonable.

Several veggie kosher sandwiches, including avocado with mixed leaf or roasted veg, and filled bagels £1.20-£2 such as veg fake chicken, houmous and salad. Italian panini with various fillings such as roasted five-bean hummous.

The soup   of the day is usually (4 out of 5 days) vegetarian or vegan, such as tomato and basil with mixed veg, or minestrone, £1 a cup or £1.30 with a roll, large cup £1.30-1.60.

Salads £1.10- £2.30 might include pasta with tomato, or couscous salad with mixed veg.

Fair Trade coffee 60p small, 70p large, espresso, cappuccino, but no soya milk.

Leon

Omnivorous cafe & take-away

73-76 The Strand, WC2R 0DE

Tel: 020-7240 3070/3071

Open: *Mon-Fri* 07.30-22.00
        Sat   09.30-22.00
        Sun   09.30-18.00

Tube: Charing Cross

www.leonrestaurants.co.uk

New fast food bar with lots of great value veggie food. See Soho branch for details (page 67) or check their website for the full menu.

The Souk

Arabian omnivorous cafe/take-away

8 Adelaide Street
London WC2N 4HZ
(opposite Charing Cross Station
next to St Martins Church
market)

Tel: 020-7240 2337

Open: *Mon-Fri*   08.00-19.00
      Thu   till 20.00
      Sat   11.00-18.00
      Sun   closed

Tube: Charing Cross

This Middle-Eastern/Arabian take-away and sit-down cafe serves really good vegan wraps such as houmus, roast veg, falafel with green beans, bean and salad wraps, stuffed vine leaves with rice, Taif bulgur with roasted red pepper and butternut squash. Also one vegan salad. All ready wrapped or sold in little containers to take away.

The sweets are fresh fruit salad, and baklava. Innocent smoothies and other drinks to take away or eat in.

Also breakfast £2.75 granola, fruit bowl, soya milk, with fresh strawberries, raspberries and blueberries on top.

Le Pain Quotidien

Omnivorous French cafe and bakery

174 High Holborn, Covent Garden WC1V 7AA (in the Aveda store, at Endell St end of High Holborn)

Tel: 020-7486 6154

Open: *Mon-Fri*   08.00-19.00
      Sat-Sun   09.00-18.00
      Sun/BH   10.00-17.00

Tube: Holborn
www.lepainquotidien.com

Veggie/vegan-friendly French cafe chain. Highlights are tofu salad £6.95 with sauces and bread, soups £2.55-£4.95, mint tea and vegan blueberry muffins. See Marylebone or Sloane for more details.

Wagamama Covent Gdn

Japanese omnivorous restaurant

1a Tavistock Street
Covent Garden
London WC2E 7PE

Tel: 020-7836 3330

Open: *Mon-Sat* 12.00-23.00
      Sun   12.30-22.00

Tube: Covent Garden

Omnivorous fast food Japanese noodle bar with some extremely filling veggie and vegan dishes. See Bloomsbury branch for menu. (page 93)

Wasabi Sushi

Take-away sushi bar

34 Villiers Street, London WC2
Tel: 020-7807 9992
Open: *Mon-Fri* 11.00–22.00
Sat-Sun 11.00–20.00
Tube: Embankmemt
www.wasabi.uk.com

They do some vegan sushi – about 10 different types at approx £1 to £1.50 per two sushi rolls. You can pick your own pre-wrapped sushi and make up your own box of food for about £6 which is quite a lot of sushi – takeaway only.

There are avocado sushi, sweet potato and mushroom sushi, tofu with onion sushi etc. All ingredients clearly marked and they sell canned drinks plus some hot food, with one vegan dish, such as stir fried tofu noodles.

We hear noodles with tofu are not vegetarian despite a V symbol. The product manual shows oyster sauce with oyster extract.

If you like this, there are other branches listed on their website around the CIty, Piccadilly, Oxford Street, Warren Street, and in Victoria station.

GNC, Covent Garden

Health food shop

37 Bedford Street, Covent Garden, London WC2E 9EN
Tel: 020-7836 9363
Open: *Mon-Sat* 9.00–19.00
Sun 12.00–18.00
Tube: Covent Garden

Lots of supplements and bodybuilding stuff. Some nuts and seeds, crackers, biscuits.

Holland & Barrett

Healthfood shop

21 Shorts Gardens
Covent Garden, London WC2H
Tel: 020-7836 5151
Open: *Mon-Sat* 10.00–20.00
Sun 11–18.00
Tube: Covent Garden,
Tottenham Court Rd

Big health food shop by the entrance to Neal's Yard with its veggie cafes. Some take-away food such as pasties and rolls. (For fresh organic fruit and veg go to the nearby Tesco Metro.) Every 4-6 weeks a qualified nutri-tionist offers food sensitivity testing for £45.

Holland & Barrett

Healthfood shop

Unit 16, Embankment Shopping Centre, Villiers St, WC2 6NN

Tel: 020-7839 4988

Open: *Mon-Fri* 08.00-19.00
Sat 09-18.00
Sun 10-18.00

Tube: Embankment
Charing Cross

Down the left side of Charing Cross station. Lots of veggie snacks and take-aways including pastries and flapjacks.

Centre Point Food Store

Omnivorous Korean/Japanese grocer

20-21 St Giles High St WC2H 8LN (under Centrepoint)

Tel: 020- 7836 9860

Open: *Mon-Sat* 10.00-22.00
Sun 12.00-22.00

Tube: Tottenham Court Rd
www.cpfs.co.uk

Handy for Japanese macrobiotic foods.

Lush Covent Garden

Cruelty-free cosmetics

11 The Piazza, Covent Garden, London WC2E 8RB

Tel: 020-7240 4570

Open: *Mon-Sat* 10.00-19.00
Sun 11.00-18.00

Tube: Covent Garden
www.lush.co.uk catalogue

Cruelty-free cosmetics, most of them vegan and clearly labelled. See Soho for details.

B never too busy to be beautiful

Cruelty-free cosmetics

Unit 13, The Piazza, Covent Garden WC2E 8RB (two doors from Lush)

Tel: 020-7836 0797

Open: *Mon-Sat* 10.00-18.00
sometimes later
Sun 11.00-18.00

Tube: Covent Garden
www.bnevertoobusytobebeautiful.com

Similar to their sister shop Lush, but more glamorous and luxurious. See Soho branch for details.

Le Pain Quotidien

Omnivorous restaurant

Upper Level, Royal Festival Hall,
London SE1 EXX

Tel: 020-7486 6154

Open: *Mon-Fri* 07.00-23.00
        Sat   08.00-23.00
        Sun/BH 09.00-22.00

Tube: Waterloo
www.lepainquotidien.com

Veggie/vegan-friendly
French cafe chain. Highlights
are tofu salad £6.95 with
sauces and bread, soups
£2.55-£4.95, mint tea and
vegan blueberry muffins. See
Marylebone or Sloane for
more details.

Paradiso

Omnivorous Italian restaurant

61 The Cut, SE1 8LL

Tel: 020 7261 1221

Open: *Mon-Sat* 12-24.00
        Sun 12-23.00

Tube: Southwark (nearby)

www.pizzaparadiso.co.uk

Loads of the usual Italian
veggie options in this small
chain of smart Sicilian style
restaurants. There are a
couple of vegan dishes and
most of the veggie pizzas
can be made with no cheese.
Of the 45 dishes, half are

veggie. Starters £2.45-5.35.
Mains £5.55-7.95. Lots of
Italian wines from £12.50
bottle, £3.15 glass. Juice
£1.65, freshly pressed
orange juice £2.55.

Children more than welcome,
baby chairs. MC, Visa, Amex.

Troia

Omnivorous Turkish/Anatolian

3F Belvedere Road,
County Hall, London SE1 7GQ

Tel: 020 7633 9309

Open: *Mon-Sat* 12.00-24.00
        Sun   12.00-22.30

Tube: Waterloo

www.waterlootroia.com

Lots of veggie and vegan
options in this restaurant
near the London Eye. A
separate vegetarian set
mixed mezze for £6.95 per
person, consisting of
tabouleh, humous, falafel,
beans etc in fact 11different
dishes (a couple need substi-
tuting if you want vegan). 10
hot and cold veggie starters
£3.50-4.25, 7 mains £7.55-
7.95.

Lots of desserts £3.25-3.75,
some vegan option.

House wine £12.50 bottle,
£3.50 glass. Children
welcome, high chairs. MC,
Visa.

Wagamama

Omnivorous Japanese restaurant

Riverside level, Royal Festival Hall, London, SE1 8XX

Tel: 020-7021 0877

Open: Mon–Sat 12.00–23.00
Sun 12.30–22.00

Tube: Waterloo

Large Japanese fast food noodle restaurant. See Bloomsbury branch, p.93.

Lower Marsh Market

Street market

Lower Marsh Street behind Waterloo Station

Open: Mon–Fri 9–14.00

Tube: Waterloo

Fruit and veg and just about everything for the home except furniture.

Bonus South Bank places next to Le Pain Quotidien:

Feng Sushi Unit 9, Festival Terrace, Belvedere Rd SE1 8XX. (Next door to Le Pain Quotidien) Part of a chain of filling Japanese restaurants. Good vegan dishes to look out for are: vegetable tempura £8, Nippon duck (tofu mock duck rolls) £6, lots of salads and vegan sushi approx £3 each. Menu at www.fengsushi.co.uk.

Ping Pong Next door to Feng Sushi at Festival Terrace. Lots of Chinese veggie food. www.pingpongdimsum.com

Los Iguanas Unit 14, next to Le Pain Quotidien, Festival Terrace , Belvedere Rd SE1. Various Latin veggie dishes – some need to be requested without cheese or sour cream for vegans. www.iguanas.co.uk

These places are not veggie but they all do ok on the veggie front if you happen to be with a posse of meat eaters at office parties or visiting the London Eye etc. The best ones are Giraffe, Wagamama and Feng Sushi. There is also Feng Sushi at Chalk Farm and London Bridge. Despite being Japanese style, plates are quite big.

Birkenstock

Non-leather sandals and clogs

70 Neal Street (north end)
Covent Garden, WC2H 7PA

Tel: 020-7240 2783

Open: *Mon–Sat* 10.30–19.00
Thur –20.00
Sun 12.00–18.00

Tube: Covent Garden
www.birkenstock.co.uk

At the back is a shelf of vegan sandals £40–47. Also multi-coloured plastic clogs £30, popular with chefs and gardeners, one of them does not have the cork insole to get soggy. Waterproof plastic sandalsfor the beach £32. Reflexology sandals £33–35.

The Natural Shoe Store

Shop with non-leather shoes

21 Neal Street, Covent Garden
London WC2H 9PU
(corner of Shelton Street)

Tel: 020-7836 5254

Open: *Mon–Tue* 10.00–18.00
Wed, Fri 10.00–19.00
Thur 10.00–20.00
Sat 10.00–18.30
Sun 12.00–17.30

Tube: Covent Garden
www.thenaturalshoestore.com

Mostly leather (animal skin) but at the back they have a few Earth vegan shoes with negative heel £75–95, Grand Step hemp trainers £30–33, Comfort nylon ladies house shoes £20.

Crocs

Plastic clogs

48 Neal Street, corner with
Shorts Gardens, London WC2

Tel: 020-3157 4005

Open: from October 2007

Tube: Covent Garden
www.crocs.eu

Forget wooden clogs, these plastic clogs are said to be ultra-light, soft, lightweight, slip resistant and fun, made from a closed cell resin that moulds to your feet when exposed to body heat and resists bacteria and odour. Originally designed for yachting, they quickly became popular with doctors, nurses, waiters, van drivers, gardeners, postmen, chefs, fashion victims and celebs, making Crocs the fastest-growing shoe company in the world. You can walk for miles in them and they are perfect for boating and gardening. 9 different models, 17 colours, under £40. See website store locator for other shops that sell them around London.

Neal's Yard Remedies

Herbs and complementary health

6 & 15 Neal's Yard, WC2

Tel: 020-7240 4145
Therapies: 020-73700 7662

Open: *Mon-Fri* 10.30-19.00
Sat 10.30-19.30
Sun 11.00-17.00

Tube: Covent Garden
www.nealsyardremedies.com

Two shops on Neal's Yard with 200 herbs and spices by weight, organic toiletries, natural remedies, cotton-wool, soaps, books on homeopathy and remedies.

Consultations available with multi-lingual staff.

All products tested on human volunteers, not animals. Mostly organic, lots of Fair Trade, 10p for every primary item of packaging you return for recycling.

They also have therapy rooms upstairs at number 2 offering dozens of healing treatments from acupuncture to zero balancing and a drop-in herbal medicine clinic on certain days.

Helios

Hoemopathic pharmacy

8 New Row, WC2N 4LJ

Tel: 020-7379 7434

Open: *Mon-Fri* 09.30-17.30
Sat 10.00-17.30
Sun closed

Tube: Leicester Square,
Covent Garden,
Charing Cross
www.helioslondon.com

Staffed by homeopaths, as well as homeopathic tablets, pills, tinctures and creams, they sell bodycare products with no animal ingredients or testing, including own brand creams, Dr Hauschka, Barefoot Botanicals, Esencia hand made herbal soaps, Kingfisher toothpaste, massage oils.

Supplements by Solgar, Bioforce, Higher Nature, Floradix, Biocare and Udo's Oil.

Everlasting crystal nail files. Loofahs. Over 400 books on homeopathy, complementary therapies, and mind, body, spirit.

Consultations by appointment. MC, Visa.

Tesco Covent Garden

Supermarket

22-25 Bedford St,WC2E 9EQ
(corner of King St & Garrick St)

Open: *Mon–Fri* 08.00–24.00
        Sat   07.30–22.00
        Sun   12.00–18.00

Tube: Leicester Square

What, a supermarket in a Veggie Guide? We've made an exception as it's one of the two places we know in Covent Garden to pick up organic fruit and veg for a snack. The other one is:

Marks & Spencer

Supermarket

107-115 Long Acre,
Covent Garden, WC2E 9NT
(opposite the tube)

Tel: 020- 7240 9549

Tube: Covent Garden

Lots of organic food, plenty of vegetarian food, though not the best place if you're looking for vegan sand-wiches.

BLOOMSBURY
Central London tranquil hotspot

This residential and university area, to the east of Tottenham Court Road and north of Covent Garden, has many midrange and budget hotels. University College London and the 800-bed Generator backpacker hostel ensure that the streets are thronged with young people from all over the world. The top attraction here is the **British Museum**, the largest of London's 150 museums, featuring Egyptian mummies, Greek and Roman antiquities and other British Empire loot.

Our favourite road is **Marchmont Street** with cafes, take-aways, a cinema nearby and a real community feel. Indian restaurant **Vegetarian Paradise** has a lunchtime bargain buffet and the superb **Alara** wholefoods store opposite has a veggie café, take-aways and extremely charming staff.

On the southern fringes of Bloomsbury are two new bargain Chinese all-you-can-eat vegan restaurants **Buffet V** at the top of Shaftesbury Avenue in a recycled McDonalds (hooray, 1 down, 20,000 to go) and **Veg** at the corner of Theobalds Road and Grays Inn Road.

Picnic tip: Fancy a day off lounging on the grass reading a novel? On a warm day load up with picnic munchies at Alara or Planet Organic (see Tottenham Court Road) and head for tranquil Russell Square, Bloomsbury Square, Gordon Square (week days only, full of students revising) or Queen Square. Or pay your respects by placing a candle in a jar at the base of the statue of Gandhi in Tavistock Square. For more typically British wet weather, next to Queen Square you'll find a lovely vegetarian café in the basement of **Mary Ward** adult education centre.

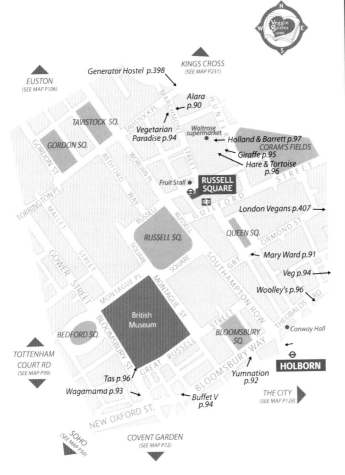

EUSTON
(SEE MAP P106)

Generator Hostel p.398

KINGS CROSS
(SEE MAP P231)

Alara
p.90

TAVISTOCK SQ.

Vegetarian
Paradise p.94

Waitrose
supermarket

Holland & Barrett p.97

GORDON SQ.

CORAM'S FIELDS

Giraffe p.95

Hare & Tortoise
p.96

Fruit Stall

RUSSELL
SQUARE

London Vegans p.407

RUSSELL SQ.

QUEEN SQ.

Mary Ward p.91

Veg p.94

Woolley's p.96

British
Museum

BLOOMSBURY
SQ.

Conway Hall

BEDFORD SQ.

HOLBORN

TOTTENHAM
COURT RD
(SEE MAP P99)

Tas p.96

Yumnation
p.92

THE CITY
(SEE MAP P128)

Wagamama p.93

Buffet V
p.94

NEW OXFORD ST.

SOHO
(SEE MAP P50)

COVENT GARDEN
(SEE MAP P72)

Alara

Wholefood store and vegetarian cafe

Open:

Mon–Fri	08.00–19.00
Sat	10–18.00
Sun	closed

MC, Visa

58–60 Marchmont Street
Bloomsbury, London WC1N 1AB
Tel: 020–7837 1172
Tube: Russell Square

See map on page 89

Big family run vegetarian healthfood shop in a lovely street that is very popular with locals, opposite an Indian vegetarian restaurant. It's near Russell Square and the British Museum. There are 12 cafe tables, each seating 4 people, and a large take-away section – one of the best places to grab lunch to go. Popular with local residents and office workers, students from the nearby universities, tourists and back-packers from the many hotels and the Generator hostel around the corner. Bustling at lunchtime and chilled out rest of the day.

Help yourself to 100% organic salads and hot food, 89p/100g, such as chickpea salad and gluten-free veg curries. Organic, gluten-free and sugar-free cakes.

Hot drinks are all organic such as herbal teas £1.09, moccaccino £1.75, soya latte £1.49, with ginger +20p.

Freshly made organic juices £2.09 small, medium £2.29, £2.89 large, such as orange, apple, carrot with ginger. Cockails £2.79–3.19 such as apple, beetroot and carrot. Smoothies with yogurt £2.19–2.69, large £3.19–4.19, can be with rice or soya milk.

Stacks of vegan and organic produce in several aisles, including fruit & veg, wide variety of bread, own brand muesli, Swedish Glace vegan ice-cream, frozen foods. Organic juices and fruit smoothies, selection of veggie beers and wines. Supplements, cosmetics, essential oils.

They have experienced and charming staff to give advice about nutrition. Every week qualified nutritionist in store, see sign in window.

If you like this you'll probably like Bumblebee, another fabulous wholefood store in Brecknock Road, north London.

Mary Ward

Vegetarian Café

Open:	Term time
Mon–Thu	9.30–21.00
Fri	9.30–20.30
Sat	9.30–16.00

Sun: First Sun of the month when the centre is open 11–15.00

Kids welcome, small portions
Cheques (add 80p) but no credit cards. Not licensed.

42 Queen Square
Bloomsbury
London WC1N 3AQ
Tel: 020–7831 7711
Tube: Russell Sq, Holborn
www.marywardcentre.ac.uk for courses
See map on page 89

Completely vegetarian cafe in an adult education centre by green Queens Square. Modern and bright with monthly changing art exhibits. Friendly Italian owners so expect a Mediterranean flavour on the menu which changes daily. Now with vegan cakes!

Breakfast served until 11.45, usually toasties, jam and Danish pastries.

The lunch menu includes daily changing salads with four choices which are vegan and wheat-free, £2.10 small, £3.10 large, with balsamic and oil or vinaigrette on the side. Lots of small things such as samosas, crostini, polenta croquettes. They bake bread on the premises such as herby garlic or spinach and cumin.

Light meals £3.20 include stuffed baguettes, such as red lentil and olive pate with lettuce; soup (always vegan); tortilla stuffed with roast butternut squash, olives and aubergine; roast veg with couscous; pasta bake; potato pie; roast onion stuffed with couscous and veg; stews such as lentil or bean especially in winter. £3.80 with mixed green salad or £4.30 with selection of 3–4 salads.

Cakes from 80p such as carob choc, muffin, wholemeal and choc biscuit, peanut butter slice.

Plenty of cold drinks such as fresh juices, Innocent smoothies (some organic), Purdeys. Herbal teas, Yogi tea, Illi coffee, soyacinno, latte, chocolate, Barleycup.

Near London Vegans' last Wednesday evening venue (see Local Groups) so a great place to unwind beforehand.

If you like this you'll probably like spending an afternoon at Pogo Cafe or the Gallery Cafe in East London.

Yumnation

Omnivorous cafe and take-away

Open:

Mon–Fri	08.00–19.00 or later
Sat	12.30–18.00
Sun	closed

Children welcome. MC, Visa., 50p charge for debit cards.

29 Sicilian Avenue, WC1A 2QH
(facing Bloomsbury Square)

Tel: 020--7430 0515

Tube: Holborn
www.yumnation.com
See map on page 89

Cafe and sandwich shop with a better selection than usual for vegetarians and vegans, including Indian wraps, meals, salads and juices. The owner is a n Asian former city profes-sional who realised there was nowhere to get proper Asian food that maintained authenticity of taste without the pungent aromas that could get you banned from eating lunch at your desk.

There is minimal unhealthy fat content as they use olive and sunflower oil but no mayonnaise or butter. Lots of seating outside and some inside.

Vegan ready meals with rice £4 include yellow lentils, aloo gobi (potato and cauliflower); spinach and lentil, or chickpeas. Veg samosa 80p. North Indian potato and cumin kathi wrap or hot chickpea wrap £2.60. Tomato or lentil soup. Chickpea salad.

Sandwiches £3-3.40 such as chickpea mix, Indian aubergine, Bombay potato, chickpea salad, others on request.

Indian sweets, flapjacks £1.30, brownies 95p.

Milkshakes £1.85 8oz up to £2.60 20oz. Soya milk +40p.

Apple, pear, orange or carrot juice freshly squeezed 9oz £1.80, 20oz £3. Cans 75p, mineral water 90p-£1.30.

55 kinds of tea from £1.40. Latte, cappuccino £1.60, espresso £1.20.

Outside catering for up to 100. Platter of 20 half sand-wiches or wraps in presenta-tion box £14 with a day's notice.

If you like this you'll probably like Health Food Centre

Wagamama

Omnivorous
Japanese restaurant

Open:
Mon–Sat 12.00–23.00 (last order)
Sun 12.30–22.00
MC, Visa. Menus and branches at www.wagamama.com

4A Streatham Street
off Bloomsbury St.
London WC1A 1JB
Tel: 020-7323 9223
Tube: Tottenham Court Rd
See map on page 89

This was the first of many Japanese noodle bars listed in this book, with over nine veggie and vegan dishes, long trestle tables and very noisy. Not great for a first date, but superb if you're out on the town for a laff. When each dish is cooked it is served straight away, so a group may get their food at different times.

Mains include saien soba wholemeal ramen noodles in a vegetable soup topped with stir-fried veg and fried tofu £7.50; yasai katsu curry of sweet potato, aubergine and butternut squash deep-fried in panko breadcrumbs served with rice, mixed leaves and pickles £7.15. Also two sauce based noodle dishes. Large salad £6.95.

Side dishes £1.35–£4.50 include miso soup, grilled asparagus; raw salad; edamame green soya beans in their pods. Vegans check whether veg dumplings (gyoza) are glazed with egg.

6 desserts £3.05–4.60, but this branch told us that now all of them contain milk, which is a real let-down with so many vegan choices earlier. On the plus side, we've always been so stuffed after a soup-noodle dish that this has not been an issue.

Raw mixed juices £2.85. Wine from £11.75 a bottle, £3.45–4.60 a glass; beers from £3.20; hot sake and plum wine with sparkling water and ice from £3.20 for a small flask.

If you like this you'll probably like their menu other branches in London. See the A–Z restaurant index.

Buffet V

Vegan Chinese buffet restaurant

40 New Oxford Street, WC1A 1ES
Tel: 020-7580 9545
Open: *Mon–Sun* 12.00-22.00
Tube: Tottenham Court Road

The newest Chinese vegan all-you-can-eat for £5.50, £6 after 5pm and Sundays and the best possible use for a closed down McDonalds, you can even see the M on the doorstep. Lovely interior with warm orange walls, wooden tables, oriental artefacts and mirrors. Lots of fake meats, vegetables, peanuts, 3 kinds of noodles, rice, fried rice, tofu, spring rolls, pancakes, salad, fruit salad.

Hot and cold drinks £1.50. Unlimited Chinese tea £1. No alcohol.

Take-away £3.50.

Cash only.

Veg

Vegan Chinese buffet restaurant

4-6 Theobalds Road, WC1X 8PN
(next to Yorkshire Grey pub on the corner of Grays Inn Road)
Tel: 07515 253798
Open: *Mon–Sat* 12.00-22.00
　　　　Sun　　closed
Tube: Chancery Lane

New all you can eat Chinese vegan buffet restaurant for £5.50 daytime, £6.50 after 5pm. Over 20 dishes including noodles, veg duck, veg beef, seaweed, dim sum, Chinese stew, Chinese pizza, boiled or special fried rice. Soft drinks and Chinese tea £1.50. No alcohol. Take-out box £3.

Vegetarian Paradise

Indian restaurant & take-away

59 Marchmont Street
Bloomsbury, London WC1N 1AP
Tel: 020-7278 6881
Open: *Mon–Sun* 12-15.00
　　　　　　　18.00-24.00
Tube: Russell Square

Indian vegetarian restaurant opposite Alara Wholefoods, offering real value for money with a lunch time buffet every day, all you can eat for £4.50 per adult.

Hot starters, £2.10–£2.50, include dal soup, ragara pattice, stuffed potato cakes with spicy chick peas. Cold starters such as pani poori – hollow wholewheat pooris served with tamarind and dates, spicy sauces and boiled chick peas for.

Curry dishes £2.40–2.50, dosas £3.95–5.15, thalis £4.95–7.95. Desserts £1.95–2.10. are milky apart from fresh fruit tropical sorbet

Bring your own alcohol, no corkage charge. Tea, coffee, soft drinks £1–1.10.

Separate party room available for up to 40 people. MC, Visa.

Giraffe, Brunswick Ctr

Omnivorous restaurant

19–23 Brunswick Shopping Centre, Brunswick Square Bloomsbury WC1N 1AF
(East side of precinct by cinema)

Tel: 020-7812 1336

Open: *Mon–Fri* 08.00–22.30
Sat 09.00–22.30
Sun 09.00–22.15

Tube: Russell Square
Children welcome, kids' menu
www.giraffe.net

Bright, lively, fun, very friendly and packed with young people. Branches all over London, with some prices slightly cheaper further from the centre.

Big breakfast/brunch menu till noon, cooked £3.95–6.95, organic porridge £3.95 with strawberries, super-foods mixed grain muesli with berries £3.95.

Starters £4.75–5.95 such as hummus with pine nuts, warm naan and veg; soup with garlic toast; mezze plate with tabouleh, hummus, Tunisian ratatouille and falafel. Salads £2.95, £6.95, £8.95. Edamame green soya beans £3.95.

Main courses inclue deluxe falafel burger and fries £8.95. Green curry and rice £7.95. Tofu veg noodles stir-fry £6.95.

No vegan desserts on the menu but they can do you a fruit bowl from the breakfast menu.

Wine £3.25–4.25 glass, £11.95 bottle. Beer around £3. Cocktails £5.50–£6. Smoothies and shakes £3.25. Teas, coffees, (soya) cappuccino, flavoured latte £1.50–2.95.

Children's menu with colouring and word game, includes sausage or falafel burger and fries £3.95, pasta with tomato sauce £2.95, brunch (till 4pm) £1.95–3.95, extra veg £1. Drinks, juices and smoothies £1.45–1.60. Mon–Fri (not bank holidays) 12.00–15.00 meal plus dessert and drink £5.50.

GM free. MC, Visa, Amex.

Hare & Tortoise

Noodle and sushi restaurant

11–13 Brunswick Shopping Centre, Brunswick Square Bloomsbury WC1N 1AF
(S.E. corner of the precinct)
Tel: 020-7278 4945
Open: *Mon–Sun* 12.00–23.00
Tube: Russell Square
w^3.hareandtortoise-restaurants.co.uk

Huge portions and low prices for central London. Starters £2.80–3.50 include green salad, tofu "duck" pancakes, spring rolls, Chinese greens, edamame steamed soy beans. Miso soup £1.60. Veggie mains £4.50 include deep–fried tofu and vegetable ramen in soup (like the massive bowls at Wagamama only cheaper); chow mein with tofu and Chinese veg; satay mixed veg and tofu with noodles and sesame.

Freshly pressed juices £1.90–2.10. Wine from £9.50 bottle, £2.50–3.40

glass. Sake or plum wine £3. Oriental beer from £1.60. Tea 60p, coffee £1.20. No cheques, only cash or card (surcharge of 30p if under £10).

Tas

Omnivorous Turkish restaurant

22 Bloomsbury St, WC1B 3QJ
Tel: 020-7637 4555/1333
Open: *Mon–Sat* 12.00–23.30
        Sun   12.00–22.30
Tube: Tottenham Court Rd
www.tasrestaurant.com

Similar menu to the Waterloo branch (see South Bank section) with stacks of veggie and vegan Turkish dishes. Licensed. Visa, MC, Amex.

Woolley's

Omnivorous take-away

33 Theobalds Road
London WC1X 8SP
Tel: 020-7405 3028
Open: *Mon–Fri* 07.30–15.30
        Sat–Sun closed
Tube: Holborn, Chancery Lane
www.woolleys.co.uk

Mostly vegetarian take–away food, fresh every day and able to cater for gluten free.

Specials change weekly and

include a salad and 4 veggie hot meals £3.80 such as korma or vegetable & lentil coconut curry, mixed bean or chickpea casserole. A different soup each day, sometimes vegan, £1.30–1.95. Also pies and pasties, baked potatoes and some cakes (not vegan).

Hummous and roast veg sandwich £2.60.

Innocent juices, drinks, bottled water, tea, coffee.

Fax your order through on 020-7430-2417. They also do catering and wholesale sandwiches.

Holland & Barrett

Healthfood store

Unit 29, Brunswick Shopping Ctr
London WC1N 1AE
(East side of precinct in middle)

Tel: 020-7278 4640

Open: *Mon-Sat* 9.30–19.00
Sun 11.00–17.00

Tube: Russell Square

Recently moved out of the arcade into larger premises in the main shopping centre, and now with a fridge that includes pastries and sos rolls. Lots of snacks and drinks. Dried fruit, nuts and seeds, teas, juices, soya/almond/rice milk, water, muesli. Herbal rememdies, vitamins and minerals, body building stuff, aromatherapy, body care products.

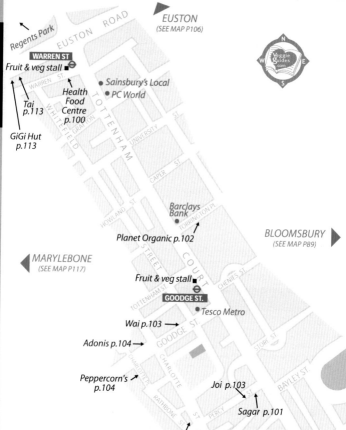

EUSTON
(SEE MAP P106)

Regents Park

EUSTON ROAD

WARREN ST

Fruit & veg stall ■

Tai
p.113

GiGi Hut
p.113

WHITFIELD ST

WARREN ST

GRAFTON

Health
Food
Centre
p.100

Sainsbury's Local

PC World

TOTTENHAM COURT ROAD

UNIVERSITY ST

CAPER ST

HOWLAND ST

TORRINGTON PL

Barclays
Bank

Planet Organic p.102

BLOOMSBURY
(SEE MAP P89)

MARYLEBONE
(SEE MAP P117)

Fruit & veg stall ■

GOODGE ST.

CHENIES ST

TOTTENHAM ST

Tesco Metro

Wai p.103 →

Adonis p.104 →

GOODGE ST

STORE ST

CHARLOTTE ST

Peppercorn's ↗
p.104

Joi p.103

Sagar p.101

PERCY ST

BAYLEY ST

RATHBONE ST

RATHBONE ST

Rasa Express
p.103

Sainsbury's

Dominion
Theatre

TOTTENHAM
COURT RD.

SOHO
(SEE MAP P51)

OXFORD STREET

COVENT GARDEN
(SEE MAP P72)

TOTTENHAM COURT ROAD

Tottenham Court Road is the street for everything electronic with computer, hi-fi and camera shops galore. There are also furniture and futon shops and a PC World at the north end. The main street has a Sainsbury's and some cafes, but there are veggie treasures awaiting you in the side-streets (that you would probably never discover without this guide and map!) At all of them you can enjoy a substantial sit-down meal for under a tenner, and at some a fiver might do it.

New in 2007 was the south Indian vegetarian restaurant **Sagar**, cousin to the original branch in Hammersmith. It's terrific value, especially at lunch time. Nearby are two Chinese vegan buffet restaurants, **Joi** in Percy Street and **Wai** on Goodge Street, just past **Tesco**. **Peppercorn's,** in a pedestrian alley, is a very friendly organic wholefood store with a nice range of take-aways in the fridge. If you fancy a change, **Adonis** Lebanese cafe has lots of vegetarian meze dishes. Afterwards you could get your hair cut at Mr Topper for only £6.

Continuing north up Tottenham Court Road, the big **Planet Organic** wholefood supermarket has a veggie cafe. One of the best things about this place is that it is open on Sundays. Also you can buy Veggie Guides here.

For the capital's best veggie sandwich selection by miles, head for **Health Food Centre**. They have dozens of amazing and unusual, and very filling, vegetarian and vegan sandwiches. There are also fabulous hot food take-aways and cakes. There's a handy fruit stall outside the station and it's only a few minutes walk from Regents Park which is the perfect place to spend a summer afternoon.

There are two more Chinese buffet restaurants on Euston Road, one with a back entrance on Warren Street.

Health Food Centre

Vegetarian health food shop & take-away

Open:

Mon–Fri	08.00–18.30
Sat	12.00–16.00
Sun	closed

Visa, MC, Amex

11 Warren Street
Euston, London W1T 5LG
Tel: 020 7387 9289
Tube: Warren Street,
Euston, Euston Square
See map on page 98

Vegetarian health food shop and take-away tucked away down the side of Warren Street tube. The owner Raj is very friendly and a committed veggie. Also a smoothies, juice and coffee bar with a table outside, weather permitting. Handy for Euston or Regent's Park.

London's biggest range of veggie and vegan sandwiches, such as (fake) chicken and salad; lentil burger and humous with salad; date, walnut and banana; veggie burger and humous; veggie BLT. Plus filled topedos, baps and baguettes. All £3.60 for two.

Savouries such as spicy Mexican slice, cartons of pasta and wide range of salads. New help yourself salad bar, large £4.60, small £2.75, includes quinoa, tofu, mixed beans, chickpeas.

Very popular hot take-away dishes include organic brown rice with vegan curries, or pasta bake, £5 large mixed box, or £3 for a small one.

All-vegan desserts such as tofu cheesecake £2.80. Lots of cakes, some sugar free or suitable for vegans such as date crumble, apricot & almond, carrot & sultana, apple slice 69p–£1.20.

The juice bar has combos such as apple, ginger and orange for £1.40, £1.90 large. Energy drinks include spirulina, echinacea or guarana around £2.50. Vegan fruit smoothie £1.50.

Coffee, teas, soyaccino £1.30 for a largish cup.

The shop packs a lot of wholefoods into a small space. Extensive range of cruelty-free toiletries, herbal remedies and oils. Vitamins, minerals, some wholefoods and natural confectionery.

10% discount if you mention this book.

If you like the sandwiches here you'll pleased to find they're also available at the Union Street Newsagent, see South Bank.

Sagar

Vegetarian
South Indian restaurant

Open:

Mon–Fri	12.00–14.45, 17.30–22.45
Sat	12.00–23.30
Sun	12.00–22.45
Bank Hols	13.00–22.45

Children welcome, high chairs.

17A Percy Street, off
Tottenham Court Rd W1T 1DU

Tel: 020-7631 3319

Tube: Tottenham Court Rd,
Goodge Street

MC, Visa, Amex
See map on page 98

The third branch of Sagar opened in August 2007, a couple of doors down from Joi and offering equally excellent value, especially the £4.95 lunch platter (Mon–Fri) and £2.95 lunch box (every day). Bright interior with wood panelled walls and wooden tables.

Mon–Fri three course lunch platter £4.95 changes daily with starters, special rice, curry, dosa, dessert (not vegan). Lunch box £2.95 every day with 2 curries, rice, chappati, salad and raita.

Starters £2–£4.75 include samosas, bhajias and veg kebab, but why not try something unusual such as Kancheepuram rice and lentil dumplings with green chili, pepper and cashew nuts; Medu vada fried lentil doughnuts; or special upma cream of wheat with fresh tomato, peas and cashews.

12 kinds of dosa stuffed pancakes, 8 variations of uthappam lentil pizzas, 15 curries £3.95-6.95. Curries include suki bhajee dry vegetable tossed in karahi with coconut, or onion and tomato sambar with fresh coconut and lentil.

Sagar thalis £10.45, Rajdani or Udupi thali £13.45, the latter can be vegan with lentils, pappadam, palaya, sukhi bhaji, kootu, veg sambar, dal, rasam, basmati rice, poori and dessert. Rice £2.25-3.45 including with garlic and spices, or lemon and peas. Vegetable biryani £4.95.

Desserts £2.25-2.75, no vegan ones on the menu but they do also have mango sorbet.

House wine £11.95 bottle, £2.85 glass. Coffee £1.50. Children welcome, high chairs.

If you like this you'll probably like their original branch in Hammersmith and the other new one in Twickenham.

Planet Organic, WC1

Natural and organic super-market and vegetarian cafe

Open:

Mon–Fri	08.00–21.00
Sat	10–20.00
Sun	12–18.00

Kids welcome
MC, Visa

22 Torrington Place
London WC1A 7JE
Tel: 020-7436 1929
Tube: Goodge St

See map on page 98

Organic wholefood super-market off Tottenham Court Road, with a juice bar and café. Most dishes, snacks and cakes have ingredients displayed and if they're gluten, sugar free or vegan.

The deli/cafe at the front has hot and cold dishes and salads, mostly vegan, for take-away or eat in at the tables by the tills and outside. Box of food £2.80, £4.50 or £5.30. Everything cooked fresh every day. Cakes and brownies £1–2.75, some vegan or dairy, wheat or gluten-free. Lots of juices and smoothies £2.50–3.00 including different kinds of soya milk.

The shop sells just about everything for veggies including organic fruit and veg, stacks of tofu and tempeh, fake meat, pastas including spelt, quinoa and amaranth, macrobiotic Japanese foods, vegan and vegetarian wines and beers.

Some bread baked daily on the premises.

Huge section devoted to health and body care, including vitamins, herbs, tinctures, homeopathy, aromatherapy oils, suncream, makeup (:Living Nature, Dr Hauschka, Lavera), shampoos and conditioners, sun cream including Weleda, Green People, Barefoot Botanicals, Urtekram, Jason, Ren, Akin, Burts Bees, Neals Yard, John Master. Staff are very friendly and knowledgeable to deal with queries, many being practitioners or in training.

A great place for presents like pretty candles and incense. Chocolate and other treats. They have magazines and books including Vegetarian Guides, fitness, pilates, yoga products and dvd's, even razors, body and tooth brushes made from recycled materials.

If you like this you'll probably like their other stores in Westbourne Grove (West London) and Fulham (Sloane Zone).

Joi

Vegan Oriental restaurant

14 Percy Street
off Charlotte Street, London W1

Tel: 020-7323 -0981

Open: *Mon-Thu*   12-22.00
       Fri-Sat   12-22.30
       Sun   12.30-22.00

Tube: Goodge Street,
       Tottenham Court Rd

Cash only.

Chinese vegan buffet restaurant specialising in fake meats and run by a relative of the proprietor of Tai in Greek Street. Eat-as-much-as-you-like buffet £5 daytime, £6 after 5pm and Sunday, children £3. Choose from chow mein, rice, sweet and sour veg "pork" balls, soya chicken, fake beef, crispy seaweed, fried aubergine, spring rolls, tofu and many more.

Desserts £2.50 such as banana or apple fritter, lychees, soya ice-cream.

No wine but you can bring your own.

£10 minimum in the de luxe area at the back. £3 or £4 for a take-away box.

Free meditatoin and cooking classes. Tai chi £5. Details in restaurant.

Wai

Vegan Chinese restaurant

32 Goodge Street, London W1

Tel: 020 7637 4819

Open: *Sun-Thu* 12-22.00
       Fri-Sat   12-23.00

Tube: Goodge Street

Chinese vegan buffet restaurant and take-away. Open every day for lunch and dinner. All you can eat £5, £6 after 5pm and Sunday. Take-away box £3 or £4 large.

Rasa Express

Omnivorous Indian cafe & take-away

5 Rathbone Street
Off Oxford Street, London W1

Tel: 020-7637-0222

Open: *Mon-Fri* 12-15.00

Tube: Tottenham Court Rd

Unlike their restaurant on the other side of the building in parallel Charlotte Street, here most of the menu is veggie snacks and take-aways. Lunch box £2.95 with 2 curries, 1 side dish (stir-fry), bread, rice, dessert (can be vegan but changes daily so call first), eat in or out. Masala dosa (vegetable stuffed pancake) £2.50. Take-away or eat-in

Typical snacks for £1.50 are Mysore potato balls with ginger curry leaves, coriander and black mustard seeds, fried in chickpea flour; or crispy spongy dumpling in a crunchy case made from urad beans and chillies, with coconut chutney.

Wine £2.95 glass, £11.50 bottle. MC, Visa over £15.

Adonis

Lebanese omnivorous restaurant

56 Goodge Street,
London W1T 4NB

Tel: 020-7637-7687

Open: *Mon-Thu* 12.00-23.00
Fri-Sat 12.00-23.30
Sun 12.00-22.30

Tube: Goodge Street

As with most Lebanese restaurants, the good stuff is in the starters £3.50-4.00 including tabouleh salad, moutabel aubergine caviar, stuffed vine leaves, okra, falafel, or pumpkin kibbeh (crushed wheat, chickpeas, onion, red cups pepper and mixed herbs). There is a Kafta veggie burger of minced veg with chickpeas, spinach and mushroom served in Lebanese bread and topped with walnuts.

Moussakant Batenjan of aubergines with tomatoes, chickpeas, garlic and sweet pepper served with rice £8.50. Set menu for £12.50 with 3-4 mezze and a main couse.

Desserts made daily include baklava selection with syrup (vegan) £2.50, sorbet £3.25, fruit salad or fresh mango £3.

Freshly squeezed juices £2.50. House wine £12.50 bottle, £3 glass. Beer £2.50. Liqueurs, teas. Coffee £2.

Peppercorn's

Wholefood shop

2 Charlotte Place, London W1

Tel: 020-7631 4528

Open: *Mon-Sat* 9.30-19.00
Sat 11.00-18.00
Sun closed

Tube: Goodge Street

10% discount for Vegetarian or Vegan Society

Organic wholefood store selling everything for veggies including tofu and tempeh, every kind of pasta and health food.

Take-away and macrobiotic specialities from around the world, some organic, with lots of vegan options including vegetarian sushi, tofu parcels, aduki pies, spring rolls, rice rolls, organic hummous, cottage pies, veggie sausages, cakes and flapjacks. Most dishes, snacks and cakes have ingredients displayed and if they're gluten, sugar free or vegan.

Also supplements, vitamins and minerals including Viridian, plus Ecover cleaning products. Natural remedies and bodycare including Jason and Weleda.

Staff are well trained and have in depth knowledge of what's what.

EUSTON Central London

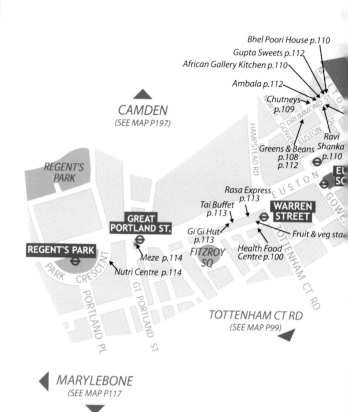

Bhel Poori House p.110
Gupta Sweets p.112
African Gallery Kitchen p.110
Ambala p.112
Chutneys p.109
Ravi Shanka p.110
Greens & Beans p.108 p.112

CAMDEN
(SEE MAP P197)

HAMPSTEAD RD
GOWE
DRUMMOND ST
EUSTON
EU SC

REGENT'S PARK

Rasa Express p.113
Tai Buffet p.113
WARREN STREET
EUSTON GOWE

GREAT PORTLAND ST.

Gi Gi Hut p.113
Fruit & veg sta

Health Food Centre p.100

REGENT'S PARK

FITZROY SQ

Meze p.114
Nutri Centre p.114

PARK CRESCENT

GT PORTLAND ST

TOTTENHAM CT RD

TOTTENHAM CT RD
(SEE MAP P99)

PORTLAND PL

MARYLEBONE
(SEE MAP P117

KINGS CROSS ▶
(SEE MAP P231)

EVERSHOLT ST

EUSTON
🚆 ⊖
Diwana p.109

ROAD

ENDSLEIGH GDNS

WOBURN PL

GORDON ST

STON
UARE

BLOOMSBURY
(SEE MAP P89)
▼

Euston rail station is the gateway to most places north or north-west of London, so you'll likely end up there sometime. Train food is awful, but there are stacks of nearby veggie places to fill up before or after your journey, grab a take-away and snacks, or meet friends for a cheap meal away from the crowds of Soho.

The big new opening is **Greens & Beans** wholefood cafe and shop on Drummond Street. As we go to print they are not open in the evenings but are considering it, so come for breakfast, lunch or afternoon tea. **Chutneys, Diwana** and **Ravi Shankar** are good value vegetarian Indian restaurants and Diwana and Chutneys have started doing vegan desserts, albeit not that exciting, or you can pop to **Gupta Sweet Centre** for vegan ladhu. **African Gallery Kitchen** offers a completely unique gourmet menu.

Euston Road has two **Chinese vegan buffet** restaurants next door to each other. Stuff yourself silly.

Health Food Centre, down the side of Warren Street tube, has a choice of dozens of vegetarian and vegan sandwiches and hot take-away food. Opposite is a fruit stall.

On the way to or from Regent's Park you can stop off at **Meze** cafe, open long hours and opposite a 24-hour grocer, Tesco Metro and two pubs.

Greens & Beans Cafe

Vegetarian organic cafe, take-away and shop

Cafe:
Mon–Fri 9.00–17.00
Sat–Sun closed

Shop and take–away:
Mon–Fri 9.00–17.00 Hot and cold take–away buffet 12–3.30pm
Sat–Sun closed

131 Drummond St, NW1 2HL
Tel: 020-7380 0857
Tube: Euston, Euston Square Warren Street
Children welcome.
www.greensandbeans.co.uk
See map on page 106

Realfood cafe downstais, take-away and shop upstairs with four seats in the window. Great for smoothies, organic juices, Fair Trade coffee and you can buy natural remedies, snacks, gifts and inspirational cards.

The cafe in the basement offers organic breakfast such as Alara Fair Trade or gluten-free or oat muesli with choice of milks £3.25. Millet or quinoa porridge £3.75. Seasonal fruit salad £3.25. All kinds of breads for toast with spreads £1.75. Cooked breakfast £4.95.

Starters: hummous with pitta £2.75, soup of the day £3.95.

Salads available till 3pm £5.50 include "Now that's a salad" (baby greens, mixed sprouts, pumpkin & sunflower seeds, avocado, tomato with healthy dressing, gluten-free, vegan; black bean and two peppers.

Pizzas £5.50–6.50. British style bangers and mash £5.95 or penne pasta with tomato and basil sauce £5.50, both served with a mixed leaf salad.

(Dairy-free) ice-cream £1.20-3.00. Cakes £1.90.

Fresh organic juices and smoothies, including green smoothies made with green barley grass, a cleansing superfood. Fairtrade coffee and chocolate.

Take–away buffet upstairs. Salads £2.95 small, £4.25 medium £5.25 large, (most vegan) include pasta with peppers and olives, black beans and peppers with cumin and mint, tabouleh, French potato salad. Hot dishes £2075 small, £4 medium, £5 large, such as penne pasta, black bean chilli, roast mixed herby veg, brown basmati rice casserole, seasonal veg. Containers and cutlery are biodegradable.

For shop see page 112.

Chutneys

Vegetarian South Indian restaurant

124 Drummond Street
Euston, London NW1 2PA

Tel: 020-7388-0604

Open: *Mon-Sat*
buffet 12.00-14.45
a la carte 18-23.00 (last orders), close 23.30
Sun 12-22.00 (last order)
buffet all day & a la carte

Tube: Euston, Euston Square

Vegetarian South Indian restaurant. Wide variety of dishes and special Keralan feast menu available most days. A popular place for a quiet romantic dinner that won't stretch the wallet.

Eat as much as you like buffet from 12 noon to 2.45pm every day for £5.95, Sunday all day.

In the evening there are 16 starters such as bhel poori, £2.95 to £3.50.

Main courses include nine kinds of dosa £5.60-5.80, 11 curries £3.95-4.20. Plenty of whole wheat breads, pickles; salad and rice from 90p.

Thalis start at £6.95. If you are really hungry try the excellent Chutney's deluxe thali for £9.50 with dhal soup, 4 curries, pillau rice, chutneys, chappatis or pooris and dessert.

Five desserts £1.60-£2.40 and they now have vegan sorbet.

House wine £1.95 glass, £8.50 bottle. Visa, MC.

Diwana

Vegetarian South Indian restaurant

121-123 Drummond Street
Euston, London NW1 2HL
Tel: 020-7387 5556

Open: *Mon-Sat* 12.00-23.30
Sun 12.00-22.30

Tube: Euston, Euston Square, Warren St

One of the larger vegetarian Indian restaurants on Drummond Street, established over twenty five years. Light wood décor and lots of potted palms give a relaxed and informal feel. The food is inexpensive and tasty. They offer an eat as much as you like lunch buffet 12-14.30 every day for £6.50 which has different dishes daily, and also a full a la carte menu all day.

Lots of starters such as dahi vada chick peas £3.00, masala spring rolls £3.50.

Thalis £5.50–7.75.

Lots of dosas £5.50–5.95 and vegetable side dishes like bombay aloo and aloo gobi £3.80–4.20.

Several desserts, including fresh fruit smoothies £3.

Visa, MC. Diwana are not licensed but you can bring your own with no corkage charge. There is an off licence next door.

Ravi Shankar

Vegetarian South Indian restaurant

133–135 Drummond Street
Euston, London NW1 2HL
Tel: 020–7388 6458
Open: Mon–Sun 12.00–22.45
(last orders 22.00)
Tube: Euston, Euston Square

One of three great value vegetarian South Indian restaurants in this street next to Euston station. Daily specials throughout the week. There's always plenty for vegans.

Thali £5.50–5.90, 2 or 3 course thali £7.30–8.95, or have a dosa or curry £4.50–5.95.

Daily specials £5.50 or £5.95. On a Monday they

serve cauliflower potato curry for £5.50, Tuesday is veg biriyani with curry for £5.95, and each day the specials are different. Sat £4.75, Sun £4.55.

Desserts £1.25–1.65, but none vegan, however vegans with a sweet tooth can score at Gupta Sweet Centre opposite.

Wine £7.95 bottle, £1.90 glass. Visa, MC. Children welcome, no high chairs.

African Gallery Kitchen

Omnivorous Afro-Carib restaurant

102 Drummond St, Euston, London NW1 2HN
Tel: 020–7383 0918
Open: Mon 17.30–22.30
Tue–Sun 12–15.30,
17.30–22.30
Tube: Euston, Euston Square

Tiny restaurant, 50% vegan, with five tables, African wood carvings on the walls and big carved giraffes in the window.

10 starters £1.95 mains £6.50. Different dishes every day such as blended beans with spices and tomatoes; fried plantain or cassava fritters; chick pea, butter beans, yam and sweet

potato porridge; black beans in bonnet chilli sauce; wild spinach; basmati rice.

They use only olive oil for cooking, no dairy or animal fats, wheat or additives, though flans for dessert contain condensed milk but vegans could have coconut date balls.

Freshly squeezed juices. Herb teas but no soya milk. Bring your own alcohol, £1 corkage, license applied for.

MC, Visa.

Bhel Poori House

Omnivorous Indian internet cafe

98 Drummond Street

Tel: 020–7383 0022

Open: *Tue–Sun* 12.00–22.00
Mon closed

Tube: Euston

Originally vegetarian, but sadly no longer, handy if you want to check your emails. Tiny restaurant with six tables and a row of internet booths down the left wall. Eat in or take-away. Buffet lunch £4.50. 14 starters £2.50. 4 dosas £4.05. Thalis £4.95 and 6.50. Lots of side dishes and drinks, coffee, cappuccino, tea. 4 desserts, none vegan, but vegans could pop next door to Gupta for some ladhu.

Unlicensed. Internet £1 per hour.

Ambala

Indian vegetarian sweet shop

112/114 Drummond Street
Euston, London NW1 2HN
Tel: 020 7387 7886 / 3521
Open: *Mon–Sun* 9.00–21.00
Tube: Euston
www.ambala.co.uk (ingredients and branch list)

The oldest branch of 32 of this vegetarian take-away and sweet shop, opposite Ravi Shankar and Diwana, for when you need to eat on the run. Samosas 40-50p, pakoras £5/kilo, Bombay mix, pickles, chutney. Indian sweets all contain dairy.

Gupta Sweet Centre

Indian vegetarian sweet shop

120 Drummond Street NW1 2HN
Tel: 020-7380 1590
Open: *Mon–Sun* 111,.00–20.00
Tube: Euston

Samosas, bhajias, veg cutlets, kachoris and Indian sweets, five of which are vegan including ladhu and jelabi. Outside catering. Another branch at 262 Watford Way, Hendon NW4.

Greens & Beans shop

Vegetarian shop & take-away

131 Drummond St, NW1 2HL
Tel: 020-7380 0857
Open: *Mon–Fri* 9.00–17.00
           Sat–Sun closed
Tube: Euston, Euston Square, Warren Street

As well as the take-away buffet (page 108), the shop sells sandwiches. Also organic fruit, snacks, rice cakes, organic drinks, Soma smoothies, AquaAid water, non-dairy milks, instant miso soup, lots of flapjacks, Viridian seed oils and vitamins, superfoods, teas, muesli, chocolate, Booja booja truffles, natural remedies and bodycare, cards, books, gifts, and you can get natural health advice.

Health Food Centre

Wholefood shop

11 Warren Street W1T 5LG
Tel: 020-7631 4528
Open: *Mon–Fri* 08.00–18.30
           Sat   12.00–16.00
           Sun   closed
Tube: Warren Street

Fabulous wholefood store with lots of take-away food, see page 100.

Gi Gi Hut

Vegan Thai Chinese buffet restaurant

339 Euston Road, NW1 3AD
Tel: 020-7383 3978
Open: *Mon-Sun* 12.00-22.00
Tube: Warren St, Euston,
        Great Portland St

Eat as much as you like buffet £5 all day including one free drink (at least when we went to press), no surcharge in the evening unlike other similar restaurants. Take-away box £3.

Veg Thahi curry, sweet and sour balls, special fried rice, Singapore noodles, sesame toast, crispy spring rolls, crispy aubergines, black beans, mixed veg, sea spiced aubergines etc.

Cash only.

Tai Buffet

Vegan Thai Chinese buffet restaurant

337 Euston Road, London NW1
Tel: 020-7387 6876
Open: *Mon-Sat* 12.00-22.00
        Sun   closed
Tube: Warren Street, Euston,
        Great Portland St

New all you can eat buffet restaurant. Lunch £5.50, after 5pm and all day Sunday

£6. Self-serve take-away box £3 or £4.

Sample menu: Pa Tai noodle, curried rice, sweet and sour balls, black beans, soya chicken, sea-spiced aubergines, special fried rice, Singapore noodles, lemon grass pot, sesame salad, seaweeds, crispy spring rolls, salad and more.

Tea, soft drinks, juice £1.50, water £1. Cash only. Children welcome.

Rasa Express

Vegetarian and fish fast food

327 Euston Road NW1 3AD
Tel: 020-7387 8974
Open: *Mon-Fri* 12-15.00
        Sat-Sun closed
Tube: Great Portland St

Indian Keralan vegetarian and fish fast food restaurant with a bright pink front just west of Tottenham Court Road. Small menu but amazing value for central London. Starters £1.50 include potato cakes with ginger and curry leaves. Masala dosa £2.75. Lunch box £2.95 for rice, bread, a stir-fried vegetable, two curries and sweet of the day. Bananas and mangoes. Cash only.

Meze Cafe

Turkish omnivorous cafe

305 Great Portland Street,
London W1W 5DA

Tel: 020-7580 9142
Open: Every day 08–23.00
Tube: Great Portland Street

Handy for Regent's Park, this is a big all-day Turkish omnivorous café next to Great Portland Street underground station and opposite International House student hostel. Tables inside and out. Open for breakfast, lunch and dinner, and chilling out at any time. Meze and salad buffet £3.90 eat in (£3 take out), large £4.90 (£3.90), including pitta bread. Choose from Turkish wraps £4.50 eat in, £4 take-away. Most of the cold (£3) and several hot (£4) meze are veggie or vegan.

House wine £9.50 bottle, £2.50 glass. Beer £2.50. Coffee £1.60 in (£1.20 take-out), tea £1.40 (£1.20).

Right opposite are an all-night grocer, Tesco Metro (07.00–midnight), a Pret-a-Manger and two pubs.

Nutri Centre

Health foods and natural remedies

7 Park Crescent W1B 1PF

Tel: Supplements & advice:
020-7436-5122
Books/education: 7323 2382
Practitioners: 7637 8436

Open: Mon–Fri 09.00–19.00
Sat 10.00–17.00
Sun closed
Tube: Regents Park,
Great Portland St

www.nutricentre.com

In the basement of the presitgiou Hale Centre natural health centre, this shop sells mainly supplements and body care products, plus a few foods such as wheat-free pasta and snacks.

There is a separate bookshop with the biggest selection of books in the UK on organic and vegetarian living, nutrition and food, yoga, aromatherapy, bodywork, homeopathy, acupuncture, Chinese medicine, energy therapies, herbalism, mind, body and spirit. Also an impressive mail order books catalogue.

VEGETARIAN
EUROPE
by Alex Bourke

MARYLEBONE
& Mayfair

It's W1, but not as you know it. Unlike the party furore of Soho, this residential area between Regent's Park and Oxford Street has wide streets and ample pavement space.

Thereis now a cluster of veggie and veggie-friendly places around Marylebone High Street. **Totally Organics** is a great new wholefood store that gets busy at lunchtime with take-aways and a small cafe area. **Le Pain Quotidien** is something we never thought we would see, a French cafe chain offering tofu salads and vegan soup and blueberry muffins. **The Quiet Revolution**, linked to the Aveda shop, is a cafe with heaps of veggie choices.

Woodlands and **Rasa** continue to offer classic South Indian dining, though sadly Chai Pani closed just before we went to press.

Eat & Two Veg has become renowned with a British and international menu plus a bar, fabulous for taking non-vegetarians to with their full English veggie breakfast, shepherd's pie and sausage and mash plus gourmet dishes from around the world.

For a fast lunch whilst fashion shopping on Oxford Street, try **Bean Juice** café, a pastie from Holland & Barrett in the Bond Street underground station, or grab a falafel from one of the Lebanese take-aways on Edgware Road. If you're working in Mayfair, **Sofra** is our first choice.

Rasa Keralan cuisine

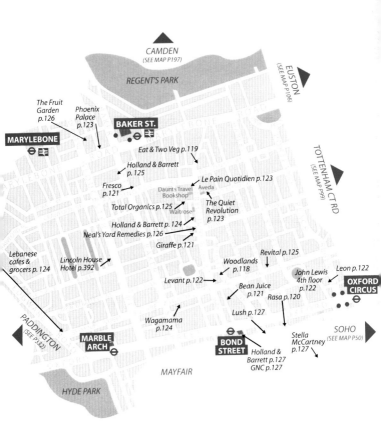

CAMDEN
(SEE MAP P197)

REGENT'S PARK

EUSTON
(SEE MAP P106)

The Fruit
Garden
p.126

Phoenix
Palace
p.123

BAKER ST.

MARYLEBONE

TOTTENHAM CT RD
(SEE MAP P99)

Eat & Two Veg p.119

Holland & Barrett
p.125

Fresco
p.121

Le Pain Quotidien p.123

Daunt's Travel
Bookshop

Aveda

The Quiet
Revolution
p.123

Total Organics p.125

Waitrose

Holland & Barrett p.124

Neal's Yard Remedies p.126

Giraffe p.121

Revital p.125

Woodlands
p.118

Lebanese
cafes &
grocers p.124

Lincoln House
Hotel p.392

Levant p.122

John Lewis
4th floor
p.122

Leon p.122

OXFORD
CIRCUS

Bean Juice
p.121

Rasa p.120

Lush p.127

SOHO
(SEE MAP P50)

Wagamama
p.124

PADDINGTON
(SEE P332)

MARBLE
ARCH

BOND
STREET

Holland &
Barrett p.127
GNC p.127

Stella
McCartney
p.127

MAYFAIR

HYDE PARK

117

Woodlands Marylebone

Vegetarian Indian restaurant

Open:
Every day 12-15.00,
18.00-23.00
MC, Visa, Amex
www.woodlandsrestaurant.co.uk

77 Marylebone Lane
(off Marylebone High St.)
London WIU 2PS
Tel: 020 7486 3862
Tube: Bond St, Baker St.

See map on page 117

Perhaps the largest vegetarian Indian chain in the world, with 4 London branches and 32 in India, from where the chefs come. This branch is smart with walnut flooing, cream linen and granite bar. Ideal for large parties, couples and business meetings. 75 dishes on the menu with many different flavours, textures and colours.

Lots of starters like idli rice balls, or deep fried cashew nut pokoda, £4.50 to £5.75, or a mixed platter for £12.50. Soups £3.75.

Nine varieties of dosa (vegetable stuffed pancake, made from rice and wheat) £6.25. Their specialty is uthappam or lentil pizza, with coconut, tomato, green chilli £5.95. 10 curries £5.50-5.95.

Thalis or set meals 16.25-17.95.

Traditional village vegetable curries £4.75-6.50 include Kootu (daily changing vegetables cooked in coconut milk) and hot breads £2.75-2.95 such as poori, chappati, bathura and soft dosa rice/lentil pancakes.

Many rice dishes such as pilau, lemon or coconut, £4.50. Indian breads such as bathura £2.95.

Unfortunately for vegans, all 9 desserts appear to be made with dairy, but they say that Jaggary dosa can be made vegan, an Indian crepe filled with pure sugar cane and cardamom at £3.95.

Glass of house wine £2.95, bottle £12.50. Beer £2.75 small, £4.95 large. Spirits £2.75-2.95.

They cater for parties.

If you like this you'll probably like their other branches in Panton Street off Leicester Square (Soho), Chiswick (West London) and the newest one in Hampstead (North London) .

Eat & Two Veg

British and International vegetarian restaurant

Open:

Mon-Sat   09.00–23.00
Sat   09.00–23.00
Sun   10.00–22.00

MC, Visa, Diners, Amex

www.eatandtwoveg.com

50 Marylebone High Street
(north end), London W1U 5HN

Tel: 020-7258 8595

Tube: Baker Street

Free parking from 6.30pm
nearby and all day Sunday.
See map on page 117

Excellent British style vegetarian restaurant and extensive bar that has been getting rave reviews from both veggies and carnivores alike. Open all day every day for breakfast, lunch and dinner with an international menu plus traditional British favourites. Your non-veggie friends will love the fake meat dishes such as full English cooked breakfast with veggie sausages, sausage and mash, burgers, shepherd's pie, and fruit crumble. Vegan dishes are clearly marked. There are lots of cocktails, juices, smoothies and wines.

Continental or full English veggie breakfast £1.50 to £7.50, served till noon Mon–Fri and till 2pm at weekends.

Soup of the day £4. Starters £4.95-5.59 such as crispl aromatic luck with pancakes; Thai spring rolls; Chinese dumplings; Thai satay skewers, Mezze with falafel, hummous, baba ghanoush and tabbouli.

12 pasta and main courses such as Thai green curry; Spaghetti/penne with fresh tomato and basil; all day breakfast; Lancashire hot pot; Schnitzel. Only a couple appear to be vegan but in fact more vegan versions can be arranged. 5 salads £3.00-7.95 such as poached pear, beet and toasted almonds with mixed leaves and seedless grapes. Sandwiches (served hot with coleslaw and fries or wedges) for £7.50 include burger, or satay soya protein in peanut sauce. Fill up with wedges, fries, mash, steamed brown rice, various veg, olives and roast almonds £1.50-2.50.

Half a dozen British desserts £5 include vegan fruit crumble, and they have Swedish Glace ice-cream.

House wine £11 bottle, £3 glass. Freshly made mixed juices £2.75. Smoothies £3.20. Cocktails £5.50-6.50.

Rasa

Open:

Mon–Sat 12.00–15.00
18.00–23.00
Sun closed

Reservations recommended

www.rasarestaurants.com

6 Dering Street
off Oxford Street
Tel: 020 7629 1346
Tube: Oxford Circus,
Bond Street
MC, Visa, Amex
See map on page 117

South Indian restaurant on two floors, specialising in Keralan cuisine. Separate vegetarian and omnivorous kitchen areas. It used to be completely vegetarian, then downstairs only, and today all the same veggie dishes are clearly marked.

Take-away Rasa Express lunchbox £2.95, upstairs Mon–Fri.

A la carte pre meal snacks £4 include nibbles made from root vegetables, rice, coconut milk, flour, lentils and seeds all beautifully spiced. Four starters, £4.25, or have a Rasa Platter £9.90 selection of starters for two people. Six pickles and chutneys £2.50. Two soups £4.25.

Three types of dosas £9.95.

Six main courses all £6.25, and five side dishes £5.25, such as vegan cheera parippu curry with fresh spinach and toot dal.

Four kinds of rice £3–£3.75, five varieties of bread £2.50.

Several desserts include banana dosa (vegan) £3.50, mango sorbet £2.75

Wine from £10.95 bottle, £2.75 glass. Champagne £26.95 or £35. Cobra beer £2.95–4.50. Spirits, liqueurs and aperitifs £2.75–3.50. Soft drinks £1.75. Coffees from £1.95, no soya milk.

Children welcome though no children's portions. High chairs. 12.5% optional service charge

If you like this you'll probably like their other branch in Stoke Newington (North London) which is 100% vegetarian.

Bean Juice

Cafe and juice bar

10a St Christopher's Place, W1

Tel: 020-7224 3840

Open: *Mon-Fri* 07.30-19.30
Sat 10.30-18.30
Sun 11.00-18.30

Tube: Bond Street

Mostly vegetarian cafe and take-away up a small alley opposite Bond Street tube. Tables inside and out.

Sandwiches £1.96-3.45, salads £3.45, hot soups £2.50-3.50 (Sept-June). Cookies, brownies, home-made coconut cake, some vegan. Fresh juices, smoothies, coffees, milk shakes (can be soya). No alcohol. Children welcome. Visa, MC.

Fresco

Juice bar & omni Lebanese restaurant

31 Paddington St, W1

Tel: 020-7486 6112

Open: *Mon-Sat* 08.00-17.00
Sat-Sun closed

Tube: Baker Street

A cross between a fresh juice bar and a small Lebanese restaurant, Fresco serves a variety of juices, smoothies and milkshakes (unfortunately no soya milk - yet!), alongside a selection of sandwiches with Middle Eastern fillings and cold mezze dishes. They also have a number of hot main dishes, about half of which are vegetarian.

Giraffe, Marylebone

Omnivorous restaurant

6-8 Blandford Street W1U 4AU

Tel: 020-7935 2333

Open: *Mon-Fri* 08.00-22.30
Sat 09.00-22.30
Sun 09.00-22.30
Bank hols 09.00-22.30

Tube: Bond Street, Baker Street
Children welcome, kids' menu
www.giraffe.net

Good selection of vegetarian dishes. See Bloombsury branch (page 95) for menu. Some outside seating.

John Lewis Coffee Shop

Omnivorous cafe

4th Floor, John Lewis department store, Oxford St, W1
Tel: 020-7629 7711
Open: *Mon–Sat* 9.30–17.30
Sun 12.00–17.30
Tube: Oxford Circus, Bond St

Good salads and freshly-squeezed juices so better for veggies than the 3rd-floor brasserie Place to Eat. Brilliant view down Harley St to Regent's Park but a bit expensive.

Leon

Omnivorous cafe & take-away

275 Regent Street W1B 2HB
Tel/Fax: 020-7495 1514
Open: *Mon–Sat* 08.00–21.00
Sun closed
Tube: Oxford Circus
Full menu at:
www.leonrestaurants.co.uk

New fast food bar with lots of great value veggie food. See Soho branch for details (page 67) or check their website for the full menu.

Levant

Omnivorous Lebanese restaurant

Jason Court, 76 Wigmore Street, London W1

Tel: 020-7224 1111
Open: *Mon–Sat* 12.00–02.30
Sun 12.00–24.00
Last food orders:
restaurant midnight, bar 02.00
Tube: Bond Street
www.levant.co.uk

Famished at midnight? Come here, between the bustle of St Christopers Place and fashionable Marylebone High St, just past Bean Juice, with lots for veggies. Mezze dishes £5–6.75 each, mains £12.50–13.00 such as baked aubergine with tomato and chickpeas. Huge wine list, bottle from £16.50–£550 (no misprint!), £4.25 glass. 12.5–15% discretionary service charge plus £1 donation to Breakthrough charity. Private bookings for up to 130 sit-down, 240 canapes. Private room for 8–12 people.

Le Pain Quotidien

Omnivorous restaurant

72-75 Marylebone High St,
London W1U 5JW
Tel: 020-7486 6154
Open: *Mon-Fri* 07.00-21.00
Sat-Sun 08.00-18.00

Tube: Baker Street
www.lepainquotidien.com

There is a French enclave at the north end of Marylebone High Street. Unfortunately the French are not noted for their vegetarian sympathies , but this cafe-style restaurant with olde worlde wooden tables is a marvellous exception.

At lunchtime it gets busy so wait just a few minutes to be seated in the patisserie at the front, which also sells jars of olives, capers, olive tapenade spread and aubergine pate.

Yummy tofu salad £6.95 comes with plenty of tofu with various sauces and hefty wedges of filling bread. Two veggie/vegan soups £2.55 small, £4.95 large. Finish with vegan blueberry muffins or mint tea.

Phoenix Palace

Chinese omnivorous restaurant

5 Glentworth St, NW1 5PG
Tel: 020-7486 3515
Open: *Mon-Sat* 12.00-23.30
Sun 11.00-22.30
Tube: Marylebone, Baker Street

Set vegan menu available both for lunch and dinner £15.80 with asparagus & cream corn, aubergine in sea spicy sauce, green bean in black bean sauce, braised bean curd 7 shitake, fried rice. It's absolutely huge, enough for 2 meals, but you can take half of it home to have the next day.

The Quiet Revolution

Omnivorous organic cafe

28 Marylebone High St, W1U 4PL
Tel: 020-7487 5683
Open: *Mon-Fri* 9.00-18.00
Sat-Sun 11.00-17.00

Tube: Baker Street
www.quietrevolution.co.uk

100% organic, mostly vegetarian, family run cafe just off Marylebone High Street, behind and with an inside doorway into Aveda cosmetics. Soft music and wooden tables.

Lentil stew with brown rice £7.95. Moroccan stew with rice or couscous £7.95. Chili fagioli (beans) with brown rice £7.95. Very big bowl of soup of the day with bread £5.95 such as sweet potato and pumpkin or spinach and potato. Detox or quinoa salad £6.95. Pasta with pesto (can be vegan), with roast veg Neapolitan tomato sauce £8.50. Roast veg and hummous ciabatta sandwich £7.95. Vegab muffins. Take-away same prices.

Freshly made juices £5.95 12oz, wheatgrass shot £2. Tea, coffee, chocolate, latte, cappuccino £1.50-2.50. Soya milk available. Cold organic drinks such as Whole Earth cola. No alcohol.

MC, Visa. Children welcome.

Wagamama

Omnivorous Japanese restaurant

101A Wigmore St W1H 9AB (behind Selfridges)

Tel: 020-7409 0111

Open: *Mon–Sat* 12.00–23.00
Sun 12.30–22.00

Tube: Bond St

Large Japanese fast food noodle restaurant. See Bloomsbury branch, page 93.

Lebanese cafes

Omnivorous cafes & grocers

South end of Edgware Road

Open: *Mon–Sun* very late

Tube: Marble Arch, Edgware Rd

There are lots of Lebanese grocers and cafes on Edgware Road. Look out for falafels, juice bars, and lovely things to take home including big tubs of tahini sesame spread for making your own hummous. (Just soak 250 grammes of chickpeas overnight, change the water, boil for 40 minutes and put in the blender with water till smooth, add lemon juice, chopped garlic and a few spoonfuls of tahini.

Holland & Barrett

Health food shop

104 Marylebone High Street, London W1U 4RR

Tel: 020-7935 8412

Open: *Mon–Fri* 9.00– 19.00
Sat 9.00– 18.00
Sun 11.00–17.00

Tube: Baker Street

The range has expanded since H&B took over what used to be a GNC store. Now as well as wholefoods you can find lots of snack foods, vitamins, flower remedies, homeopathy, ginseng, aloe vera products, echinacea, sports nutrition, bodycare, essential oils, incense, juices and water, soya desserts.

---

78 Baker St, London W1M 1DL
Tel: 020-7935 3544
Open: *Mon-Fri* 8.30-18.00
      Sat   9.30-17.30
      Sun   closed
Tube: Baker Street

Medium sized branch with some take-away food

Revital Health Shop

Health food shop

22 Wigmore St W1U 2RG
(between Wimpole & Harley St)
Tel: 020-7631 3731
Open: *Mon-Fri* 9.00-18.00
      Sat   10.00-17.00
      Sun   closed
Tube: Bond St, Oxford Circus
www.revital.co.uk

The flagship central London branch of this chain of health food stores, opened 2006, not just for locals but also the nearby Harley Street healthcare practitioners and their patients.

Juice bar and fresh food counter. Health foods

including gluten and wheat-free and organic. This branch has organic beers, wines, ales and spirits.

Bodycare and natural beauty products including Dr Hauschka. Vitamins and minerals. Healthnotes touch-screen information kiosk. Revital Education Centre downstairs offers seminars, classes and workshops with a discount on anything you buy that day.

Total Organics

Wholefood shop, take-away, juice bar

6 Moxon Street, Marylebone, London W1U 4ER
Tel: 020-7935 8626
Open: *Mon-Sat* 10.00-18.00
      Sun   10.00-15.00
      (juice bar closes 30mins earlier)
Tube: Baker Street

New totally organic wholefood store, take-away and cafe with 9 seats. People who used to love Country Life will love this place.

Salad bar £1.20/100gr or box £4.50, giant box £5.99, eat in on a pate £5.75 for all you can pile on it. Vegan soup £3 take-away, £3.50 eat in or with bread. Lots of sandwiches, made to order from £3.50.

Juice bar £3, and specials such as Brazilian acai (a fruit that tastes like chocolate milkshake), wheatgrass, echinacea from £3.50.

The shop has fruit & veg, wheat and non-wheat pastas, tinned beans, raw food section with chocolate and Wolfberries, lots of mueslis, olive oil refills. Gleten-free section. Baby foods. All the Ecover and Bio-D household products.

Visa, MC. Fri-Sat they also run a stall in Borough Market with salad bar, soups and tofu/veggie-burgers.

The Fruit Garden

Health food shop

21 Melcombe St, NW1 6AG

Tel: 020-7935 5161

Open: *Mon-Sat* 08.00-21.00
         Sun   closed

Tube: Baker Street, Marylebone

Big shop with health and organic food near Marylebone station. MC, Visa.

There is a branch of **Neal's Yard Rememdies** at 112 Marylebone High St. Open Mon-Sat 10-19.00, Thu till 20.00, Sun 10-18.00.

Chor Bizarre, Mayfair

Omnivorous Indian restaurant

16 Albemarle Street, London W1

Tel: 020-7629 9802

Open: *Mon-Sat* 12.-15.00
         Mon-Sun 18-23.00
         (Sun 22.30) (last orders 15 min before cosing)

Tube: Green Park

www.chorbizarrerestaurant.com
chorbizarrelondon@
oldworldhospitality.com

Big, very upmarket Indian with quite a bit of vegetarian food, though not vegan desserts. £30-35 per person a la carte. Thali £25. House wine £16 bottle, £4 glass. You can book the whole restaurant for 30-50 people.

Sofra Mayfair

Omnivorous Turkish restaurant

18 Shepherd Street, W1Y 7HU

Tel: 020-7493 3320

Open: *Mon-Sun* 12.00-24.00

Tube: Green Park
www.sofra.co.uk

Excellent Mediterranean food. Veggie meze £3.45-£5.75 each, or a mixed platter for £7.45. Healthy meal of 13 dishes £8.95 till 6pm, then £11.95. House wine £3.50 glass, £11.65 bottle. Children welcome, high chairs. Another branch at 1 St Christopher's Place near Bean Juice.

Lush

Cruelty-free cosmetics

44 South Molton St, W1K 5RT

Tel: 020-7491 3443

Open: *Mon–Wed* 10.00–19.00
       Thu–Sat 10.00–19.30)
       Sun   11.00–19.00

Tube: Bond Street

Lovely cosmetics, all vegetarian and most of it vegan and clearly labelled. See Soho branches for more details.

Stella McCartney

Non-leather shoes & accessories

30 Bruton Street, Mayfair, W1J 6LG (south end of New Bond St)

Tel: 020-7518 3100

Open: *Mon–Sat* 10.00–18.00
       Thur   till 19.00
       Sun   closed

Tube: Bond Street, Green Park, Oxford Circus

www.stellamccartney.com

The highest of vegetarian high fashion with no leather or fur, though vegans beware of silk and wool. Allow £300–£500 for shoes or boots.

GNC, West One

Health food shop

Unit G14 West One Centre, Oxford Street, London (corner Davis Street), W1C 2JS

Tel: 020-7629 8535

Open: *Mon–Fri* 08.00–20.00
       Sat   9.00–20.00
       Sun   12.00–18.00

Tube: Bond Street

In the same shopping centre as a big Holland & Barrett, this one is more for body-building and supplements.

Holland & Barrett

Health food shop

Unit C12, West One Shopping Centre corner of Davis St & Oxford St, W1C

Tel: 020-7493 7988

Open: *Mon–Fri* 08.00–20.00
       Sat   09.00–20.00
       Sun   13.00–18.00

Tube: Bond Street

In the Bond St tube shopping complex downstairs. Larger than usual selection of take-away savouries including sandwiches and vegan pasties and pies.

THE CITY

The Square Mile of the financial capital still has a few pinstriped suits and brollies, though these days you're more likely to see smartly dressed young and not so young men and women heading for the gym or a healthy lunch, as fitness clubs and multicultural food continue to expand and thrive in London.

At breakfast and lunchtime everyone is fuelling their brains for work at take-away specialists such as **Futures**, **Gujarati Rasoi**, **Pure** and **Tiffin Bites**, but once a week they might treat themselves to a sit-down lunch (or breakfast) at **The Greenery** or **The Place Below**.

If you're not in workaholic mode, enjoy a relaxing time at the small cafe areas within tranquil food shops **Rye Wholefoods** or **Antimony Balance**, or try the new internet cafes **Coffee@** which have a fridge full of vegan munchies.

At night the City can feel eerily empty, but you can still enjoy a feast at Chinese buffet restaurants **Veg** and **Zen Garden** or Turkish **Tas** in the west. In the east there are vegetarian restaurant **Carnevale** and lots of **Wagamamas**. The big new vegan restaurant opening of 2008 is **Saf** (p.134) in trendy Hoxton, a short walk north of Liverpool Street station.

If you work around Liverpool Street, check out the start of the East London section of this guide for **Spitalfields Market** (page 154) with lunchtime falafel and Asian food stalls. Some people hop on a bus or walk or cycle up to **Shoreditch** to have lunch at **Lennie's** (page 184). Between Spitalfields and Brick Lane is the delightful new vegan gourmet "bus-teraunt" **Rootmaster**. (p.156)

Carnevale, p.130

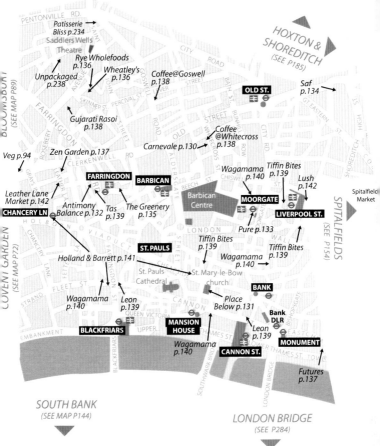

ISLINGTON
(SEE MAP P229)

PENTONVILLE RD.

Patisserie
Bliss p.234
Sadliers Wells
Theatre

Rye Wholefoods
p.136

Wheatley's
p.136

Coffee@Goswell
p.138

HOXTON &
SHOREDITCH
(SEE P185)

Unpackaged
p.238

CITY   ROAD

OLD ST.

Saf
p.134

BLOOMSBURY
(SEE MAP P89)

FARRINGDON

Gujarati Rasoi
p.138

SKINNER ST.   PERCIVAL ST.

GOSWELL   STREET

OLD   STREET

Coffee
@Whitecross
p.138

Carnevale p.130

Wagamama
p.140

Tiffin Bites
p.139

Lush
p.142

Veg p.94

Zen Garden p.137

CLERKENWELL   RD.

Spitalfields
Market

COVENT GARDEN
(SEE MAP P72)

Leather Lane
Market p.142

FARRINGDON

BARBICAN

Barbican
Centre

MOORGATE

LIVERPOOL ST.

SPITALFIELDS
(SEE P154)

CHANCERY LN

Antimony
Balance p.132

Tas
p.139

The Greenery
p.135

LONDON

Pure p.133

Holland & Barrett p.141

ST. PAULS

Tiffin Bites
p.139

Tiffin Bites
p.139

Wagamama
p.140

BANK

Wagamama
p.140

Leon
p.139

St. Pauls
Cathedral

St.Mary-le-Bow
church

Place
Below p.131

Bank
DLR

BLACKFRIARS

MANSION
HOUSE

Leon
p.139

MONUMENT

Wagamama
p.140

CANNON ST.

Futures
p.137

SOUTH BANK
(SEE MAP P144)

LONDON BRIDGE
(SEE P284)

Carnevale

Mediterranean vegetarian restaurant and deli

Open:

Mon–Fri	11.30–23.00
Sat	17.30–23.00
Sun	closed

Children welcome (no high chairs)
Visa, MC. Menus online at
www.carnevalerestaurant.co.uk

135 Whitecross St.
London EC1Y 8JL
Tel: 020-7250 3452
Tube: Old Street, Barbican, Moorgate
See picture on page 128
See map on page 129

Lovely little restaurant, snack bar and take-away with a glass roofed area out back. Near Barbican Centre and Museum of London.

Set menu £13.50 (3 courses, or 2 courses and a drink): for example soup of the day; risotto with giroles, mascarpone and herbs; plum and almond tart.

Lots of **lunchtime** hot and cold sandwiches £2.25–4.50 such as baba ghanoush with roasted peppers, artichoke hearts with olive relish and leaves, auberines and peppers with pesto or sun-dried tomatoes. 25p extra for ciabatta, walnut or organic sourdough bread. Extra fillings form 25p. Hot take-away £5.75 such as spring veg casserole with broad beans, artichokes and chilli polenta fritters. Eat in deli plate £5.95. Lots of salads £2.25–£4.25.

A la carte starters include vegan soup of the day £3.95; quinoa, wild mushroom, spinach and chilli cakes with apricot and ginger chutney.

Main courses £11.50 such as homemade sausages with Colcanon mashed potato and red wine rosemary gravy,; potato cakes with fennel, lemon and basil with provencal vegetable casserole and mixed rocket salad; butternut squash risotto; stuffed red peppers.

Five **puddings** £4.95, vegan options include cinammon crusted pears with spiced red wine and vanilla cream sauce.

House wine £7.50 half pichet, £3 glass. Organic wines from £14.95/£3.95.

Minimum food order £5.50 per person. Small organic **health food shop** with Green & Black's chocolate.

If you like this you'll probably like Manna in Hampstead (North London) or 222 in West London which also offer gourmet vegetarian and vegan dining.

The Place Below

Veggie restaurant & take-away

Open:

Mon–Fri 07.30–15.00
lunch 11.30–14.30
Sat–Sun closed

Children welcome. MC, Visa
Today's menu at
www.theplacebelow.co.uk

Crypt of St Mary-le-Bow Church
Cheapside EC2V 6AU (Bow Lane)
Tel: 020-7329 0789
Tube: St Paul's

See map on page 129

Located in the Norman Crypt of a Wren church, this large vegetarian restaurant provides a quiet retreat. 80 seats inside plus 40 in the churchyard. Global food, especially Mediterranean and Middle Eastern. Menu changes daily.

Breakfast (vegan friendly) 07.30–11.00. They make their own granola, muesli £1.90 (£2.30 eat in), organic porridge £1.50, muffins £1.30, croissants £1.50, fresh fruit, freshly squeezed orange juice £1.75–1.95, and Illy coffee, which Italian customers say is the best in the world, 90p with food.

Soup £3.20 eat in, take-away £2.90. Salads £7.75 eat in, £6.45 off-peak or take-away, such as tabouleh, lemon spiced carrots, aubergine puree and marinated green beans in tomato dressing.

The hot dish of the day £7.75 in, £5.20 out or off-peak, might be ratatouille with Asian flavours, spiced chickpeas and coconut rice; or green risotto with asparagus. Off-peak is 11.30–12.00 or 13.30–14.30.

Healthbowl £5.65 in, £4.65 out, contains wholegrain rice, puy lentils, seasonal veg, sesame and ginger dressing.

Desserts like apple, raspberry and almond cake, £2.80 in or £2.20 to go, or fruit salad.

From 14.30 they gear up for espresso, sandwiches and cake.

Evening private hire available.

Antimony Balance

Wholefood shop and cafe

Open:

Mon–Fri	08.00–19.00
Sat	10.00–16.00
Sun	closed

Visa, MC over £5.

47 Farringdon Road
London EC1M

Tel: 0870–3600 345
Tube: Farringdon
See map on page 128

Spacious wholefood store, very well stocked, with lots of bodycare products, take-away foods and a small cafe area at the back.

The cafe and fridge have lots of take-away food including veggie sandwiches £2.70–2.90; falafel, hummus and salad wrap £2.65;, pies and pastries; nuts and seeds and flapjacks. Lots of snacks, cereal bars, chocolatey things.

Coffees whether espresso, latte or cappuccino all £1.50. Hot chocolate and teas £1. Soya milk available. Lots of herbal teas.

Extensive range of vitamins and supplements including Solgar, Quest, Higher Nature, BioCare, Gillian McKeith.

Bodycare includes Dr Hauschka, Neal's Yard, Barefoot Botanicals, Burt Bees, Weleda, Spizia Organics, Jäson, Jurlique, Ren.

Natural gifts include aromatherapy, incense, lavender wheat bag hot/cold compresses.

Big range of vegetarian health and diet books.

A homeopath and nutritionist are sometimes available.

If you like this you'll probably like Bumblebee in North London, which also sells just about everything and has nice take-away food.

Pure

Almost vegetarian take-away

Open:

Mon–Thu	06.00–22.00
Fri	06.00–16.00
Sat	08.00–17.00
Sun	08.00–15.00

MC, Visa
Specialists in wheat-free, low fat

In one of the entrances of Moorgate tube at the corner of Moor Place and Moorfields, opposite Currys electrical store.

Tel: 020-7588 7800
Tube: Moorgate
See map on page 129

Fabulous take-away with an astonishing range of food, most vegan except some sandwiches and the cooked breakfast. Fridge with wraps and boxes of food, a counter with salads and hot food to choose from, and a big range of fresh juices and smoothies. Open long hours from during the week.

Falafel with hummous and avocado (or tabouleh, or grilled veg) in wheat-free pitta £3.65. Soups £2.95, £3.95.

Box of food £2.25, £3.95 or £4.30, such as grilled veg, hummous, avocado; curry & rice; moussaka; lentils with rice; couscous.

9 salads £3.45 small, £3.95 large, include country veg with pasta, beans and lentils with sundried tomatoes; heart of palm with brown and red rice, sweet corn; red pepper with broccoli and red, black and brown rice,

Moroccan chickpea/pepper.

6 kinds of wraps, single or double, white £2.95–4.50, gluten free. Lots of fresh veg juices, fruit juices and smoothies in various sizes £3.25–4.95, wheatgrass add £1.65–2.75. Many coffees and teas £1–£2.35.

Vegans beware of egg in all the muffins except the banana one, but you could have a fruit salad for dessert.

Breakfast porridge £1.60–2.60 with raisins or banana, served with fresh fruit. 40p each extra portion if fruit or berries. Gluten-free tropical or fruit and nut muesli, puffed rice cereal, or whole-grain bread. Soya and rice milk available.

Food Doctor dry roasted soya nuts, Green & Black's mini choc bars, Alpro soya drinks, Copella apple juice, Purdey's.

If you like this you'll probably like some of the take-away food stalls in Spitalfields Market, weekday lunchtimes and Sun morning and early afternoon.

133

Saf

Vegan organic raw and international restaurant and bar

Open:

Mon–Sat 11.00–23.00 last orders
Closes midnight, 01.00 Fri–Sat.
Sun closed, will be 12–23.00
Take–away available 11.00–17.00.
www.safrestaurant.co.uk
rawchef.com   MC, Visa, Amex

153–154 Curtain Road
Shoreditch EC2A 3AT
(corner Old Street)
Tel: 020–7615 0007
Tube: Old Street,
Liverpool Street
See map on page 129

Opened April 2009, The City now has a big gourmet vegan restaurant right by the bars and clubs of trendy Shoreditch. The menu is huge, 80% of it raw, and there are over 100 organic and biodynamic wines. Out front is a restaurant seating 78 with a long bar and open kitchen. Behind this is an courtyard where you can enjoy a bevvy, and at the back another area for courses and the library of 150 health and recipe books you can browse.

Head chef Chad Sarno leads an international team to bring London the kind of green cuisine that you can find in American vegan and raw restaurants, creating innovative raw and plant-based versions of many traditional dishes foods.

Lunch: Take–away lunch £5–6 such as salads, garden wraps, TTS or TLT (see below). Eat in snacks £3.50–6.50 such as edamame, nachos with dips, nettle and onion dumpling, "Boursin" trio. Main dishes £5–8.50 such as tofu and lettuce sandwich (TLT), teriyaki tempeh sandwich (TTS), cashew cream cheese garden wrap, hummus wrap, salads, miso soba soup, Buddha bowl, truffle lasagne, ravioli. 3–course tasting lunch £17, or £28 with paired wines.

Dinner: Starters £4.50–£7 include gazpacho, miso soba soup, beetroot ravioli, "caviar", spinach rolls, spring dumplings, macadamia or cashew or almond cheese plate, salads.

Mains £8.50–£13 such as lasagne, mushroom and truffle plate, sushi plate with aloe sashimi and parsnip "rice", cauliflower risotto with sage polenta, gnocchi, Buddha bowl (with forbidden rice, green tea smoked tofu, garlic greens, wakame, kimpira, sambal).

5–course chef's tasting menu

£35, or £50 with paired wines selected for each course by their somelier.

Fabulous desserts £5.50-£6 such as berry cheesecake with peppercorn ice-cream, brownie sundae, champagne poached fruits with hemp praline, superfood lucuma cookie with maca ice-cream and goji syrup, jasmine poached pears with matcha ice-cream and green chocolate, or try a 3-course dessert menu whcih can be paired with wine.

Freshly squeezed fruit and vegetable juices and shakes made with almond milk and agave syrup £2.75-3.50. Beer £3.50. House wine £3.50 glass, £14.50 bottle. 100 organic and biodynamic wines, with vegetarian and vegan marked. Lots of organic cocktails. Coffee £2.25. Bar snacks available till midnight.

Courses at back and there is a library of 150 books to browse on lifestyle and diet. Their associated business Lifeco runs courses and advises. You can hire the space.

The Greenery

Vegetarian café & take-away

5 Cowcross St EC1M 6DR
Tel: 020-7490 4870
Open: Mon-Fri 07.00-17.00.
        Sat   07.00-16.00
        Sun   closed
Tube: Farringdon

Busy wholefood vegetarian café with big take-away trade near Farringdon tube, with a juice bar.

Breakfast around £2 with muesli, porridge, wholemeal or chocolate croissants, fruit scones, toast etc.

Soup £1.80 small, £3.20 large, £4 eat in including bread or baps. 10 salads £2-£4.50. Mains such as Homity pie, pasta, curries, paella, roast veg. £2.10-£4.75 take-away, £4.75 eat in, £5.50 with salad platter. £5 meal deal any take-away with drink.

Desserts are mostly non-vegan cakes plus fruit salad.

Fresh juices and smoothies £2-3.85 and they have soya milk. Teas and coffees 90p-1.70.

No credit cards. At the time of printing this cafe was up for sale.

Rye Wholefoods

Wholefood store and vegetarian cafe

35a Mydeltton Street,
London EC1R (off Rosebery Ave
near Sadlers Wells)

Tel: 020-7278 5878

Open: Mon-Fri 9.00-19.00
       Sat   10.00-18.00
       Sun   closed

Tube: Angel

Wholefood store containing a great value cafe and take-away. Vegetarian hot dishes and salads, mostly vegan, with vegan dressings. Soup small £1.35, large £1.95 take-away, eat in £1.80-2.50.

Mixed salads, stir-fries, eat in medium plate £2.95, large £3.95; take-away £1.80, £2.90, £3.90. Pasties £1.39. Sandwiches and wraps from £1.70.

Brownies and cakes fom 85p, vegan ones on the way as we go to press. Lots of herb and fruit teas from 60p, coffee and alternatives like barleycup, filter 85p, hot choc £1.

Huge range of wholefoods in a small space, flapjacks, biscuits, vitamins, body care.

Children welcome, no high chairs. No credit cards.

Wheatley's

Vegetarian café

33-34 Myddelton Street,
London EC1R 1UA

Tel: 020-7278-6662

Open: Mon-Fri 8.00-16.00
       Sat-Sun closed

Tube: Angel, then 38 or 341 bus

Veggie family run café with friendly vegetarian proprietors Jane and mum, not far from Saddlers Wells. There is a garden with a canopy for summer showers and heaters in winter. Plenty for vegans.

Soup £2.30. Sandwiches £2.95 made to order. Around 15 salads, small £3.50, medium £4.75, large £5.

Many hot lunch possibilities around £3.95 including tortillas, savoury crepes and falafel wraps.

Vegan cakes £2.20.

Freshly squeezed juice and , smoothies £2, herbal teas 80p.

Seating outside for 15, inside for about 10. They welcome parties and office lunches.

Futures VTA

Vegetarian take away

8 Botolph Alley, EC3R 8DR
(off Eastcheap between Botolph
Lane and Lovat Lane)
Tel: 020-7623 4529

Open: *Mon–Fri* breakfast
                08.00–10.00
            lunch: 11.30–14.30
            Sat–Sun   closed

Tube: Monument
Cash only or luncheon vouchers

www.futures-vta.net menu

Vegetarian take-away only, in a pedestrianised alley in the heart the City. Heaps for vegans, also wheat-free. The whole menu changes daily.

Soup of the day £2.35, large £3.15. Choose from several hot dishes £4.85 such as bake of the day, fusilli with spinach and mushroom in a tomato and basil sauce, or stir fry veg with rice.

Four salads such as mixed bean; cabbage, apple and raisin with grain mustard dressing; mixed leaves, cucumber, mustard and cress with dill dressing. £1.90 single portion, £3.55 combos.

Desserts £1.50 include apricot Bakewell tart, apple crumble.

Smoothies £1.50 during breakfast, tea, coffee and juices.

Companies can check the website then order 10.30-13.00 by phone or fax to 020-7621 9508. Orders over £12 delivered. Parties and outside functions catered.

Zen Garden

Vegan Chinese/Thai buffet

88 Leather Lane
The City, London EC1
Tel: 020-7242-6128

Open: *Mon–Fri* 12.00–22.00
            Sat–Sun   closed

Tube: `Chancery Lane,
            Farringdon. Bus 55, 243

Completely vegan oriental buffet restaurant on the north side of the city. All you can eat for £5 (all day) or you can have a take-away box for £3 or £4. Typical dishes include veg Thai curry, sweet and sour veg balls, lemon grass pot, spring rolls, crispy aubergine and black bean with mixed veg, seaweed spiced aubergine, several veg curries with tofu and all kinds of fake meats.

Licensed for alcohol.

Veg

Vegan Chinese buffet restaurant

4-6 Theobalds Road, WC1X 8PN
(next to the pub on the corner
of Grays Inn Road)

Tel: 020-7831 9268
Open: *Mon–Sun* 12.00-22.00
Tube: Chancery Lane

All you can eat for £5.50
daytime, £6 after 5pm and all
day Sunday. See page 94.

Gujarati Rasoi, EC1

Vegetarian Indian food stall

Exmouth Market, EC1
Tel: 020-7394 1187
Open: Wed–Fri 11.00-15.00
www.gujaratirasoi.com

Real Indian home cooking, by
mother and son team Lalita
and Urvesh Patel, has
attracted raving fan
customers. Samosa Chaat is
their signature dish £5, a
mildly spiced chickpea and
potato curry with crunchy
chaat plus a samosa and two
sauces. There is also a daily
special with rice £5.50, made
with locally grown veg.
Bhajias and samosas £1.
Take-away masala sauce in
jars.

Outside catering for parties,
festivals and corporate
events from their Tower
Bridge base. They are also at
Broadway Market, E8, on
Saturdays.

Coffee@Goswell Road

Organic coffee bar & cafe

160 Goswell Road EC1V 7DU
Tel: 020-7336 6538
Open: *Mon–Sun* 07.00-20.00
Tube: Barbican, Old St, Angel

Funky new internet and wifi
coffee bar chain with vegan
cappuccino and food. See
Brick Lane (East London) for
details.

Coffee@Whitecross St

Organic coffee bar & cafe

161 Whitecross St EC1Y 8JL
Tel: 020-7403 1525
Open: *Mon–Sun* 07.00-20.00
Tube: Old Street

The sixth branch of this
brilliant new chain of
veggie/vegan friendly
internet/wifi cafes with
vegan food in the fridge.
Near Carnevale vegetarian
restaurant. Opening end
2007 or early 2008. See Brick
Lane (East London) for
details.

Tas

Omnivorous cafe & take-away

37 Farringdon Rd EC1M 3JB

Tel: 020-7430 9721

Open: *Mon-Sat* 12.00-23.30
Sun 12.00-22.30

Tube: Farringdon

www.tasrestaurant.com

Similar menu to the Waterloo branch (see South Bank section) with stacks of veggie and vegan Turkish dishes. Licensed. Visa, MC, Amex.

Leon

Omnivorous cafe & take-away

12 Ludgate Circus EC4M 7LQ

Tel: 020-7489 1580

Open: *Mon-Fri* 08.00-23.00
Sat-Sun closed

Tube: St Paul's, Blackfriars

www.leonrestaurants.co.uk

86 Cannon Street EC4N 6HT

Tel: 020-7623 9699

Open: *Mon-Fri* 07.30-22.00
Sat-Sun closed

Tube: St Paul's, Blackfriars

www.leonrestaurants.co.uk

New fast food bar with lots of great value veggie food. See Soho branch for details (page 67) or check their website for the full menu.

Tiffin Bites

Indian cafe and take-away

22-23 Liverpool St EC2M 7PT

Tel: 020-7626 5641

Open: *Mon-Fri* 06.30-21.30
Sat-Sun 11.00-17.00

Tube: Liverpool Street

24 Moorfield, Moorgate
London EC2T 9AA

Tel: 020-7638 3951

Open: *Mon-Fri* 06.30-21.30
Sat-Sun closed

Tube: Moorgate

23 Russia Row, off Gresham Street, St Pauls EC2V 7PG (north side of Cheapside, half way between St Pauls and Bank)

Tel: 020-7600 4899

Open: *Mon-Fri* 11.30-22.00
Sat-Sun closed

Tube: St Pauls, Bank

www.tiffinbites.com

New chain of omnivorous cafe style Indian places with lots of vegetarian offerings. Light, healthy Indian foods rather than the usual lager and curry. No ghee, no colouring, GM free. Tiffin is a stackable metail food box used in Bombay to deliver lunch, and here you'll find stacks of see-through plastic ones for take-aways.

Main course tiffin boxes include vegetable biryani, chana masala and jeera aloo baked potato wedges £5.29. Gujarati daal, potato bhaji and steamed rice £4.64. Smokey aubergine, black eye bean thoran and lemon rice £4.64. Snacks £1.50 such as 2 samosas, 3 onion bhajis with mango chutney or 3 hara bara kebab.

Eat in biryani £6.95 day, £7.95 evening, with spicy potato and chickpea masala. Evening thali £12.95. Samosas or bhajis £2.75. Chaat spicy nibbles £3.95–4.50.

Teas, herb teas, coffees and Indian chai tea £1.50–£3, no soya milk. Juices £2. Wine £4.50 glass, £14 bottle. Cobra Indian beer from £1.75. Spirits £3.50. Cocktails £5.

Wagamama

Japanese omnivorous restaurant

1a Ropemaker Street EC2Y 9AW
Tel: 020-7588 2688
Open: Mon–Fri 11.30–22.00
Sat–Sun closed
Tube: Moorgate

109 Fleet Street EC4A 2AB
(between Farrington St & Poppins Ct)
Tel: 020-7583 7889
Open: Mon–Fri 11.30–23.00
Sat–Sun closed
Tube: Blackfriars, St Paul's

22 Old Broad Street EC2N 1HQ
Tel: 020-7256 9992
Open: Mon–Fri 11.30–22.00
Sat–Sun closed
Tube: Liverpool Street, Bank

2b Tower Place(by Tower of London), London EC2Y 9AA
Tel: 020-7283 5897
Open: Mon–Sat 11.30–21.00
Sun 12.30–21.00
Tube: Tower Hill

4 Great St Thomas Apostle, between Garlick Hill and Queen Street, EC4V 2BH
Tel: 020-7248 5766
Open: Mon–Fri 11.30–22.00
Sun closed
Tube: Mansion House

www.wagamama.com

We're not padding the book out, Wagamama are handy when veggie restaurants are closed or your mates veto them. For menu see Bloomsbury page 93, or check the website.

Holland & Barrett

Health food shop

8 High Holborn WC1V 6DR

Tel: 020-7430 9346

Open: *Mon-Fri* 08.00-19.00
Sat 11.00-16.00
Sun closed

Tube: Chancery Lane

New branch with fridge and freezer and some take-away food.

Holland & Barrett

Health food shop

Unit A, Leadenhall Court
Leadenhall Street EC3 V1PP

Tel: 020-7621 0165

Open: *Mon-Fri* 08.00-19.00
Sat-Sun closed

Tube: Bank, Monument

Fridge but no freezer, a few lunchie things like pies.

Holland & Barrett

Health food shop

5 Ludgate Circus EC4M 7LF

Tel: 020-7353 9380

Open: *Mon-Fri* 09.00-19.00
Sat-Sun closed

Tube: Blackfriars, St Pauls

New branch with fridge and freezer, including some veggie food to take-away and microwave.

Holland & Barrett

Health food shop

139-140 Cheapside
London EC2V 6BJ

Tel: 020-7600-7415

Open: *Mon-Fri* 8.00-18.00
Sat-Sun closed

This small store packs a lot in. Nibbles such as dried fruit and nuts, also vegan chocolate, flapjacks, supplements also some toiletries, toothpaste and chiller cabinet with vegan yogurts. No take-away food.

Leather Lane Market

Street market

Leather Lane, EC1
Open: *Mon–Fri* 10.30–14.30
Tube: Farringdon,
Chancery Lane

Fruit and veg, clothing and household goods. The market has two juice bars and a stall selling fruit, nuts and olives. The Oasis Mediterranean cafe sells falafels.

Lush Liverpool St Stn.

Cruelty-free cosmetics

Unit 55, Broadgate Link
Liverpool St Station, EC2M 7YP
(next to Boots on ground floor)
Tel: 020–7247 6983
Open: *Mon–Fri* 08.00–19.30
Sat 11.00–18.00
Sun closed
Tube: Oxford Circus
www.lush.co.uk

Hand–made cosmetics, most of them vegan. See Soho for details.

Fruit and Veg stall

Market stall

Liverpool Street Station
Open: Open every day all day
Tube: Liverpool Street

By the ticket barriers going into the underground inside the mainline train station.

Unpackaged

Wholefood shop

42 Amwell Street, EC1R 1XT
Tel: 020–7713 8368
Open: *Mon–Fri* 10.00–19.00
Sat 10.00–18.00
Sun closed
Tube: Angel
www.beunpackaged.com

Bring your own bags, boxes and jars to this new Fair Trade wholefood shop that doesn't believe in useless packaging, near Exmouth Market. See page 238.

SOUTH BANK

Central London *by Christine Klein*

Waterloo is not a part of London you associate with vegetarian or vegan food!! Close by along the River Thames are the London Eye, Festival Hall, Gabriel's Wharf (an interesting place by the

river to meander if you like craft shops and bars), the IMAX cinema, the National Theatre, National Film Theatre, the Young Vic and Old Vic Theatres, and County Hall which contains the Dali Universe exhibition and has some of his giant sculptures in front. But where can a hungry veggie eat?

Tucked away behind Waterloo Station lies a street called **Lower Marsh**, where there is a

bustling s**treet market**. There has been a market here since the mid 19th century and this road is now a conservation area, in recognition of its special character, and also that the earliest records (1377) of this area show that it was the sight of the ancient Lambeth Marsh. Here you can buy cheap vegetables and fruit of a high quality, plus inexpensive clothes, shoes and cd's. Here and there are a few unusual shops selling trendy and ethnic jewellery, antiques, cards, not forgetting the fetish shop, with its black plastic ensembles, and art gallery – truly something for everyone!!

Lower Marsh also has a few street food stalls as well, which all offer veggie options. Crossing Waterloo Road, Lower Marsh becomes **the Cut**, which also has numerous cafes and bars where a hungry herbivore can eke out a few meals.

143

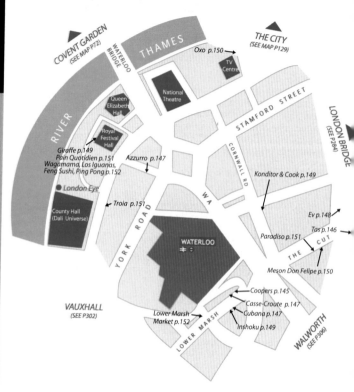

Although Waterloo has only one truly veggie eating place, **Coopers** – sadly not open in the evening, don't despair, tasty veggie and vegan food can be found elsewhere in the vicinity and for a reasonable price. The place has been changing and there are numerous trendy bars and cafes springing up all over, as well as some lovely cosy back street pubs such as the Kings Arms in the Cornwall Road / Roupell Street area.

Coopers

Vegetarian cafe, deli and wholefood shop

Open:
Mon–Fri 08.30–16.30 (Fri 16.00)
Sat–Sun closed
Children welcome, no high chairs.
No mobiles. Visa, MC min £5.

17 Lower Marsh
London SE1
Tel: 020–7261 9314
Tube: Waterloo
See map on page 143

Long established and very popular vegetarian family run cafe, deli and health food store, popular with non-veggies too. All dishes are cooked fresh on the day on the premises. Good value for both veggies and vegans, with excellent and imaginative vegan rolls and sandwiches to take away or eat in. Better than other sandwich bars for quality and size of fillings. A good spot to have lunch or afternoon tea. 30 seats inside and now an outside garden area with 24 seats.

They serve a variety of tortillas, quiche, pizza, it changes daily. Also salads, rolls and sandwiches. Appetizers too such as olives, dolmades, vine leaves and humous. There are amazing salads and at least one is vegan. Salads change every day, soups too, e.g. noodles with roasted mushroom, cherry tomatoes, or avocado and roasted almonds. Soup and large salad take-away £5. Vegans note the soup probably contains stock made with whey. Containers are biodegradable.

Several types of organic bread sandwich £2.20–3.20 such as veg sausage and pickle, Swiss herb paté and humous, peanut butter, all with salad.

Normally a choice of 5 cakes daily such as chocolate and walnut, carrot and coconut, apple and sultana, at least one is vegan. Vegan oat bars.

Hot chocolate and organic coffees (soya milk available) and herb teas.

Wonderful health food store with lots of the latest products and lovely breads and deli type food.

Staff are very helpful and will always order things for you if they don't have them in stock.

If you like this you'll probably like the cafes inside the Planet Organic stores in Fulham (West London) and off Tottenham Court Road (Central).

Tas

Turkish/Anatolian
omnivorous restaurant

Open:

Mon–Sat 12.00–23.30
Sun 12.00–22.30
Children welcome, 2 high chairs
MC, Visa, Amex.
12.5% service charge.

33 The Cut, Waterloo,
London SE1 8LF
Tel: 020-7928 1444
Tube: Waterloo, Southwark
www.tasrestaurant.com
See map on page 143

Turkish omnivorous. Anatolian restaurant that received the Time Out Best Vegetarian Meal Award 2000. Almost all starters (meze) are veggie. The menu has a veggie section with 10 main dishes.

11 cold starters £3.75 to £4.15 include soup; kisir: crushed walnuts, hazelnuts, bulgur wheat, tomato sauce, herbs, fresh mint, and spring onions; zetin yagli patlican: aubergine, tomatoes, garlic, peppers and chickpeas cooked in olive oil; and the classic Turkish dolma: stuffed vine leaves with pine kernels.

Also several veggie hot starters £4.35 such as sebzeli kofte, which is falafel with broad beans.

Vegetarian main dishes £6.95–7.75 such as patli–canli: grilled aubergine with tomatoes, peppers and couscous; spinach with potaotes; okra with herbs;

baklali enginar: artichokes, broad beans, fresh tomatoes with garlic; vegetarian couscous. 9 veggie salads and 10 rice dishes like bademli pilaf with almonds and kayisili pilaf with apricot for £2.15 to £2.45.

Many desserts £3.45–4.25 though according to their online menu only the fruit salad is vegan.

Wines £11.95–19.50 bottle.

Live guitar music in the evenings. Parties and special occasions welcome.

There are four more branches between Waterloo and London Bridge called Tas, Tas Cafe, Tas Pide and Ev (see London Bridge section), plus Tas branches by the British museum (Bloomsbury) and Farringdon Road (City).

If you like this you'll probably like Tas Firin in Bethnal Green Road (East London) or The Dervish in Stoke Newington (North London).

Azzurro

Italian restaurant and wine bar

Arches 145/146, Sutton Walk,
London SE1 7ND
Tel: 020 7620 1300
Open: *Mon-Sat* 12-23.00
Sun 12-22.30
Tube: Waterloo

Good place for large mixed groups/entertaining with a cavernous dining area under the arches of the railway line. Food is Italian with quite a few veggie options and a couple of vegan ones, such as bruschetta – tomatoes, garlic and basil on slices of bread; Toscana soup, various salads, lots of pizzas. Quite a good place for a light snack and a drink pre theatre.

House wine £11.75 bottle, £2.95 glass. Visa, MC.

Casse-Croute

Continental style sandwich-deli bar

19 Lower Marsh, SE1 7RJ
Tel: 020 7928 4700
Open: *Mon-Fri* 06.30-16.00
Sat 08.30-15.00
Ssun closed
Tube: Waterloo

Lovely cafe, a few yards from Coopers, to get a take-away lunch, with just a couple of seats inside. 18 different sandwiches for veggies £2.20-2.80, 6 of these vegan. Also fresh salads, cakes, and hot snacks such as veg pasta £3.50, curry etc. They are open to suggestions, so you can create your own fillings, for example avocado and salad with aubergine pate on a carrot and herb bap; humus, alfalfa, sundried tomatoes and sunflower seeds on a carrot/herb bap; roasted veg plus sundried tomato pesto on herb and tomato bread etc They do usual teas, coffees etc, no soya milk. Cakes are excellent – but not vegan! Cash only.

Cubana

Omnivorous Cuban/Creole

48 Lower Marsh, SE1 7RG
Tel: 020 7928 8778
Open: *Mon-Tue* 12-24.00
Wed-Thu 12-01.00
Fri 18-03.00
(kitchen closes 02.00)
Sat 18-03.00
*Closed Sun, bank hols
except good Friday.*
Tube: Waterloo
www.cubana.co.uk menus

Another omnivourous restaurant, however, they serve a few unusual veggie options (all clearly marked on the menu) such as chickpea creole stew, sweet potato fritter with salsa, vegetable turnovers with plantain, sweet potato and veggies with salsa, and papaya salad with mango and avocado etc they also do a mixed veggie Cuban tapas for approx £7.95. Cantina lunch 12-3pm two courses £5.95, three for £7.95.

Smoothies and juices £3.25, jug £5.95, and lots of cocktails, made with freshly squeezed juices from fruit delivered daily. House wine £9.95 bottle, £2.95 glass.

Service can be slow sometimes – but this is a young, lively place and gets crowded Wed-Sat, popular with large groups. Salasa and Latin live music 11pm (Wed 10.30pm) till close. Children welcome till 7pm. MC, Visa min £5.

Ev

Omnivorous Turkish restaurant, bar and delicatessen

The Arches, 97-99 Isabella St
SE1 8DA

Tel: 020-7620 6191/2
Cafe: *Mon-Sat* 12.00-23.30
       Sun 12.00-22.30
Deli: *Mon-Fri* 07.30-22.30
       Sat-Sun 08.30-22.30
Tube: Southwark

www.tasrestaurant.com menus

Three arches, the first with a bakery and delicateseen with Mediterranean organic foods, meze and vegetarian dishes; second a fish and meze restaurant in the style of Tas Pide with lots of vegetarian dishes; the third a wine bar that seats 100. Outside tables in summer. Part of the Tas chain but with a completely different name.

House wine £12.65 bottle, £3.40 bottle. Children welcome, high chairs. MC, Visa, Amex.

Giraffe, South Bank

Omnivorous restaurant

Unit 1&2, Riverside Level 1
SE1 8XX (by Royal Festival Hall)
Tel: 020-7928 2004

Open: Mon–Fri   08.00–23.00
        Sat   09.00–23.00
        Sun/BH   09.00–22.30

Tube: Waterloo

Children welcome, kids' menu
www.giraffe.net

Good selection of vegetarian dishes. See Bloomsbury branch (page 95) for menu. Some outside seating.

The nearby EAT sandwich bar sells hummous wraps,

Inshoku

Omnivorous Japanese restaurant

23/24 Lower Marsh, SE1 7RJ
Tel: 020 7928 2311

Open: Mon–Fri   12–15.00,
                  17.30–22.30
        Sat   17.30–22.30
        Sun/BH   closed Sun

Tube: Waterloo

Large menu with lots of vegan choices such as sweet corn cake with sweet and sour sauce, tofu with spring onions in tempura sauce for starters; and veg tempura, tofu steak with veg sauce, veg ramen/curry. They also

serve the usual sushi rolls, noodle dishes and miso soup. Starters £2.80–5.20, main £5.20–5.80.

House wine £9 bottle, £2.50 glass. Small flask sake £5, large £6.50, cold sake £7. MC, Visa min £10.

Konditor & Cook

Omnivorous take-away

22 Cornwall Road, SE1 8TW
Tel: 020 7261 0456

Open: Mon–Fri   07.30–18.30
        Sat   08.30–14.30
        Sun   closed

Tube: Waterloo
www.konditorandcook.com

This fantastic shop, on the corner of Roupell Street and Cornwall Rd, is very popular at lunchtime. Excellent for veggies with some vegan options, this is mostly a cake shop. Everything freshly baked –lots of wonderful breads, pizzas, cakes by the the slice or whole if you're feeling greedy! At the back there is a take-away counter with soups, bakes, salads and drinks. The menu changes every day. They also serve food at The Young Vic cafe in The Cut. MC, Visa.

They also have a shop in the West End in the Curzon Cinema cafe/bar on

Shaftesbury Ave. No tables. Tel: 020-7292 1684.

Meson Don Felipe

Omnivorous Spanish bar

53 The Cut , SE1 8LF
Tel: 020-7928 3237

Open: *Mon–Sat* 12.00–23.00
Sun closed
Tube: Waterloo, Southwark

Omnivorous Spanish bar with 10 vegetarian tapas snacks like lentils and fresh vegetables, artichoke heart salad, chickpeas with spinach, soup, and deep fried aubergines for £2.75-5.25. House wine from £11.25 bottle, £2.95 glass. Visa, MC.

It gets crowded prior to performances at the Old or Young Vic theatres nearby.

OXO Tower Restaurant

Omnivorous restaurant

Oxo Tower Wharf, Barge House Street, SE1 9PH
Tel: 020-7803 3888
Open: *Mon–Sat* 12.00–14.30
18.00–23.00
Sun 12.00–15.00
18.30–22.00

Tube: Waterloo
www.harveynichols.com

Finally a posh restaurant where the head chef understands the importance of a separate vegetarian menu that is not entirely based on cheese and eggs, with half the dishes vegan and clearly marked. The dishes are fairly basic for such high prices, and their website's description of the vegetarian menu as fabulous is a gross exaggeration compared to what you would get at The Gate, Manna or 222, however it's still far cheaper than the omnivore menu. So if you're fairly affluent and with a gang of meat-eaters, it's worth a look. It can be cheaper at lunchtime or in their brasserie.

4 starters £9.50 might include melon soup with watermelon and roast fig, or artichoke barigoule with girolles and potato

4 mains £18.50-19.50 such as falafel with imam bayildi, or an asparagus salad.

Discretionary 12.5% service charge, though for wines over £150 it is capped at £18.50.

* Brick Lane & Spitalfields 154
* Broadway Market 162
Canary Wharf 168
* East Ham 170
* Forest Gate 172
* Globe Town 174
Hackney 179
Hoxton & Shoreditch 185
Leyton, Stratford, Wanstead 189
Walthamstow & Chingford 191
Essex 193

EAST LONDON

Gallery Cafe page 177

BRICK LANE
& Spitalfields, veggie hotspot

Spitalfields market on a Sunday morning and afternoon is packed with small designers and their clothes, hand-made jewellery, a secondhand record stall, and heaps of veggie food. Look out for **Rainforest Creations** with their salad boxes and amazing raw cakes, the falafel stall, the wholefood shop, the fresh tofu stall, juice bars and organic wine.

The south end of Brick Lane is packed with Bangladeshi restaurants, all offering veggie options. But the big new opening in 2007 was **Rootmaster**, a red double-decker bus fitted out as a gourmet vegan restaurant between Spitalfields and Brick Lane with absolutely stunning food.

Two cafes on Brick Lane have a fridge full of vegan food: **coffee@154** in the middle, and **coffee@157** at the north end between two 24-hour bagel bakeries. **Hookah Lounge** and **Tas Firin** are also a good bet for some mezze for around a tenner.

Spitalfields Market, a delightful way to spend Sunday morning.

Ambala

Vegetarian Indian sweet shop

55 Brick Lane E1 6PU

Tel: 020-7247 8569

Open: *Mon–Fri* 10.00–20.00
        Sat   10.00–19.45
        Sun   09.30–19.30

Tube: Aldgate East
www.ambalafoods.com

Indian sweets and savouries to take away.

Coffee@157

Organic coffee bar & cafe

157 Brick Lane, London E1 6SB
(north end between two 24-hr bagel bakeries)

Tel: 020-7729 2666

Open: *Mon–Sun* 07.00–20.00

Tube: Liverpool Street

The best cafe on Brick Lane for veggie, and especially vegan, food, with biodegradable take-away packaging and as many organic and Fairtrade products as possible, particularly tea and coffee. Carbon neutral, even the cleaning products.

Breakfast panini, croissants, pastries or yoghurt-style tofu with apricots and muesli.

Makhlouta (organic roasted veg) and mini-pitta £3.50; hummous, tabouleh and pitta £3.40; falafel and spicy aubergine wrap £2.90; bean feast with rice £4; lentil and potato meal £4; rainbow salad, chickpea salad, pasta fantasia.

Cakes £1–£2 and they told us they are getting vegan ones. Also bags of dried fruit and nuts and dark chocolate with ginger.

Coffees, cappuccino, hot choc, chai £1–2.30. Smoothis and shakes £2.80–3.50. Soya and oat and rice milk available.

This is one of six Coffee@ branches, the others are in the City (Central London) and London Bridge (South). All have the same menu and facilities. Child-friendly with high chairs and toys. No alcohol. No credit cards, but there are cash machines in all the branches. Internet £1 half hour; wi-fi free with purchase. Cool tunes playing as there are a few DJ's among the staff. Dog friendly, free veggie dog biscuits. The only downside is that the enticing-looking sofas are all unfortunately covered in leather.

Rootmaster

Nouveau vegan bustaurant – a restaurant in a bus

Open:
Mon–Sun 11.00–22.00
Children welcome
Visa, MC, Amex
Menus at www.root-master.co.uk

Ely's Yard, The Old Truman Brewery car park, Hanbury Street (2nd left coming from Spitalfields) E1 6QR
Tel: 07912 389314
Tube: Liverpool Street

Finally Brick Lane has a vegetarian restaurant and what an absolute cracker it is, gourmet vegan in a classic, nay iconic, Routemaster double decker red bus, situated in the car park of the Old Truman Brewery. Downstairs is an open-plan fully fitted galley, the top deck is a swish 28-seat bustaurant, and there are 26 more seats at tables outside under an awning. The staff are very friendly and funky, the owner is a dancer, one of the chefs dresses Japanese style, drinks are organic, bread is baked on the bus, there are candles on tables at night, even the flowers are sustainable cacti and sunflowers in pots. It's manically popular already so best to reserve and that's absolutely essential on Friday and Saturday nights.

Come at opening time for elevenses with a luxurious warm fruit muffin for £1.50 which will probably sell out by lunchtime as they appear to be the best vegan muffins in London.

Lunch lite bites include olives with thin-sliced sundried tomatoes and herbs £2.50; edamame soya beans £3; green salad £3; soup with bus baked bread £4. Main courses are Rootmaster burger with roast veg, hummus, salad and wedges £6.50; pasta of the day £6.50; seasonal curry with organic brown rice £5; roast veg salad £6.50; Mexican bean wrap £5.

Add to any dish organic brown rice £1.50, organic local tofu £2.

Sinful vegan **desserts** are lacking in many veggie restaurants, but not here! For a fiver you can have triple chocolate fudge cake with ice-cream, or a platter of assorted ice-cream with organic wild berries and maple syrup.

Rootmaster

Dinner appetizers: gyoza veg wraps with ponzu dip £5; soup £4; stuffed mushrooms £6; wild mushroom medley £8; tempura veg with wasabi and ponzu sauce £7 for 2.

Main courses include teriyaki stir-fry tofu with cashews £9; grilled marinated tofu tower with crispy wontons, with creamy coconut vegetable curry sauce £10; mixed lentil filo purse with soft garlic polenta, veg and chilled gravy £11; aubergine tempura stack salad with sake and soy £11; purple sprouting broccoli with ginger cream, sun blushed tomatoes and organic maple wild rice £12.

Dinner desserts include the lunchtime ones plus gyoza seasonal fruits in wonton pastry with ice-cream and maple syrup £6, and tempura banana with ice-cream and maple syrup £6.

Classy **wine** list up to £37 with organic vegan wines. Champagne £30–£56. House wine £12 bottle, £3.95 glass. Bottled lager £3, Sheppy's cider and Stoodley stout £3.75. Soft drinks £1.50. Organic juices £2. Fair Trade organic coffee £1.80, teas £1.50.

Service is not included, but they say "tipping is sexy."

If you must you can smoke in the outside area, though this is discouraged when busy. (They have only two ashtrays/)

You can hire the top deck for up to 30 people. Bespoke birthday cakes, they can even make a destination sign for the birthday boy or girl. They cater to all dietary needs, especially with notice.

Coffee@Brick Lane

Organic coffee bar & cafe

154 Brick Lane, London E1
(corner Buxton St)
Tel: 020-7247 6735
Open: *Mon–Sun* 07.00–20.00
Tube: Liverpool Street

Very trendy coffee bar with internet, soya cappuccino and now a fridge full of Laura's Idea veggie food such as beanfeast, special lentils, various salads such as rice and lentil, vegan rice pudding, fruit salad, £1.95–3.50 out, £1.95–£4 in. Soup £2.95, £3.50 large, usually something vegetarian or vegan.

Coffees, cappuccino, hot choc, chai £1–2.30, soya and oat and rice milk available.

Internet £1 per half-hour; free wifi if you buy something.

Spitalfields Market

Hookah Lounge

Omnivorous Moroccan style cafe

133 Brick Lane (near the top)
London E1
Tel: 020 7033 9072
Open: *Mon–Thu* 11.00–23.00
        Fri–Sat 11.00–02.00
        Sun   11.00–22.30
Tube: Liverpool Street

This place is something quite unusual, just south of the bagel shops at the top of Brick Lane, with comfy chairs you can collapse into with a cup of mint tea, or a plate of Sultan's or veg cold mezze £4.50–6.95. The best deal is the £5 vegetarian lunch. Vegan almond and apricot energy balls £1.50 Free wifi.

Tas Firin

Omnivorous Turkish restaurant

160 Bethnal Green Road
London E2 6DG
(corner Chilton Street near north end of Brick Lane)
Tel: 020 7729 6446
Open: *Mon–Sun* 12.00–24.00
Tube: Liverpool Street)

Several vegetarian mezze dishes. You and a friend can have a few between you with Turkish flat bread (pide) and eat well for £10 or less.

Giraffe, Spitalfields

Omnivorous global restaurant

Unit 1, Crispin Place, Spitalfields
E1 6DW (between Lamb St and
Brushfield St)

Tel: 020-3116 2000

Open: *Mon–Fri* 10.00–23.00
      Sat 9.00–23.00
      Sun 9.00–22.30
      Bank hols 9.00–22.30

Tube: Liverpool Street
Children welcome, kids' menu
www.giraffe.net

Good selection of vegetarian dishes. See Bloomsbury branch (central London) for menu.

Leon, Spitalfields

Omnivorous cafe & take-away

3 Crispin Place, Spitalfields
E1 6DW ((between Lamb St and
Brushfield St)

Tel: 020-7247 4369

Open: *Mon–Wed* 08.00–23.00
      Thu–Sat 09.30–23.30
      Sun 10.00–22.00

Tube: Liverpool Street

www.leonrestaurants.co.uk

New fast food bar with lots of great value veggie food. See Soho branch for details or check their website for the full menu.

Soup + Salad

Omnivorous take-away

34 Brushfield Street, London E1

Tel: 020-7377 5756

Open: *Mon–Fri* 12.00–23.00
      Sat closed
      Sun 11.00–16.00

Tube: Liverpool Street

Omnivorous take-away and juice bar with lots of veggie food in three sizes near Spitalfields. Soups £1.95, 2.95, 3.95. Salads £2.49, £3.49, £4.49. Smoothies 99p.

Holland & Barrett, E1

Health food store

1 Whitechapel High St
London E1 1AA

Tel: 020-7481-3791

Open: *Mon–Fri* 08.00–17.00
      Sat–Sun closed

Tube: Aldgate East

Situated under an office block, this store caters for the surrounding workers. Small take-away selection along with dried foods, supplements and toiletries.

Spitalfields Organics

Wholefood store

103a Commercial Street
Spitalfields, London E1
(SW corner of the Market)

Tel: 020-7377 8909
Open: *Mon–Sun* 10.30–19.00
Tube: Liverpool Street

Large completely vegetarian wholefood shop on the side of Spitalfields market, with a huge range of food products, frozen and chilled, and lots of take-away food, plenty of which is vegan. Also toiletries and Ecover refills.

Spitalfields Market

Market with organic fruit & veg

Commercial Street, London E1
between Brushfield St & Lamb St

Open: *Tue–Fri* 10.00–16.00
Sat, Mon closed
Sun 9.00–17.00

Tube: Liverpool St.
www.spitalfields.co.uk

Covered market with lots of food stalls on weekdays, but Sunday is the mega day with a maze of clothes and craft stalls and an organic fruit and veg stall. Look out for **Rainforest Creation**s raw foods (next page), **Mother Nature's** raw organic foods, the Iranian dried fruit and nuts (picture page 158),

Sedlescombe organic wines, juice bars, **Clean Bean** organic tofu factory, and **The Eco People** (see p.167, here Thu, Fri, Sun).

On weekdays there are a only a handful of the usual stalls so it's mainly a place for local workers to get lunch. As on Sundays, there is an east Asian style food market with a wide range of foods where you can eat cafe style at wooden tables or take-away, and a falafel café.

Spital Felafel

Falafel shop in Spitalfields market

North side of Spitalfields Market, Commercial Street, London E1 between Brushfield St & Lamb St

Open: *Sun* 10.30–17.30
Mon–Fri 10.30–15.30
Sat closed

Tube: Liverpool Street

In a row of food vendors with lots of trestle tables to eat at. Falafels £2.70, with hummous £3, deluxe £3.50. Mezze salad box £4.20 with falafel, hummous, olives, dolma, pittta. Pitta and salad £2.30, with hummous £2.50, with dolma £2.70. Self serve salad box £2.40. Soup £1.80. Freshly squeezed orange juice £2, pint £3, carrot and celery £2.50 half pint.

Rainforest Creations

Raw food stall in Spitalfields Market

Old Spitalfields Market
Brushfield St E1
Open: *Sun* 10.00–18.00
Tube: Liverpool Street
www.rainforestcreations.co.uk

Vegan raw food heaven. £5 for a box of your selection of salads (tropical coleslaw, Caribbean sunrise, red quinoa, wild rice, mungbeans and lentils, chickpeas, kale and avocado), sprouted hummous, akashe ball and dressing. Your box can include a slice of egg-free and flour-free Caribbean or spinach flan. Caribbean roti wrap £5 with wholewheat corn split lentil roti spread with sprouted hummous, salads and dressing. Hummous £3.

Mango-banana, tropical or berry cake £3, free of wheat, sugar and dairy but satisfyingly cakey. Sweets £1.

They have another stall in the nearby **Bishopsgate Market** on Sunday, which is right next to Spitalfields Market. It is opposie Giraffe, Leon and the other eating establishments along that area.

You can also catch them at Hammersmith Lyric Square Thursdays 10–3pm and the 1st and 3rd Saturday of the month; Chelsea Market on Saturdays 10–4pm; and Alexandra Palace Farmers Market Sundays 10–3pm, if they're not doing a special event elsewhere.

East End emergencies

'Ideous East End kebab shops

If all else fails late night in the East End, you can find hummous and salad in pitta in almost any Turkish kebab shop to keep you going while waiting for the night bus. If you're lucky they may have falafels too. Or grab a pot of hummous and some Turkish flatbread in a 24-hour grocer.

The **Zero** kebab shop on the corner of Old Street, Kingsland Road and Shoreditch High Street is open half the night and does hummous and salad in pitta, chips and samosas. Handy for Hoxton.

In the daytime, most **greasy spoon** British cafes will fix you an **all-day breakfast** with baked beans, mushrooms, onions, toast and coffee for around £4. But honestly mate your stomach will thank you for jumping on a bus to Pogo Cafe or Gossip in Hackney or the Globe Town. See also page 183.

BROADWAY MARKET
veggie hotspot

Broadway Street Market

Amazing Saturday street market

Length of Broadway Market, a street running due south from London Fields Park to the canal, Hackney, London E8

Open: *Sat* 9.00–17.00

Tube: Bethnal Green
London Fields BR

www.broadwaymarket.co.uk

On Saturdays, Broadway Market is pedestrianised to become the best little street market in London with a host of veggie delights. Refuel after a swim and sunbathe at the **heated open-air pool** at the other end of adjacent **London Fields** park, or before a day in Victoria Park. There are excellent pubs at the north end of the market and on the east side of London Fields.

North end: Hot food stalls are concentrated here and two are vegetarian: **Gujarati Rasoi**, selling curry with crunch, and **Arabica** falafels and Lebanese dips. Next door are a wholemeal bread stall; exotic mushrooms; and

Chegworth Valley fruit juices and fruits. You'll also find **Café Gossip** (open all week), with over 60 kinds of tea, vegan cake, and a range of wholefoods.

Middle: The highlight is the **Eco People** stall, which sells everything you could find in a wholefood stall except the food. There are several fruit & veg stalls, a coffee stall, flowers, and **Prelabito** Italian foods with jars of antipasti. The post office here doubles as a cashpoint and on Saturdays is conveniently open till 5pm.

South end: Near the canal are a completely **vegan food stall**, freshly squeezed juices, an olive oil stall and an olive stall. Throughout the week you can have a feast of Turkish mezze dishes at **Solché Cilician** restaurant, buy wholefoods at the new little shop **Broadway Organic Foods**, and browse **Broadway Books**, one of London's treasured independent bookstores.

Detailed listings follow.

Solché Cilician

Open:

Mon–Sat 11.00–23.00
Sun 10.00–23.00

Children welcome, high chair.
Cheques and credit cards min £15
Birthday parties welcome.
80 seats, canal view at rear.

1 Broadway Market, London Fields, E8 4PH (south end, by bridge over canal)

Tel: 020-7249 8799
Train: London Fields BR
Tube: Bethnal Green

Cilicia is an ancient name of the Mediterranean coast of Turkey, and if you've ever been there then you'll love this authentic restaurant with warm red walls, wooden tables and carvings, paintings ornate lanterns and mirrors. There is a covered garden area at the back (good for smokers) with a view of the canal.

Cafe menu till 5pm. Veggie cooked breakfast £5.50 served till 3pm. Lunch special every day 11–5pm is very good, 2 course meal £7.50, 3 courses £8.50, choose from cold and hot meze and various main dishes.

Dinner offers 9 mixed mezze for £8.50 each or 12 for £10.50, minimum 2 people. Set menu of 7 mixed mezze, any main, dessert and coffee £17 each for minimum 2 people. A la carte cold and hot mezze £3.50–£4 include broad beans, humus, tabule, artichoke with veg, aubergines, broad bean and humus falafel, salad. Main courses £8–8.50 include penne pasta, falafel, artichoke casserole with broad beans, tomatoes and rice, imam bayildi, or oven baked mixed veg. Side veg £2. Soup £3.25. Various desserts but none vegan.

House wine £2.95 glass, £7.25 pichet (500ml), £11.95 bottle (750ml). Turkish Efes beer £3. Spirits and liqueurs £2.50–£3.

Tea or coffee £1, Turkish coffee £1.75. Herb teas, Turkish apple or lemon tea, soft drinks, latte, cappuccino all £1.50. Soya milk available weekends when busy.

Cafe Gossip

Vegetarian cafe, take-away and shop

Open:

Mon–Sun 08.00–19.00
Sat–Sun 08.00–19.00 or later

Children welcome, no high chairs
MC, Visa. Wifi. No alcohol.
www.cafegossip.co.uk

62 Broadway Market, Hackney
London E8 4QJ

Tel: 020-3215 2062
Train: London Fields (nearest)
Hackney Central
Tube: Bethnal Green (15 mins)

Gorgeous cafe in trendy Broadway Market just below London Fields park. Good music, friendly people, cozy. Warm, brightly coloured walls, wooden tables. Beautiful large selection of teas and tea accessories. Wholefoods for sale. Open kitchen. Part organic.

Combine a trip here with the Saturday farmers' market, sunbathe in London Fields park or its fantastic heated open air 50m Olympic swimming pool and lido, or just relax with a friend then go on to the nearby pub.

Breakfast muesli £2.40, +50p for soya milk.

Health plate £4.70 with bio nuggets or vegan sausages or falafel plus salad, bread and hummous.

Sandwiches include Ahimsa vegan ham salad sandwich £3.20, take-away £2.80.

Vegan cakes £2.80 (£2.40 take-away) such as chocolate, banana or pear and nut. Banana tofu cheese-cake. Fruit and nut bars £1.20. Gluten- and sugar-free millet munchie (highly addictive) £1.70 (£1.50 take-away), Ploughshares carob and nut fridge cake £2 (£1.70).

Gossip is tea-drinkers' heaven, with over 60 kinds in jars to drink or buy by weight and take home. Most places have a wine list, here there is a magnificent 7-page tea list, with Little Buddha being the most popular. Mug of tea £1.50, pot £2.20, large pot for two £4. They also sell teapots and cups from Poland, Czech Republic, China, Mexico etc, metal tea-balls and bamboo strainers.

Organic Fair Trade coffee comes in Italian roast or their own medium blend that's easy on the stomach. Single or double espresso £1.60. Cappuccino, latte or mocha

£1.80. Large soya hot chocolate £2.20.

Organic Whole Earth cola, lemonade and elderflower £1.50 (£1 take-out).

The shop area at the front has what you won't find in Hackney Tesco, most of it organic, including ready foods, grains, meatless meats etc. There is a fridge with 4 kinds of tofu including smoked or hazelnut; spelt and almond cutlets; mini burgers; wheat and soya steaks; Redwood Cheatin' ham; sausages. Sojasun yogurts, Alpro chocolate and strawberry soya drinks.

Organic bread delivered daily, reduced price after 5pm. For fast cooking try organic pasta, quinoa, polenta, and big jars of Danival organic Disney-free ratatouille, veg in pumpkin sauce, or lentils and tofu with veg.

Soya mince, Cheatin' gravy. Plamil mayo. Bouillon powder. Organic cocoa powder. Kallo chocolate rice cake thins. Maple syrup.

On Saturday the farmers' market on the street includes a falafel stall and fruit & veg amongst the non-veggie stuff.

165

Broadway Organic Foods

Wholefood shop and greengrocer

25 Broadway Market, E8 4PH
Open: Mon–Sat 08.00–20.00
     Sun   09.00–19.00

Opened December 2007, this small but gorgeous store packs in both organic and now (to satisfy customer demand) non-organic fruit and veg, all organic wholefoods, nuts, dried fruit, muesli, oat and rice cakes, pasta sauces, mayo, nut butter, baby food, bottled juices (pomegranate is very popular), teas, even Dead Sea salt. Shampoo and toothpaste. Recycled toilet tissue.

Gujarati Rasoi, E8

Vegetarian Indian food stall

Saturday stall at Broadway Market, north end
Tel: 020-7394 1187
Open: Sat 10.00–17.00
www.gujaratirasoi.com

Real Indian home cooking, by mother and son team Lalita and Urvesh Patel, has raving fan regulars. Samosa Chaat is their signature dish £5, a mildly spiced chickpea and potato curry with crunchy chaat plus a samosa and two sauces. There is also a daily special with rice £5.50, made with locally grown veg. Bhajias and samosas £1. Take-away masala sauce in jars.

Outside catering for parties, festivals and corporate events from their Tower Bridge base. They are also at Exmouth Market, EC1, Wed–Fri 11.00–15.00.

Vegan Stall

Vegan food stall

Saturday stall, Broadway Market, south end near the canal
Open: Sat 11.00–16.00

Yummy nut burgers served in a bap with salad, pasties, tofu and veg pies, blackeye beans and sweet potato stew with brown rice, dahl, cookies and different cakes. All vegan plus wheat-free and gluten-free options both for sweet and savoury.

Arabica Food & Spice

Vegetarian Lebanese food stall

Saturday stall at Broadway Market, E8, middle/north end
Open: Sat 11.00–16.00
www.arabicafoodandspice.com

Lebanese falafel £3.50–4.50 and take-away dips.

They also run a stall Fri-Sat in Borough Market (page 287).and Pulse take-away at London Bridge (page 284).

The Eco People

Vegetarian eco-stall

Saturday stall, Broadway Market
Open: *Sat* 10.00–17.00
www.theecopeople.com

While Broadway Organic Foods and Gossip sell wholefoods, these guys sell everything else on a "green but not weird" enviro-friendly stall with cleaning products, Jäson cosmetics, biodegradable and organic and vegan baby stuff, even can crushers.

Also at Spitalfields Thu, Fri, Sun. Deliveries to East, North and EC London, see website.

The Wholemeal Shop

Health food shop

190 Well St, E9 6QT (NW side of Victoria Park, a few minutes' walk east of London Fields)
Tel: 020-8985-1822
Open: *Mon-Sat* 9.00–18.00
Sun closed

Vegetarian shop with good range that includes organic bread, vegan ice-cream, vitamins, body-building products. Veggie take-away pasties and sandwiches. Bodycare. Homeopathic and herbal remedies. Ecover full range and refills. No credit cards, but cashpoint outside.

Frizzante @ City Farm

Italian omnivorous cafe

Hackney City Farm
1a Goldsmiths Row E2 8QA
(off Hackney Road, south of Broadway Market)
Tel: 020-7739 2266
Winter *Tue-Sun* 10.00–16.30
Summer *Tue-Sun* 10.00–17.30
Sun/BH closed
Bus: 48, 55, 26
www.frizzanteltd.co.uk

Vegan dishes available every day such as pasta with fruity tomato sauce and chargriled veg topped with grilled tofu £5.75.

At least two flavours of dairy-free ice-cream. Freshly squeezed orange juice £1.95. Coffee and cappuccino £1-1.90, soya milk available. Organic drinks including lemonade, ginger beer, £1.90.

Some Italian deli pacakaged foods such as porcini mushrooms and jam. They tell us that they don't eat the animals in the farm.

Canary Wharf

Canary Wharf doesn't have a vegetarian restaurant, but a lot of people work there or visit for business. Here are some suggestions from vegan reader Simon England who worked there in 2007.

Coffee and (herb) teas, chilled drinks. Around £1.49 for filter coffee and free top-up. Latte or cappuccino £1.79, £2.09 large (20oz). Soya milk available. Also fruit smoothies.

Bagel Factory

Omnivorous bagel cafe & take-away

Columbus Courtyard
7 West Ferry Circus
Canary Wharf E14 4HB

Tel: 020-7513 0737

Open: *Mon-Fri* 07.30-16.30
Sat-Sun closed

Tube: Canary Wharf 5 mins
bagelfactory.co.uk

The bagels are vegan, GM-free and made to order. Don't be frightened by the very meaty and eggy samples on their website, fillings include Marmite, guacamole (avocados, peppers, onions, oil), salads, peppers, sundried tomato. Average price £2.80. Veggie platter of 7 bagels (14 open sand-wiches) is £20 and can be delivered if you order before 10a.m.

Crussh, Canary Wharf

Omnivorous juice bar and cafe

Tower Concourse Level, Canary Wharf E14 5AB

Tel: 020-7513 0076

Open: *Mon-Fri* 07.00-19.00
Sat/BH 10.00-18.00
Sun closed

Tube: Canary Wharf

Unit 21 Jubilee Place
Canary Wharf E14 5AB

Tel: 020-7519 6427

Open: *Mon-Fri* 07.30-18.00
Sat/BH 10.00-18.00
Sun closed

Tube: Canary Wharf
www.crussh.com

Juices made in front of you, soups, salads and sand-wiches to eat in or take away.

Soups & Salads

Omnivorous salad bar

Promenade Level, Cabot Place
West, Canary Wharf E14 4QT

Tel: 020-7513 0040
      020-7512 8112

Open: *Mon–Fri* 10.30–15.00
      Sat–Sun closed

Tube: Canary Wharf
www.birleysandwiches.co.uk

A lot of vegetarian and probably vegan menu items. including a lovely veggie chilli. Certainly the salads are mostly vegan. Friendly staff and cheap too!

Tiffin Bites

Indian cafe and take-away

22–23 Jubilee Place, 45 Bank St
Canary Wharf, London E14 5NY

Tel: 020-7719 0333

Open: *Mon–Sat* 11.00–22.00
      Sun 11.00–21.00

Tube: Heron Quays,
      Canary Wharf
www.tiffinbites.com bookings

Lots of vegetarian dishes in 3-box stacks based on the tiffin lunchboxes of Bombay. See City (Central) for details. Order online for delivery too.

Leon

Omnivorous cafe & take–away

Promenade Level, Cabot Place
West, Canary Wharf E14 4QS

Tel: 020-7719 6200

Open: *Mon–Fri* 07.00–22.00
      Sat 10.00–18.00
      Sun 12.00–18.00

Tube: Canary Wharf
www.leonrestaurants.co.uk

New branch, see page 67.

Wagamama

Omniovorous Japanese restaurant

Jubilee Place, 45 Bank St
E14 5NY (by Canary Wharf tube)

Tel: 020-7516 9009

Open: *Mon–Sat* 11.30–22.00
      Sun 12.00–21.00

Tube: Canary Wharf
www.wagamama.com

Big restaurant with several veggie/vegan noodle based dishes. See page 93 or online.

Also in Canary Wharf, **Singapore Sam** (next to Burger King) do a veggie stir fry. There are also plenty of places to get **sushi** which they assure us can be vegan, very tasty, very expensive.

East Ham

Chennai Restaurant

Vegetarian South Indian restaurant

309 High Street North, E12 6SL
(junction Byron Ave)

Tel: 020-8472 0255

Open: Mon–Sun 09.00–23.00

Tube: East Ham

www.madrasrestaurant.co.uk

Set lunch £2.75, with unlimited rice £3.75, special set meal £5.95. Tiffin deal £3.25–3.40. Curry dishes £1.50–1.95. Desserts 95p–£1.45 include halva. Tea and coffee 45–60p. Soft drinks and juices 60p–£1.20. No alcohol, but their omnivorous Madras restaurant next door does have it. Children welcome, one high chair. MC, Visa.

Chennai Dosa Vegetarian

Vegetarian South Indian restaurant

339 High Street North
Manor Park, London, E12 6PQ

Tel: 020-8470 6566

Open: Mon–Sun 09.00–22.30

Tube: East Ham

www.chennaidosa.com

Rasam tamarind soup 95p. Starters 30p–£2.99. Dosas, uthapam and curries £1.60–2.95. Executive packed lunch Mon–Fri £3.50 with plain rice, veg sambar, porial, pachadi and poppadum. Look out for their 6-foot family dosa. No alcohol.

Omnivorous branches nearby at 177 and 353. MC, Visa.

Saravana Bhavan

Vegetarian South Indian restaurant

300 High Street North,
Manor Park, London E12 6SA

Tel: 020-8552 4677

Open: Mon–Sun 10.00–23.00

Tube: East Ham

www.saravanabhavan.co.uk

New and very good vegetarian restaurant. Starters £1.95–3.45 including Chinese items such as chili mushroom.

Main courses include dosas of course. South Indian meal with sweet, curries, rice £5.99. North Indian meal £6.99 with biryani or pilau rice, tandoori curry, gulab jaman, starters or soup.

Vegans will be pleased with the dessert choice of fruit salad, halva, ladu or gulab jamun without milk.

Juices £2.25–2.45. Tea 95p, coffee £1, no soya milk. No alcohol and you can't bring it in. Children welcome, high chairs. MC, Visa.

Holland & Barrett East Ham

Health food shop

133a High Street North, E6 1HZ
Tel: 020–8552 6090
Open: *Mon–Sat* 9.00–17.30
       Sun   10.00–16.00

Fridge and freezer, some take-aways food such as pasties.

TLC Dental Surgery

Vegetarian dentists

4 Terrace Road, Plaistow, London, E13 0PB
Tel: 020 8552 7552
        020 8586 7241

Open: *Mon–Fri* 9.00–17.30
       Sat   9.00–13.00
       Sun   closed

Tube: Plaistow
www.tlcdental.co.uk

Sunita Chaudhuri and her brother Sanjit offer NHS and private treatments, mercury free dentistry. Nervous patients cared for. Wheelchair and pram accessible. Interpreters available. Free treatment to under 18's and those receiving benefits.

Afterwards you could go for a curry at nearby veggie hotspot Green Street. Or a bowl of soup if your teef 'urt.

Forest Gate

Green Street is like a more multicultural Southall or Brick Lane, full of Asian shops run by Sikhs, Muslims, Hindus, Buddhists, even Hare Krishnas, selling henna, incense, clothes and with several restaurants.

Chawalla

Indian vegetarian restaurant

270 Green Street E7 8LF
Tel: 020-8470 3535
Open: *Every day* 11.00-21.00
Tube: Upton Park

Indian vegetarian restaurant with South Indian, Gujarati and Punjabi food. Really good and vegan friendly. Eat for around £7 a head. Some unusual dishes such as spicy masala potato chips garnished with lime juice, cassava chips with tamarind sauce, lentil and rice dosa pancakes. Every day there is a dish of the day £5-7.

Desserts include vegan made from gram flour and sugar such jelabi, gulab jamun.

No alcohol. Visa, MC over £5. Children welcome, high chairs.

Ronak Restaurant

Vegetarian South Indian restaurant

317 Romford Road
Forest Gate, London E7 9HA
Tel: 020-8519 2110
Open: *Tue-Sun* 12-21.00
Mon closed
all January closed
Tube: Stratford, Upton Park, Forest Gate BR

Vegetarian South Indian restaurant and take-away still going strong after over 30 years.

Masala dosa £4, thali with two curries £7.50. Lots of snacks like bhel puri, samosas, kachori.

Sunday buffet £5.99 eat as much as you want all day.

Desserts include vegan halva and monthar (made fom chickpea flour).

Wine £7.50 bottle, £1.80 glass. Lager £2.80. Children welcome, high chairs, Disabled friendly. No credit cards.

Amita

Vegetarian Gujarati Indian restaurant

124–126 Green Street, E7 8JQ
Tel: 020-847 16638 / 21839
Open: *Mon–Sat* 12.00–23.00
Sun closed mon.
Tube: Upton Park

North and South Indian and Chinese dishes. The Chinese dishes and Gujarati thalis are especially popular. Thalis £5.99, £6.99, £7.99.

Lots of sweets, and gulab jamun or jelabi are vegan.

House wine £9 bottle, £2-3 glass. Children welcome, high chairs. Visa, MC. Outside catering up to 1000.

Spice Green

Vegetarian Indian restaurant

149–153 Green Street E7 8LE
Tel: 020-8472-8887
Open: <u>Winter</u>
Mon–Sun 12.00–21.30
<u>Summer</u>
open half hour later
Tube: Stratford, Upton Park
Train: Forest Gate BR

Formerly called Sakonis, the new owners offer the same menu. Lunch buffet 12-4pm £5.99. Dinner buffet 6-9.30pm £7.99. No alcohol. MC, Visa. Kids welcome, high chairs.

Ambala

Vegetarian Indian sweet shop

253 Green Street, E7 8LJ
Tel: 020-8470 4946
Open: *Mon–Sun* 10.00–21.00
www.ambalafoods.com

Indian sweets and savouries to take away.

City Sweet Centre

Vegetarian Indian take-away

510–512 Romford Rd E7 8AF
Tel: 020-8472 5459
Open: *Wed–Mon* 10.00–20.00
Tue closed
Bus: 25, 86 Stratford 10mins

Sweets (some vegan including ladhu, jelbai, bundi)and Indian savouries, chaats, bhel puri, samosas.

GLOBE TOWN
East London hot spot *by Claire Ranyard*

When I moved to **Roman Road** in East London, I was immediately struck by the character of the area and the real sense of community. The borough of Tower Hamlets is the most ethnically diverse region of the UK so the influence of lots of different cultures is clearly evident in the types of restaurants, cafes and shops.

I particularly love the wide range of **pubs**, from the most traditional East End type that almost feels like sitting in your front room to the wonderful organic gastro-pubs around the park.

Victoria Park is a place I really appreciate. It's deceptively big and you can lose yourself and

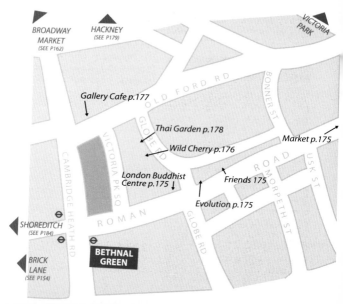

BROADWAY
MARKET
(SEE P162)

HACKNEY
(SEE P179)

VICTORIA PARK

OLD FORD RD

BONNER ST

Gallery Cafe p.177

Thai Garden p.178

Wild Cherry p.176

Market p.175

VICTORIA PK SQ

GLOBE RD

CAMBRIDGE HEATH RD

London Buddhist
Centre p.175

Friends 175

ROAD

MORPETH ST

USK ST

Evolution p.175

SHOREDITCH
(SEE P184)

ROMAN

GLOBE RD

BRICK
LANE
(SEE P154)

**BETHNAL
GREEN**

forget for a while that you're in the middle of the city. It even has its own little deer park.

The area is also great if you're a cyclist. The canal provides a lovely traffic-free route all the way to Hoxton, Angel or King's Cross to the west and Limehouse and Docklands to the south.

For bargain hunters, **Roman Road Market** (Tue, Thur, Sat) is a must. It sells mainly clothes, shoes and household goods but also has a few good fruit and veg stalls that are extremely cheap. Don't miss the excellent olive stand where the Turkish owner insists that you try everything first!

The **London Buddhist Centre** (www.lbc.org.uk) offers meditation classes. Next door is the Buddhist run **Wild Cherry** cafe-restaurant, **Thai Garden** restaurant, **Gallery Cafe** (now open evenings and weekends and with more vegan options), a Buddhist run wholefood store and the gift shop **Evolution.**

This area has a real vibrancy to it. It's obviously not the most prosperous borough of London but it's the people and the rich cultural mix which make it such a wonderful place to live.

Friends Organic

Wholefood & organic shop

83 Roman Road, London E2 0GQ

Tel: 020 8980 1843

Open: *Mon-Fri* 9.30-18.30
        (*Tue* 10.30-18.30)
        Sat   10.00-18.00
        Sun   closed

Tube: Bethnal Green

Buddhist right livelihood wholefood co-op with take-away food and sandwiches, vegan pies, hot and cold snacks and samosas, which they'll heat up for you.

Organic fruit and veg. Non-dairy ice-cream and cheeses. Fair trade range. Bodycare products. Natural remedies, supplements. Cleaning products, mainly Ecover. MC, Visa.

Roman Road Market

Street market

Eastern end (Parnell Rd) of Roman Road, E3

Open: *Tue,Thu and Sat*
        08.30-17.30

Tube: Mile End

Street market with mainly clothes, shoes & household goods but also has a few good fruit and veg stalls that are extremely cheap.

Wild Cherry

Vegetarian cafe and restaurant

Open:

Sun–Mon closed
Tue–Fri 10.30–19.00.
Sat 10.30–16.30
Kids welcome, 2 high chairs, baby changing. MC, Visa.
Outside catering & cakes

241 Globe Road, Bethnal Green
London E2 0JD
Tel: 020–8980 6678
Tube: Bethnal Green
See map on page 174

Cooperatively run cafe-restaurant which has a light, spacious feel to it, combined with elegant décor. Sit inside and enjoy the ambience or pop outside to the secluded garden and take a break from the city. They use as much organic produce as possible whilst retaining affordable prices.

They regularly change the artwork on display, primarily from local artists. Jambala bookshop next door and Evolution gift shop opposite are all linked to the Buddhist centre on the corner. Vinyl and second-hand bookshop next door.

Start with soup of the day £2.70 or a huge range of salads £5.25–5.95. For mains there is always a vegan option or two, such as aubergine and courgette pilau plus salad £5.95; or veg with spicy & fruity peanut sauce and rice £5.75.

Wide range of homebaked cakes, including vegan, sugar-free and wheat-free, such as banoffee pie £3.25, carrot cake or chocolate brownies.

Saturday has a different menu. All day breakfast £5.95 includes pancakes, scrambled tofu, veg sausages with tomatoe basil sauce, roast potatoes, baked beans , large flat mushrooms, unlimited toast and filter coffee with free top-up. Vegan smoothies. Also wraps £3.95 with salad garnish, lentil or butterbean paté or falafel and hummous.

Next to the London Buddhist Centre and many meditators pop in before or after classes to enjoy a vast range of herbal teas, (decaf) coffee or tea, lemonade and cordials, organic GM-free soya milk. Bring your own alcoho and pay £1 corkage.

The Gallery Cafe

Vegetarian restaurant & cafe

Open: *Mon–Fri* 9.00–20.00
Fri when concert 9.00–22.00
Sat 10.00–18.00 or later
Sun 11.00–16.00 or later
2 high chairs, baby changing table
Cheques, Visa, MC over £5. Wifi.
See picture on page 153

St Margarets House,
21 Old Ford Road,
Bethnal Green, E2 9PL
Tel: 020-8983 3624
Tube: Bethnal Green
See map on page 174

Cosmopolitan vegetarian cafe with an international menu, now open evenings and weekends, and from earlier in the morning. The food is getting more varied and exotic, with a Jamaican chef, more is organic and they now have vegan desserts.

Outside umbrella seating in summer on the flower-filled south-facing terrace. Comfy sofas at front. Concerts first or last Friday evening of month.

Sandwiches served from 9am: bagels £1.90, panini or ciabatta £3.10, with lots of fillings including smoked tofu with roast red pepper and black olive tapenade. Burger £2.60.

Hot dishes from 11.30a.m. Soup of the day £3.10, with bread £3.50. Salads £1.50. Falafel in pitta with houmous, veg and mint soya yoghurt £3.90. Jacket potato £2.40, add £1 for salad, £2 for 2, 50p for toppings, chili £1.50.

Main courses £3.90, such as sausage, mash and peas with gravy; spaghetti bolognaise; chili sin carne. Salad add £1.

Vegan desserts include muffins £1.80 (chocolate, raspberry etc), spicy biscuits 50p, cakes £2.50, brownies and flapjacks £1.40, tofu cheesecake £2.50.

30 kinds of tea and herbal tea £1, half litre pot £2.50, litre £3.90, served with warmers to keep it hot. Organic Fair Trade coffee, latte etc £1.30–1.80. Organic hot chocolate £2. Juices £1.20, freshly squeezed £1.50. Organic soft drinks £1.60, mineral water £1.

Weekend menu has bean roast with potatoes and veg £5.30, home-made bean-burger in wholemeal roll with wedges and mushy peas £4.70. Wraps with falafel, beans or tofu £3.50.

Wine is available when there is a concert. House red/white £2.40 glass, £8.90 bottle. Whitstable Bay beer £2.80, Freedom lager £2.10.

Thai Garden

Vegetarian & fish
Thai restaurant

Open:

Mon–Fri 12.00–15.00 then
18.00–23.00

Sat–Sun 18.00–23.00

Kids welcome, hlgh chairs
MC, Visa

249 Globe Road
Bethnal Green London E2 0JD
Tel: 020–8981 5748
Tube: Bethnal Green

See map on page 174

Thai vegetarian and seafood restaurant where you'll pay a lot less than in the West End. Over 40 vegetarian dishes of which many are vegan. Intimate dining on two floors, the staff are friendly and attentive.

Starters from £4, or £9 for a combination platter for 2 people sharing, such as satay shitake mushrooms in peanut sauce, spring rolls, deep fried vegetable tempura, papaya salad.

4 veggie soups £4.

There are 14 vegetable main dishes and another 11 noodle and rice dishes, £4.50–5.00. Gang phed ped yang jay was full of flavour, consisting of Thai aubergine, mock duck, pineapple, tomatoes, grapes, bamboo shoots and sweet basil leaves in a red curry with coconut cream. Lard na with fried rice noodles, mushrooms, mixed veg and black bean sauce was also very filling. Other dishes include spicy potato deep fried in chilli sauce; stir-fried morning glory with garlic and chilli; Pahd gra prou chopped mushroom fried with veg and basil leaf in hot chilli. And of course there are Pad Thai fried noodles with peanuts, parsnip, bean sprouts and veg.

Desserts $3 include fruit salad or banana with coconut milk.

House wine £2.25 glass, £4.95 half bottle, £8.50 bottle, beer £2.50.

Tea or coffee about £1 but no soya milk.

If you like this you may also like the big Thai Square restaurant on Islington High Street. (North London)

Hackney

Hackney, a pleasant bike ride or walk along the canal from Islington, is an ethnically diverse area, with a beautiful mix of cultures. It's also the best value place in inner London. (At least until the new tube line opens in 2010 and the Olympics turns it into the next Islington.)

Alternative types flock to **Pogo** co-operative vegan cafe for London's best selection of vegan cake and cheesecake.

The other vegetarian cafe is **Gossip**, with over 60 kinds of tea to enjoy in trendy Broadway Market (see page 162). Market day is Saturday.

Locals enjoy several very different independent wholefood stores spread throughout the borough. Late night you can find wholefoods in the many Turkish grocers.

As well as street markets in Dalston and Broadway Market, there are fruit & veg stalls once a week at various community centre.

Pembury Tavern

Real ale pub with vegetarian food

90 Amhurst Rd, Hackney E8 1JH
Tel: 020-8986 8605
Open: *Mon–Sun* 12.00–23.00
Food *Mon–Sat* 12.00–15.00
18.00–21.00.
Sun 12.00–21.00
Train: Hackney Central, Hackney Downs
Today's menu at www.individualpubs.co.uk/pembury

EAST Hackney

Big pub near Pogo and Hackney Central with a lot more than the usual token veggie dishes. Hummus with pitta £4.75. Nut and pulse haggis with neeps, tatties and gravy £7.95. Mushroom and artichoke risotto with salad £7.95.

Wine from £9 bottle, £2.20–3.10 glass.

Pool table, bar billiards and lots of games. Supervised quiet children welcome till 8pm. Well-behaved dogs welcome.

POGO CAFÉ

DELICIOUS VEGAN FOOD & ALTERNATIVE CULTURE

www.pogocafe.co.uk

76 CLARENCE ROAD • HACKNEY • LONDON E5 8HB • TEL: 020 8533 1214

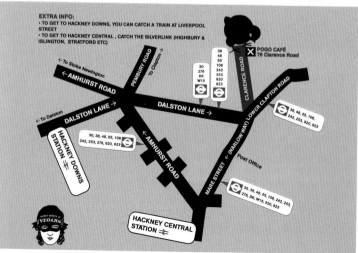

EXTRA INFO:
- TO GET TO HACKNEY DOWNS, YOU CAN CATCH A TRAIN AT LIVERPOOL STREET
- TO GET TO HACKNEY CENTRAL , CATCH THE SILVERLINK (HIGHBURY & ISLINGTON, STRATFORD ETC)

Pogo Cafe

Open:
Wed–Sat 12.30–21.00 (last order)
Sun 11.00–21.00
Mon–Tue closed, private parties
Children welcome, kids' books.
No credit cards.
Gluten/wheat/sugar-free cakes.

76a Clarence Road, Hackney
E5 8HB (top of Mare Street)
Tel: 020-8533 1214
Train: Hackney Central BR

www.pogocafe.co.uk
See advert and map page 152

100% vegan, Fair Trade, mostly organic, cooperatively run cafe with cooks from six continents. An oasis in Hackney with comfy sofas, tables big enough for large groups, children's corner, wooden floor, art exhibtions on the walls, spot lighting and cool music. Tasty food with many healthy options, and cakes that customers cross London for.

Sunday full British cooked vegan breakfast £5, served until they run out, can feature French toast, scrambled tofu and potatoes, Pogo special spicy beans, nut burger or sausage, garlic mushrooms and even broccoli.

Lite bites such as quesadillas (wrap with vegan rashers and cheese), burritos, hummous wrap £2.50–3.50.

Starters and snacks such as garlic mushrooms on garlic toast or a bed of salad £2.50; smoked tofu salad with spicy peanut satay sauce £3.

Main courses £6.95 such as curried black-eyed bean ragout with couscous, pitta salad and yoghurt dip; bean burritos with guacamole; cashew nut roast with red cabbage and apple, sweet potato mash and mushroom gravy; Feijoada Brasileira (black beans, vegan sausages, sundried tomato) served with stir-fried cabbage, wholemeal rice and farrofa (stir-fried manioc flour).

The best vegan cakes and cheesecake in London, £1.30–£2, knickerbocker-glory, cookies, muffins. And vegan ice-cream!

Shakes, deluxe smoothies with vegan ice-cream, freshly squeezed fruit and veg juices £1.60–2.00. Teas, herbal teas, fair trade Zapatista coffee, soyaccino, latte, soft drinks. Bring your own alcohol, offie 5 doors down.

EAST Hackney

181

Wholsum

Organic wholefood shop & take-away

16 Dalston Lane, E8 3AX
(corner Beechwood Road)
Tel: 020-7249 9601
Open: *Mon-Sat* 08.00-19.30
Sun 10.00-16.00
Train: Dalston Kingsland BR
info@wholsum.co.uk

Gorgeous new wholefood store close to Dalston Junction, that has now added hot take-away food. Light meals from £2.79 such as couscous, quinoa salad, sandwiches, jacket potatoes. Soup £3.39. Organic freshly-squeezed juices, coffee tea.

Almost everything is organic including beans, brown rice, nuts and seeds, soya products. Fresh organic bread including sourdough, rye and spelt. Organic fruit and veg. Vegan chocolate.

The fridges have vegan ice-cream, yoghurt, non-dairy milks, cheezly, tofu and seitan steaks, pies, sprouts, burgers, spreads.

Bodycare products include Faith in Nature, Mistry, Tom's, Natracare. Baby products. Supplements. Ecover full rage and refills.

Event catering service.

Back to Eden

Organic wholefood store

120a Lower Clapton Road
Clapton, London E5 0QR
Tel: 020-8525-4092
Open: *Mon-Sat* 10.00-22.00
Sun 11.00-21.00

Completely veggie wholefood store with an Afro-Caribbean flavour. Organic fresh herbs, food and spices, fruit and veg such as coconuts, yam. Also some toiletries such as Yaoh hemp shampoo. Highlights include vegan hot dogs, tempeh, fishless fishcakes, vegan chicken chunks, spicy bean quarterpounders, soya yoghurt, soya dessert, soya, oat, almond and even quinoa milk. Lots of herb teas. Ecolino cleaning. No take-away but it's near Pogo vegan cafe.

Organic & Natural

Organic grocer

191 Lower Clapton Road, E5
Tel: 020-8986 1785
Open: *Mon-Sun* 09.00-21.00
Train: Hackney Downs

Nuts, fruit, grains, body care, cleaning products, fresh daily bread.

Holland & Barrett Dalston

Health food store

Unit 2B, Kingsland Shopping
Centre, Dalston E8 2LX

Tel: 020-7923 9113

Open: *Mon–Sat* 9.00–17.30,
Sun 11.00–16.00

Tube: Dalston Kingland BR

Health food store near Ridley
Road market. Take-away
Jamaican, veg and Cornish
pasties. Soya cheese and ice-
cream. Frozen pasties,
soysage rolls, porkless pies.

In front of the shop is a stall
selling sweetcorn and
another nearby with hot nuts
and dried fruit.

Holland & Barrett Mare St

Health food shop

376 Mare Street, Hackney E8
1HR (top end, north of Tesco, in
the one way bit)

Tel: 020-8985 2906

Open: *Mon–Sat* 9–17.30
Sun 11–17.00

Train: Hackney Centra BRI

Freezer and fridge.

Haggerston Store

Fresh fruit & veg co-op

Haggerston Community Centre
179 Haggerston Road, E8 4JA

Open: *Thur* 10.00–16.00

Cheap fruit & veg stall in a
community centre,
purchased from Spitalfields
wholesale market. Best to
come in the morning or place
an order beforehand. Over
50's club too in the
afternoon.

It's a community initiative
started by the tenants and
residents association with
funding from the council,
NHS and East London Food
Access. They also deliver
fresh fruit to schools.

Landfield Fruit & Veg

Fresh fruit & veg co-op

Landfield Community Centre,
by Nightingale Estate,
Stellman Close (NW corner)
Lower Clapton E5 8QZ

Open: *Thur* 10.30–14.30

Train: Hackney Downs BR

As above.

Granard House Fruit & Veg

Fresh fruit & veg co-op

In the nursery playground,
Hartlake Rd, Homerton E9 5BN
Open: *–Tue*   11.00–13.30
Train: Homerton

As above.

Pembury Fruit & Veg

Fresh fruit & veg co-op

Pembury Community Hall,
Pembury Close, Lower Clapton
Open: *Thur*   15.00–17.00
Train: Hackney Downs BR

As above.

Ridley Road Market

Fruit & veg market

Ridley Road, E8, off Kingsland
High Street, Dalston
Open: *Mon–Sat* 9–17.00
        Sun   9. half day##
Tube: Dalston Kingsland BR
         (right opposite)

This is yer genuine great
value East End street market
with bustling fruit and veg
stalls, some Caribbean food
and household goods. Lots
of bowls of fruit for a quid.

Late night munchies

'Ideous 'Ackney kebab shops

There are lots of lovely
Turkish people in Hackney
with shops and yummy
grocers galore, especially
along the length of
**Kingsland Road, Kingsland
High Street** and all the way to
Stoke Newington. As anyone
who has been to Turkey
knows, or to Solché Cilician
in Broadway Market, it's the
best country outside India
for veggie dining. Even the
greasiest of kebab shops will
have one or two vegan possibilities. So after a late night
at the Hackney Empire or a
classic boozer such as **The
Pub on the Park** in London
Fields park, you can find
hummous and salad in pitta
(with chips) in just about any
kebab shop. If you're lucky
they'll have falafels too.

In the daytime, most
Hackney greasy spoon caffs
serve hearty **all–day breakfasts** with baked beans,
mushrooms, onions, toast
and coffee for around £4. But
your stomach will appreciate
much more a trip to **Pogo** at
the north end of Hackney
(wicked Sunday full English
breakfasts), **Gossip** in the
middle, or the **Globe Town
cafes** on the southern
border, all easily reached by
bus.

HOXTON
& Shoreditch

Saf

Vegan gourmet restaurant

153-154 Curtain Road (corner Old Street) Shoreditch EC2A 3AT

Tel: 020-7615 0007

See page 134.

Lennie's Larder

Omnivorous take-away

16 Calvert Avenue E2 7JP (off Shoreditch High Street)

Tel: 020-7729 1199

Open: *Mon-Fri* 11-15.00
         Sat-Sun closed

Tube: Liverpool Street
          Old Street

Originally a veggie cafe and still with lots of veggie food, with some nice salads and pasta dishes. They want people to eat more healthily and have more fruit. It's great value, people get the bus up from the City to get lunch. Everything is home-made with vegetarian food prepared separately. You can take it to their other cafe a few doors to the right to sit down and eat with a drink, or collect a plate there first. There are tables outside too.

Soups £1.25 for 12oz, £1.50 with half a baguette toasted in olive oil.

Take-away £3 small, £4 for a 750ml box and they pile it high. Free piece of fruit with salad box. They aim for a balanced meal, dishes can include pasta or new potatoes or rice; roast veg with butternut squash or sweet potatoes; broccoli;, green beans and mange-tout mixed with peppers roasted in olive oil; organic lentils with lemon juice; cucumber and tomato in horseradish sauce; raw beetroot and red cabbage grated; big bowl of green salad; falafels and spring rolls; Brazilian, Thai or Caribbean salad; wild mushroom risotto with porcini mushrooms picked and dried by the owner. Jacket potato with baked beans and salad.

They use dairy-free horse-radish instead of mayonnaise. MC, Visa 35p per £5.

Lennie's Snack Bar

Omnivorous daytime cafe
and evening Thai restaurant

6 Calvert Avenenue E2 7JP
(off Shoreditch High Street)

Tel: 020-7739 3628

Cafe: *Mon–Fri*   08.00-15.30
      Sat   closed
      Sun   09.00-14.00

Thai restaurant:
      Tue–Sat   19.30-20.00
      Sun–Mon   closed

Tube: Liverpool Street
      Old Street

This is a very homely place. Thai proprietor and chef Mama Irene says that all her customers become her friends. If you say what you fancy, she will cook it for you. You can get take-away veggie lunch from their other branch a few doors to the left, though this cafe also does several vegetarian cooked lunches for £5 such as veg curry, or £5.50 with a drink.

Several Sunday veggie cooked breakfasts £4.50-£5 including tea/coffee and orange juice.

Tea £1, herb tea or coffee espresso £1.20. Cappuccino or latte £1.50. Hot chocolate £1.40. They have soya milk.

Evening Thai restaurant with some vegetarian dishes £5.50 with rice such as Thai veg curry; Chinese veg stir-fry with garlic; pumpkin and tofu curry; morning glories with soya sauce; five-spice aubergine; veg pad Thai with rice noodles.

Sweet and sour soup £4, Singapore laksa £6 with coconut milk, rice noodles and veg in a big bowl like at Wagamama. Veg spring rolls £4. Mushroom warm salad £3.50.

If you have any room for dessert, which 90% of pepole don't, they have banana or pineapple fritters with coconut milk £2.50-£3.

Bring your own wine, £1 corkage per table. Children welcome, no high chair.

Hoxton Fruit & Veg

Greengrocer

183 Hoxton Street, N1 6RA

Tel: 020-7603 0833

Open: Mon–Sun 08.00-20.00

Hackney is a fast food nightmare, so it's brilliant to find a proper old-fashioned greengrocer that also sells grains, beans, lentils, nuts, olives, dates and halva.

mOrganics Cafe

Vegetarian and fish cafe

231 Kingsland Road (corner
Nuttall St) E2 8AN

Tel: 020-3222 0090
(yes it really does start with a 3)

Open: *Mon–Sat* 07.00-20.00
    Sat 08.30-20.00
    Sun 08.30-19.00

Bus: 67, 149, 242, 243

Opened September 2007,
this mostly vegetarian cafe
adjoins a new organic
wholefood shop. Vegan
items are clearly marked. It's
only slighlty more to eat in
than take away. Tables inside
and out.

Soup £3, take–away £2.50.
Rolls and sandwiches £1.60-
4.35. Salad bar portions
£1.50-4.35 such as tofu veg,
lemon couscous or stuffed
vine leaves. Big slice of vegan
mixed veg boreka £2.50.
Jacket potaoes £2.95-3.95,
toppings include beans,
vegan cheese, tofu with
horseradish mustard.

Muffins £1.20 and cakes (not
vegan). Hot drinks £1-1.60
include Turkish tea, Fair
Trade coffee, cappuccino,
latte, mocha, hot choc. Soya
and rice milk available. Juice
£1.30-1.60. Smoothies
£3.60-3.95.

mOrganics

Organic wholefood shop

229 Kingsland Road (corner
Nuttall St) E2 8AN

Tel: 020-3222 0090
(yes it really does start with a 3)

Open: *Mon–Sat* 08.30-20.00
    Sat 09.30-20.00
    Sun 10-19.00

Bus: 67, 149, 242, 243

New shop packed with
wholefoods plus breads,
sandwiches, snacks, drinks,
fruit and veg, vitamins. Tofu,
burgers. Soya milk, yogurt
and dessert. Hummous.
Bread. Juices. Booja Booja
truffles. Swedish Glace,
Tofutti and Booja Booja
dairy-free ice-creams.

Lots of bodycare including
Jäson. Herbatint, Faith In
Nature. Urtekram, A. Vogel.
Henna.

Sprouters. Ecover refills.
Baby products. Health Aid
supplemements. Natural
remedies.

Viet Hoa

Omnivorous Vietnamese restaurant

70–72 Kingsland Road E2 8DP
(south end)
Tel: 020-7729 8293

Open: *Mon–Sun* 12.00–15.30
last order, 17.30–23.30

Tube: Liverpool Street then 242
or 149 bus, Old Street then 243
or 55 bus.

Of the Vietnamese cafes and restaurants clustered at the bottom of Kingsland Road, this is our favourite for its amazing tofu dishes £4.95, with for example pickled greens, tamarind and tomato sauce, or steamed with mushrooms and chili lemongrass sauce. Rice £1.80–2.20.

Desserts £2.20–2.80 include lychees or banana/apple/pineapple fritter.

Wine £1.80 glass, £8.50 bottle. 12.5% service charge. Visa, MC. Children welcome, high chairs.

For midnight munchies in Hoxton, see page 161,

The Grocery

Organic wholefood supermarket

54–56 Kingsland Road E2 8DP
(south end by railway bridge)
Tel: 020-7729 6855

Open: *Mon–Sun* 08.00–22.00
Bus: 48, 55, 67, 149, 242, 243
www.thegroceryshop.co.uk

With the closure of Fresh & Wild at Old Street, this big new mostly organic shop appeared at just the right time to fill the gap. They source stock from a range of local producers and wholesalers. Bread, veg, fruit, wholefoods, Clearspring Japanese foods, household, natural remedies, organic wines, Freedom organic vegan-certified lager.

You can email or phone in your shopping list (minimum order £20, you can specify a maximum spend) before 3pm and the order will be ready to collect from 6pm onwards.

The shop is mostly vegetarian, but the organic cafe is rather meaty. Open for breakfast, lunch and afternoon tea Mon–Fri 9.00–18.30, Sat–Sun 10.00–18.30.

Leyton & Stratford

Swaad

Omnivorous South Indian restaurant

715 High Rd, Leytonstone, London E11 4RD
Tel: 020-8539 1700
Tube: Leytonstone
Open: *Mon–Sun* 12.00–15.00,
18.00–23.00
(*Fri–Sat* 22.30)
www.swaadrestaurant.com menu

This used to be Chandni Indian vegetarian restaurant and still has lots of veggie dishes.

Sunday buffet £5 all day.

Starters £1.50–2.75 include samosas, spiced mixed veg, Uzhunnu Vada black lentil doughnut with sambar and chutney, hot chilli Bhaji, pakora, Cashew Pakwada, spicy tomato and tamarind soup.

Dosas £1.75–3.75, 18 curries and vegetable side dishes £2.50–2.75 include some unusual ones with coconut. Lots of breads and rices 90p–£2.25. Green salad £1.

Drinks and fresh juices 90p–£1.50.

4 outside tables. Bring your own alcohol, no corkage charge. Children welcome, high chairs.

Ambala

Vegetarian sweet shop

680 High Road, Leyton E10 6JP
Tel: 020-8558 0385
Open: *Mon–Sun* 11.00–23.00
Tube: Leyton
www.ambalafoods.com

Indian sweets and savouries to take away.

Nature's Choice

Health food shop

47 Church Lane
Leytonstone, London E11 1HE
Tel: 020-8539-4196
Open: *Mon–Sa*t 9.00–18.30
Sun closed
Tube: Leytonstone

Health food shop with organic bread, magazines and books, body care and a small savoury and sweet take-away selection. Ecover and refills.

Natural remedies, supplements. Chinese medical centre, nutritionist, Reiki, food allergy testing, hypnotherapy, every day by appointment. MC, Visa.

Applejacks

Health food store & take-away

Unit 28, The Mall, The Stratford Centre, London E15 1XD
Tel: 020-8519 5809
Open: Mon–Sat 9.00–18.00
Thu/Fri 9.00–18.30
Sun 10.30–16.30
Tube: Stratford
www.applejacks.co.uk

Excellent funky general healthfood shop. If they don't have it they'll get it within a week.

Full range of vegan, gluten-free, organic pasties 99p–£1.50.

Aromatherapy, homeopathy, herbal. Bodycare such as Lavera, Jäson, Weleda, Earth Friendly Baby. Cleaning products include Ecover, Enviroclean.

Supplements including Solgar, Viridian and FSC. Lots of bodybuilding stuff such as Met-Rx, EAS, U.S.N., Maximuscle. Books.

Holland & Barrett Stratford

Health food shop

90 East Mall, Stratford Centre London E15 1XQ
Tel: 020-8536 0467
Open: Mon–Sat 9.00–18.30
Sun 10.30–17.00
Tube: Stratford

Health food store with soya sausage rolls, pasties, but no sandwiches. But they do have soya ice-cream.

Simply Natural

Wholefood shop

3A High St, Wanstead E11 2AA
Tel: 020-8530 8892
Open: Mon–Sat 10.00–18.00
Sun closed
Tube: Snaresbrook, Wanstead

Fridge with veggie burgers, escalopes, sausages, mince, Linda McCartney, B'Nice rice-cream. No take-away.

Lots of wheat-free stuff, seaweeds, big range of teas.

Bodycare especially Weleda. Baby foods, soap, oil and cream. Natural remedies, homeopathy, herbs, vitamins, minerals, omega oils. People come for miles for their Nag Champa incence.

Walthamstow

Hornbeam Cafe

Vegetarian cafe

Hornbeam Environmental
Centre, 458 Hoe St,
Walthamstow, London E17 9AH
(1 min from Baker's Arms)

Tel: 020-8558 6880
Cafe: *Sat* 10.00-16.00
maybe also Friday
Stall: *Sat* 10.00-15.00
Tube: Walthamstow Central
www.hornbeam.org.uk

A mainly vegan cafe has re-opened in this eco-centre, with a fruit & veg stall outside selling organic produce from Eostre farmer's co-operative, other local growers and bakers, jams and pickles.

Food is cooked by a collective of local people. Depending who's there it could be Korean such as noodle soup, rice balls wrapped with seaweed, or pancakes; or Turkish or Italian dishes. Main meals £3.50-4.50. Toasties and salads around £2. Homemade cakes, usually vegan, £1-1.50. Tea or coffee 70p.

The centre is open Mon, Wed Friday. It enables practical sustainable environmental activity at a local level. They hold community events, run school programmes and offer meeting space, office space and a mail collection service for groups."

Ambala

Vegetarian sweet shop

480 Hoe Street, Walthamstow
London E17 9AH

Tel: 020-8539 6695
Open: *Mon-Sun* 10-20.45
Tube: Walthamstow
www.ambalafoods.com

Indian sweets and savouries to take away.

Holland & Barrett, E17

Health food shop

3 Selborne Walk, Walthamstow
London E17 7JR

Tel: 020-8520 5459
Open: *Mon-Sat* 9.00-17.30
Sun 10.30-16.30

Fridge-freezer with pasties and pies to take away.

Second Nature

Organic wholefood store

78 Wood Street, Walthamstow
London E17 3HX

Tel: 020-8520 7995

Open: *Mon–Sat* 8.00–17.30
Sun closed

Tube: Train Wood Street BR

Good selection of organic foods, supplemements, sandwiches £2.70 such as humous and carrot, pies and various snacks for veggies and vegans such as mixed bean & salsa, veg sausage. The focus is on fresh and packaged organic produce and they cater for special diets. Also cruelty-free toiletries, handmade cards, fair-traded gifts, incense, oil burners. No credit cards.

Vita Health

Wholefoods shop

565 Lea Bridge Rd, Leyton
London E10 7EQ

Tel: 020-8539 3245

Open: *Mon–Sat* 9.00–18.00
Sun closed

Tube: Leyton

Usual range of wholefoods and chilled and frozen veggie foods including veggie sausages and burgers, but no fresh take-away. Small toiletries section with cruelty-free shampoos and soaps and a few books. Vitamins and supplements including Solgar.

Walthamstow Market

Street market

The entire length of Walthamstow High Street

Open: *Mon–Sat* 9.00–17.00

Tube: Walthamstow Central

The greatest East End street market with hundreds of stalls, mostly food, and some incredible bargains. At the Blackhorse Road (west) end are some amazing value grocery stores.

Food & Fitness

Health food store

43 Old Church Road,
South Chingford, London E4 6JS

Tel: 020-8524 0722

Open: *Mon–Sat* 9.00–17.30
Sun closed

Train: Chingford BR

Specialise in vitamins, supplements, body-building and sports products. No take-away food.

Essex

Ambala

Vegetarian sweet shop

213–215 Ilford Lane, Ilford
Essex IG1 2RZ
Tel: 020-8553 0159
Open: *Mon–Sun* 11.30–22.30

---

52 Ilford Lane, Ilford
Essex IG1 2RZ
Tel: 020-8553 0159
Open: *Mon–Sun* 11.30–21.00
www.ambalafoods.com

Indian vegetarian sweet shop.

GNC, Romford

Health food shop

N16 Laurie Walk, Liberty Centre
Romford, Essex RM1 3RT
Tel: 01708-747192
Open: *Mon–Sat* 9.00–17.45
Sun 10.30–16.30

Next door to Holland & Barrett. H&B sell more dried fruit and nuts and vitamins, GNC sell more bodybuilding stuff.

Holland & Barrett Barking

Health food shop

49 East Street, Barking IG11 8EJ
Tel: 020-8591 8017
Open: *Mon–Sat* 9-17.30
Sun closed

Freezer and fridge with some take-away food.

Holland & Barrett Ilford

Health food shop

52 Cranbrook Road, Ilford
Essex IG1 4PG
Tel: 020-8553 2808
Open: *Mon–Sat* 9.00–18.00
Sun 10.30–17.00

Freezer and fridge with some take-away pasties, couscous etc.

Holland & Barrett Loughton

Health food shop

212 High Road, Loughton
Essex IG10 1DZ
Tel: 020-8532 1163
Open: *Mon–Sat* 9.00–17.30
            Sun   10.00–16.00

Freezer and fridge, sometimes take-away sos rolls.

Holland & Barrett Romford

Health food shop

Unit 17, Laurie Walk
Romford RM1 3RT
Tel: 01708-722349
Open: *Mon–Sat* 8.30–18.00
            Sun   11.00–17.00

Freezer and fridge with take-away pasties etc.

Lush Romford

Cruelty-free cosmetics

The Liberty shopping centre,
Swan Walk, Romford RM1 3DH
Tel: 01708-769 379
www.lush.co.uk

Gorgeous hand-made cosmetics, most of them vegan and clearly labelled. Worth coming in here just for the lovely smells. Blokes, this is the place to get 'er indoors a present as the staff will be delighted to help you. See Soho for details or enjoy the website, though you can't smell it.

* Camden 196
Finchley 208
Finsbury Park & Archway 211
Golders Green 215
Hampstead 218
Hendon & Brent Cross 222
Highbury 224
Highgate 227
* Islington 229
Kings Cross 238
Kentish Town 240
Muswell Hill & 243
Crouch End 245
* Primrose Hill 246
* Stoke Newington & 250
Newington Green 257
Wood Green 259
Rest of North London 260
Hertfordshire 262

NORTH LONDON

Indian Veg page 231

CAMDEN
North London hotspot

Camden, on the north-east edge of Regent's Park, features some of the best bars, clubs and pubs in London which are the basis of a lively music scene. The various huge and unique covered markets attract an eclectic mix, who flock there at the weekend in their thousands. We've divided Camden into four sections:

Camden Market p.198
Parkway p.201
Camden Town p.204
Chalk Farm Road p.206

Camden Market (actually six markets) off the High Street and around the Lock, gives you the best choice of hip new and secondhand clothes in town, jewellery, crafts, hippy and Goth stuff galore. There are many food stalls and cafes with veggie and vegan options including two falafel bars and a Morrocan cafe **Marrakech**. Recently opened on the bridge over the canal is a fabulous new organic cafe and restaurant **InSpiral Lounge** with lots of events and something for everyone.

Parkway, running from the tube station to Regents Park, has a **Fresh & Wild** wholefood supermarket where you can pick up supplies for a summer's day in the park. **Green Note** is London's only vegetarian pubrestaurant with live music most nights (see website for listings)

Right outside **Camden Town** tube station is Tai all-you-can-eat vegan Chinese buffet – eat till you can't walk for £6. **Max Orient** up the high street towards the market is a new buffet with quite a bit of veggie stuff too.

Past the market on **Chalk Farm Road** is a terrific new wholefood store **My Village** with a cafe area at the back. We had a lovely time browsing here and sipping smoothies and chai. Nearby is a branch of **Neal's Yard Remedies** with 200 herbs and spices sold by weight.

10 minutes walk away (bring your A-Z or risk getting lost!) is tranquil **Primrose Hill** (page 246) with terrific views over London. There's gourmet food at **Manna**, or relax at **Madder Rose** or **Cafe Seventy-Nine**.

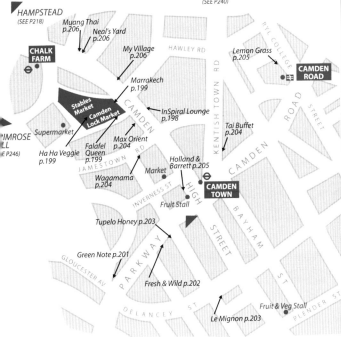

KENTISH
TOWN
(SEE P240)

HAMPSTEAD
(SEE P218)

Muang Thai
p.206

Neal's Yard
p.206

My Village
p.206

HAWLEY RD

Lemon Grass
p.205

CHALK
FARM

CAMDEN
ROAD

Marrakech
p.199

RYL COLLEGE ST

KENTISH TOWN RD

Stables
Market

CAMDEN

InSpiral Lounge
p.198

Camden
Lock Market

Supermarket

Tai Buffet
p.204

PRIMROSE
HILL
(SEE P246)

Ha Ha Veggie
p.199

Falafel
Queen
p.199

Max Orient
p.204

JAMESTOWN RD

Holland &
Barrett p.205

Market

Wagamama
p.204

CAMDEN

INVERNESS ST

CAMDEN
TOWN

HIGH

Fruit Stall

BAYHAM

Tupelo Honey p.203

STREET

Green Note p.201

GLOUCESTER AV

PARKWAY

ST

Fresh & Wild p.202

DELANCEY ST

Fruit & Veg Stall

PLENDER ST

Le Mignon p.203

EUSTON
(SEE MAP P106)

197

InSpiral Lounge

Vegetarian organic restaurant, cafe and music venue

Open:

Tue-Thu	10.00-20.00
	(later if event is on)
Fri-Sat	10.00-24.00
Sun	10.00-22.00

Free internet/wi-fi. Smokers' jetty
www.inspiralled.net (events,menu)

250 Camden High St, Camden Lock NW1 8QS (next to bridge over canal by Camden Market)

Tel: 020-7428 5875

Tube: Camden Town

Kids welcome. MC, Visa
See map on page 197

Newly opened on two floors in an amazing location. InSpiral Lounge serves organic visionary cuisine, lots of raw foods, and is licensed for alcohol with all drinks organic and vegan or vegetarian. Have a healthy meal or afternoon tea with vegan cake after shopping in the market or at nearby My Village, or wind down with a glass of wine by the outside canal seating.

InSpiral is already a hotspot for events featuring ambient/downbeat electronica, multimedia performances, talks, film screenings, acoustic sessions, dance, healthy living and conscious being.

There is a buffet with portions for £1.50-£3. You can mix from hot dishes and raw gourmet items. Combination plates start from £5.50. Sandwiches £3.28-3.95. Soup with bread £3.50.

Organic cakes £2.50, cheesecakes and brownies include a vegan banana and date cake. Raw chocolate balls £1.50, guarana truffles £1, super cubes £2, hemp hearts.

Homemade Chai £2.55, herbal teas and fair traded organic coffee from £1.30. Superior "superfood" smoothies with goji, macca, spirulina etc. £3.85-4.95. Organic ciders, spirits, wines, champagne. House wine £3 glass, £12 bottle. Innovative cocktails from £5. Bottle of beer or ale £3, Cannabia hemp beer £3.20. Sensatonics alcoholic herbal elixirs in cocktails, £2 shot or £2.25 for a little bottle to take home.

Every Friday is Electronica Eclectica, Saturday night is Inspiral nights, free entry.

They sell superfoods, books on raw, vegan, conscious and eco-living. And for parents it offers a nice child-friendly space downstairs with toys and books.

Falafel Queen

Vegetarian take-away

Camden Lock, West Yard near the boats by the weeping willow

Tel: 020-8806 4460

Open: *Sat-Sun* 10.30-17.30
Mon-Fri closed

Tube: Camden Town

Queen Falafel £4, with a superior selection of salads including sweetcorn, spinach leaves, tabouleh, red beans etc, hummous and toppings. King Falafel £4.50 adds a topping of warm chickpeas in tomato sauce. Add another 50p for some chips. Portion of chips £1.50, made on site from real potatoes, not frozen. Scrumptious salad box £4.50. Help yourself to dressings. Soup £2.

Ha Ha Veggie Bar

Vegetarian & vegan take away

In Camden Lock market. From West Yard entrance 4 (under the railway bridge) go straight ahead and it's on the left after the pizzeria.

Open: *Sat-Sun* 10.00-17.00
Mon-Fri usually closed

Tube: Camden Town

Stall selling falafels £3, drinks and large, homemade veggie burgers with a range of toppings such as avocado and pineapple. All are vegan except the cheeseburger. Salds and hummous in pitta £2. Prices £2-3.00. Fair trade tea and coffee 70-80p.

InSpiral Lounge, Camden's new visionary veggie venue

Marrakech

Omnivorous Morrocan and
Mediterranean cafe & take-away

In the entrance of Camden
Stables market, Chalk Farm Rd.
Also another branch opening
nearby further into the market.

Tel: 07944 774155

Open: *Sun–Thu* 09.00–24.00
Fri–Sat 09.00–04.00

Tube: Camden Town, Chalk Farm

If you've ever been to
Morocco or you miss the low
tables and cushioned seating
of the recently closed nearby
Psychedelic Dream Temple
Cafe, then you'll love this
place. Some outside tables
and lots more upstairs,
which is elaborately
decorated with lanterns, low
brass tables and cushioned
seating. Arabic music. Shisha
water pipes. The lanterns
and furniture are for sale. Eat
in or take away.

Veg tagine or veg couscous
wrap £4. (Chili) falafel. Meze
dishes £2.25 include
hummous, olives, tabouleh.
Salad selection £3.75.

Almond and pistachio
baklava, some without
honey, 50p. Sweet dates
£2.25.

Fresh fruit juices and
smoothies made to order
£1.95–2.60. Cold drinks
95p, £1.35. Pot of mint tea
£2.25, large £4.25. Coffee
£1.25–1.75.

In the food court on
weekdays you can also find
(from left to right) Japanese
tofu teriyaki with veg
noodles; hummous salad
bagel; Indian veg curry;
Indonesian veg curry and
noodles (no egg).

Inverness Street Market

Street market

Inverness Street,
off Camden High Street

Open: *Mon–Sat* 08.00–17.00
Sun closed

Tube: Camden Town

A few fruit and veg stalls,
which you won't find in the
main Camden markets,
which are all clothes and
jewellery. There's also a
handy fruit stall (Mon–Sat
08.00–18.30) on the corner
of Parkway and Camden High
Street, and a few more stalls
down the High Street at the
corner with Plender Street.

Green Note

*Vegetarian bar, live music
& organic cafe–restaurant*

Open:

Mon–Tue –closed
Wed–Thu 18.00–23.00
Fri–Sat 18.00–24.00
Sun 18.00–23.00
*Can vary throughout the year, see
website for latest info.*

106 Parkway, London NW1 7AN
Tel: 020-7485 9899
Tube: Camden Town
www.greennote.co.uk events
12.5% service charge. MC, Visa
Cover charge for live events.
See map on page 197

*Founders Immy and Risa
have created a place where
you can enjoy quality live
music and have good veggie
food, while being in a laid-
back, friendly atmosphere.
Live music most nights
includes blues, jazz, folk,
roots, world, alt-country
and singer-songwriter.*

*The menu draws inspiration
from around the world, with
international tapas and a
daily main course special.
All ingredients are GM free
and all basic ingredients are
organic.*

Lunch sandwiches, wraps and
burgers £6.95.

Salad plate £8.95 with mixed
leaves, toasted seeds, vinaigrette and your choice of 5
from marinated baked tofu,
falafel, avocado, cherry or
sun-blushed tomato, roasted
Mediterranean veg, humous,
olives, marinated artichoke
hearts, hearts of palm.

18 kinds of tapas, 12 vegan,

£1.45–4.95, include humous
and grilled pita, guacamole
and tomato salsa with tortilla
chips, Indian potato patties,
mock duck spring rolls with
hoisin sauce, falafels, potato
wedges, marinated artichoke
hearts with capers,
dolmades, marinated baked
tofu, mixed leaf salad,
focaccia bread, mixed olives.
Tapas platter for two £17.95.

Main course daily special
£7.95–9.95 such as Peruvian
style baked pineapple served
with shitake mushrooms and
sesame roasted potatoes; or
sweet potato and spinach
curry.

6 desserts £4.95, 4 vegan
such as cheesecake, fruit
crumble or ice-cream.

House wine £3.45 glass,
£11.50 bottle. Beer £3 bottle
£3.15 pint. Coffee £1.50.
Soya milk and cappuccino.
Kitchen closes 9.30 Sun–Thu,
10pm Fri–Sat. Reservations
recommended. See website
for full menu and music
listings.

Fresh & Wild Camden

Organic supermarket and cafe

Open:

Mon–Fri	08.00–21.00
Sat	08.00–21.00
Sun	08.00–21.00

Visa, MC, Amex.
Masseuse and iridologist once a week. Special events.

49 Parkway, Camden Town
London NW1 7PN
Tel: 020-7428 7575
Tube: Camden Town

See map on page 197

Big wholefoods super-market, with cafe tables outside. They sell everything from tea to toothpaste and have a big take-away food and juice bar. Load up for a day in Regents Park or fashionable Camden Lock market. 60-80% of fresh produce is organic with lots of local suppliers.

Take-away food bar by weight, £1–1.19 per 100g, with salads, baked tofu and savouries (not all vegetarian). Muffins, cakes £1.99-2.29 include gluten- free, vegan carrot and chocolate, and soyaccino.

Great choice of organic fruit and vegetables. Lots of fresh breads including gluten-free. Big range of own brand value foods such as rice and oat cakes. Clive's pies in the winter. Artesan chocolates including amazing slabs of Venezuelan dark choc with nuts and dried fruit. Lots of mueslis and everything you need to make your own.

Big vegan fridge at the back packed with cheeses, tempeh, seitan, tofu, fish fingers. Vegan ice-cream heaven including Booja booja amazing new cashewnut and agave (low GI), B'Nice, Swedish Glace and Tofutti. Frozen ready meals including Linda McCartney.

Vegan wines, Weston's cider and beers.

Bodycare from top-end Ren, Dr Hauschka and Jurlique to the great value Weleda range. Green People, Barefoot Botanicals, Jäson, Lavera makeup. Hair dyes.

Aromatherapy, natural remedies and supplements include Viridian, Solgar, Biocare, New Chapter. Books and magazines, yoga and pilates dvd's, Putumayo world music CD's. Organic baby clothes.

If you like this you'll probably like their other stores in Soho, Clapham and Stoke Newington and the Wholefoods Market in Kensington.

Tupelo Honey

Omnivorous café

27 Parkway, Camden NW1 7PN
(corner of Arlington St)

Tel: 020-7284 2989

Open: *Tue–Sat* 9.30–23.30
       Sun   12.00–20.00
       Mon   9.30–18.00

Tube: Camden Town
www.tupelo-honey.co.uk

Very popular and chilled out café with several rooms on three floors with wooden tables, a ground floor terrace area that is set back from the street, and a roof garden.

Several veggie dishes e.g. couscous, slightly curried root veg £7.95.

Desserts include carrot cake, vegan version on the way.

House wine £11.50 bottle, £3 glass, beer £3.50 bottle. Illy cappuccino £1.80, latte £2, they have soya milk.

Children welcome, no high chair yet. MC, Visa.

Le Mignon

Omnivorous Lebanese

9a Delancey Street,
corner of 98 Arlington Rd
Camden Town, London NW1

Tel: 020 7387 0600

Open: *Mon–Sun* 12.00–15.00
                18.00–24.00

Tube: Camden Town

Sweet little Lebanese restaurant with a couple of outside tables on a quiet side street off Camden High St, round the back of Woolworths.

Like virtually all Lebanese places, main dishes are meat based and starters are vegetable based. Dairy products and eggs are rarely used. Staff are very friendly and it is clear from the menu what is veggie/vegan and what isn't.

There are around 22 hot and cold vegan starters £3.95–5.00, so if you and a friend order 3 different ones each, you can create a tasty feast.

House wine £2.50 (125ml glass) –3.00 (175ml), £11.75 bottle. Beer £2.20. MC, Visa, Amex.

Tai Buffet

Vegan Chinese Restaurant

6 Kentish Town Road,
Camden, London, NW1
(just up from the tube)
Tel: 020-7284 4004
Open: *Mon–Sun* 12.00–22.30
Tube: Camden Town

Chinese vegan buffet restaurant and take–away with lots of fake meat. Open every day for lunch and dinner. All you can eat £5.50, £6.50 after 5pm and Sunday, plus 10% service charge, so it's actually £6.05 and £7.15. Take–away box £3 or £4 large.

House 2ne £10 bottle, £2.50 glass. Chinese beer £2.50 bottle. Soft drinks or tea £1.50.

Max Orient Buffet

Omnivorous Oriental restaurant

273–275 Camden High Street
London NW1 7BX
(just south of the canal, between railway bridge & Jamestown Rd)
Tel: 020-7485 5466
Open: *every day* 11.00–23.00
Tube: Camden Town

Opened July 2007, big Malaysian, Chinese, Japanese and Thai buffet £7.60, £4.30 children under 130cm (4'3"). Take–away £4.50. Half is veggie and labelled, including salad bar, spring rolls, samosa, sea spice aubergine, bok choi, sweetcorn soup, veg chicken wrap with pandan leaf, Thai green curry, beancurd, cashew rice, noodles (brown with egg, yellow udon without).

Fresh juice £1.80, smoothies £3.50, soft drinks £1.50. House wine £3.50 glass, £11.90 bottle. Coffee £1.50.

High chairs. Disabled toilet, but some steps into the seating area.

Wagamama Camden

Omnivorous Japanese

11 Jamestown Road,
Camden Town, NW1 7BW
Tel: 020-7428 0800
Open: *Mon–Sat* 12.00–23.00
        Sun 12.00–22.00
Tube: Camden Town
www.wagamama.com

Omnivorous fast food Japanese noodle bar with over nine veggie and vegan dishes. See Bloomsbury, WC1 branch for menu.

Lemon Grass

Omni Cambodian/SE Asian restaurant

243 Royal College Street
Camden Town, London NW1

Tel: 020-7284 1116

Open: *Every day* 17.30-23.00
Last orders 22.30

Tube: Camden Town
Camden Road BR

Small, and brightly-lit restaurant, there is a separate vegetarian menu with mostly stir-fry dishes.

Starters £3 include golden triangles of curry potato, veg spring rolls, garlic lemon mushrooms, fried leek cake with chilli sauce. Plate of the last 4 with ginger/shallots for 2+ people for £11 each.

Mains £5.40 such as Buddhist cabbage with peppers, rainbow stir-fry, pak choy ginger, spicy veg. Mango salad £4.30. Steamed rice £1.90. Veg set feast £16.80 per head, minimum 2 people, of 5 treats with dips, mango salad, Buddhist cabbage, fresh asparagus or spiced veg, steamed rice, fresh mango/pineapple or lychee.

Desserts include fresh mango, lychees, pineapple or banana fritters.

Wine £3.30 glass, £12.60 Children welcome, high chairs.

Holland & Barrett, NW1

Health food shop

191-200 High St, Camden
London NW1 0LT

Tel: 020-7485-9477

Open: *Mon-Sat* 09.00-19.30
Sun 10.30-19.30

Tube: Camden Town

One of the largest London branches of this national chain. They have lots of take-away items such as pies, pastries, Mexican slices, cakes, sprouts. A whole aisle of nuts, seeds and dried fruit. Oat cakes, patés, vegan chocolate.

Large range of soya milks, dried goods, frozen ready meals, nut roasts, toiletries, non-dairy cheeses, yoghurt and ice-creams. Bodycare, aromatherapy. Supplements, hardcore bodybuilding. Relaxing music CD's at the back.

My Village

Vegetarian wholefood store and cafe

Open:
Mon–Fri   Summer 9.00–21.00
             Winter 9.00–20.00
Sat–Sun   10.30–21.00
Bank hol   11–21.00, 20.00 winter
Last orders 1 hour before close.
High chairs for kids. Visa, MC.

37 Chalk Farm Road, NW1 8AJ
(after Stables Market but before
Roundhouse, on opposite side)
Tel: 020–7485 4996
Tube: Camden, Chalk Farm
www.freshandorganic.co.uk
See map on page 197

Fabulous new wholefood store and deli-cafe, opened in 2007 by two Kurdish brothers, half way between Camden Town and Chalk Farm tubes. Rustic style brick walls and old timber fittings, tables and flooring, with subtle lighting.

For a take-away or chill-out at the timber tables at the back, try fast lunches from the fridge £1.69–2.29 such as Laura's Idea vegan calzone or tofu spinach pancake, salads, lentils or beanfeast with rice, sushi, croquettes. Falafels, hummous, fresh olives, sundried tomatoes.

Vegan cakes are hard to find in Camden, but at the counter are vegan chocolate cake £2.50, carob fridge cakes £1.50, organic muffins, all with ingredients lists.

Fresh juices, smoothies and shakes £1.75–3.25. Teas, freshly roasted coffee, cappuccino, latte, mocha, hot choc, hot soya milk, tea latte, Bombay chai (amazing with soya milk), £1.40–2.65. Brazilian frozen juices include açai.

Oasis organic soysages and burgers, herby tofu. Organic fruit. Bottled juices, bread, loose walnuts and small figs. All kinds of oils and dressings. Soya dessert. Rice and oat milk. Muesli bars, flapjacks, Green & Black's chocolate. Goji berries, nuts, seeds. Alara mueslis, Dr Karg and Amisa crispbreads, jams, herbs, seaweeds, miso, a wall of teas, even rice-quinoa spaghetti. Date syrup to put in your porridge.

Bodycare includes Tom's of Maine, Organic Blue, Kingfisher, Urtekram, Faith In Nature. Soaps.

Ecover, BioD and Faith In Nature cleaning products. Soft recycled toilet paper.

Everything is veggie though they may add fish in future.

Muang Thai

Omnivorous Thai restaurant

71 Chalk Farm Road, NW1 8AN
(between Belmont and Ferdinand
Street, opposite Roundhouse)
Tel: 020-7916 0653
Open: every day 18.00-23.00
Tube: Chalk Farm

Thai restaurant with amazing coconut rice and garlic rice (butter optional) £3 plus over a dozen veggie dishes £4.50-£6.95 including pad thai veg and noodles, red or green curry, stir-fry tofu and cashew. Special yellow curry with tofu £7.95. Thai soups £3.50. Hot food is marked with one or two chilis.

Desserts £3.50 include banana fritter, steamed banana with sweet coconut milk, lychees, sweet sticky rice and bananas, rambutan.

House wine £2.95 glas, £11.50 bottle. Chang or Singha Thai beer £3. Spirits £2.70, liqueurs £2.40. Warm saké £4 qtr bottle, very popular in winter. Tea and coffee £1.50, no soya milk.

Children welcome, high chair. MC, Visa, cheques over £10.

Neal's Yard Remedies

Herbs and complementary health

68 Chalk Farm Road NW1 8AN
Tel: 020-7284 2039
Open: *Mon-Sat* 10.00-18.00
  Fri till 18.30
  Sun 11.30-17.30
Tube: Chalk Farm
www.nealsyardremedies.com

200 herbs and spices by weight, organic toiletries, natural remedies, cotton-wool, soaps, books on homeopathy and remedies. Consultations available with multi-lingual staff. All products tested on human volunteers, not animals. Mostly organic, lots of Fair Trade, 10p for every primary item of packaging you return for recycling.

Finchley

Man Chui III

Chinese omnivorous restaurant

84 Ballards Lane,
Finchley Central N3
Tel: 020-8349 2400
Open: *Mon–Sun* 12–14.30,
18–23.30
Tube: Finchley Central

Chinese restaurant near the tube station with extensive and tasty vegan section on the menu. Apart from the tofu and veggie dishes, there are many fake meat items, around £4.90 each. Wine £2.70 glass, £9.90 bottle. Children welcome, 3 high chairs. MC, Visa, Amex.

The Ottomans

Turkish omnivorous restaurant

118 Ballards Lane,
Finchley Central N3
Tel: 020-8349 9968
Open: *Mon–Sun* 12.00–23.00
Tube: Finchley Central
www.theottomans.co.uk

This Turkish restaurant has 21 veggie dishes of which 14 are vegan, such as red lentil soup; vegetable stew with onion, courgette, aubergine, potato and green beans served with salad; imam bayildi – stuffed aubergine on a bed of salad and stuffed vine leaves with rice, sultanas, parsley, onion, dill and pine nuts and salad. The cold starters are all vegetarian and can be eaten separately for £2.90–4.90 each or 7 of them (5 cold and 2 hot) as a mezze for £3.50 per person, minimum 2 people. Sweets are baklava, cooked pears stuffed with pistachio and chocolate sauce etc – check the ingredients if you are vegan.

They also do take away and special lunch menus which include roast vegetable wraps, and the usual humus/falafel sandwich wrap – all served with chips and salad for £4.95–5.50.

Wine £2.95 glass, bottle £11.50. Children welcome, 2 high chairs. MC, Visa.

Rani

Open:

Mon–Sat   18.30–22.00
Sun   13.00–15.30
          then 18.00–22.00

MC, Visa, Amex

7 Long Lane, Finchley,
London N3 2PR
Tel: 020-8349 4386
Tube: Finchley Central

www.rani.uk.com

Home–style Gujarati cooking at the top of Long Lane. Rani won the Good Curry Guide Best Veggie Restaurant Award 2001. Vegan friendly as they don't use egg at all and only vegetable ghee.

5 cold and 11 hot Indian starters, 3 soups, and 2 appetisers £3.80–£4.

Daily evening buffet 7pm to 9pm arrivals, buffet closes 10pm, £13.90, or £14.90 Friday/Saturday. Sunday buffet £11.90, 1pm to 2.30pm arrivals, buffet closes 3.30pm.

There are 12 main dishes £5.10-6.50 such as bhindi fried ladies fingers (okra) delicately spiced and slow cooked with whole baby potatoes and onions; matar gobi cauliflower florets and garden peas slow cooked with fresh spices. Some dishes have an African influence such as akhaa ringal, Kenyan aubergine slit with ground peanuts and potato. Masala dosa £8.50. Thali £10.80. Set meals £15–17 per person.

Excellent breads such as mithi roti, a sweetened lentil mix with cardamon and saffron, parceled in unleavened dough, roasted in vegetable ghee, sprinkled with poppy seeds.

10 desserts £3.20–3.80, but only fruit salad is vegan.

House wine £1.90 glass, £9.70 bottle. Small Cobra Indian beer £2.50, large £4.40. Tea or coffee £1.50.

Rani's indicate on the buffet and menu which items contain dairy products although one contributor has caught them out a couple of times when they've mislabelled, but at least they are doing their best.

If you like this you'll probably enjoy a trip to the many Indian vegetarian restaurants in Wembley.

B Green Health Food Plus

Health food shop & take away food

104-106 Ballards Lane.
London N3 2DN

Tel: 020-8343 1002

Open: *Mon-Sat* 9.30-17.30
Sun closed

Tube: Finchley Central,

Wholefood shop with sandwiches and pasties takeaway selection with vegan options including cakes. Lots of gluten-free, vegan cheeses and yogurts, tofu, sprouts. Cruelty-free toiletries include Weleda, Jason, Dr Hauschka, Faith In Nature (without sodium lauryl sulphate). Whole Ecover range. Nelsons homeopathy range.

Finchley Health Food

Healthfood shop

745 High Road, London N12 0BP

Tel: 020-8445 8743

Open: *Mon-Sat* 9.00-18.00
Sun closed

Tube: Woodside Park

Vegetarian take-away salads, sandwiches, pies and pasties, some of which are vegan. Cakes, biscuits, chocolate, confectionery. Fridge freezer including vegan ice-cream. Herbal teas. Some cruelty-free cosmetics, toiletries, cleaning products. Natural remedies. Books,

Natural Health

Wholefood store

339 Ballard's Lane
London N12 8LJ

Tel: 020-8445 4397

Open: *Mon-Sat* 9.00-17.30
Sun closed

Tube: Woodside Park
www.whybehealthy.co.uk

Take-away veggie and vegan pies, sandwiches. Vegan ice-creams and cheeses. Meat substitutes including Realeat, Frys, Tival, Linda McCartney. Gluten-free and special diet ranges. Good quality vitamins. Homeopathic and herbal remedies, aromatherapy oils. Cruelty-free bodycare and cosmetics. Cleaning products including Ecover, Enviroclean and Ecolino. Books, CDs.

Book for alternative clinic with relexology, acupuncture, food intolerance testing, massage, Reiki, homeopathy, herbalist, nutritionist. MC, Visa.

Finsbury Park

Jai Krishna

Vegetarian Indian restaurant

161 Stroud Green Road
Finsbury Park, London N4 3PZ

Tel: 020-7272 1680

Open: Mon-Sat 12-14.00
                    17.30-23.00
           Sun   closed

Tube: Finsbury Park

Vegetarian South Indian and Gujarati restaurant not far from the old 'Gunners' ground.

There is a wide range of veg and vegan starters such as pakoras, katchuri (lentils in puff pastry) from £1.80.

Mains such as dosas, 35 kinds of curry, £2.95-3.75 with some up to £4.95 such as Thai mixed vegetable. Thalis £6.95. Try the coconut and lemon rice, and they have brown rice. There are lots of special dishes such as pumpkin curry £3.25.

The usual Indian desserts plus mango slice or mango pulp for £1.95.

Very good value and can get busy, so worth booking for big groups especially Fri- Sat evening. Corkage £1.35 bottle of wine, 30p a bottle or can of beer, and there's an off-license opposite. Coffee or tea 80p, masala chai 95p, no soya milk. Soft drinks £1.

Children welcome, no high chairs. No credit cards, only cash or cheque with card.

St Gabriel Cafe, N4

Ethiopean omnivorous cafe

12 Blackstock Rd, Finsbury Park, London N4

Tel: 020-7226 1714

Open: Mon-Sun 09.00-20.00
                    or later

Tube: Finsbury Park

This tiny cafe has lovely vegetarian salads and roast vegetables, which you wrap in Ethiopian Enjera flatbread and eat with your hands. The menu is in Amharic so just ask for a selection of vegetarian dishes with Enjera for £4.50, which is probably enough to share. It's smaller than the Kennington branch (south London). Dishes include cabbage and carrot, chickpea, or lentil, watch out for the spicy one.

After they close you could go on to the French cafe a few doors to the right to finish off with a coffee or herb tea, open till 10pm.

Gallery Cafe, N7

Mostly vegetarian cafe

in Islington Arts Factory
2 Parkhurst Road, Holloway
London N7 0SF
(opp. Holloway Prison entrance)

Tel: 020-7607 0561

Open: *Mon–Fri* 10.30–18.30
Sat–Sun open if events on or live music, maybe veggie BBQ in the garden in summer

Tube: Holloway Road
www.islingtonartsfactory.org.uk

Almost veggie cafe (apart from the odd tuna sandwich) in an arts centre offering dance, visual art and music classes, courses and workshops.

Hot and cold daily special £5. Sandwiches £3.50 with salad.

Cakes and hot drinks and organic juices. Tea £1, Fair Trade organic coffee £1.20, £1.50 large, soya milk available.

Kids meals and playground out the back. Eat in or take-away. Outside catering available. Cash only.

The space is available to hire to put on your own events with their catering.

Holland & Barrett, N7

Health food shop

452 Holloway Road,
London N7 6QA

Tel: 020-7607 3933

Open: *Mon–Sat* 9.00–17.30
Sun 11–17.00

Tube: Archway

Fresh take-away food delivered on a Monday like veggie pies, pastries and sandwiches. Dairy-free ice-cream.

Archway

OHFS Natural Foods

Organic store and off-licence

758 Holloway Rd
London N7 6QA
(corner St John's Villas)

Tel: 020 7272 8788

Open: *Mon–Fri* 07.00–20.30
Sat 19.00–23.00
Sun closed

Tube: Archway
www.eles–dietary.co.uk

Really well stocked store. Great selection of soya products, tofu steaks. Lots of organic fruit and veg. Massive selection of organic wine, beer and unusual imported low/non alcohol drinks. Vegan yogurt, cheese and ice-cream.

Take-away pies, salads, cakes (mostly vegan), sometimes sandwiches. They can make anniversary cakes for you.

Ecover refills, Ecolino and sometimes BioD cleaning products. Environmentally friendly organic paint, towels, clothing.

Bodycare products include Weleda, Anika, Lavera, Urtekram, Faith in Nature.

Supplements including Viridian and Bioforce.

Weleda homeopathy and natural remedies, Karela (Momordica Charantia) herbal tinctures. By appoint-ment facials, massage, aromatherapy, reflexology, Indian head massage, manicure, pedicure. Visa, MC, Amex.

They take local council vouchers for natural washable nappies and have liners, wipes and baby foods.

Peking Palace

Vegan Oriental restaurant

Open:

Mon–Fri   12.00–15.00,
              18. 00–23.00
Sat–Sun   18.00–23.00

MC, Visa. No alcohol.
Half buffet portions for children.
Catering for private parties.

669 Holloway Road
London N19 5SE
Tel: 020-7281-8989
Tube: Archway (closest)
           or Holloway Rd then bus
www.thepekingpalace.com

Lovely vegan Asian restaurant with western specials in the centre of North London with London's biggest vegan menu, currently over 100 options. Chinese, Vietnamese and Malaysian chefs. The décor is modern, bright and clean with deep reds and ochre yellows and beautiful paintings and flower displays that give the restaurant a lavish feeling.

Take–away lunch buffet with 18–20 dishes Mon–Fri £3 small, £4 large, or one large plate eat in £5. Half portion for children £2.50.

18 appetizers £3.00 to £4.80 like grilled Peking dumpling; vegetarian satay; asparagus tempura; soya drum sticks or capital soya spare ribs. Range of soups from £2.50 such as spinach, tofu and "chicken".

Second course could be crispy aromatic "duck" served with pancakes and hoi sin sauce for £6.50.

The main course menu is divided into soya meat, tofu dishes, and curries. Try the sizzling soya beef steak Peking style which is very filling for £5.50, fried soya fish in black bean sauce with olive £5, or Kung Po soya king prawn for £5. 7 kinds of tofu dishes such as big braised tofu steak in black pepper sauce on a bed of cabbage £4.50.

Fake fish steaks and even **vegan fish and chips** with a big plate with two pieces of fake fish with mushy peas and grilled tomatoes £6.80.

Desserts include several flavours of vegan ice-cream £3.25. Toffee and banana with ice-cream, or rambutan stuffed with pineapple in lychee syrup £2.20.

Ame non–alcoholic wine £4.50–8.50 bottle, £1.60 glass. Low alcohol beers £1.60–1.70. Fresh pressed juices £2–2.30. Teas/coffee £1–1.20. Organic hot chocolate £1.80.

Golders Green

CTV

Asian vegan buffet restaurant

22 Golders Green Rd, NW11 8LL
Tel: 020-8201 8001
Open: *Every day* 12.00–22.00
Tube: Golders Green

Mouthwatering eat-as-much-as-you-like buffet for £5, or £6 after 5.30pm and on Sunday. Fill up on pa tai noodle, curry or special fried rice, sweet and sour balls, black beans soya chicken, sea-spiced aubergines, spring rolls, Singapore noodles, lemon grass pot, sesame salad, seaweeds, salad and more.

Unlimited Jasmine tea £1. Detox, organic green or ginseng tea £1.50. Orange or apple juice £1.50. Wine £10 bottle, £2.50 glass.

Cash only. 10% service charge. Fill your own take-out box £3 or £4.

Coby's

Israeli vegetarian and fish cafe

115a Golders Green Rd NW11 8HR
Tel: 020-3209 5049/54
Open: *Sun-Thu* 08.30–01.00
      Fri 08.30–dusk
      Sat dusk–late
Tube: Golders Green
www.cobys.co.uk

Kosher cafe attached to a florist. Pasta dishes and salads £6.45–8.95. Veggie burger made from Portobello mushrooms with baked chips, salad and fried sweet beans £11.80. Jacket potato with topping £5.50.

Fresh juices £2.50, smoothies and shakes £2.95–3.80. Teas and coffess £1.30–2.80, add 30p for soya milk.

Milk 'n' Honey

Vegetarian & fish Kedassia cafe

124 Golders Green Rd,
London NW11 8HB

Tel: 020-8455 0664

Open: *Sun–Thu* 10.30–23.00
Fri 10.30–19.00
Sat closed

Tube: Golders Green

Mediterranean, Italian and Chinese kosher and parve food. The only place in the UK with a Kedassia licence, with vegetables growin in an insect-free environment in Israel washed and checked to ensure clean of insects.

Starters £3.95 such as spring rolls, breaded mushroom with garlic dip, hummous with pitta, spinach filo. Soups include mushroom, onion or vegetable.

Main course salad $7.95. Jacket potato with soya and mushroom sauce or beans £4.95. Several pastas £7.95 with tomato sauce or mushrooms and olive. Pizzas £6.95, cheese optional. Veggieburger with salad, chips optional, £5.95. Stir-fry with rice or noodles £7.95.

Desserts £4.75 such as fruit crumble, fresh fruit salad, sorbet surprise with mango, blackcurrant and lemon.

Juices £1.50–1.95. Tea £1.50, coffee/cappuccino £1.95 and they have soya milk.

No alcohol. High chairs. 10% service charge. Visa, MC.

Pita

Falafel bar

98 Golders Green Rd, NW11 8HB (corner of Hoop Lane by railway bridge over the main road, next to Baskin-Robbins)

Tel: 020-8381 4080

Open: *Sun–Thu* 1-23.00
Fri -16.00
Sat 19.00–23.00
Closed Jewish holidays

Tube: Golders Green

Green herby or yellow spicy falafels with humous £3.25. Other nice take-aways such as salads £2 small, £3.50 medium, £6 large. Humous with chips and salad £3. Humous and 2 pita with broad beans or mushrooms £4. Three kinds of bread: pitta, baguette or laffa wraps. Soft drinks 70p–£1.20. Tables inside and out. No longer completely veggie but the other stuff is not on display at the front.

Novellino

Kosher vegetarian and fish restaurant

103 Golders Green Road
London, NW11 8EN
Tel: 020-8458 7273
Open: *Mon-Thu* 08.30-23.30
　　　Fri 　08.30-dusk
　　　Sat 　dusk-late
　　　Sun 　09.00-23.30
(may close 23.00 if not busy)
Tube: Golders Green

Mostly Italian, also pad Thai.

Taboon Bakery

Vegetarian café & take away

17 Russell Parade
Golders Green Road NW11 9NN
Tel: 020-8455-7451
Open: *Sun-Thu* 9.00-midnight
　　　Fri 　9.00-15.00
　　　Sat 　18.00-01.00
Tube: Golders Green

Kosher veggie bakery with lots of take-away snacks including hot potato, mushroom or aubergine latkas, pizza and falafel. Some vegan snacks available but advisable to check which ones are parve (dairy free) such as falafel and some salads. There is a small seating area

Holland & Barrett, NW11

Healthfood shop

81 Golders Green Rd, NW11 8EN
Tel: 020-8455 5811
Open: *Mon-Sat* 9.30-18.00
　　　Sun 　11.00-17.00
Tube: Golders Green

This store has a freezer section with veggie sausages, burgers and dairy-free ice-cream but no take-away section.

Temple Health Foods

Health food shop

17 Temple Fortune Parade NW11
Tel: 020-8458 6087
Open: *Mon-Fri* 9.00-18.00,
　　　Sat 　9.00-17.30
　　　Sun 　10.00-14.00
Tube: Golders Green

Lots of take away food: pies, falafels, pasties, sandwiches, salads, many vegan including Laura's Idea things. They stock vitamins and minerals and they are happy to order anything for you. Sports nutrition. Homeopathy, aromatherapy, herbal medicine, Bach and Original Bach. All the leading bodycare brands. Two trained nutritionists on site to advise. Herbalists and reflexologist available.

Hampstead

Woodlands Hampstead

Indian vegetarian

102 Heath Street, NW3 1DR

Tel: 020-7794 3080

Open: *Sun*   11.00–23.00
Mon   closed lunch
Tue–Sat 12–15.00
Mon–Sat 18–23.00

Tube: Hampstead

MC, Visa, Amex
Children welcome, high chairs
www.woodlandsrestaurant.co.uk

One of four branches of this excellent chain with chefs from India. Seating for 55, warm red and brick walls.

14 starters and soups £4.25–4.95, or variety platter for 2 for £12.50. Main dishes, uthappam lentil pizzas, curries and dosas £4.75–£7.25. Rice £2.75–5.95. Thalis £15.25–26.95, including a vegan one.

Among the desserts, jaggery dosa crepe £4.50 can be made vegan.

House wine £12 bottle, glass £3.25. Tea or coffee £1.75, no soya milk.

For more of the menu see Marylebone (page 118) or the website. Discretionary 12.5% service charge. Minimum £25 for groups of 12 or more when ordering a la carte.

Friendly Falafels

Falafel stall

15–17 South End Rd
Hampstead, London NW3
(In front of House of Mistry shop)

Open: *Wed–Sat* 19.30–24.00
Sun   13.30–24.00

Tube: Hampstead Heath

Since 1989, falafel stall in front of the House of Mistry health food shop next to Hampstead Heath.

Falafel £3.40, with hummous £3.90. Salad in pitta £2.50, or with hummous too. 6 falafel balls £1.50. Also Whole Earth cola, lemonade, tea, coffee.

Giraffe, Hampstead

Omnivorous global restaurant

46 Rosslyn Hill, NW3 1NH

Tel: 020-7435 0343

Open: *Mon-Fri* 08.00-23.00
Sat 09.00-23.00
Sun 09.00-22.30
Bank hols 09.00-22.30

Tube: Hampstead
Children welcome, kids' menu
www.giraffe.net

Good selection of vegetarian dishes. See Bloomsbury branch (page 95) for menu.

Fungus Forays

Forays on Hampstead Heath

Tel: 07958 786 374
Tube: West Hampstead
www.fungitobewith.org
mush.room@fungitobewith.org

Join Andy Overall for workshops on identifying edible and poisonous fungi and go on fungus forays to Hampstead Heath where there are hundreds of species. See website for full details. Not a vegetarian group but the fungi are.

Hampstead Health Food

Vegan & veggie health foods
& take-away shop

57 Hampstead High Street
London NW3 1QH

Tel: 020-7435 6418

Open: *Mon-Sat* 10.00-18.00
Bank holiday: 11.00-17.00
Closed: 25-26 Dec

Tube: Hampstead

Health foods and a wide selection of take-away, some organic, with lots of vegan options including cottage pies, veggie sausages, rice and curry, cakes and flapjacks. Organic dried fruit, nuts and seeds. Complete Ecover range. Natural cosmetics. Supplements. Homeopathic and herbal remedies.

Holland & Barrett NW3

Health food shop

14 Northways Parade,
Swiss Cottage, London NW3 5EN

Tel: 020-7722 5920

Open: *Mon-Sat* 9.00-18.00
Sun 11.00-18.00

Tube: Swiss Cottage

Usual range of health and wholefoods.

House of Mistry

Health food shop

15–17 South End Rd,
Hampstead, London NW3

Tel: 020-7794 0848

Open: *Mon–Fri* 9.00–18.30
Sat 9–18.00
Sun closed

Tube: Belsize Park or
Hampstead Heath BR

Health food shop owned by Mr Mistry, a renowned vegetarian health food nutritionist who is producing organic products such as insect repellent for plants and humans, and won the Indian equivalent of an M.B.E. for his outstanding achievements with neem, an Indian tree from which many products are made. He has a catalogue of products which are available by mail order worldwide. Cosmetics, body products, oils and toiletries, all of which are definitely not tested on animals.

All vegetarian take-away sandwiches includluding gluten-free. Lots of gluten-free and diabetic products. They can advise on products suitable for diabetic, blood pressure, IBS, psoriasis and eczema.

Peppercorn's

Healthfood shop & take-away

193-195 West End Lane,
West Hampstead,
London NW6 1RD

Tel: 020-7328 6874

Open: *Mon–Fri* 9.00–19.30
Sat 9.00–19.00
Sun closed

Tube: West Hampstead

Organic wholefood store selling everything for veggies including tofu and tempeh, every kind of pasta and health food.

Wide selection of take-away and macrobiotic specialities from around the world, some organic, with lots of vegan options including vegetarian sushi, tofu parcels, aduki pies, spring rolls, rice rolls, organic humous, cottage pies, veggie sausages, rice and curry, cakes and flapjacks. Most dishes, snacks and cakes have ingredients displayed and if they're gluten, sugar free or vegan.

Also supplements, vitamins and minerals. Ecover cleaning products. Bodycare including Jason and Weleda.

Staff are well trained and have in depth knowledge of what's what.

10% discount for Vegetarian and Vegan Society members, and senior citizens on Wed.

Revital Health Shop

Health food shop

197 Haverstock Hill, Belsize Park London NW3 4QG (between Belsize Ave and Glenloch Rd)

Tel: 020-7443 5725

Open: *Mon–Fri* 9.00-19.00
Sat 9.00-18.00
Sun closed

Tube: Belsize Park
www.revital.co.uk

New health food store with a juice and smoothie bar and a fresh food bar. Opened May 2007, and handy for those commuting into central London.

Bodycare and natural beauty products including Dr Hauschka. Lots of vitamin and mineral supplements, sports nutrition, herbal and homeopathic remedies, aromatherapy, books. Staff are trained in nutrition and products and you can browse the Healthnotes touchscreen kiosk for further information on health conditions, diet plans or interactions of food and herbal supplements with pharmaceutical medication.

Hampstead Cuisine School

Vegetarian cookery schol

The Artisan House, 70 Fortune Green Rd, West Hampstead, London NW6 1DS

Tel: 0844 8842788

Tube: West Hampstead
www.hampsteadcuisineschool.
co.uk

Vegetarian Cookery School run by well-travelled former Vegetarian Society chef Chico Francesco and nutritionist Vanessa Ough. Courses include Thali, Mezze and Tapas; Gluten and Dairy-Free; Children's cuisine; Moroccan, Tunisian and Lebanese; European Christmas; even Cooking for Blokes – intro, intermediate or advanced. It's not just recipes, they teach basic techniques to demystify the art of cooking such as differences in olive oil grades, veg preparation, sautéing spices, knife skills and types of pans.

Private restaurant for students where you can invite family and friends to eat what you've prepared, or come for a taster evening to help you choose a course. Full schedule and prices on website.

Healthy Image

Natural remedies store

231 Finchley Rd, NW3 6LS

Tel: 020-7794 4586

Open: Mon–Fri 9.30–18.30
Sat 9.30–18.30
Sun closed

Tube: Finchley Road

Small selection of health foods. No take-away. Snacks such as sugar- or wheat-free. Raw living. Organic natural beauty and bodycare, hair dyes, Ayurvedic products. Sports nutrion. Magazines such as Lifescape. Massage therapist and treatments. The manager has a degree in nutrional therapy. MC, Visa.

Holland & Barrett, NW3

Health food shop

14 Northways Parade
Swiss Cottage NW3 5EN

Tel: 020-7722 5920

Open: Mon–Sat 9.00–18.00
Sun 11.00–18.00

Tube: Swiss Cottage

No fridge or freezer in this branch.

Hendon

Rajen's Thali Hut

Veggie Indian restaurant & take-away

195-197 The Broadway
West Hendon, London NW9 6LP

Tel: 020-8203 8522

Open: Mon–Sun 11.00–22.00
Restaurant:
Wed–Mon 12.00–15.00
18.00–22.00
Tue closed

Tube: Hendon BR

Excellent value and close to the mega-crossroads where the M1 meets the North Circular meets the Edgware Road.

Don't miss their speciality eat as much as you like buffet thali £5.90 weekdays 12 till 3pm, £7.50 evenings and all weekend. Also an a la carte menu with lots of fast food items such as bhel poori, kachori, masala dosa, onion uttapam, idli, spring roll.

They now have wine £2.25 glass, £8 bottle. Free car park at the back. Children welcome, can share with parents if under 5, 2 high chairs. MC, Visa over £10.

& Brent Cross

Chandni Sweet Mart

Indian vegetarian take-away

141 The Broadway,
West Hendon, London NW9 7DY
Tel: 020-8202 9625
Open: Mon-Sat 9.00-18.00
Sun 9.00-16.00
Tube: Hendon Central
www.chandnisweetmart.co.uk

Take-away only. Samosas, bhajias, but mostly sweets such as jelabi, barfi, ladu, some of them vegan as they use vegetable ghee. Visa, MC. Catering parties & weddings.

Gupta Sweet Centre

Indian vegetarian sweet shop

262 Watford Way,
Hendon NW4 4UJ
Tel: 020-8203 4044
Open: Tue-Sun 10.00-18.00
Mon closed
Tube: Hendon Central

Samosas, bhajias, veg cutlets, kachoris and Indian sweets, five of which are vegan including ladhu and jelabi. Outside catering.

Wagamama Brent Cross

Omnivorous Japanese restaurant

Brent Cross Shopping Centre
London NW4 3FP
Tel: 020-8202 2666
Open: Mon-Fri 11.00-19.45
Sat 11.00-18.45
Sun 12.00-17.45
Tube: Brent Cross
www.wagamama.com

Just off junction 1 of the M1 motorway, where the North Circular Road meets the A41 Hendon Way. See Bloomsbury (p.93) for menu.

Holland & Barrett, NW4

Health food shop

Unit W16, Shopping Centre,
Brent Cross, London NW4 3FP
(opposite Waitrose)
Tel: 020-8202 8669
Open: Mon-Fri 10.00-20.00
Sat 9.00-19.00
Sun 12.00-18.00
Tube: Brent Cross

Open late to accommodate shoppers. Jumbo sausage rolls, porkless pies, pasties, non-dairy ice-cream.

Highbury

The Straw Bale Cafe

Vegetarian cafe

at Freightliners City Farm
entrance on Sheringham Road,
Highbury, London N7 8PF

Tel: 020-7609 0467

Open: *Wed-Sun* 11.00-16.00
Mon-Tue closed

Tube: Highbury & Islington
Caledonian Road
Holloway Road

www.FreightlinersFarm.org.uk

Officially opened June 2007,
London's newest vegetarian
(rather than vegan except for
the soup) cafe has been built
by farm volunteers out of
traditionally jointed green
oak with straw bale insulated
walls and a green roof. The
café seats around 24 people
with outdoor seating for a
further 20 in the garden.

Freshly made soups, salads
and snacks. Blackboard
specials change daily and
there are cakes and pastries
as well as a healthy eating
children's menu.

Coffee, teas, fresh juices and
fruit smoothies. All proceeds
from the café will go towards
keeping the farm open,
though note that they do
keep animals. The café is
partly run by volunteers and
provides a training
programme and work expe-
rience for young people.

Eostre Organics Co-op

Organic fruit & veg stall

Freightliners City Farm (above)

Tel: 020-7609 0467 (farm)

Open: *Sat* 10.00-15.00

www.eostreorganics.org

An East Anglian co-operative
is one of the Saturday stalls
at Freightliners City Farm
with organic fruit & veg,
bread, garden plants, pasta,
apple juice.

Mother Earth, Highbury

Organic wholefood store

Open:

Mon–Fri	08.00–20.30
Sat	09.00–19.00
Sun	10.00–18.00

www.motherearth-health.com
healthylivingcentre.co.uk

282–284 St Pauls Road
Islington N1 2LH (near tube)

Tel: 020-7354 9897 shop
020-7704 6900 centre

Tube: Highbury & Islington

See map on page 229

New organic natural Fair Trade food store by the big Highbury & Islington round-about, with a complementary therapies space upstairs.

Large range of organic food such as artisan breads, fruit, veg and sprouts, healthy take-aways, baby foods and natural body-care products.

The fridge has lots of take-away food including Laura's Idea, Taste Matters, Hoxton Beach. Sandwiches £2.35, spelt muffins, falafel, salads £2.40, breakfast muesli £2.55, tofu cheesecake £2.55, bean feast £3.75, veg pakoras £1. Village Bakery cakes. Apricot slices. Vegan or sugar-free muffins.

Different varieties of tofu including locally produced Clean Bean. Lots of margarines. Dairy-free ice-creams: Booja booja, Swedish Glace and Tofutti cones.

Bottled and sparkling juices.

Water filters. Juicers, sprouters, water purifiers, eco-household products.

Bodycare includes Barefoot Botanicals, Dr Hauschka, Jurlique, Weleda.

Supplements include Nature's Own, Viridian, Higher Nature. Omega oils. Homeopathy, aromatherapy.

The Healthy Living Centre upstairs offers beauty treatments, acupuncture, Alexander technique, aromatherapy, Ayurvedic and herbal medicine, counselling, psychotherapy, NLP, chiropractic and osteopathy, homeopathy, hypnotherapy, kinesiology, craniosacral (for children, mother and baby and M.E.), various massages, shiatsu, rolfing, lymphatic drainage, meditation, naturopathy (with food, vitamin and blood testing), nutrition, pilates, reflexology and yoga.

NORTH Highbury

If you like this you'll probably like their other two shops, see Stoke Newington.

Five Boys

Health food shop & drugstore

17 Highbury Park, Highbury,
London, N5 1QJ

Tel: 020–7359 3623

Open: *Mon–Sat* 10.30–20.00
        Sun   closed

Tube: Highbury & Islington

Small but well-stocked
health food shop. Large
chilled section with many
vegan products such as
Redwood and Scheese, tofu,
tempeh, Swedish Glace, milk
alternatives. Fresh bread.
Vegan Parmazano.

Cosmetics, hair colour.
Cleaning stuff,

Organic baby food. Nappies
and wipes.

Lots of herbs. Homeopathy.
Even D–I–Y stuff.

Highgate

The Pavilion

Omnivorous cafe in Highgate Wood

in Highgate Wood, Muswell Hill
Road, London N10 3JN

Tel: 020-8444 4777

Open: *Every day* 09.00–16.00
Summer till 18.00 or as
late as 21.30/22.00 (half an
hour before park closes at dusk)
Food after 12.00.

Tube: Highgate

Formerly Oshobasho vege-
tarian cafe and still catering
well for us. Mezze type
starters are mostly vege-
tarian, around £3–£3.50,
such as falafel, roast
artichoke, cannellini bean
dip. Soup with bread £3.85.

Two out of five main courses
are veggie, average cost
about £7, such as salad with
tomato and basil sauce
£6.25. There's a different
menu Fri-Sun, e.g. spiced
couscous and minted
hummous £7.

Coffees, teas, they have soya
milk. Organic juices. Freshly
squeezed juices. Homemade
cakes such as lemon polenta,
can be wheat-free.

Beer and cider £2.90–3.30.
Wine £3.70 glass, £11 bottle.
Spirits £1.80–2.50.

A good place to bring
children as they can run
around freely and it's full of
young mums. High chairs,
children's menu £3.50.

GM free. MC, Visa. The cafe
closes half an hour before
the park, which closes at
dusk.

Queens Wood Cafe

Omnivorous cafe in Queens Wood

42 Muswell Hill Road
Highgate Woods, N10 3JP

Tel: 020-8444 2604

Open: *Every day*
Summer 10.00–18.00
Winter 10.00–16.00

Tube: Highgate

No longer completely vegetarian, but much of it is, and
some nice vegan dishes until
you get to the desserts. And
hey it is in the middle of a
tranquil wood with a lovely
relaxing vibe to the place, a
cute sofa at one end,
verandah tables with a sense

of woodland energy, and now open weekdays too.

Cooked breakfast £5. Main courses £5–£6 such as falafel salad with hummous £6.50; Jamaican chickpea and sweet potato curry with herb rice and mango chutney; bean burrito with salsa and mixed salad. Toasted ciabatta sandwiches with salad £4.75.

Teas £1. Coffee, cappuccino, latte, choc, £1.20–2.80. Soya milk available. Ginger beer, lemonade, elderflower, freshly squeezed orange juice £1–£2.70.

The Red Hedgehog

Music venue, vegetarian cafe & bar

255-257 Archway Rd
Highgate, London N6 5BS

Tel: 020-8348 5050

Open: *Every day &
some evenings*

Tube: Highgate.
Buses 43, 134, 263
www.theredhedgehog.co.uk

Live music and events venue. Vegetarian, vegan & raw foods. Keep an eye on their website for updates, or the free Veggie Guides updates pages for this book with new openings in London at:

www.vegetarianguides.co.uk
/updates

ISLINGTON
plus Kings Cross & Highbury

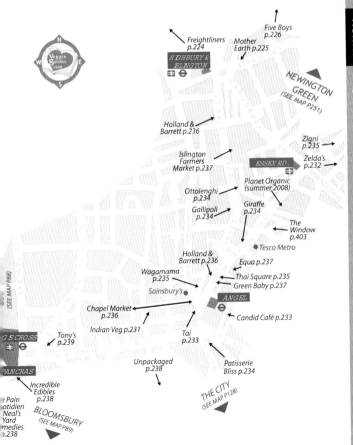

Freightliners p.224

Five Boys p.226

Mother Earth p.225

HIGHBURY & ISLINGTON

NEWINGTON GREEN
(SEE MAP P251)

Holland & Barrett p.236

Islington Farmers Market p.237

Zigni p.235

Zelda's p.232

ESSEX RD.

Planet Organic (summer 2008)

Ottolenghi p.234

Gallipoli p.234

Giraffe p.234

The Window p.403

● Tesco Metro

Holland & Barrett p.236

Equa p.237

Wagamama p.235

Thai Square p.235

Green Baby p.237

Sainsbury's ●

ANGEL

Chapel Market p.236

Indian Veg p.231

Tai p.233

Candid Café p.233

(SEE MAP P88)

KINGS CROSS

Tony's p.239

Unpackaged p.238

Patisserie Bliss p.234

THE CITY
(SEE MAP P128)

PANCRAS

Incredible Edibles p.238

e Pain
otidien
Neal's
Yard
medies
.238

BLOOMSBURY
(SEE MAP P89)

229

ISLINGTON
veggie hotspot

Islington is a shopping and cafe area that's great for designer gifts, antiques and a big Borders bookstore. Enjoy a relaxing cafe rendezvous at **Candid Cafe** or **Patisserie Bliss**.

Diners converge from all over to meet friends for a bargain buffet at either **Indian Veg** or **Tai Buffet**. You could follow

The Candid Cafe behind Angel tube station

with a cheap movie at the nearby Vue cinema if you pay for and print off a voucher a lastminute.com before 4pm (click on "Going out"). Collec tickets before your meal to ensure your first choice of film

New shop **Equa** in the antiques zone sells Fair Trade women's high fashion and a few Beyond Skin non-leather shoes. Some shops in **Chapel Market** (fruit and veg) have bargain non leather jackets. You can pick up organic fruit & veg at the Sunday **Farmers' Market** near the Town Hall.

As well as two branches of **Holland & Barret**, on the fringes of Islington are four gogeous wholefood stores: **Zelda's Pod** (north-east), a new **Mother Earth** (north), the new **Unpackaged** (south of Angel), and **Tony's** vegan cafe and wholefood store, which is handy for **King's Cross** (see next section) and the new **Eurostar** station at St Pancras. **Planet Organic** will open a fourth wholefood supermarket on Essex Road summer 2008.

Indian Veg Bhelpuri

Vegetarian and Vegan
Indian restaurant

Open: *Every day:* 11.00–23.00
MC and Visa
No alcohol
See map on page 229
See picture page 195

92–93 Chapel Market
Islington
London N1 9EX
Tel: 020-7837 4607
Tube: Angel

Best value veggie restaurant in London with a great bargain all-you-can-eat-buffet that runs all day long. Fantastic value for money here on the edge of trendy Islington, where you could easily stretch your wallet beyond the total bill here by going to nearby Upper Street for just starters or a couple of drinks. Indian Veg promotes the benefits of a vegetarian diet and were serving organic brown rice long before it ever got fashionable in this part of town. Come to think of it, how many Indian restaurants can you think of that even serve it or have non-dairy lassi?

Eat as much as you like for £2.95 (the only place in this book to drop its price since the last edition) from the buffet which has 3 types of rice, 3 curries, onion bhaji, poori, 3 sauces and lentil dhal. You can go back as many times as you like.

If you prefer a la carte there are snacks and starters from £1.95 like veg kebab or brinjal (aubergine slices) deep fried in gram flour. Mains include five thalis £3.95, dosas £3.50.

One of the few Indian restaurants that will make fresh vegan lassi for you with soya or rice milk in different flavours, £2.15. Juices 99p. 14 kinds of organic fruit juice in cans £1.65. Tea 85p, herb tea 95p, coffee or cappuccino £1.60.

They even some vegan desserts (other Indian restaurants please note!), and so are a popular restaurant with London Vegans.

They use vegetable oil not butter ghee.

From 2008 this restaurant, like many other Indian places, is now alcohol free.

If you like this then keep coming back because you won't find better value in London.

Zelda's Pod

Wholefood store

Open:
Mon–Sat 10.00–19.00
Sun closed

www.zeldaspod.co.uk

95 Southgate Rd, London N1 3JS
(just south of Northchurch Rd)
Tel: 020–7226 2524
Buses: Southgate Rd 141, 76;
Essex Rd 38, 56, 73, 341, 476
See map on page 229

This very well stocked and friendly wholefood shop is a fantastic find, between Essex Road and Kingsland Road.

Locally grown organic fruit and veg plus Fair Trade bananas. At least 5 varieties of UK apples. Salads in summer, warming roots in winter, sprouted seeds.

Fridge has Plamil mayo, veggie sausages, Sojasun and Provamel vegan yogurts, Clive's pies, unpasteurised miso, marinated tofu, Ploughshares fridge cakes. In the freezer you'll find dairy-free ice-cream from Swedish Glace and Tofutti, convenience foods, meatless meat and spinach.

Lots of nibbles including the Kallo and Clearspring range of rice cakes, biscuits and cakes, Green & Black's chocolate, Booja Booja truffles (which are not so much a snack as a vegan miracle for your mouth.

Organic tinned tomatoes and baked beans. Dozens of sauces, dressings and spreads. Juices, Fair Trade teas and coffees.

Baby foods. Lots of natural remedies. Viridian supplements. Omega oils. Aromatheraphy.

Bodycare products include House of Mistry, Kingfisher, Nelson's, Urtekram, Desert Essence, Green Things, Organic cotton bleach-free tampons and towels.

Wide variety of eco cleaning products and refills including linen window cloths, Vertue, Ecover, BioD, Urtekram, Ecolino. Kenwood universal water filter refills.

If you like this you'll probably like Bumblebee in central North London, which also has a big selection of foods.

Tai Buffet, N1

Chinese vegan restaurant

11 Islington High St, N1 9LQ
(opposite Angel tube)
Tel: 020-7833 9399
Open: *every day* 12-22.00
Tube: Angel

Previously called Tai Buffet, this is another wonderful Chinese vegan eat-as-much-as-you-like buffet, right opposite Angel tube station.

£5.50 daytime +10% "service charge" (in a self-serve buffet restaurant), so you actually pay £6.05. £6.50 after 5pm and Sunday, +10%, so that's £7.15. £3.50 for a take-away box.

Choose from chow mein noodles, rice, sweet and sour veg "pork" balls, soya chicken, fake beef, crispy seaweed, fried aubergine, spring rolls, tofu, fruit salad and many more.

Chinese beer £2.50. Wine £2.50 glass, £10 bottle. Or bring your own, free corkage. Soft drinks and Chinese tea £1.50.

Candid Café

Omnivorous restaurant

3 Torrens Street, Islington
London EC1V 1NQ
Tel: 020-7278 9368
Open: *Mon-Sat* 12.00-22.00
Sun 12.00-17.00
Tube: Angel

Turn left out of the tube station and walk right around to the back of the block, then climb the stairs to get to this lofty arthouse style omnivorous café. Faded renaissance interior with red velvet and chipped gold leaf chairs, with some very interesting pieces of art work to gaze at!

Several veggie offerings such as stuffed aubergine with herbs and veg for £5.50-6.00 (day), £7 (evening), which comes with salad. Also lentil and butternut squash soup or coconut curry soup with bread for £4. The menu changes daily.

Several sweets £3.50 such as cakes, but none vegan. Coffee or cappuccino £1.80, tea and herbal teas £1.50. They have soya milk. House wine £8 bottle, £2.50 glass. Beers £2.80 bottle.

Visa, MC. Children welcome; some books and games, further donations welcome.

No disabled access, second floor of an old building.

Patisserie Bliss

Vegetarian French cafe

428 St. Johns Street, junction of Upper St. & Pentonville Rd Islington, London EC1V 4NJ

Tel: 020-7837 3720

Open: *Mon–Sat* 8.30–18.00
Sat 8.30–18.00
Sun: 9.00–14.00

Tube: Angel

Vegetarian French cafe patisserie and bakery with seating inside and take-aways. It was in fact the first coffee shop with patisserie in Islington in 1989, now there are lots of them, but this is the only French one.

They serve a range of sweet and savoury filled croissants, filo parcels and puff pastry, as well as sweet items such as almond croissants, fruit tarts and cakes. Unfortunately they are rather keen on using eggs, butter and cream so nothing vegan in the French department, but they also do panini and filled baguettes without butter or mayo such as roasted veg or hummous falafel salad baguette £2.95 in, £2.50 take-away.

Various continental coffees:

cappuccino, latte, mocha £1.80 in, £1.50 take-away.

Cash or cheque only. Children very welcome, 2 high chairs.

Giraffe, Islington

Omnivorous global restaurant

29–31 Essex Road, N1 2SA (south end)

Tel: 020-7359 5999

Open: *Mon–Fri* 08.00–23.00
Sat 09.00–23.00
Sun 09.00–22.30
Bank hols 9.00–22.30

Tube: Angel
Children welcome, kids' menu
www.giraffe.net

Good selection of vegetarian dishes. See p. 95 for menu.

Stop press: On Upper Street, **Ottolenghi** (Mediterranean) at 287, and **Gallipoli** (Turkish meze) at 102, 107 and 120 are also quite good for veggies.

Bliss Cafe is the only French vegetarian patisserie in Londres

Thai Square

Thai omnivorous restaurant & bar

347–349 Upper Street
Islington, London N1 0PD
Tel: 020-7704 2000
Open: *Mon–Fri* 12.00–15.00
18.00–23.00
(Fri –23.30)
Sat–Sun 12.00–23.30
Tube: Angel
www.thaisq.com

Big classy Thai restaurant with a whole page of veggie dishes. 6 starters £3.95–4.55 such as tempura, fried bean curd, crispy seaweed, spring rolls, corn cake with sweet chilli sauce, or have a mixed selection £10.95 for two people. 3 soups £4.25–4.45.

8 main courses £6.25–6.95 such as green or red or hot curry, stir-fry, fried bean curd with ginger or cashew, £1 for extra bean curd. Rice sticky, steamed or with coconut £1.90–2.50. You can ask for extra veg.

House wine £10.95 bottle, £3.20 glass. Liqueurs £2.95, spirits, champagne £6 glass, bottle £29–120. Soft drinks from £1.25.

MC, Visa, Amex. Children welcome, no high chairs.

Wagamama Islington

Omnivorous Japanese restaurant

First floor, The N1 Centre,
Parkfield St, Islington N1
(next to Borders bookshop)
Tel: 020-7226 2664
Open: *Mon–Sat* 12.00–23.00
Sun 12.00–22.00
Tube: Angel
www.wagamama.com

Inside the N1 shopping centre at the junction of Upper Street and Liverpool Road, on the first floor next to the upper level of Borders bookshop. See page 93 or website. Disabled access.

Zigni House

Eritrean omnivorous restaurant & bar

330 Essex Road. N1 3PB
Tel: 020-7226 7418
Open: *Mon–Thu* 12.00–23.30
Fri–Sun 12.00–late
Tube: Angel,
Highbury & Islington
www.zignihouse.com

Chef Tsige Haile serves up exotic East African cuisine with plenty for veggies. Like Ethiopean restaurants, food is served with Injera, a soft pancake-like flatbread, or rice if you prefer.

Starters £2.75–3.00 are all vegetarian such as tabuleh, slow cooked peas, pan-fried veg or lentil rolls. Salads £3.30–4.50. Falafel £5.75.

Mains £6.50–9.25 such as red lentils in zigni (spicy) sauce, vegetables cooked in olive oil. Starter, main and drink deal £10.99. Vegan platter of dishes for two with injera £20.

Fri-Sat night self-serve buffet from 8pm, half veg, £15 including one soft drink, beer or glass of wine, with menu dishes such as chickpeas, mixed veg, salad, injera, rice. Sometimes they have special events with live music and dance.

Eritrean beer £3, sambuca £3–5.50. Take-away can be delivered, minimum £8.

Chapel Market

Yer actual London street market

Chapel Market (a street), N1

Open: Tue–Wed,
      Fri–Sat 9.00–18.00
      Thu, Sun 9.00–16.00

Tube: Angel

Full on London street market with all sorts of bargains for the home, fruit and veg, clothing, and great cheap veggie eateries nearby.

Holland & Barrett, N1

Health food shop

31 Upper St, Islington, N1 0PN

Tel: 020-7359 9117

Open: Mon–Fri 08.20–20.00
      Sat   19.00–18.00
      Sun   10.00–18.00

Tube: Angel

This shop has a small take-away section with own-brand and Goblins pastries and also a chiller cabinet with vegan ice-cream, vegan yogurt, veggie sausages and fishless fishcakes.

212 Upper Street
Islington, London N1 1RL

Tel: 020-7226 3422

Open: Mon–Fri 9.00–19.00
      Sat   9.00–18.00
      Sun   12–17.00

Tube: Highbury & Islington

Take-away section with snacks and own-brand pastries such as veg Cornish pastie, porkless pie, soysage roll, not necessarily vegan.

Planet Organic, Islington

Natural & organic supermarket

Essex Road, Islington N1
(near junction Packington St)
www.planetorganic.com

Opening summer 2008.

Equa Boutique

Fair Trade & organic women's wear

28 Camden Passage, London N1
Tel: 020-7359 0955

Open:	Mon	12–18.00
	Tue	11–18.00
	Wed–Fri	11–18.30
	Sat	10–18.00
	Sun	12–17.00

Saturday is best market day.

Tube: Angel
www.equaclothing.com catalogue
www.beyondskin.co.uk shoes

Ladies, high fashion eco-chic has arrived at the north end of trendy little Camden Passage market, normally known for antiques and old furniture and not to be confused with the massive punky-gothy Camden Lock market. Everything here is Fair Trade, lots of organic cotton sourced from third world cooperatives, English organic hemp and recycled. Enamore's 1960's hemp designs, Ciel, Loomstate jeans, People Tree, Hug jeans, Edun from Ali Hewson.

Beyond Skin high fashion non-leather shoes and boots, as worn by Natalie Portman. If the high fashion price for the sexiest vegan shoes in the world scares you, look out for end of season sales such as shoes down from £177 to £85 or boots for £95.

Canadian Matt & Nat non-leather bags £65–110, wallets £25–40. Also jewellery from Nature Creations and People Tree. Hand-woven cotton bags from Martha Evatt and Enamore. Children's ranges from Eternal Creation, Bishopston Trading, Hug and Organics for Kids.

Green Baby

Organic baby clothing

345 Upper Street, N1 0PD (just north of Angel tube station)
Tel: 020-7359 7037

| **Open:** | Mon–Fri | 10.00–17.00 |
| | Sat | 10.00–18.00 |

Tube: Angel
www.greenbaby.co.uk

Organic cotton baby and children's clothing, organic nappies.

Islington Farmers' Market

Food market

William Tyndale School (behind the Town Hall), Upper St, N1
Open: Sundays 10.00–14.00
Tube: Highbury & Islington

Quite a lot of animal produce, but good for organic fruit & veg and there's a stall with many varieties of apples.

Kings Cross

Incredible Edibles

Fast food take-away

opposite King's Cross station
Open: *Mon–Sun* till late night
Tube: King's Cross

In an emergency you can get hummous and salad in pitta bread here.

Le Pain Quotidien

Omnivorous French cafe and bakery

Unit 4, St Pancras International Station, Euston Road, NW1 2OL
Tel: 020–7486 6154
Open: *Mon–Fri* 06.00–24.00
             Sat   07.00–24.00
             Sun/BH   07.00–22.00
Tube: King's Cross
www.lepainquotidien.com

Get in the mood for a trip on Eurostar to Paris or Brussels from St Pancras station with a meal at this veggie/vegan-friendly French cafe chain. Highlights are tofu salad £6.95 with sauces and bread, vegan soups £2.55–£4.95, mint tea and vegan blueberry muffins.

St Pancras Station has a new branch of **Neal's Yard**

Remedies (see page 207). Open: Mon–Fri 07.30–21.00, Sat 9.00–20.00, Sun 10.00–20.00. Tel 020–7833 4162.

Unpackaged

Organic Fair Trade wholefood shop

42 Amwell Street, EC1R 1XT
Tel: 020–7713 8368
Open: *Mon–Fri* 10.00–19.00
             Sat   10.00–18.00
             Sun   closed
Tube: Angel
www.beunpackaged.com

Bring your own bags, boxes and jars to fill with organic wholefoods and eco-cleaning products at this new Fair Trade organic wholefood shop. Loose organic grains, pulses, flour, dried fruit, nuts, seeds, herbs, spices, "superfoods". Fresh fruit and veg. Refillable cleaning products. Recycled toilet paper. Baby products. Organic wine and beer. Recycled cards, gift wrap and stationery.

If you forget to bring bags, they also have reusable containers.

Tony's Natural Foods

Vegan organic cafe, shop and juice bar

Open:
Mon-Fri 08.30–17.30
Sat-Sun closed
(May open Sat, phone to check)
MC, Visa.
Children welcome, no high chairs.

10 Caledonian Road
Kings Cross, London N1 9DU
Tel: 020-7837 5223
Tube: Kings Cross
No mobiles, no laptops.
See map on page 229

Bustling, very friendly vegan organic shop with juice bar and garden cafe just a short walk from the madness of King's Cross station. Come and take respite and relax beneath a great 150 year old fig tree in their 150 foot garden, or sit inside the shop.

Different soup every day, £2 small take-away (£2.45 eat in), £2.75 large (£3.45).

Hot food, all vegan or wheat free and organic, £4 take-away (£4.45 eat in), such as vegan curry cooked in fresh coconut oil, mung bean stew, and pies. Pizza £1.95 take-away, £2.30 eat in. Home made spring rolls and samosas £1.50 out, £1.40 in.

Vast selection of salads including sprouted quinoa, sunflower and hemp seeds, £1.40 per 100 grammes.

Sandwiches £2.20–2.50, including burger or falafel. Vegan cake £1.50 (£1.75 in)

such as apple and date or chocolate.

Raw chocolate £4 per 100 grammes. Raw nut cheese also available and raw houmus made with sprouted sunflower seeds. Raw dehydrated crackers made with linseeds.

Spirulina and fruit smoothies £2.95 drink out (£3.50 in), large £4.95 (£5.50), with freshly made nut and hemp seed milk. Flavours include mango, banana, strawberry, and green juice with seasonal fruits and supergreens such as spirulina and Kiki superfoods.

Also wholefoods, supplements, hemp seed and oil (great for omega essential fatty acids) and some literature on the history of hemp products and its many beneficial uses. Cruelty-free toiletries. Ecover cleaning products.

If you like this you'll probably like Bumblebee in Kentish Town, which also has a big selection of foods.

Kentish Town

Phoenicia

Mediterranean cafe and food hall

186-192 Kentish Town Rd,
NW5 2AE (corner Patshull Rd,
opposite Somerfield)

Tel: 020-020-7267 1267

Open: *Mon-Sat* 09.00-20.00
Sun 10.00-16.00

Tube: Kentish Town

Great Lebanese cafe and
grocery with deli counter.
Point to what you want from
20 dishes, nearly all vegetarian, aubergine and chick
pea, dolmades, broad beans,
salads, falafel, hummous,
baba ghanoush (aubergine)
dip, mixed vegetable grill,
wraps, panini. Plate of food
£3, salads 99p. Hot drinks
£1.25-1.75. Juices £1.45-
1.69. Soft drinks 75p.

Meat is out of sight in a
separate section. The big
groceries area includes 17
kinds of self-serve (stuffed)
olives by weight, fresh
roasted nuts, fruit and veg,
fresh herbs, Mediterranean
breads. Wholefoods and
organic section on the far
left. 30 kinds of halva. Lots
of olive oils.

Outside catering. Free local
delivery delivery over £20.
Children welcome, no high
chairs. MC, Visa.

Paradise Foods

Health food shop,
organic greengrocer and grocer

164 Kentish Town Road,
Kentish Town, London NW5
(near Patshull Rd,
opposite Tesco Express)

Tel: 020-7284 3402

Open: *Mon-Sat* 09.00-18.00
Thur 12.00-18.00
Sun closed

Tube: Kentish Town

Health food shop that stocks
a great selection of herbs
and spices, range of organic
bread, also organic fruit and
veg delivered 3 times a week.
Lots of frozen vegetarian
ready meals such as Linda
McCartney, Beans/Frys, Bio
frozen veg, Realeat, Goodlife
and Cheezly. Gluten-free
and sugar-free foods. Dairy-
free ice-cream. Bodycare,
shampoos and soaps
including Weleda.
Supplemements including
Solgar and Bioforce (A.
Vogel). MC, Visa.

Bumblebee

Wholefoods store, organic greengrocer, bakery, take-away and natural remedies

Open:
Mon–Sat 9.00–18.30
Sun closed
Pay and display parknig on street.
MC, Visa, Amex

30, 32, 33, 35 Brecknock Road
London N7 6AA
Tel: 020-7607-1936
Tube: Kentish Town
Bus: 393, 390, 29, 253

Independent wholefoods heaven! Four shops close together: a bakery/deli, a dry/sauces shop, a greengrocer/dairy shop, and a natural remedies shop.

Massive selection of wholefoods, health foods, organic fruit and veg, macrobiotic foods and the bakery has organic bread delivered daily from organic bakers.

Lots of unusual hard-to-find items, for example they usually have Canadian Tinkyada pasta. Big range of south European foods and olive oils.

Takeaway foods and lunches 11.30–15.00 £2.15–3.90. Always at least two vegan hot dishes based around rice. Tofu quesadillas, tofu pasties, burritos, samosas, Salads made in house. Soup £1.15.

Box scheme for organic fruit and veg. Trade delivery service for other produce.

Nice things in the fridge include tofu, fake meats by Redwood and Beanies/Frys, frozen and chilled ready meals. Every dairy-free ice-cream: Swedish Glace, Tofutti, B'Nice rice-cream, Booja booja soya-free.

Enormous selection of vegan and organic wines and beers, probably the biggest in London.

Household products such as Ecover, Ecolino, BioD, Clearspring. Moltex nappies.

Natural Remedies shop at 35 has herbal, homeopathy and flower essences. Vitamins and minerals including Solgar, Viridian, Biocare, Nature's Own. Lots of bodycare, creams, shampoos and cosmetics by Dr Hauschka, Green People, Jäson, Lavera, Urtekram, Weleda. Mother and baby things. Complementary clinic by appointment with various practitioners.

Large selection of herbs and spices that you can weigh out yourself.

Earth Natural Foods

Wholefoods shop and take-away

Open:
Mon–Sat 08.30–19.00
Sun closed

MC, Visa
www.earthnaturalfoods.co.uk

200 Kentish Town Road
NW5 2AE (corner Gaisford St, opposite Rio's health spa)
Tel: 020-7482 2211
Tube: Kentish Town (nearest)
Camden Town
Kentish Town West BR

Fabulous and huge new wholefood store, more like a mini-supermarket, set up by people who used to work at Bumblebee. Packed with organic vegetarian wholefoods, bodycare, cleaning products and a big range of organic vegan wine.

Lots of organic fruit and vegetables, herbs, fresh bread. Pasta made from kamut, spelt, rice and corn, rice quinoa. Tinkyada pasta. Self-serve nuts pulses, grains and coffee beans which you can have fun grinding in their electric grinder. Soya, rice, oat, hazelnut and even quinoa milk. Stacks of vegan margarines, dips, nut butters. Japanese foods.

Exclusive and unusual chocolate such as Rapunzel, Demeter, New Tree, Green & Black's. Vegan ice-cream includes Booja Booja, B'Nice, Swedish Glace cornets. Cake slices from 99p, some vegan.

Deli counter at back with salad bar £3.30, £4.95 large, point to what you want. Veggie and vegan dishes of the day £2.15-4.55. Wheat-free vegan soup in winter. In a hurry? The fridge in the middle of the shop has Laura's Idea tofu spinach pancakes, croquettes, sushi, tofu cheesecake, Sempura Puran Potali broccoli lime chili wrap, Hoxton Beach falafel salad, Natural Rise seitan pies, Clive's pies, Wild Oats penne salad. Several soups £2.50.

Big organic wine section, mostly vegan and labelled, beers and ciders, juices.

Bodycare includes Desert Essence, Jäson, Faith In Nature, Weleda, Yaoh, Culpeper, Eco Cosmetics, Lavera, Avalon, Avena. Organic cottonwool and buds. insect repellant.

Ecover, BioD, Ecolino cleaning products. Vitamins include BioCare and Nature's Plus. Magazines. Baby section.

Muswell Hill

Giraffe, Muswell Hill

Omnivorous global restaurant

348 Muswell Hill Broadway,
N10 1DJ (by the roundabout)

Tel: 020-8883 4463

Open: *Mon-Fri* 08.00-23.00
Sat 09.00-23.00
Sun 09.00-22.30
Bank hols 09.00-22.30

Tube: Finsbury Park, then W7
bus

Children welcome, kids' menu
www.giraffe.net

Good selection of vegetarian
dishes. See Bloomsbury
branch (central London) for
menu. Some outside seating.

GNC , N10

Healthfood shop

243 The Broadway, Muswell Hill
London N10

Tel: 020-8444 7717

Open: *Mon-Sat* 8.30-18.00
Sun 12.00-17.00

Tube: Finsbury Park, then W7
bus

Vegan cheeses, yogurt, but
no freezer. Non-dairy
chocolate. Dry fruits, nuts,
wheat-free and sugar-free
snacks.

Not exclusively vegetarian as
some of their supplements
contain gelatin. Herbal
supplements, vitamins,
minerals, sports nutrition.
Bach flower remedies, homeopathy.

Holland & Barrett, N10

Health food shop

121 Muswell Hill Rd, N10 3HS

Tel: 020-8883-1154

Open: *Mon-Fri* 9.30-17.30
Sat 9.00-17.30
Sun 11.00-17.00

Tube: Finsbury Park, then W7
bus

Fresh take-away snacks such
as pies and soya sausage
rolls, pastries. Also dried
foods, seeds, supplements.
Vegan Swedish Glace ice-
cream, yogurts and cheeses.

Victoria Health Foods
Health food store

99 Muswell Hill Broadway, N10
Tel: 020-8444-2355
Open: *Mon–Sat:* 9.00–18.00
  Sun: 11–18.00
Tube: Finsbury Park, then W7
  bus

Great little health food store, with visiting food allergist every 6 weeks. The manageress Vanya is a nutrition consultant and can give advice.

Very well stocked with large fridge freezer section that has 3 varieties of vegan ice-cream. Plenty of choice for chocoholics also as they stock Booja booja gourmet vegan chocs amongst their naughty but nice goodies.

Wide range of dry foodstuffs including wheat-free and diabetic sugar-free sections, and some unique pioneering products from overseas such as candida, IBS, weight loss and skincare products.

Also huge range of herbal and homeopathic remedies and cruelty-free toiletries, toothpaste and household products. Visa, MC.

Crouch End

Just Natural
Organic shop & take-away

304 Park Road, Crouch End
London N8 8LA
Tel: 020-8340 1720
Open: *Mon–Fri* 9.00–19.00,
  Sat 10–19.00
  Sun 11.00–15.00
Tube Finsbury Park, W7/W3 bus
  Alexandra Palace BR

Organic food shop, although not veggie. On the hill not far from Alexandra Palace, so good for picnic supplies. Organic foodstuffs including pastas, noodles, breads, fruit and veg. Soya yogurts, Tofutti organic ice-cream and hemp ice-cream. Organic baby foods. Homeopathic remedies. Veggie and vegan wines. Local box scheme for delivering organic veg.

They do daily changing fresh lunch vegetarian take-aways Mon–Fri such as Moroccan stew with dates, couscous and chickpeas, Tuscan salad with bread, Thai coconut & lentil soup, all £3.25 for small and £3.95 for a large carton. Salads £2.75, £3.25. Fresh juices, coffees, they have soya milk.

Crouch End

Organic bodycare including Weleda, Lavera, Jason, Barefoot Botanicals, Urtekram, Yaoh hemp moisturiser, Dr Bronner soaps.

Visa, MC, Amex over £10.

Haelan Centre

Wholefood shop

41 The Broadway, Crouch End, London N8 8DT

Tel: 020-8340 4258

Open: *Mon–Thur, Sat*
              9.00–18.00
    Fri   9.00–18.00
    Sun   12.00–16.00

Train: Crouch Hill, Hornsey BR

Large independent wholefood shop located in hip Crouch End since 1971, one of the oldest wholefood centres in London. Complementary health clinic upstairs. A great place to buy presents or just little cruelty-free luxuries to pamper yourself.

Ground floor is food, including organic fruit & veg, large fridge/ freezer section with several types of vegan cheese, ice-creams and selection of veggie foods. Well stocked fresh take-away food with vegan options, sandwiches, pasties, pancakes, pies and cakes. Herbs, teas, amazing amount of dry wholefoods and pulses and a good selection of Japanese seaweeds and oriental sauces.

The second floor is an Aladdin's cave of non-food items which always smells lovely thanks to the fab toiletries. There is a clinic with a counter which is usually staffed for those wanting to make appointments. Great variety of cruelty-free toiletries, oils, perfumes, soaps, moisturisers, and more cruelty-free shampoos than you've ever seen. Many household products, like environmentally friendly cleaning stuff and vegetable wash.

Homeopathics, herbalists, acupuncturist, osteopath, all types of massage therapy, food allergy testing, nutritionist, Chinese herbalist, relexology, Reiki. Visa, MC.

PRIMROSE HILL
North London hotspot

Sesame Health Foods

Wholefood shop & take-away

128 Regents Park Road
Primrose Hill, London NW1

Tel: 020-7586 3779

Open: *Mon–Frid* 9.00–18.00
Sat 10.00–18.00
Sun 12.00–17.00

Tube: Chalk Farm

Wholefoods, fresh foods. and everything you need for a summer picnic on nearby Primrose Hill. Take-away items include soups, salads, rice and vegetables, snacks, pasta, stir-fries, cakes. Lunch rice and veg £3. Medium salad £3. Cup of soup always vegan £1.50. Organic juices, wide range of teas, cups of tea. One table outside.

Organic fruit and veg. Bread comes from several different bakers. Lots of snacks for picnickers. Wide range of supplements especially Viridian. Natural remedies and body care. Ecover full range. Organic baby food. MC, Visa, Amex.

Holland & Barrett, NW8

Health food shop

St Johns Wood High St, NW8 7NL

Tel: 020-7586 5494

Open: *Mon–Sat* 9.00–17.30
Sun Closed

Tube: St Johns Wood

This one doesn't have a freezer cabinet so no vegan ice-cream here.

Primrose Hill's finest

Manna

Vegetarian restaurant

Open:

Mon–Sat 18.30–23.00
Sun 12.30–15.00
18.30–22.30

Children welcome. High chairs.
MC, Visa.
www.manna-veg.com

4 Erskine Road, Primrose Hill,
Hampstead, London NW3 3AJ
Tel: 020 7722 8028
Tube: Chalk Farm
Service charge 12.5%.

See photo page 246

Very classy international gourmet vegetarian restaurant with lots of vegan food, set in a picturesque street near Primrose Hill, still going strong since 1966, with incredibly friendly and efficient service by staff from all over the world. There is some seating in the conservatory and outside. The menu is constantly changing with the seasons.

Starters £5.25–7.25, include gyoza pan stickers half moon dumplings filled agé tofu, water chestnut and bamboo shoots; shoyu ginger juice swirl with Chinese leaf and arame salad.

3 salads £3.95–6.75 such as crispy mock duck.

Manna Meze of any 3 starters or salads for £14.95.

Mains £9.50–13.50, half vegan, such as Organic Tagine with chickpeas, sweet potatoes, green beans, prunes and saffron in a roast squash with onion and sesame seed bread twists and pomegranate and mint yogurt (can be vegan); Green curry and Malay coconut pancakes.

Desserts £3.50 to £6.95, plenty vegan, such as petits fours, a plate of truffles, chocolates and biscuits. Organic fruit crumble, pecan and apricot brownie. Rich chocolate cake served with rum spiked custard. Vegan ice cream.

Lots of liqueurs and vegan wines. Beer from £2.60, house wine £3.50 a glass or £11.50 a bottle. Champagne £29.25, half bottle £15.95.

Kosher wine and food no problem. They even use organic soya. They serve till 11pm and it's advisable to book as not surprisingly they are very popular.

If you like this you'll probably like The Gate in Hammersmith which also serves gourmet food, desserts and wine.

Madder Rose Cafe

Vegetarian organic cafe and juice bar in yoga centre

Open:

Mon–Fri	08.00–20.00
Sat	08.00–19.00
Sun	08.00–19.00

No mobile phones. No credit cards. Children' portions. www.triyoga.co.uk classes

in Triyoga Centre
Unit 4, 6 Erskine Road
Primrose Hill, London NW3 3AJ
(almost opposite Manna)

Tel: 07949 882540
020–7483 3344 (centre)

Tube: Chalk Farm

New organic and 50% raw cafe in the tranquil setting of a yoga and pilates centre in Primrose Hill, with raw breakfasts and lunches, wheatgrass and energy juices. Chef Matthew Neel formerly worked at top veggie restaurant The Gate and took over here in July 2007. Come after a walk on Primrose Hill or check the website for yoga and pilates classes – they can prepare your meal while you stretch.

Lots of healthy breakfast options: sourddough toast with jam or Marmite £2; home-made granola (may contain honey) £3.50, banana and strawberries add 50p, soya milk add 50p; living buckwheat cereal with bananas, dates and strawberries with almond milk £4.

Lunch: soup £4; salad of the day £4; toasted sourdough sandwiches £5; raw avocado sushi rolls £5.50 with sprouted quinoa, salad and spicy Thai dipping sauce; raw mezze platter £6 with onion bread, falafel, courgette humous, oven-dried tomato, guacamole.

Fruit juices (12oz) £3, energy cocktails £3.50, smoothies £4. Organic wheatgrass shots £2.

Mug of organic tea or coffee £1.50. Cappuccino, latte, double espresso £2. Chai latte £2.50. Hot chocolate £2.50. Soya milk add 50p. No alcohol.

Wheat/gluten-free no probs.

The adjacent Triyoga shop has everything for yoga practice, Dr Hauschka products for face and body, books including pilates, Buddhism and even baby massage, world and New Age music CD's and videos for yoga, pilates and meditation at home.

If you like this you'll probably like the very healthy food and juices at VitaOrganic in Soho (Central London).

Cafe Seventy-Nine

Vegetarian cafe and take-away

Open:
Mon–Sat 08.30–18.00
Sun 09.00–18.00
Kids welcome, one high chair
MC, Visa.

79 Regents Park Road
Primrose Hill
London NW1 8UY
Tel: 020-7586 8012
Tube: Chalk Farm

Modern vegetarian café and take-away with a small number of seats outside in one of London's most picturesque streets on the edge of Primrose Hill. Catering for the lunchtime and weekend trade predominantly.

There is an extensive menu, though vegans will find almost all of the dishes contain dairy or eggs, but they can make something for you.

All day full English cooked breakfast £6.45. Croissants, bagels and toast £1.95.

Organic soup of the day with organic Neal's Yard roll £4.45.

Houmous and warm wholemal pitta £3.65. Veggie burger and salad £4.45. Baked potato £2.75, or £3.95 with a filling then £1.45 per extra filling. Side salads £2.45. Baked beans or grilled tomatoes on toast £3.95.

Sandwiches, toasted sandwiches, baguettes and bagels from £2.65.

Main courses such as pasta with pesto, pine nuts, cherry tomatoes and green salad £6.25. Bagel burger and deep fried new potatoes £5.75.

Lovely large salads £6.95.

Nine kinds of cakes and desserts from £1.45-3.25, but nothing vegan.

Lots of teas, coffees and soft drinks, with a pot of tea for one £1.65.

Freshly squeezed orange juice £2.65.

Milkshakes £2.95, can be made with soya milk. (Soya) cappuccino £1.65-1.95.

Bring your own alcohol.

If you like this after a walk on Primrose Hill, you might also enjoy Queens Wood cafe in Highgate (North London).

STOKE NEWINGTON
& Newington Green – hotspot

The vegetarian republic of Stoke Newington is one of the bes
areas to live if you're into cruelty free living. Although not on th
tube, it's smack in the middle of north London and quite easy t
get to by train or bus. There are some excellent parks nearby.

Stoke Newington Church Street has a big **Fresh & Wild** store and
lots of great eateries of which the Keralan Indian vegetarian **Rasa**
is our favourite. **The Dervish** is family run with lots of Turkish
meze and just one of many restaurants that have stacks of choice
for veggies.

HIgher Taste – The ultimate in veggie sweet shops!

Newington Green has excellent East Mediterranean grocers for
hummus, baba ganoush aubergine dip, olives, flatbreads etc and
even a Turkish vegetarian patisserie and café **Higher Taste**.
Mother Earth wholefood store has expanded with new branches
here and at Highbury & Islington.

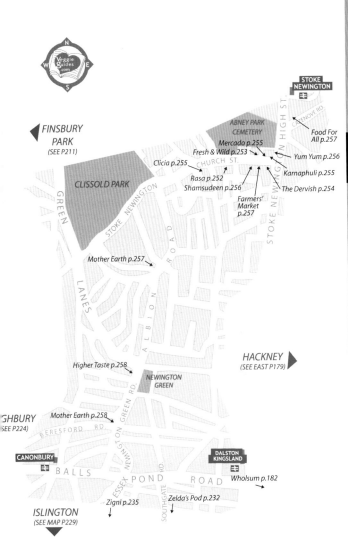

FINSBURY
PARK
(SEE P211)

ABNEY PARK
CEMETERY

Mercado p.255
Fresh & Wild p.253
Clicia p.255   CHURCH ST.
          Rasa p.252
Shamsudeen p.256
          Farmers'
          Market
          p.257

Yum Yum p.256
Karnaphuli p.255
The Dervish p.254

STOKE
NEWINGTON

Food For
All p.257

CLISSOLD PARK

STOKE NEWINGTON ROAD

STOKE NEWINGTON HIGH ST.

CAZENOVE RD.

Mother Earth p.257

ALBION   ROAD

LANES

HACKNEY
(SEE EAST P179)

Higher Taste p.258

NEWINGTON
GREEN

HIGHBURY
(SEE P224)

Mother Earth p.258

BERESFORD   RD.

GREEN ROAD

CANONBURY

BALLS   POND

ESSEX

SOUTHGATE RD.

ROAD

DALSTON
KINGSLAND

Wholsum p.182

Zigni p.235

Zelda's Pod p.232

ISLINGTON
(SEE MAP P229)

Rasa N16

Open:

Sun–Thu 18–22.45
Fri–Sat 18–23.30 (last orders)
Sat–Sun lunch 12.00–15.00
Kids welcome, but no high chairs.
Visa, MC, Diners, Amex
Optional service charge 12.5%

55 Church Street, Stoke
Newington, N16 0AR

Tel: 020-7249 0344
Tube: Stoke Newington BR
Bus 73 from Angel
www.rasarestaurants.com
See map on page 251

One of London's top vege-tarian restaurants and great for parties. Rasa means taste, and not only of the food. Here you experience a taste of Kerala's villages and dishes from other south Indian states. The atmos-phere is relaxed with classic Indian music in the back-ground, with pink walls and tablecloths. Dishes that don't seem vegan can be veganized.

Starters £2.75–£3.00 such as banana boli with plaintain slices in a batter of rice and chickpea flour, seasoned with black sesame seeds and served with peanut and ginger sauce; medhu vadai spongy urad bean and chilli dumpling. Two soups such as peppery lentil broth with garlic, tomatoes, spices and tamarind.

Main courses feature a large dosa (stuffed pancake) selection and 11 curries from £3.70–5.95.

Salad and side dishes £3.50–4.00 such as amazing Kerala salad of guava, avocadoes, stir-fried Indian shallots, fresh coconut, lemon juice and chilli powder; vendakka masala of fresh okra fried with shallots, garlic, chillis, mustard seeds and curry leaves; kovakki olathiathu with tindori (like baby cucumbers), cashew nuts dry roasted with coconut mustard seeds and curry leaves. 6 kinds of rice from £2 including brown, tamarind, lemon, coconut, tomato & cashew.

Desserts £2.20–3.00 include vegan ice-cream and mango halva.

Kerala feast £16.50 per head with pre-meal snacks, starters, curry selection, side dishes, breads and a tradi-tional Keralan sweet.

House wine from £11.95 bottle, £2.95 glass.

If you like this then try their other omnivorous branch in Dering Street (see Marylebone, Central London). The other Rasa in N16 opposite isn't veggie.

Fresh and Wild

Wholefood supermarket, cafe and juice bar

Open:
Mon–Sat 08.00–21.00
Sun 09.00–20.30

www.wholefoodsmarket.com

32–40 Church Street,
Stoke Newington N16
Tel: 020 7254 2332
Tube: Stoke Newington BR
Bus 73, 476 from Angel
106 from Finsbury Park
See map on page 251

Big natural food shop and café concentrating on organic produce. No artificial colourings, sweeteners, preservatives or hydrogentated fat. Large range of veggie and vegan food, natural remedies department, an area devoted to natural skincare and supplements. Trained advisers are on hand to answer all queries.

Deli section with freshly prepared organic hot food, macrobiotic and raw food selections, and a cake section where you can buy juices, coffee, soyacinno and tea. Cake ingredients are clearly labelled and usually one is vegan. Outside cafe seating for around 25 people.

Highlights include 12 kinds of tofu, veggie ready meals, wheat-free pasta, breakfast cereals, organic juices, non-dairy cheeses and yoghurts, hemp and soya ice-cream. Big selection of organic fruit

and veg as well as organic herb plants, organic wine, beers and ciders with clear veggie/vegan signs.

Another area is given over to all kinds of toiletries, aromatherapy oils, supplements and herbal remedies, many of which are veggie and vegan, including Dr Hauschka and Ren. There is always a staff member who can advise you, and a cardfile available for local alternative health practitioners.

Well stocked range of books on many subjects adjacent to the toiletries counter. There is a small bulletin board at the front of the shop for local events.

If you like this then don't miss their other five stores in Soho, Clapham, Westbourne Grove, Camden, and the *Wholefoods* superstore in Kensington.

The Dervish

Open:
Mon–Sun 10–23.00
(Fri/Sat till midnight)

Children welcome, high chairs.
Visa, MC. Licensed.

15 Church St,
Stoke Newington, London N16
Tel: 020-7923 9999
Tube: Stoke Newington BR
Bus 476 from Angel
106 from Finsbury Park
See map on page 251

With its bright purple facade, it's hard to miss this family run Turkish restaurant opposite Fresh & Wild. Orange, red and brick walls with dozens of small lamps suspended from the ceiling. As in Turkey the front is open and there are some outside tables.

All day veg breakfast £4.45.

Falafel sandwich £3.10 if you want a quick meal. Lots of veggie starter mezze dishes £2.55-4.25, or £4.25 for a platter of 7 cold and 2 hot starters including their famous tasty home-made stuffed vine leaves, zeytinyagli bakla broad beans, aubergine purée with tahini and garlic.

7 veggie mains £5.35-5.65 of which two are vegan: falafel with broad beans; Imam bayildi delicately fried aubergine stuffed with traditional onion mixture. Others have vegan option such as spicy spinach with potatoes and leeks, kisir (crushed wheat, mint, spring onion, nuts, tomato paste, lemon and olive oil), blackeye beans with green olives, sweet coriander, peppers and herbs.

Belt-busting set meal of mezze, main, tea/coffee and dessert £11.95 per person, minimum two people, though after a big starter plate of mixed mezze, two of us were so stuffed we had no room for the main.

Turkish desserts £1.60-4.40, but none vegan.

Juice, soft drinks, tea and apple tea, (Turkish) coffee £1.20-1.85.

House wine £9.95 bottle, £2.55 glass. Beer £2.70. Liqueurs and shorts £2.90.

If you like this you'll probably like the Tas Turkish restaurants in central London with lots of veggie food.

Clicia

Omnivorous cafe-grill and mezze bar

97 Church St, Stoke Newington,
London N16 0UD
(corner of Defoe Rd)

Tel: 020-7254 1025

Open: *Mon–Sun* 08.00–24.00

Tube: Stoke Newington BR

Omnivorous Turkish restaurant with 20 hot and cold veggie mezze starters all clearly marked £2.70–3.50. 6 mains £7.50–9.25.

Veg full English breakfast £4.95. Cafe menu veg, hummous and salad sandwich £3.50.

Wine £10.95 bottle, £2.95 glass. Visa, MC. 6 outside tables.

Karnaphuli

Omni Tandoori Indian restaurant

20 Stoke Newington Church St

Tel: 020-7254 5888 / 0661

Open: *Mon–Sun* 12.00–14.00
17.30–24.00
Fri–Sat till 00.30

Train: Stoke Newington BR

Vegetarian starters from £2.29. 15 mains £4.99–7.89 include veg jalfrezi, dansak, masala, bhuna, korma.

Thalis £8.99–9.49. No additives, GM or service charge. Visa, MC.

Mercado Cantina

Omnivorous Mexican restaurant/bar

26-30 Stoke Newington Church Street, London N16 0LU

Tel: 020-7923 0555

Open: *Mon–Sun* 12.00–15.00
18.00–24.00

Train: Stoke Newington BR
www.mercado-cantina.co.uk

Bright walls with Mexican prints and vintage film posters. Vegetarian (though not vegan) dishes marked on the menu. Starters £4.50–5.25 include guacamole with corn chips, ensalada mexicana (spinach, lettuce, tomato, cactus leaves and amaranth, with hibiscus dressing). Several mains £7.95–9.80 include fajitas.

Shamsudeen

Omnivorous Malaysian
& South Indian restaurant

35 Church St, Stoke Newington
N16 0NX (opposite Fresh & Wild)
Tel: 020-7241 4171
Open: *Wed–Mon* 12.00–15.00
Mon–Sun 18.00–24.00
closed Tue lunch
Tube: Stoke Newington BR

Set lunch £5.95 such as popadom, bajia, masala dosa, cenda wang kacary (mushroom and lentils). Vegetarian "feast of unusual size" menu for two people £23.60. House wine £9.75 bottle, £2.75 glass. Free delivery 6–10.30pm.

Yum Yum

Omnivorous Thai restaurant

183–187 Stoke Newington High
Street, London N16 0LH
Tel: 020-7254 6751 restaurant
020-7241 5678 orders
Open: *Mon–Fri* 12.00–15.00
18.00–23.00
Sat–Sun 12.00–23.30
Tube: Stoke Newington BR
www.yumyum.co.uk menus

Recently moved into a stunning Grade II listed building with seating for over 200, with entry through a Thai garden where you can drink cocktails on a summer evening. Hand carved cocktail bar. They make their own coconut milk and curry pastes in-house and have introduced seasonal specials menus. Vegetarian dishes marked on menu.

Starters £3.70 such as spring rolls, tempura, sweet corn cakes, crispy tofu with peanut sauce, Monk's vegetable on toast, or have a platter for two £11.50. Thai soups and salads £4.40–4.90. Curries £5.80 such as pumpkin curry with tofu, green or red curry. 9 vegetable dishes £3.70–4.95 including aubergines, mushrooms with tofu, long beans, stir-fry, spinach with garlic, sweet and sour tofu with veg. Rice £1.85–2.65.

Set vegetarian menu for two £16.50 each with assorted starters, Thai red curry with veg, sauteed aubergines, mixed mushrooms with cashew nuts and jasmine rice.

House wine £11 bottle, glass white £2.80, red £3.20. Children welcome, high chairs. Evening deliveries. Outside catering. Downstairs lounge bar with large screen TV for private events. MC, Visa.

Mother Earth, N16

Organic wholefood shop & take-away

5 Albion Parade, Albion Road
Stoke Newington N16 9LD

Tel: 020-7275 9099

Open: *Mon-Thu* 9.30-20.30
Fri 9.30-20.00
Sun: 10.00-19.00

Train: Canonbury BR

Colourful wholefood shop with fresh organic fruit and veg, macrobiotic and organic products. Veggie sausages. Bread and assorted veggie snacks. Bulk produce, weigh and pay, discount on cases.

The freezer counter has vegan ice-cream, choc ices and fruit ice-lollies in various flavours.

Lots of take-away prepared salads, meals, pies, cakes and brownies. Hot drinks. One table and chairs.

Cruelty-free toiletries such as shampoos, lip balms, soaps and veggie toothpaste. Ecover refills. Water purifying service. Natural remedies and friendly advice. Homeopathy, herbal, supplements. Superfoods including goji berries, macca, spirulina. Green/environmental magazines. Small selection of books.

Food For All

Vegetarian wholefood store

3 Cazenove Road
Stoke Newington, N16 6PA

Tel: 020-8806 4138

Open: *Mon-Fri* 9.00-18.00
Thu 9.00-19.00
Sat 10.00-18.00
Sun: 10.00-16.00

Tube: Stoke Newington BR

Popular veggie wholefood shop with alternative medicine, herbs and spices. Over 300 brands of herbal remedies, and dried herbs sold by weight. Great chilled section with many vegan cheeses and sausages. Take-away has samosas, falafels, pakoras. Bodycare. Cleaning products including Ecover refills. There is a free notice-board in the shop and a yoga centre upstairs.

Farmers Market, N16

Organic market

Schoolyard of William Patton School, Stoke Newington Church Street, opposite Fresh & Wild

Open: *Sat* 10.00-14.30

Train: Stoke Newington BR

Fruit & veg, and there is a food stall with some vegan pasties, pies and cakes.

Mother Earth, Newington Gr

Vegetarian café and shop

101 Newington Green Road,
London N1 4QY

Tel: 020-7690-6811

Open: *Mon–Fri* 8.30-19.00
Sat 9.00-18.00
Sun 10.00-18.00

Train: Cannonbury BR

www.motherearth-health.com

Veggie café and food shop.
Eat in or take away.

Around 4 salads, usually pies
or pastries, all made on the
premises. The deli has a
gourmet selection of olives
and Sicilian patés. Filled rolls
with some vegan options like
red pepper and houmous, or
veggie sausage and vegan
mayo with salad. They make
their own cakes and scones.
Plenty of herbal teas, coffees,
and cold juices.

They have a new kitchen
specialising in really good
gluten-free and sugar-free
baked products and also
supply their other two nearby
shops. Organic bread and
gluten-free ranges. Organic
baby food. Unusual and
sometimes handmade cards,
aromatherapy oils, candles,
cruelty-free toiletries and
toothpastes. Ecover refill
service.

Previously called 2 Figs then
Pilgrims and now taken over
by Mother Earth and with a
much expanded range.

Higher Taste

Vegetarian Turkish patisserie & café

47 Newington Green, N16 9PX

Tel: 020-7359-2338

Open: *Mon–Sat* 07.00-20.00
Sun 09.00-18.00

Train: Cannonbury BR

Hot and cold vegetarian
mezze such as aubergine
£2.50 or humous. Lots of
Turkish savoury and sweet
pastries 75p-£1.25 with
many fillings like potato and
spinach, various cakes and
Turkish style biscuits.
Amazing baklavas, sweets
with pistachio nuts and
syrup, which have to be
tasted to be believed, some
without honey we thought
were good for vegans but
have been recently told that
there is egg on everything.

Tea and coffee £1 as well as
cold drinks.

Wood Green

Rainforest Creations, N22

Raw food stall

Alexandra Palace Farmers
Market, Hornsey Gate entrance
Wood Green N22
Open: *Sun* 10.00–15.00
Train: Alexandra Palace BR
www.rainforestcreations.co.uk

Vegan raw food heaven with
a big box of salad and
savouries for £5, cakes £3.
See Spitalfields (East London)
for more info.

The Greenhouse

Vegetarian café, take away and
wholefood store

Unit 63, Market Hall
Wood Green, London N22
Tel: none
Open: *Mon-Sat* 9.30–18.00
        Sun   11.00–17.00
Tube: Wood Green

Vegetarian café (90% vegan),
snack bar, take-away and
wholefood shop inside
covered market hall in Wood
Green Shopping Centre.

Homemade soup with bread,
pate and toast, various sandwiches £1.20–3.00. Lite bite
salads and savouries £1.20–
2.50, mains £3.50–4.00 such
as sos roll with meat substitutes, fishless fishcakes,
curries, pasta, pies, flans,
pasties, chilli sin carne,
stews, bean bakes, burgers,
risotto.

Desserts 60p–£1.50 like
homemade cakes and
crumbles, flapjacks, always a
vegan option.

Special diet such as candida,
diabetic etc. can be catered
for. Cheques but no credit
cards. Private functions.

Wholefood store has a well
stocked with vegan ice-
cream, veggie sausages and
burgers.

Ambala, Turnpike Lane

Vegetarian sweet shop

61 Turnpike Lane, Wood Green
London N8 0EE

Tel: 020-8292 1253

Open: *Mon–Sun* 10.00–20.00

Tube: Turnpike Lane
www.ambalafoods.com

Indian sweets and savouries
to take away.

Holland & Barrett, N22

Wholefood shop

129-131 High Street,
Wood Green, London N22 6BB

Tel: 020-8889-4759

Open: *Mon–Sat* 9.00–18.00
         Sun   11.00–16.00

Tube: Wood Green

Usual health foods here. This
shop has a freezer section
with veggie burgers and
sausages and vegan fish-
cakese. Vegan cheese and
yoghurt. Some take-away
such as sausageless rolls,
porkless pies.

Alternative Health Store

Health food shop

1369 High Road, Whetstone,
London N20 9LN

Tel: 020-8445 2675

Open: *Mon–Sat* 9.00–18.00
         Sun   closed

Tube: Totteridge and Whetstone
then 15 minute walk

Vegetarian healthfood shop.
No take-away. Cleaning
products such as Ecover.
Also body care, supple-
ments, natural remedies,
homeopathy. Clinic by
appointment with homeop-
athy, Reiki, reflexology,
acupuncture, nutritionist.

Ital and Vital Takeaway

Caribbean take-away

134 High Road
Seven Sisters, London N15 6JN

Tel: 020-8211 7358

Open: *Mon–Fri* 9.00–21.00
         Sun   closed

Tube: Seven Sisters

Small take-away only with
Caribbean flavour. Some
veggie options such as
salads, pea soup, steamed
vegetables, and ackee, pea
and tofu stew.

Pure Health

Wholefoods shop

56 Chaseside, Southgate,
London N14 5PA

Tel: 020-8447-8071

Open: *Mon–Sat* 9.00–17.30
Sun closed

Tube: Southgate

Wholefoods, cosmetics, bodycare and vitamins. Some fresh take-away such as samosas, pies and sausageless rolls. Herbal and homeopathy, ayurvedic, sports nutrition. Staff have 20 years experience and training in nutrition. Ecover and Earth Friendly cleaning products. Local delivery.

Holland & Barrett, N9

Health food shop

7 North Mall, Edmonton Green
London N9 0EQ

Tel: 020-8807 6711

Open: *Mon–Sat* 9.00–17.30
Sun closed

No fridge or freezer, but the bigger branches at Enfield and Wood Green do have them and are open Sundays.

Holland & Barrett

Health food shop

332 Green Lane, Palmers Green
N13 5TW

Tel: 020-8886 6769

Open: *Mon–Sat* 9.00–17.30
Sun closed

No fridge or freezer, but the bigger branches at Enfield and Wood Green do have them and are open Sundays.

Seven Sisters BR

Kiosk with vegan snacks

Seven Sisters railway station
(overground, not the tube)

Open: *Mon–Sat* 9.00–17.30
Sun closed

Vegan food on trains and in stations is quite frankly non-existent, except here! A reader reports that the little kiosk on the platform of Seven Sisters railway station sells things like the Organica vegan "Bounty" bar and the nougat/"Mars" bar. They also do vegan brownies, Blue Sky cola and the like. Other stations in veggie hotspots take note....

Hertfordshire

Spizzico

Mediterranean omnivorous restaurant

135 High Street,
High Barnet EN5

Tel: 020-8440 2255

Open: *Mon–Sun* 12.00–24.00

Tube: High Barnet

Modern Mediterranean Italian style, pizzas and pastas with lots of veggie options, salads, fajitas. Ali the owner is happy to adapt for vegans.

Gritz

Italian onmivorous restaurant

135 High Street,
High Barnet EN5

Tel: 020-8275 9985

Open: *Mon–Sun* 12.00 till late

Tube: High Barnet

The usual Italian food in this very popular restarant with a large wood fired oven and 8 veggie pastas such as penne rusticana with mixed char grilled vegetables, or spaghetti napoli with tomato and basil sauce. salads. Pizzas are freshly made and can be without cheese for vegans. Also salads. Pasta and pizza dishes £7.50–£8.

House wine £10.95 bottle, £3.85 large glass, £2.95 small. Children welcome, high chairs. MC, Visa.

Holland & Barrett, Enfield

Health food shop

38 Church Street, Enfield
EN2 6BA

Tel: 020-8367 3944

Open: *Mon–Sat* 9.00–17.30
      Sun 10–16.00

Tube:

Freezer and fridge with take-away food such as pasties.

Holland & Barrett, Barnet

Health food shop

Unit W115 High Street, Barnet

Tel: 020-8449 5654

Open: *Mon–Sat* 9.00–17.30
      Sun 10.00–16.00

No take-away, just vegetarian sausage rolls.

Daniel Field

Hairdresser

5 Greenhill Parade, Station Road
New Barnet, Herts EN5 7ES

Tel: 020-8441 2224

Tube: High Barnet
Free parking.
www.danielfield.com
www.danielfield.net
www.danielfieldmailorder.co.uk
www.freefromproducts.com

Celebrity hairdresser who is also a chemist and has developed his own range of hair care products now certified by the Vegan Society, with a 1984 testing cut-off date, no animal ingredients, hypo-allergenic, toxin-free, Fair Trade and with minimal packaging. 10 freelance stylists, or be styled by the man himself if you book well ahead. There is also a private studio if you need privacy.

Brixton 266
Clapham & Battersea 270
Crystal Palace 278
Greenwich 281
Kingston 282
London Bridge 284
Putney 288
Richmond 289
Streatham 293
* Tooting & Balham 296
* Vauxhall 302
Walworth 306
Wimbledon 308
Rest of South–East 309
Rest of South–West 317

SOUTH LONDON

Riverside Vegetaria page 283

Brixton

Euphoria @Lorentson's

Vegetarian stall in market

Trailer on Pitch 16, Brixton market, on Brixton Station Road (the next one north from Atlantic Road) Between the Recreation Centre and Brixton High Street, next to the Hive Cafe

Tel: 07956039676

Open: *Mon-Tue* 9.00-18.00
*Wed,Sun*i closed
Thu-Sat 9.00-18.00

Tube: Brixton

New food and drinks trailer on one of the quieter market streets next to Hive cafe. They are aiming at all vegan but sometimes they are vegetarian depending on supplies. Over half is organic and they are "working on" this. Already they have vegan spreads, rolls, soya milk and smoothies, children's portions, gluten/wheat-free and diabetic, and the manager is vegan.

Millet/oat porridge £2. Soup and roll £2. Snacks from 50p. They have started to experiment with African doughnuts and chocolate cakes.

Canadian recipe Euphoria 100% fruit smoothies £2.95. Chai tea £1.95. Big mochaccino £2, chilled £2.95. Fruity Bubble tea from £2. Herbal teas £1.

All served with a friendly smile!! Cash only. Outside catering and private hire.

Eco, Brixton

Omnivorous Italian restaurant

4 Market Row, Electric Lane
Brixton SW9 8LD
(in the covered market)

Tel: 020-7738 3021

Open: *Coffee* 08.30-11.30
Full menu 11.30-17.00
Wed, Sun closed

Tube: Brixton

Tiny restaurant in the market with a few tables inside and out, next to Brixton Foodland grocer, though the sight of the fishmonger almost opposite may put some veggies off sitting outside. Antipasti £1.80-4.95 include olives, bruschetta, side

Lounge Bar

Omnivorous pub
with vegetarian food

Open:

Mon–Wed	11.00–23.00
Thu–Sat	11.00–24.00
Sun	11.00–17.30

Children welcome, high chairs
MC, Visa

56–58 Atlantic Road, Brixton
London SW9 8PX
(opposite Atlantic Wholefoods)
Tel: 020-7733 5225
Tube: Brixton

The original urban retreat, a very chilled out pub opposite the wholefood store, with an eclectic selection of wholefood vegetarian dishes, snacks by day and lots of tapas and mezze by night and some Caribbean food.

Day menu served till 5.30pm include vegi breakfast £6.45 with sausage, grilled tomatoes, mushroom, beans and toast, £4.95 without sausage.

Vegiburger with two large portabello mushrooms, grilled peppers and rocket £6.50. Side salad £2.50. Toasted panini with humous £3.10, add 35p for ciabatta or 45p for focaccia. Falafel with pitta and salad £5.50. Hot jacket potato with two fillings £3.75. Soup and ciabatta £3.

Evening menu from 6pm. Bar bites such as chilli peanuts or crackers, pan Asian snaps, mixed olives and dip £4; chargrilled pitta strips £2; spicy chickpeas £2.95; balsamic roasted tomatoes or mixed olives £2.95. Choice of 3 dips and pitta strips £3.50 per item such as humous, guacamole or aioli, falafel and hummous, tabouleh, grilled Med veg, cumin spiced potato salad, fried plantain, crispy new potatoes. Mezze platter £12 which can be shared.

House wine £9.75 bottle, £3.60 glass. Beer £1.60–£3.

Apple or orange juice £2, mixed juices £2.95. Soft drinks 90p–£1.45. Tea and all kinds of coffee £1–2, add 20p for soya milk.

If you like this you'll probably like Carmen tapas bar by Clapham South tube station, which also has stacks of veggie food.

salads, avocado vinaigrette. Garlic bread £2.90. Pasta mains £3.90, £5.50, £6.50. Pizzas £5.40–7.50 and you can order extra toppings from 50p to £2. Avocado and sundried tomato salad £6.90, or have an insalata vegetariana £7.50 with roast veg, artichoke, avocado, grilled asparagus, leaves and balsamic dressing. Aubergine and artichoke pizza bread sandwich £6.50.

Hot drinks, freshly squeezed orange juice and sodas £1.60–1.90. Not licensed for alcohol. MC, Visa.

Hive Bar & Restaurant

Omnivorous Modern European cafe-restaurant

11–13 Brixton Station Road
London SW9 8PA

(Turn right out of tube station)
Tel: 020-7274 8383

Open: *Mon–Wed* 12.00–24.00
        Thu   12.00–02.00
        Fri–Sat   11.00–03.00
        Sun   11.00–last
                        customer
Tube: Brixton

What used to be Jacaranda Garden still has veggie food and a new vegan manager. Everything is made from scratch, so you can ask for a vegan version of their mezze platter, £6 for 1, £10 for 2. Also vegan chickpea cakes, bruschetta, soup or salad.

Beer £3. House wine £4.50 large glass, £13 bottle. Kids welcome till 8pm. MC, Visa.

Honest Foods

Omnivorous British cafe

424 Colharbour Lane SW9 8LF
Tel: 020-7738 6161

Open: *Mon–Fri* 9.00–16.30
        Sat   10.00–18.00
        Sun   11.00–16.00
Tube: Brixton

Recommended by the folks at Brixton Wholefoods, this used to be vegetarian Cafe Pushkar and the new owners are still serving up lots for the old regulars. Organic freshly squeezed juices, (toasted) sandwiches, some veggie foods.

Really good salad bar £2.95 for a plate which is a meal in itself. All soups £3.25 with bread are vegan and they have stews. (Toasted) sandwiches £3.25 e.g. marinate roast peppers, or mixed pulses and herb pate. They make their own pies and cakes too, 90% vegetarian. MC, Visa. Children welcome, high chair. British scrumpy cider £3.50 large bottle, sometimes they have British wine. Veggie cooked all-day breakfast £5.95. Lentil and aubergine stew £3.95 eat-in (bargain) with bread. Fair Trade coffee £1.20, cappuccino £1.30, soya milk available.

Brixton Wholefoods

Wholefood shop

59 Atlantic Road
Brixton, London SW9
Tel: 020-7737 2210
Open: \ Mon-Sat 9.30-17.30
Mon -19.00, Fri -18.00
Sun closed
Tube: Brixton

Great wholefood store behind Brixton market with take-away pies, pasties, some vegan. Huge range of 'serve yourself' herbs and spices which you weigh so you can have as little or as much as you want. Large range of vegan foods including non-dairy cheese and ice-cream. Organic fruit and veg. Homeopathic remedies. Bodycare. Lots of raw superfoods and chocolate. Ecover cleaning products and refills, BioD and Earth Friendly.

Brixton Market

Street market

Behind Brixton underground station
Open: Mon-Sat 8.00-17.30
not Wed afternoon
Tube: Brixton

This market is much bigger than it at first seems and falls into various areas both indoors and out. Loads of fruit and veg on Electric Avenue and Pope's Road, especially Caribbean stuff like yam and plantain. There are arcades and a covered market full of shops. Unfortunately Zionly Manna vegan cafe has closed but you can still chill out at Hive or Lounge Bar, or get a fruit smoothie or vegan munchies from Lorentson's.

Esme

Organic grocery store

16A Market Row, Brixton SW9
(in covered market)
Tel: 020-7733 2065
Tube: Brixton

Organic/alternative grocery store in the covered market, with lots of wholefoods, fresh vegetables and teas.

R Green Grocery (Food

Brixton

Africa) next door has lots of fruit, spices, pulses and starchy grains.

S.G. Manning

Health food shop & pharmacy

34–36 New Park Rd.
Brixton, London SW2

Tel: 020-8674 4391

Open: *Mon–Fri* 9.00–18.00
Sat 9.15–17.00

Tube: Brixton

Small health food store in a pharmacy towards the south end of Brixton Hill. An astonishing range of wholefoods, non-dairy cheese, organic bread, frozen foods including vegan ice-cream, nut and chocolate spreads. Great for vegans.

BATTERSEA

CLAPHAM JUNCTION

Fresh & Wild p.273

LAVENDER

ELSPETH

Yum Yum p.276 ← *Holland & Barrett p.277*

Jasmin p.275

CLAPHAM COMMON N. SIDE

WANDSWORTH

BATTERSEA RISE

Market p.277

CLAPHAM COMMON W. SIDE

Giraffe p.274

NORTHCOTE ROAD

LAKEHURST

ROAD

Neal's Yard Remedies p.277

BELLEVILLE

Dandelion p.277

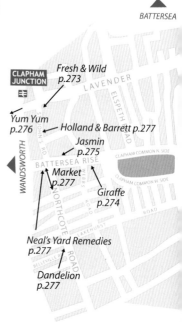

CLAPHAM
& Battersea

Clapham and Battersea are well endowed with green open spaces, a theatre, plenty of shopping and a fine variety of veggie-friendly eateries and shops, though nowhere 100% veggie.

Eco is a regular pizza restaurant that really likes veggies and has vegan calzone. **Carmen** is a fun tapas bar with stacks of veggie food.

There are three wholefood stores as well as Holland &

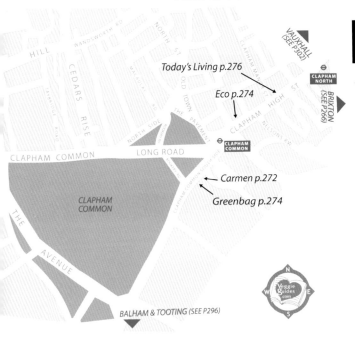

Today's Living p.276

Eco p.274

Carmen p.272

Greenbag p.274

CLAPHAM COMMON

BALHAM & TOOTING (SEE P296)

Barrett. **Dandelion** has heaps of take-aways. **Greenbag** is a deli-cafe right by Clapham Common tube that also sells wholefoods. **Fresh & Wild** wholefoods supermarket has a café and juice bar. You can find more shops down the road in **Balham** (p.300),

Not far from Clapham is **Brixton** (p.266), with its street market, or catch a bus down to new veggie hotspot **Tooting** (p.296) for its many vegetarian Indian shops and a couple of restaurants.

Carmen

Omnivorous Spanish tapas bar

6 Clapham Common South
London SW4 7AA

Tel: 020-7622 6848

Open: *Mon-Thu* 18.00-24.00
         Fri-Sat 12.00-01.00
         Sun   12.00-24.00

Tube: Clapham Common

Andalusian-style tapas restaurant with Spanish staff. If you've ever been to Spain you will think you are there again. Almost half the menu is vegetarian and half of that is vegan or vegan-option. Ask for the separate version of the menu showing what is vegan and vegan option,

wheat-free, or has nuts. There are warm yellow walls, covered with Spanish pictures, posters and a few farm tools. Wooden tables, discrete lighting, long bar. Don't wait for a table, you can eat at the bar like in Spain.

16 veggie tapas and salads £3.50-4.50 include gazpacho soup, patatas bravas, lentil or chickpea casserole, garlic mushrooms, asparagus and artichoke salad. Pimientos de padrón (on main menu only) are mixed mild and hot peppers, so you can have fun with your friends trying to guess which ones are hot.

6 desserts £6.50, vegans can have pears cooked in red wine and cinammon without the cream.

Wine £3 glass. Beers £3. Soft drinks £1.90. Tea/coffee £1.70. No soya milk but we think we persuaded them to get some.

They love children, one high chair. 10% service charge for parties of 6+. Visa, MC. No drinking without food.

Fresh & Wild

Natural & organic wholefood supermarket, deli & cafe

Open:

Mon–Fri	9.00–20.00
Sat	9.00–19.30
Sun	11.00–18.00

Visa, MC, Amex
www.wholefoods.com

305–311 Lavender Hill
London SW11 1LN

Tel: 020-7585 1488
Train: Clapham Junction BR
Tube: Clapham Common
then bus

Big organic wholefood supermarket with a cafe (not veggie but plenty for us) and a huge range of organic produce, fruit and veg, take-away food, remedies and books.

Organic wholefood supermarket with a huge range of organic produce, fruit and veg, take-away food, remedies and books.

Lots of gourmet, artisan and specialist foods including locally made bread, gluten/wheat free foods. The natural remedies and bodycare section has qualified naturopaths. Organic and vegetarian wines.

Café, juice bar and deli with seats and tables. The café has heaps of organic hot and cold food made daily by the in-store chefs, £1.28-1.79 per 100gr, salad bar £1.29/100gr, plus individual items, such as falafel 75p. Vegetarian lunch deal £4.50 eat in or take-away, such as brown rice, broccoli and dahl or bean casserole or Thai curry. Sandwiches made daily £2.45-3.49.

Health, body and skincare includes Dr Hauschka, Ren, Weleda, Faith in Nature, Jason, Urtekram, Green People. Aso aromatherapy, herbs, probiotics, flax oil, supplements, world music and books. There is always a staff member who can advise you, most are qualified naturopaths with varying specialities. There is a cardfile available for local alternative health practitioners who have been vetted.

Customer toilet.

Eco

Omnivorous pizza restaurant

162 Clapham High Street
Clapham, London SW4
Tel: 020-7978 1108
Open: *Mon–Fri* 12.00–16.00
18.30–23.30
Sat 12–23.30
Sun 12–23.00
Tube: Clapham Common
www.ecorestaurants.com

The best pizzas are vegetarian according to the manager, though they weren't sure if the dough base was dairy free. Hhowever the vegan calzone is great with pepper and aubergine. This is a pizza place with panache, smartly decorated in light wood and sculptured steel. Allow £6.50-7.50 for a pizza. The garlic bread is done in olive oil not butter. Salads £2.20-3.90, main course £5.90-8.95.

Aubergine and artichoke pizza bread sandwich £6.90. £10.95 for a bottle of wine or £2.75 a glass. Gets pretty crowded so reservations advisable and you are encouraged to leave after an hour and a half, but great fun if you've got the energy. MC, Visa.

Giraffe, Battersea

Omnivorous global restaurant

27 Battersea Rise, SW11 1HG
Tel: 020-7223 0933
Open: *Mon–Fri* 10.00–23.00
Sat 09.00–23.00
Sun 09.00–22.30
Bank hols 09.00–22.30
Train: Clapham Junction BR
Children welcome, kids' menu
www.giraffe.net

Good selection of vegetarian dishes. See Bloombsury branch (page 95) for menu.

Greenbag

Organic natural deli-cafe & shop

18 Clapham Common South Side
London SW4 7AB
Tel: 020-7627 2943
Open: *Mon* 09.30–18.00
Tue–Fri 08.00–19.30
Sat 09.00–19.00
Sun 10.30–17.30
Bank hols 09.30–17.00
Tube: Clapham Common

Originally 100% vegetarian, now 75%. A good place to come and eat, and then buy stuff to cook at home. Seating inside for 10 plus 4 more outside.

Eat in full all-organic veggie breakfast £6 gets you veggie sausages, toast, mushrooms, baked beans, marinated tofu.

Muesli with fresh fruit £2.99, £3.99 with yogurt (vegans let them know to get soya yogurt in).

Sandwiches such as hummous salad £2.49 take-away, £2.99 in. Hummous and avocado panini. Soup of the day

Lunch daily special £4.99 such as chickpea stew with brown rice and side salad, or stuffed red peppers. Vegan savoury tomato and basil tart with side salad £4.75.

Small salads £2.50, large £3.99 take-away, £4.50 eat-in for a big plate.

Vegan ginger cake is available £2 slice, cookies 69p.

Teas 99p take-away, £1.30 drink in. Fair Trade organic coffee £1.69 take-away, £2–2.10 drink in, latte, cappuccino, Americano, espresso. Soya and rice milk available. Fresh cold-squeezed organic juices £2.95. Smoothies £3–£4. Wheatgrass shot £1, double £2. No alcohol.

Children welcome and they get lots. Visa, MC minimum £6.

The small shop has some amazing and unusual products. Organic veg.

Gluten-free heaven. Rice and oat cakes, muesli, sweet potato and buckwheat noodles, pumpkin ginger and rice noodles, rice and millet pasta, brown rice penne, buckwheat or spelt pasta. Wheat/gluten/dairy free biscuits. Oat digestives. Nuts and nut butters. Almond and quinoa milk. Miso soup. Tea. Some books.

Jasmin

Omnivorous Chinese restaurant

50 Battersea Rise SW11
Tel: 020-7228 0336
Open: *Tue–Sun* 12.00-14.30
          18.00-23.00
          Mon closed
Train: Clapham Junction BR

Selection of veg dishes such as pak choi, tofu, aubergines, average £4. Rice or noodles £2–£4. 10% discount for take-away.

House wine £3.50 glass, £13.50 bottle.

Children welcome, 2 high chairs. MC, Visa.

Yum Yum

Omni Chinese–Malaysian restaurant

112 St John's Hill SW11 1SJ
Tel: 020-7585 1802
Open: *Mon–Sun* 18.00–23.00
Train: Clapham Junction BR

Average £8.50 for Malaysian veggie dishes, or £5.50 take-away. Wine £11.95 bottle, £3.20 glass. Children welcome, high chairs. MC, Visa, Amex.

Dandelion

Health food shop & veggie take-away

120 Northcote Road, Battersea London SW11 6QU
Tel: 020-7350 0902
Open: *Mon–Sat* 9.00–18.00
Sun closed
Tube: Clapham South
Clapham Junction BR

Vegan take-away sweet and savoury food a speciality here. Main dishes £23 cooked on the premises with at least 20 options including rice dishes, spring rolls, bhajis, samosas, salads, mung bean burgers. Salads £1.95 small, £2.80 large. Some vegan cakes. Organic fruit and veg arrives Tuesday and Thursday. Many other organic products. One table outside.

Bodycare products. Bach and Australian flower remedies, herbal and homeopathy, supplements, nutritional advice. Ecover cleaning products.

Visa, MC over £5.

Today's Living

Health food shop

92 Clapham High St.
Clapham, London SW4 7UL
Tel: 020-7622-1772
Open: *Mon–Sat* 9.00–18.30
Sun closed
Tube: Clapham Common

Supplements, oils, frozen foods, remedies and body building products. Sandwiches and pasties, several vegan. Vegan ice-cream and meat substitutes.

Holland & Barrett

Health food shop

51 St Johns Rd, Clapham
London SW11 1QP

Tel: 020-7228 6071
Open: *Mon–Sat* 09.00–18.00
         Sun 11.00–17.00

Train: Clapham Junction BR

This branch has a freezer
section and small amount of
take-away food.

Holland & Barrett

Health food shop

Unit 29, The Arndale,
Wandsworth, London SW18 4DG

Tel: 020-8871 3706
Open: *Mon–Sat* 9.00–17.30
         Sun 11–17.00

Train: Wandsworth BR

Take-away pasties, sos rolls,
drinks. Freezer section.

Neal's Yard Remedies

Herbs and bodycare

6 Northcote Road, SW11 1NT

Tel: 020-7223 7141

Open: *Mon–Wed* 10.00–18.00
         Thu–Fri 10.00–19.00
         Sat 9.00–18.00
         Sun 11.00–17.00

Train: Clapham Junction BR
www.nealsyardremedies.com

Herbs and spices by weight,
organic toiletries, natural
remedies. Mostly organic,
lots of Fair Trade.

Also therapy rooms offering
healing treatments.

Northcote Road Market

Health food shop

Northcote Rd, Battersea Rise end

Open: *Fri–Sat* 9.00–17.00
         (best days)

Loads of fruit and veg and
upmarket food stalls, definitely a cut above most street
markets, but then this is
Clapham.

The Spirited Palace

Organic vegan
Caribbean cafe

Open:

Tue–Fri   11.00–22.00
Sat–Sun   14.00–22.00
Mon   closed
No alcohol

105 Church Road
Crystal Palace, London SE19 2PR
Tel: 020-8771 5557
or 07939 474 507
Train: Crystal Palace. Near Crystal Palace bus station, bus 63/363 from Central London.

Finally south-east London has a vegan cafe, run by Sister Matana from Grenada and her team. The cafe feels more like a family and is friendly, relaxing and cheerful, and open long hours too. Upstairs food counter and open kitchen with two tables. More tables and sofas in the basement which has warm red walls.

Rotis and wraps £3.50, sandwiches, rolls. Eat in £7 for a max plate. Takeout £5 small, £6 large. Choose from vegan cheese, sausages, bacon, chick pea or veg fritters, roasted mixed veg, curried chick peas, curried veg, seasoned tofu and pumpkin, sprouted seeds and salad. If you're into raw food they can make up a plate for you.

Soup of the day £3–4. Organic raw veg and sprouted seeds platter £4.50. Patties (veg, spinach/potato, or wheatmeat/coriander), pasties and pizza £1.30.

Sweets and cakes £1–2 might include sweet potato pie, apple crumble; choc chip slice; ginger squares; coconut rock cake; fridge cake (dry and raw fruits and nuts set in the fridge); pineapple cup cake; fruit cake; coconut, carrot, ginger, or vanilla cake.

Freshly made organic juices £2.50 small, £3 large, from apple, carrot, kiwi, celery, cucumber or ginger. Ginger beer, sorrel, lemonade, soya drinks, organic canned drinks, smoothies. Herbal teas, chai, Jamaican mocha spice tea, with soya or almond milk.

Special events featuring live music, poetry, seminars, cultural evenings.

They sell some Veganicity supplements, One Love bath crystals, Queen Makeda facial and body scrub, crystals, Rastafarian books.

It's A Green Thing

Eco-shop plus wholefoods

Open:

Mon-Tue, Thu-Fri	10.00-13.00
	14.00-17.00
Sat	10.00-17.00
Sun	closed
Wed	closed

79 Church Road, Crystal Palace
London SE19 2TA

Tel: 020-8771 1178

Train: Crystal Palace. Near Crystal Palace bus station, bus 63/363 from Central London
www.itsagreenthing.biz

Finally Crystal Palace has a place to buy Fair Trade organic food. Opened July 2007 by a husband and wife team, this fabulous little shop on the way to Spirited Palace has all the lovely green gadgets you normally only find in catalogues. Perfect for present buying too. Why not come down for a walk in Crystal Palace park, go shopping here then chill out at Spirited Palace or Domali.

Organic Fair Trade foods include rice, pasta, passata, muesli, tea, Montezuma and Green & Black's chocolate, rice milk, high energy snacks.

Toiletries include Organic Blue, Earth Friendly, Kingfisher.

If it's recycled, renewable or reduces carbon, it's here. Wind-up, solar, water-powered or low-energy radios, kettle, torches, battery chargers, light bulbs.

Stackable recycling bins. Recycled wrapping paper and cards. Washing balls and refills. BioD and Ecover cleaning products and refills. Recycled aluminium foil.

Women's things include Mooncups. Biodegradable and real nappies and all kinds of baby stuff. PlayMais toys.

People Tree and Gossypium organic Fair Trade cotton clothes. Baby and maternity clothing made from bamboo fibre. Fitting room and mirror. Onya and Doy bags.

They offer advice on anything to benefit the environment from solar panels to composting. Browse the directory of recommended suppliers for products and services they don't stock. Magazines including the Ecologist.

If you like this you'll probably enjoy a visit to the Centre for Alternative Technology in Machynlleth, Wales. See *Vegetarian Britain* for details and places to stay and eat in the area.

SOUTH Crystal Palace

Domali

Omnivorous international cafe-bar-restaurant

Open:
Mon–Sun 9.30–23.00
Child portions, 5 high chairs.
MC, Visa minimum £5. Licensed.
www.domali.co.uk

38 Westow Street, Crystal Palace
London SE19 3AH
Tel: 020–8768 0096
Train: Crystal Palace BR,
Gypsy Hill BRA

Big tapas bar style café with a young and lively feel to it. Chill-out lounge with sofa, plus a big garden with tables out back. Global menu, 90% veggie and plenty for vegans apart from desserts. They love to cater for eveyone from die-hard vegans to carnivores who don't even notice it's mostly veggie. Local artists' work is exhibited and it's for sale.

Veggie breakfast served until 6pm, includes muesli, veggie bacon and sausages from £1.90 to £5.90 for the full English.

At lunchtime they have vegan soup £3.50. Weekday specials £4.50 9.30am–6pm, £6.90–8.90 evening, include wild mushroom paté with farmhouse bread, olive oil and mixed leaf garnish; pasta of the day; veg tagine; butternut squash casserole; spinach and coconut curry served with rice and tomato salsa.

Toasties £3.90 include veggie sausage with mustard and tomato. Vegan sandwiches include humous and carrot, veggie BLT £2.60–2.90, or humous Mediterranean veg and veg bacon £3.90. Thick chips with homemade chilli tomato sauce £2.50.

Several cakes but none vegan as yet.

Coffee and juice bar with soya smoothies £2.20, double juices £2.50, singles £2.20. Add a shot of St. John's Wort, echinacea, gurarana or milk thistle for 40p. Tea £1. Coffee £1..20, cappuccino £1.30, latte £1.50, soya milk available.

Large drinks list includes house cocktails and wine £2.20 glass, £9.90 bottle. Organic wine £3.50 glass, £12.90 bottle. Cocktails £4.90–6.90. Happy hour every evening 6–8pm, half price cocktails and wine, i.e. £1.45 for a glass of wine!

Greenwich

Royal Teas

Almost vegetarian cafe/coffee shop

76 Royal Hill, Greenwich SE10

Tel: 020-8691 7240

Open: *Mon–Fri* 9.30–17.30
   Sat 10.00–18.00
   Sun 10.30–18.00

Train: Greenwich BR, but more fun by boat from Westminster or Embankment Pier.

www.royalteascafe.co.uk

Vegetarian cafe and tea house, apart from salmon in the cream tea and one sandwich. However vegans beware all the breakfasts, sandwiches and cakes are made with dairy or eggs, though the chef has told us this will be looked at. Phone ahead to find out if today's special £4.25 with salad, or soup £2.75 with baguette, is vegan. They always have hummous with salad and pitta for £4.

However if you want a cuppa after doing the Observatory, this is the business with lots of teas and coffees to choose from. Tea £1.40 small pot (2 cups), £2.80 for 2, £3.80 for 3. Filter coffee £1.20. Big latte or cappuccino £1.40. Soya milk available.

Greenlands Health

Wholefood shop

Unit 3a, Greenwich Craft Market Greenwich, London SE10 9HZ

Tel: 020-8293 9176

Open: *Mon–Sun* 9.30–18.30

Tube: Greenwich

All vegetarian take-away pies, pasties, snacks £1–3.75. Sandwiches from £1.79, salads £1.79. Cakes (including vegan) and health drinks. Bodycare. Cleaning products including Ecover. Herbal and homeopathy.

Green Baby

Organic baby clothing

52 Greenwich Church St, SE10

Tel: 020-8858 6690

Open: *Mon–Sat* 9.30–17.30
   Sun 10.00–17.30

Tube: Greenwich

www.greenbaby.co.uk

Organic cotton baby and children's clothing, organic nappies.

Kingston–upon–Thames

Wagamama Kingston

Omnivorous Japanese restaurant

16–18 High St, Kingston-upon-Thames, Surrey KT1 1EY
Tel: 020-8546 1117
Open: *Mon–Sat* 12.00–23.00
Sun 12.00–22.00
Train: Kingston BR

Omnivorous fast food Japanese noodle bar with veggie dishes. See Bloomsbury branch for details.

Food For Thought

Wholefood shop

38 Market Place, Kingston Surrey KT1 1JQ
Tel: 020-8546-7806
Open: *Mon–Sat* 9.00–17.30
Sun closed
Train: Kingston

Lots of organic and gluten-free. Fridge with humous, beansprouts, pies, tofu. Frozen foods include dairy-free ice-cream.

Supplements. Skin-care ranges, aromatherapy, homeopathy. Cleaning products include Ecover, Enviroclean, Earth Friendly, Faith in Nature,

Holland & Barrett

Health food shop

12–13 Apple Market, Kingston Surrey KT1 1JF
Tel: 020-8541-1378
Open: *Mon–Sat* 9.00–17.30
Sun 11.00–17.00

Fresh take-away snacks may be vegan such as pasties and pies. Also frozen food.

Lush, Kingston

Cruelty-free cosmetics

27 Market Place, Kingston, KT1 1JH
Tel: 020-8974 9929

Hand-made cosmetics, most vegan. See Soho (page 69).

Neal's Yard Remedies

Herbs and organic bodycare

25–27 Church Street, Kingston-upon-Thames, KT1 1RW
Tel: 020-8549 7077
Open: *Mon–Sat* 9.30–18.00
Thu till 20.30
Sun 11.00–17.00
www.nealsyardremedies.com

Also therapy rooms with treatments. See page 70.

Riverside Vegetaria

International vegetarian restaurant

Open:
Every day 12.00–23.00
Sun till 22.30
Kids welcome, 5 high chairs
Gluten and wheat free no problem.
MC, Visa.
Menus at www.rsveg.plus.com

64 High Street, Kingston-upon-Thames, Surrey KT1 1HN
Tel: 020-8546 7992
Tube: Kingston BR
Booking advised a week ahead for weekends and outside.
Outside catering.

Superb riverside vegetarian restaurant with large windows that open out over the Thames. Idyllic in summer but well worth the trip at any time of year. In warm weather you can eat under the sky in the outdoor area on the towpath beside the river. 70% vegan with awesome desserts.

Starters £4.50–£5.50 like potato balls with chilli sauce, sweet potato soup, garlic mushrooms, and falafel, veg bowl with coriander sauce, nutty parsnip soup, turnip and chestnut soup.

Main dishes £6.95–£8.75 include masala dosa; string hopper biriyani with fine noodles; tofu marinated in teriyaki sauce, mushroom and lentil bake; all served with veg, salad and/or rice.

A truly great vegetarian restaurant is memorable for its desserts and vegans especially will love scoffing the chocolate cake or baked figs with orange and brandy. They even have soya custard. From £3.50.

Lots of soft drinks, liquor, organic beer and even champagne from £28.95. Organic wines and Disos vegan red and white.

10% discount on the total food bill for Vegetarian and Vegan Society members and 20% for eople presenting this book! Take-away including frozen soup by the litre. Vegetarian Society best restaurant 2002, best local restaurant 2004 from Kingston LBA.

London Bridge

London Bridge

Pulse

Vegetarian Middle Eastern take-away

London Bridge south side, 10m north of Dukes Street Hill where it joins Borough High Street, near Evans Cycles.

Tel: 020-7403 7638

Open: *Mon-Fri* 07.00-18.00
      Sat-Sun closed

Tube: London Bridge

www.pulsefoodislife.com (menu)

6 kinds of falafel £3.25-4.45. Meze lunchbox £3.95 for any 3 from hummus, roast red pepper salad, babaganoush, couscous with orange zest and dates, char-grilled butternut squash with toasted pine nuts, 5-bean salad, tabouleh, falafel etc. Wholemeal flatbread 35p.

Omega-3 flapjacks, fruit and nut/seed bags, pistachio and date biscuits, 65p-£1.40.

Oat milk smoothies £2.60. Freshly pressed orange or carrot juice £2-2.20. Cold drinks 95p-£1.30. Teas and coffees £1.30-1.95.

Much of the Middle Eastern produce comes from women's cooperatives. All packaging is sustainable and biodegradable and napkins and take-away bags are made from recycled materials. Corporate buffets.

Arlington Cafe, SE1

Omnivorous cafe

73-81 Southwark Bridge Road, London SE1 0NQ

Tel: 020-7407 2825

Open: *Mon-Fri* 08.00-18.00
      Sat-Sun closed

Tube: Southwark

www.novas.org, search on "cafe"

Café Arlington, run by Charity of the Year for 2007 Novas, is a 100% not for profit business that believes in providing a fair deal for everyone, from team members to the growers of its products. Every penny spent on lunch and coffee goes towards providing training and employment for people experiencing home-lessness or social exclusion.

They sell the Fresh! range of sandwiches, some of which are vegan/veg, Clive's pies and snacks, fresh falafel and hummus ciabatta sandwiches which they can toast for you, a bunch of different soups that are all vegan (so far anyway), plus vegan chocolate cake. Soya milk available.

Coffee@tower bridge rd

Organic coffee bar & cafe

173 Tower Bridge Road SE1 2AW (corner of Druid St)

Tel: 020-7407 4273

Open: *Mon-Sun* 07.00-20.00

Tube: London Bridge, Tower Hill

One hour's free Wifi token when you buy something. See Brick Lane branch (East London) for details.

Coffee@Bermondsey St

Organic coffee bar & cafe

163 Bermondsey Street SE1 3UW (south end)

Tel: 020-7403 7638

Open: *Mon-Sun* 07.00-20.00

Tube: London Bridge

Popular with local veggies and their laptops. Wifi. See Brick Lane branch (East London) for details.

Hing Loong

Chinese omni restaurant/take-away

159 Borough High Street, SE1

Tel: 020 7378 8100

Open: *Mon-Fri* 12.00-23.30
Sat-Sun 12.00-15.00
Sat 17.00-23.30
Sun 17.00-23.00

Tube: Borough, London Bridge

Recommended by staff at the nearby PETA office. They do fab fake meat dishes like sweet and sour 'pork' and stir fried 'duck', and an extensive veggie menu with 5 different tofu dishes. Tasty tasty. House wine £7.80 bottle, £2 glass. Children welcome, 2 high chairs. Visa, MC.

Leon, Bankside

Omnivorous cafe & take-away

7 Canvey Street
The Blue Fin Building SE1 9AN (Behind the Tate Modern)

Tel: 020-7620 0035

Open: *Mon-Fri* 08.00-22.00
Sat 10.00-22.00
Sun 11.00-19.00

Tube: London Bridge, Southwark

www.leonrestaurants.co.uk

New fast food bar with lots of great value veggie food. See Soho (p.67) for details or website for the full menu.

Tas

Omnivorous Turkish restaurant

72 Borough High Street, SE1 1XF
Tel: 020-7403 7200/7277
Open: *Mon-Sat* 8
Sun 9
Tube: London Bridge, Borough
www.tasrestaurant.com

Similar menu to the Waterloo branch (p.145) with stacks of veggie and vegan Turkish dishes. Licensed. Visa,MC.

Tas Pide

Omnivorous Turkish restaurant

20-22 New Globe Walk SE1 9DR
Tel: 020-7928 3300/7633 9777
Open: *Mon-Sat* 12.00-23.30
Sun 12.00-22.30
Tube: London Bridge, Southwark
www.tasrestaurant.com

Pide is a traditional Anatolian dish made from dough in the shape of a boat, baked in a wood fired oven producing a crispy outer crust, with a variety of highly flavoured, aromatic fillings, best eaten by hand. Vegetarian Pide £6.35-6.95 such as Pirasali with leek, green lentils, potatoes, raisins, fresh tomatoes, sesame seeds, red basil, vegans ask for it without the cheese topping. See page 145 for menu.

Tas Cafe

Omnivorous Turkish restaurant

76 Borough High Street SE1 1QF
Tel: 020-7403 8557
Open: *Mon-Sat* 12.00-23.30
Sun 12.00-22.30
Tube: Borough, London Bridge
www.tasrestaurant.com

See page 145 for menu.

Wagamama

Japanese omnivorous restaurant

1 Clink Street, (opposite Vinopolis), SE1 9BU
Tel: 020-7403 3659
Open: *Mon-Sat* 12.00-23.00
Sun 12.00-22.00
Tube: London Bridge
www.wagamama.com

See page 93 for menu.

Union Newsagents

Newsagent with veggie sandwiches

77-79 Union Street., SE1 1SG
(next to League Against Cruel Sports office)
Tel: 020-7407 2652
Open: *Mon-Fri* 06.00-20.30
Sat 07.00-20.00
Sun 07.00-14.30

Great veggie sandwiches by Health Food Centre (p.100).

London Bridge SOUTH

Neal's Yard Remedies

Herbs and organic bodycare

4 Bedale Street, Borough Market
London SE1 9AL

Tel: 020-7940 1414

Open: *Mon–Thu* 10.30–18.30
        Fri–Sat   9.00–18.30
        Sun   11.00–17.00

www.nealsyardremedies.com

Also therapy rooms. On Monday they run graduate clinics £25 for 1 hour. See also page 70.

Borough Market

Huge covered food market

Between Stoney Street
and Bedale Street, SE1
Open: Fri   12.00–18.00
        Sat   9–16.00
Tube: London Bridge

This food market is the Daddy. An astounding array of stalls with exotic foods from around the world. For a great foodie day out or something like truffles to impress your dinner guests, no other market comes close. Plenty of organic normal fruit and veg too.

Look out for the **vegan stall** that sells raw chocolate bars, slabs of choccy fudge cake, and raw chocolate energy bars. There is a **vegan organic burger stall** and an organic drinks stall with freshly squeezed juices – all in one corner – fantastic place! **Arabica Food & Spice** (see page 166) is a falafel and Lebanese dips stall.

Next door is the sushi restaurant **Feng Sushi** which has bowls of noodle dishes with several vegan options: vegetable tempura, mock duck pancakes, and salads.

The tapas bar **Brindisi**, next to the market, does several veggie dishes and a few vegan ones such as patatas bravas, spinach with pinenuts and raisins, various toasts with dips, salads and one vegan dessert which is mixed berries.

Total Organics

Vegetarian food stall

Borough Market SE1, behind
Roast Restaurant

Tel: 020-7935 8626

Open: *Fri*   12.00–18.00
        Sat   09.00–17.00
Tube: London Bridge

The new organic store in Marylebone also has a food stall in Borough Market with salad bar, soups and tofu/veggie-burgers.

Putney

Hare & Tortoise, Putney

Noodle and sushi restaurant

296-298 Upper Richmond Road,
Putney, London SW15 6TH
Tel: 020-8394 7666
Open: *Sun-Thu* 12.00-23.00
Fri-Sat 12.00-23.30
Tube: East Putney
w3.hareandtortoise-restaurants.co.uk

Huge portions and low prices. Starters £2.90-4.20 include green salad, tofu "duck" pancakes, spring rolls, Chinese greens, edamame steamed soy beans. Miso soup £1.60. Veggie mains £4.75-5.75 include deep-fried tofu and vegetable ramen in soup (like the massive bowls at Wagamama only cheaper); chow mein with tofu and Chinese veg; satay mixed veg and tofu with noodles and sesame.

Freshly pressed juices £1.90-2.10. Wine from £10 bottle, £2.50-3.40 glass. Sake or plum wine £3. Oriental beer from £1.60. Tea £1, coffee £1.20.

No cheques, only cash or card (surcharge of 30p if under £10). Optional 10% service charge for groups of 6+.

Wagamama Putney

Japanese omnivorous restaurant

50-54 High Street, Putney,
London SW15 1SQ
Tel: 0208 785 3636
Open: *Mon-Sat* 12.00-23.00
Sun 12.30-22.00
Tube: Putney Bridge
www.wagamama.com

Opened October 2004. See Bloomsbury, Central London, for menu, or their website.

Holland & Barrett

Health food shop

137 High St, Putney, SW15 1SU
Tel: 020-8785 7018
Open: Mon-Sat 8.30-19.00
Sat 9.00-18.30
Sun 10.00-17.00

This branch has some fresh take-away such as sos rolls and and pasties, also a freezer section.

Putney SOUTH

GNC Putney

Health food shop

151 Putney High St, SW15 1SU

Tel: 020-8788-0944

Open: Mon-Sat 9.00-19.00
Sun 11.00-19.00

Train: Putney BR

Freezer products like veggie sausages and burgers and veggie mince.

Herbs, vegan chocolate, but no fresh take-aways at this branch. Large range of vitamins and minerals, some veggie and vegan, sports nutrition, body-building. Same foods as the nearby Holland & Barrett, but more sports orientated.

Richmond –upon–Thames

Hollyhock Café

Vegetarian cafe

Petersham Road, Richmond, Surrey TW10 6UX

Tel: 020-8948 6555
Open: Daylight hours..

Child friendly, high chairs.

Another vegetarian café, linked to Tide Tables, in the middle of a park overlooking the Thames, with really lovely views. Very child friendly, parents sit on the verandah while kids play on the grass.

Lots of juices and smoothies, (soya) cappuccino. Salads and baked dishes. Cakes, but not vegan. They do veggie breakfasts.

The Green Cafe

Vegetarian café and juice bar

29 The Green, Richmond, Surrey TW9 1LX.
Tel: 020-8332 7654

Open: Winter:
Mon-Fri 07.30-17.30
Sat-Sun 08.00-17.30
Summer:
Mon-Sun 07.00-18.00
or later if busy

Train: Richmond BR
Smoking outside only. No cards. Very child friendly but no high chairs here as less seating and bar chairs.

Similar to Tide Tables, on picturesque, historic Richmond Green tucked behind the main high street, with outside seating. This one is more of a specialist juice bar. Smoothies £3.45, fresh fruit and veg juices £2.90, wheatgrass available. Organic tea and coffee. They always have soya milk. Also salads, falafel £3.20, soups £2.90.

Giraffe, Richmond

Omnivorous global restaurant

30 Hill Street, Richmond
TW9 1TW

Tel: 020-8332 2646

Open: *Mon-Fri* 08.00-11.00
Sat 09.00-23.00
Sun 09.00-22.30
Bank hols 09.00-22.30

Tube: Richmond
Children welcome, kids' menu
www.giraffe.net

Good selection of vegetarian dishes. See p.95 for menu.

Wagamama, Richmond

Omnivorous Japanese restaurant

3 Hill Street, Richmond, TW9 1SX

Tel: 020-8948 2224

Open: *Mon-Sat* 12.00-23.00
Sun 12.00-22.00

Train: Richmond BR

See p.93 for details.

Holland & Barrett

Health food shop

50a George St, Richmond, TW9

Tel: 020-8940 1007

Open: *Mon-Sat* 9.00-18.00
Sun 10.30-16.30

Fresh take-away snacks such as sos rolls. Frozen foods.

Oliver's Wholefood

Wholefoods shop

5 Station Approach, Kew Gardens, Richmond TW9 3QB (next to the tube station)

Tel: 020-8948 3990

Open: Mon-Sat 9.00-19.00
Sun 10.00-19.00

Tube: Kew Gardens

Wide selection of produce, not all veggie. Pick up munchies for a trip to Kew Gardens such as sandwiches, wraps, pastries, salads and seaweed rice.

Organic fruit and veg. Vegan wines. Some homeopathic remedies. Cleaning products include Ecover, Ecolino.

Trained nutritionist and beauty therapist for advice. Regular lectures in-store on topics like living food and digestive health.

Tide Tables

Open:

Open every day, daylight hours, phone ahead as they close if weather is bad.

Child friendly, high chairs
Smoking outside. Free corkage.

2 The Archways,
Richmond Bridge,
Richmond, Surrey TW9 1TH
Tel: 020-8948-8285
Train: Richmond BR
Cash or cheque, no cards.

Vegetarian café under the arch of a bridge near the town centre, with beautiful views of the Thames, a riverside terrace and outside seating in summer, though people sit ouside year round when it's sunny for the view.

All food is GM free and menu items are clearly marked up for gluten-free, organic and vegan.

Child and dog friendly, a nice place to meet friends for lunch.

For breakfast (or anytime!) you could have muesli, toasted muffin with jam, almond twist (vegan) or pain chocolat from £1.35 to £2.90. They have soya milk.

For lunch and tea there's vegan soup, spinach pastie with salad, stuffed focaccia, vegan shepherdess pie with salad, falafel with hummous and salad, from £2.55 to £6.25. Everything is served with salad. Also samosas and bhajias.

Handmade cakes, including vegan almond twists, £2.55, and slices from 95p.

Hot and cold drinks or bring your own alcohol (free corkage). Juices, freshly squeezed organge juice £2.50 for half pint. Latte or cappuccino £2.15 big mug, £1.50 smaller one, soya milk no problem.

They also sell some second-hand books for charity, £1 each or 3 for £2.

If you like this you'll probably also like The Green Cafe and Hollyhock Cafe nearby.

SOUTH Richmond

Neal's Yard Remedies

Organic baby clothing

15 King Street, Richmond-upon-Thames, Surrey TW9 1ND

Tel: 020-8948 9248

Open: *Mon-Sat* 10.00-18.00
Sun 11.00-17.00

www.nealsyardremedies.com

Herbs and spices by weight, organic toiletries, natural remedies. Mostly organic, lots of Fair Trade. Also therapy rooms offering over 20 kinds of treatments from acupuncture to Swedish massage.

Green Baby, Richmond

Organic baby clothing

4 Duke Street, Richmond TW9

Tel: 020-8940 8255

Open: *Mon-Fri* 10.00-17.00
Sat 10.00-17.30
Sun 11.00-17.00

www.greenbaby.co.uk

Organic cotton baby and children's clothing, organic nappies.

Revital Health

Health food shop

The Quadrant, 2 Quadrant House, Richmond TW9 1BP

Tel: 020-8334 1049

Open: *Mon-Sat* 9.00-18.00
Sun closed

Tube/Train: Richmond
www.revital.co.uk

Health food store near the HQ of the Institute for Optimum Nutrition, handy for their students and their clients, while the in-store juice and smoothies bar is popular with people waiting at the bus stop outside. Fresh food counter.

Bodycare and natural beauty including Dr Hauschka. Vitamins, minerals, herbs, homeopathy, essential oils, health books. Healthnotes touch-screen information kiosk.

Streatham

Wholemeal Café

Wholefood vegetarian restaurant

1 Shrubbery Road, Streatham
London SW16 2AS

Tel: 020-8769 2423

Open: *Every day* 12.00–22.00
closed on all bank
holidays

Tube: Streatham BR,
Streatham Hill BR

Wholefood veggie restaurant with Thai, Indian, Mediterranean and world cuisine. Large vegan selection. Typical dishes include garlic mushrooms with pitta £3.25; guacamole and warm pitta £3.25, or soup of the day £2.60, usually vegan.

Main dishes £2.50–6.95 include homity pie, hot bake of the day, casserole of the day, red Thai curry, spinach and mushroom crumble.

Desserts from £2.85 such as banoffee pie or wholemeal fruit crumble with vegan custard.

Soft drinks such as organic lemonade. Freshly squeezed juices £2.75. Teas £1.20, coffees £1.40. They have soya milk. House wine £3.55 glass, £14.50 bottle. Organic wines, beers, ciders, ales.

Child portions, high chair. MC, Visa.

Wholemeal Cafe, Streatham

Shahee Bhelpoori

Indian vegetarian & vegan restaurant

Open:

Mon-Sat	17.30–23.00
Sun	12.30–23.00

Children's menu, high chairs
Visa, MC.

www.shaheebhelpoori.co.uk

1547 London Road
Norbury,
London SW16 4AD
(opposite Norbury BR Station)
Tel: 020-8679 6275
Train: Norbury BR

Indian vegetarian restaurant with 100 dishes, many of them vegan and virtually anything can be made vegan for you. Also vegan desserts, milkshakes and lassi, which makes this place immensely popular with local vegans.

13 hot and cold starters £2.10-3.70 such as vegetable kebab. 20 side orders from £2.30 include vegetable kofta at £2.90.

Main courses from £4.50. 8 dosas £4.10-5.50. 8 thalis £5.50-7.50.

14 desserts £1.90-2.70 include vegan ice cream. They also do vegan kashmiri faluda milkshake £2.30 and mango lassi £1.80. Not that you need to be vegan to enjoy a dairy-free dessert anymore than you need be Indian to eat a curry.

Exotic Sunday buffet lunches only £4.95, eat as much as you like, 12.30-10pm.

Children under 6 half price.

Children's menu £4.10 with mild masala dosa or French fries with veggieburger and salad, followed by ice-cream on request, can be vegan.

Beer £2.90 pint, £1.80 bottle. Wine £6.90 bottle or £1.80 glass. Tea £1, coffee £1.10, soya milk available.

10% discount to Vegetarian or Vegan Society members. If you present this book you also get 10% discount. Free delivery within 2 miles, minimum £12.

Croydon Vegans meet here, see local contacts, and the local MP comes here for bhel poori.

On the A23 Brighton to London road, so handy on you way back from a trip to the seaside.

If you like this you'll probably like the Indian vegetarian restaurants Kastoori and Milan in Tooting (also south London).

Nature's Way

Health food shop

252 Streatham High Road,
Streatham, London SW16 1HS

Tel: 020-8769-0065

Open: *Mon-Sat* 9.30-18.30
Sun closed

Train: Streatham BR

Two floors wotj a very large range of foodstuffs on the lower floor, while on the upper floor are supplements, remedies, oils, green products, stationery and cruelty-free cosmetics. Ecover and Ecofriendly cleaning products. People come from a long way to shop here.

There's plenty for vegans including the whole Plamil range. All the take-aways are veggie or vegan and include carrot cutlets, eccles cakes, pies, soya rolls, samosas, date or apricot crumble, carrot cake.

Allergy testing. 5% discount for Vegetarian and Vegan Society members. MC, Visa.

Holland & Barrett

Health food shop

110 Streatham High Road
Norbury, London SW16 1BW

Tel: 020-8769 1418

Open: *Mon-Sat* 9.00-17.30
Sun 10.00-16.00

Sandwiches, sos rolls, pasties and will even order things on customer request. Freezer too.

TOOTING
& Balham – veggie hotspot

Upper Tooting Road is the new Brick Lane with heaps of Indian take-aways and sweet shops. Long-established **Kastoori** and the new **Saraswathy Bavans** (pp.298-9) are authentic vegetarian Indian restaurants.

Ambala Sweets, Tooting

Indian vegetarian take-away

48 Upper Tooting Road,
SW17 7PD (corner Mandrake Rd)
Tel: 020-8767 1747
Open: *Mon–Sun* 10.00–20.00
Tube: Tooting Bec
www.ambalafoods.com

Indian sweets, samosas, pakoras.

Chennai Dosa

Veggie S,Indian/Sri Lankan restaurant

33 Upper Tooting Rd SW17 7TR
(corner Foulser Rd)
www.chennaidosa.com

Opening summer 2008. They already have branches in East Ham and Wembley.

David Wong

Omnivorous Chinese restaurant

108 Mitcham Rd, Tooting
Broadway, London SW17 9NG
Tel: 020-8672 9886
Open: *Mon–Fri*   12.00–14.30
                18.00–23.45
Sat   17.30–23.45
Sun   14.00–23.30
Last orders 30 mins before close
Tube: Tooting Bec

If you need a change from Indian, the menu here has 14 veggie dishes £3.40 such as monk's vegetables, various stir-fried veg, assorted deep fried bean curd such as with yellow bean and cashews. Veg spring roll £1.20. Plain rice £1.80, veg fried rice £3.

Banana or pineapple fritters £2, lychees £1.60.

House wine £2.20 glass, £8.50 bottle. Children welcome, high chair. Visa, MC. Free home delivery 6-11pm over £10 within 2 miles. Eat-in and take-away same price.

The Health Store

Health food store

246 Upper Tooting Road
London SW17 7EX

Tel: 020-8672 5417

Open: *Mon–Sat* 9.00–18.00
Sun closed

Tube: Tooting Broadway

Chilled and frozen foods but no take-away. Large range of wholefoods, gluten-free,

Lots of bodycare products, sports nutrition and supplements. Cleaning products include Ecover, Ecolino, Earth Friendly. Natural remedies, flower remedies, homeopathy, aromatherapy. 3 qualified staff on all aspects of natural health and nutrition. Books.

Holland & Barrett, Tooting

Health food shop

3 Mitcham Rd, Tooting
London SW17 9PA

Tel: 020-8767 8552

Open: *Mon–Sat:* 9.00–17.30,
Sun 10–16.00

Freezer section for those important purchases of vegan ice-cream. They also stock some fresh take-away item like pasties, sos rolls and porkless pies.

Pooja

Vegetarian take-away

168–172 Upper Tooting Road
SW17 7ER (corner Hebdon Rd)

Tel: 020-8672 4523

Open: *Mon–Sun* 09.00–21.00

Tube: Tooting Bec,
Tooting Broadway

www.poojasweets.com

Chaat house, Indian bakery, Indian savouries and sweets, Lebanese sweets. Breakfast, lunchtime meals, take-away only. Lunch thali only £2.50.

Shiv Darshan Sweets

Vegetarian Indian sweet shop

169 Upper Tooting Road
London SW17 7TJ

Tel: 020-8682 5173

Open: *Mon–Sun* 08.00–20.00

Tube: Tooting Bec

Indian savouries and sweets, snacks, curry. All take-away.

You can also find a fair selection of veggie dishes, at **Ah Mirage** at 215 Upper Tooting Road or **Mirch Masala** at 213 (also 1416 Norbury Rd SW16).

Kastoori

Open:

Mon–Tue 18.00–22.30
Wed–Sun 12.30–14.30
    then 18–22.30
Children's portions, no high chairs
Visa, MC over £10

188 Upper Tooting Road
Tooting, London SW17 7EJ
Tel: 020–8767 7027
Tube: Tooting Broadway

There is an east African influence to this vegetarian Indian Gujarati restaurant which doesn't use eggs.

7 starters are marked vegan such as Mogo bhajia, bhel (mix of puffed rice, sev, potato and onions in a sweet and sour sauce), or dahi vada (crispy puris filled with diced potatoes, chickpeas, pani puri sauce and sweet and sour sauce and topped with sev) £1.95 to £4.25.

12 curries, 8 vegan. You could try the Kastoori kofta – mixed vegetable balls, roasted aubergine curry, or a potato curry with the chef's sauce £4.75–5.25.

Thalis £8.50 to £17.50.

Other dishes include dosas, and the range of Kastoori family specials like Kasodi – which is sweetcorn in coconut milk with ground peanut sauce, or kontola curry – made with a crunchy mountain vegetable with garlic sauce.

Lots of side dishes, plus a choice of six desserts – alas only one vegan, the fresh fruit.

House wine £2.25 glass, £9.95 bottle. Coffee and teas £1.25. £ 7 minimum change.

They do outside catering.

Note that Sakonis and Milan vegetarian restaurants in Tooting have closed.

If you like Gujarati food you'll find lots more restaurants, some also with East African food, in Wembley. (West London)

Sarashwathy Bavans

Vegetarian
South Indian restaurant

Open:
Mon–Sun 11.00–23.00
Children welcome, high chairs.
MC, Visa, cheques minimum £10.
No alcohol.
www.sarashwathy.com

79 High Street, Tooting,
London SW17 0RN
(opposite Sainsbury's)
Tel: 020-8682 4242
Tube: Tooting Bec

Amazing value and with a huge menu, this sister to the Wembley branch is part of the transformation of Tooting into the new Brick Lane with lots of veggie-friendly restaurants and Indian sweet shops. The chefs are from Chennai and if you've been to India you will recognise how authentic it is right down to the stainless steel thali dishes and complementary tumblers of water. Very bright inside and lots of Indian diners.

Top value are the thalis from £2.75. The amazing special thali £6.95 has 20 items. Business lunch Mon–Thur 12.30–15.00 £2.50–2.95 such as dosa or idly, methu vadai and sweet, or biryani and sweet, or mini thali.

A la carte 30 starters from 40p for individual samosas, papadam or methu vadai, to £5.75 for a plate of starters. 25 dosas £1.50–3.25. Lots of uthappam £1.95–4.95, the special one has onion, chilli, tomato, capsicum, corn, pineapple, coriander, and mushroom. Curries £1.50–3.50. 5 Chinese dishes £3.95–4.50 such as garlic Gobi Manchurian. Sri Lankan stringhoppers fry with ginger oil or veg kottu roti £3.95. Rice from £1.25 up to £4.50 for a special biryani.

Separate dessert menu, all made with milk, but from the main menu vegans can have fruit salad or kesari (made with oil and sugar).

Fresh juices £1.95–2.95. Tea and coffee 75p–£1.50.

Most items can be without onion or garlic and are indicated on the menu.

Outside catering: their mobile dosa unit will make fresh dosas, idly, vadai etc at your home or garden.

If you like this you'll probably like their other vegetarian branch in Wembley, and their two omnivorous restaurants called Sarasas in Wembley and Hayes.

As Nature Intended

Organic & health food shop

186–188 Balham High Road,
Balham, London SW12 9BP

Tel: 020-8675 2923

Open: *Mon–Fri* 9.00–21.00
Sat 9.00–20.00
Sun/ 10.30–18.30

Tube: Balham

www.asnatureintended.uk.com

95% organic store that aims to combine the variety of a supermarket (over 5,000 products) with the product range found in traditional health food shops. Many items are suitable for those with food allergies such as sugar-, gluten-, salt- or yeast-free. Bread and gluten-free muffins. Wide range including sandwiches and pies to take away. Not completely vegetarian. Many Japanese and tofu-based foods and tempeh. Vegan and veggie wines are clearly labelled and there is a leaflet in case you're unsure what constitutes a vegan wine.

Herbal and homeopathic remedies, aromatherapy oils, New beauty and skincare products. Vitamins and minerals. Lots of books.

Everyone in the remedies section is a practitioner or has had training. Certain days therapists offer treatments. Lots of information on recommended treatments for various conditions on their website.

Other branches in Ealing and Chiswick (West London).

Balham Wholefood

Health food shop

8 Bedford Hill, Balham
London SW12 9RG

Tel: 020-8673-4842

Open: *Mon–Sat* 9.30–18.00
closed 13.30–14.30
Sun closed

Tube: `Balham BR

Large range of dried fruit, seeds, pulses etc, both organic and non-organic. Vegan cheeses, meat yogurts, Swedish Glace ice-cream, meat substitutes. Supplements, homeopathic remedies. Toiletries. Cleaning products including Ecover and Clearspring. Books. No take-away.

No credit cards, cash/cheque only.

Health Food Centre

Health food shop

156 Balham High Road, Balham
London SW12 9BN

Tel: 020-8265 7532

Open: Mon-Sat 9.30-18.00
Sun 11.00-17.00

Tube: Balham

Health foods but no fresh take-away. Vitamins, homeopathic remedies, aromatherapy oils. Cleaning products. Complementary therapies, massage by appointment.

VAUXHALL
South London veggie hotspot

Courtyard Cafe

Vegetarian cafe in garden museum

at Museum of Garden History
Lambeth Palace Rd, SE1 7LB
(by Lambeth Bridge, midway
between Vauxhall and Waterloo)

Tel: 020-7401 8865

Open: *Tue–Sat* 10.30–16.45
Sun Mon closed

Tube: Waterloo, Vauxhall
Bus: 77 or 507 from Waterloo;
77 or 344 from Vauxhall;
507 from Victoria.

www.museumgardenhistory.org

If you are into gardening
you'll love this place, a
museum with a vegetarian
cafe in a church by Lambeth
Palace, plus garden of
course. Home-made dishes
and light snacks from across
the globe. All food is organic
and changes with the
seasons. Very good prices.

Soup £4 changes daily. Six
mains £6, two vegan, such as
aubergine tagine with
cinnamon and almonds and
apricot; stuffed pepper with
ratatouille and chestnut.

Big slice of brownie or
flapjack or cakes £2.50,
including vegan.

Filter coffee and teas £1.20,
soya and oat milk available.
James White organic juices
£1.80. Organic wine £2.75
glass, £12.50 bottle with
food.

Children welcome, no high
chairs. Cash only.

The museum is open the
same hours and Sunday. It's
free if you eat in the cafe, or
by donation.

Synergy Centre

Vegetarian cafe in community centre

220 Farmers Rd, Oval, SE5 0TW

Tel: 020-7793 1083

Centre open:
Mon–Sun 09.30–22.00

Tube: Oval then bus 36,436 or
185 towards Camberwell, get off
by Co-op supermarket with
Union Tavern on your right.
www.thesynergycentre.org ok
www.myspace.com/
synergytuesday

Brilliant community centre with occasional all-veggie cafe, check the website for what's on this month.

Alternate Tuesday nights for example is acoustic night with a non-alcohol bar selling teas, coffee and home-made vegan food. You can bring your own alcohol too or veggie food to share, but no drinking outside.

Loads of classes and events such as yoga, belly dancing, capoeira, spinning poi.

Basic Wholefoods

Wholefood shop & therapy centre

49 Denmark Hill, Camberwell SE5 8RS

(junction with Colharbour Lane)

Tel: 020-7701 8888

Open: *Mon-Sat* 10.00-19.00
Sun closed

Train: Denmark Hill BR

Almost everything is organic except the things you can't get organic. Fruit & veg, fresh bread, lots of cakes

The whole range of Laura's Idea take-away such as vegan calzone £2.69, sushi, vegan cheesecake, and very popular locally made samosas.

Lots of local cakes and brownies made with Green & Black's chocolate, some gluten or sugar-free 79p-£2.50.

Vitamins including Solgar, Quest, Bioforce, Higher Nature.

Bodycare including Jäson, House of Mistry, Urtekram, Tom of Maine.

Clearning products such as Ecover and refills, BioD, Ecolino, Clearspring, Faith In Nature.

Bush flower remedies, homeopathy. Incence, books, crystals.

Therapy centre in the basement with Reiki, every kind of massage, reflexology, Indian head massage, homeopathy, nutrition, counselling, spiritual healing. Phone the shop or pick up a leaflet or check the window profiles for details.

You can park free for 2 hours in the nearby Somerfield.

Bonnington Cafe

Veggie international wholefood restaurant

Open:
Every day 12.00–14.00
　　　　　18.30–22.30
www.bonningtoncafe.co.uk

11 Vauxhall Grove, Vauxhall
London SW8 1TA
Tel: 020–7820 7466
Tube: Vauxhall

Vegetarian wholefood restaurant and garden in a quiet square. Run by a cooperative of member cooks from all over the world, with a different cook and their recipes each night, such as Japanese, French, Italian or new American. The atmosphere is very laid back and it's incredible value at £10 for a three course dinner. Regulars love the candlelight, burning fire in winter, and community feel.

Main courses £6. On the day they were roast pepper, red onion and rocket pizza with salad; and spinach and blackeye bean tart with roast potatoes and salad.

There is usually vegan food and Thursday is vegan night.

Visit their website for a map of the exact location behind Vauxhall underground/rail station and for tonight's chef's email and phone number for enquiries such as the availability of vegan food and reservations. On second, fourth and fifth Sunday in the evenings it's raw chef Anya Ladra of Raw Fairies food delivery service.

Bring your own alcohol, corkage is free and you can buy booze at the off-licence opposite. Somethimes there is piano music. Individual cooks may set a minimum charge or service charge on large bookings.

If you like this you'll probably like Pogo Cafe in Hackney (East London), which is run in a similar style as a cooperative with different cooks each day.

Spring Gardens Cafe

Vegetarian English & Mediterranean cafe

Open:

Mon–Fri   08.00–14.00
Sat–Sun   closed

Children welcome, no high chair

Outside catering if you collect

In Vauxhall Gardens Community Centre, 100 Vauxhall Walk, SE11 5EL

Tel: 07723 023625
       0795 6381560

Tube: Vauxhall

English and Mediterranean style cafe in community centre, started by people who cook at Bonnington on Saturday nights, including an Italian chef. Everything is organic and prices are very affordable. Outside porch with some tables, weather permitting.

Breakfast till 10am can be coffee, cake and croissants, homemade flapjacks, fruit.

Sandwiches only 10 till 12, made with crusty bread bloomer slices or wholewheat £2, or ciabatta £2.70. Fillings include aubergine pate, guacamole, red kidney bean pate with some salad veg.

Lunch 12 till 2. Soup £2 is always vegan and main course specials £4.50 often are, otherwise have a jacket potato or pasta. Specials include mushroom and green bean or curried parsnip pie; pumpkin curry; chilli; tagines; mung beans in satay sauce; spinach or spicy potato strudel; nut and lentil burger.

Pasta with various sauces such as tomato or lentil bolgnaise or pesto. Jacket potatoes with toppings such as hummous and roast veg, aubergine pate, guacamole, red kidney bean pate.

Cakes £2 though rarely vegan, but crumble when available is.

Organic Fair Trade coffees and teas. Espresso £1.20, cappuccino £1.60, latte £1.80. Soya milk available. Juices £1. Smoothies £2. Homemade ginger lemonade £1. No alcohol.

Catering if you collect, or book the cafe for an event such as a birthday party which can be in the evening for up to 100 people.

The centre has artists' studios, social clubs at the weekend, Portuguese groups, Latin American refugee groups, bingo night.

Walworth

St Gabriel Cafe, SE11

Ethiopean omnivorous cafe-deli

154 Newington Butts,
Kennington, London SE11 4RN
(in an alley along the back of the
triangular junction of Newington
Butts, Kennington Lane and
Kennington Park Road, next
door to Sisay Hairdresser)

Tel: 020-7587 0199

Open: *Mon-Sun* 09.00-20.00
Tube: Elephant & Castle,
         Kennington

Lovely vegetarian salads and
roast vegetables, some with
quite a lot of oil, which you
wrap in Ethiopian Enjera
flatbread and eat with your
hands. Have a veggie
selection for a fiver, which is
probably enough to share
with a friend. Also fresh
juices and some groceries.

Baldwin's Health Food

Health food shop

171 Walworth Road
Walworth, London SE17 1RW

Tel: 020-7701 4892

Open: *Mon-Sat* 9-17.30
         Sun   closed

Tube: Elephant & Castle
www.baldwins.co.uk online shop

Hot and cold take-away
selection of sweet and
savoury goodies including
sandwiches, pasties, ready
meals.

Organic bread. Vegan
cheeses, yogurts, and ice-
cream, meat substitutes.

Bodycare such as Weleda,
Wild Rose. Ecover and Earth
Friendly cleaning products.
Homeopathic remedies.
Supplements include Quest,
Bioforce, Viridian, Nature's
Plus. Informative notice-
board.

FareShares Food Co-op

Vegan organic wholefood cooperative

56 Crampton Street, Walworth, London, SE17 3AE

Tel: none

Open: *Thu*   14.00-20.00
Fri   15.00-19.00
Sat   15.00-17.00
Sun-Wed closed

Tube: Elephant & Castle, Kennington

www.56a.org.uk
fareshares@hotmail.com

Established by local people back in 1990, and now with a new 10 year lease from Southwark Council, FareShares is a non-profit community-run food co-op which aims to make healthy food affordable. They buy in bulk and resell at minimal mark-up to cover some expenses.

They stock a range of dry goods, fresh organic fruit, veg, bread and various household products. All stock is sourced as locally and ethically as possible, much of it is organic and all produce is animal-, sugar- and GMO-free.

FareShares relies on individual's time and energy and everyone is a volunteer. They always welcome new people to get involved – as well as doing shifts, there are plenty of other ways to help out. They operate as a collective, with meetings on the first Sunday of the month.

Wimbledon

Giraffe, Wimbledon

Omnivorous global restaurant

21 High St, Wimbledon Village
SW19 5DX

Tel: 020-8946 0544

Open: *Mon–Fri* 08.00–11.00
Sat 09.00–23.00
Sun 09.00–22.30
Bank hols 09.00–22.30

Tube: Wimbledon
Children welcome, kids' menu
www.giraffe.net

Good selection of vegetarian dishes. See Bloombsury branch (central London) for menu.

GNC Wimbledon

Health food shop

Centre Court Shopping Centre
Queens Road, Wimbledon,
London SW19

Tel: 020-8947 3583

Open: *Mon–Fri* 9.30–19.00.
Thur –20.00
Sat 9.00–18.00
Sun 11–17.00

Tube: Wimbledon

Fridge with tofu and veggie meals and a freezer section.

Holland & Barrett

Health food shop

68 The Broadway, Wimbledon
London SW19 1RQ

Tel: 020-8542 7486

Open: *Mon–Sat:* 9.00–17.30
Sun 11.00–17.00

Small shop, no fridge or freezer.

Health Zone Ltd

Health food shop and
complementary health clinic

30 Wimbledon Hill Road
Wimbledon, London SW19 7PA

(corner of Walpole Rd, opposite the library)

Tel: 020-8944-1133

Open: *Mon–Fri* 9.30–19.00,
Sat 9.30–18.00
Sun 11–17.00

Tube: Wimbledon

Much more than your average health food shop, with a vegan manager and a complementary therapy clinic attached.

They stock a wide range of veggie and vegan foods, many organic, supplements and organic body-care products. Ecover cleaning products.

Also veggie/vegan sandwiches, falafel in pitta, pasties, pies, salads such as couscous, from £1.65 upwards and a gluten-free range. Vegan ice-cream.

Yoga and pilates equipment. Wide selection of books on health, magazines, CD's.

Clinic treatments include acupuncture, massage, shiatsu, aromatherapy, relexology, Reiki, facial rejuvenation, herbal medicine, homeopathy, nutritional therapy, hypnotherapy, crystal therapy.

Lush, Wimbledon

Cruelty-free cosmetics

5 Wimbledon Bridge,
Wimbledon SW19 7NH
Tel: 020-8944 1299
www.lush.co.uk

Hand-made cosmetics, most vegan. See p.69 for details.

Rest of South-East

Santok Maa's

Indian vegetarian restaurant

848 London Road,
Thornton Heath, Surrey CR7 7PA
Tel: 020-8665-0626
Open: *Thu-Tue* 12.00-22.00
         Wed closed
Train: Thornton Heath BR,
          Norbury BR
Children welcome, high chairs.
Visa, MC, Amex

North and South Indian dining and take-away, with some spicy Chinese dishes like stir-fries. Nearly 100 dishes. Starters average £2.95, main courses £3.95, rice £1.75. Desserts from £1.50 and they now have vegan ice-cream. Bring your own wine, £1 per person corkage. Special offer on Monday, all food half price excluding dessert and take-away. Outside catering for weddings and parties. Eggless cakes.

Cafe Crema

Open:

Mon-Sat	10.30–18.30
Sat	12.00–18.30
Sun	closed
	Evenings as advertised

Children welcome, toys and swing.

306 New Cross Rd, SE14 5AF
(between New Cross and
NewCross Gate tube stations)

Tel: 020-8320 2317

Tube: New Cross,
New Cross Gate

Great value, friendly cafe that has been going for three years, with red walls and a big sunny garden with tables, toys and swing. It's full of students from nearby Goldsmiths College. Art event posters and a big bulletin board. Look out for special film and food nights

Design your own late breakfast/brunch from toast, baked beans or mushrooms 80p each, pototaoes fried with herbs in olive oil £1.80.

For a main meal, Macaxeira is the house speciality £4.50, with cassava and soya meat in veg sauce and lettuce. Polenta £4 comes with veg and sunflower seeds. Big veg pasty £3.50. Couscous with chickpeas and coriander £4.50. Pizzas £4.50, vegan option.

For a light bite try toasted sandwiches and big wraps £2.50-3.50 such as Macaxeira or roast veg. Veg soup with bread £2.50–£3.50. Tomato salad £2, garlic bread £1.80.

Flapjacks, brownies, muffins and sometimes vegan carrot cake £1.

Banana and pear smoothie £2. Coffee £1.20 espresso. Cappuccino, latte, mocca, hot choc £1.60. Tea 80p, herb tea or chai £1. Soya milk available. In summer they have home-made lemonade and mint tea made with mint from the garden. Wine £8.50 bottle, £2.50 glass.

Palestinian Fair Trade olive oil for sale, £5 for 500ml, £6.50 for 750ml.

Film nights £6 including meal, such as children's world cinmea, cult films, private groups, inside or out.

Children welcome, toys and swing in the garden. Cash or cheque only. Waste is composted.

Pepperton UK

Open:

Tue–Sat 12.00–22.00
Sun–Mon closed (except for group bookings of 10 or more)
Licensed. Therapy rooms upstairs
www.peppertonuk.co.uk menu and gallery info

25 Selhurst Road
London SE25 5PT
(opposite the Selhurst Arms)
Tel: 020-8683 4462
Tube: Selhurst BR,
buses 75, 157

Vegetarian restaurant and contemporary art gallery. The red front makes it unmissable. A favourite of Croydon Vegans who tell us the food is delicious and most artistically presented, looking more attractive even than some of the paintings and delightful photographs. There are two upstairs rooms for the gallery, and the beautiful staircase was made by the owner from a fallen fruit tree from France. The owner-manager has a huge smile. Vegan and wheat-free items are marked on the menu and you can call ahead with any special requests. Vegan cake specialists, including wheat, gluten or sugar-free. Organic where possible.

Starters and salads £3–4.50 include mung bean pakoras on a bed of fresh salad; hummus with pitta and crudités; Pepperton salad of avocado, artichoke, tomato and kalamati olives; garlic mushrooms with olive bread. Soup with bread £5.

Main courses are no more than £7 such as almond and vegetable fried rice with spinach dhal; West African stew; pizzas; wild rice with vegetable curry. Jacket potato with beans £4.50,.

Double chocolate fudge cake, walnut cake, mocha cake £2.75, fruit cake £3, fruit crumble £3, dairy-free ice-cream £2.50.

Teas and herb teas £1, large pot £2.50, hot chocolate £1.50, all kinds of coffees £1.10–1.90. Mineral water and soft drinks £1–1.75. House wine £9.50 bottle, £2.20 glass. Fruit and organic wines £11.50. Organic beers £2.20–£2.75.

Service charge not included other than 10% for groups of four or more.

If you like to look at art with your food, you'll probably like Pogo Cafe or Wild Cherry in East London.

Pili Pili

Indian vegetarian restaurant

26 Embassy Court, **Welling**, Kent
DA16 1TH (mid-way between
Greenwich and Dartford)

Tel: 020-8303 7636

Open: *Tue–Thu* 11.00–21.30
Fri–Sat 12.00–14.30
18.00–23.00
Mon closed
(except bank holidays)

Train: Welling
www.pili-pili.co.uk

Indian vegetarian restaurant
with some Chinese food on
the way out of London
towards Canterbury and
Dover. Much of the food is
vegan and they can make
non-vegan items with soya
milk on request.

Over 35 bites £3.50–9.95
include uttapam lentil pizza,
dosas, dhokla rice and lentil
pancake, lentil doughnuts,
pani puri, bhel puri, chilli
corn on the cob, potato
fritters, idli, samosas, sev
puri, spring rolls.

Main specials include potato
curry with daal bhajia £4.50,
sag aloo £5.95, vegetable
sizzler £8.50, or veg with
rice, noodles and rice cutlet.
Indo-Chinese soups and
dishes such as Szechuan
noodles with veg, sweet and
sour veg £4.50.

Desserts £2.50-3.95 include
carrot halwa, lychees.

Tea £2, cappuccino £2.50.
Sodas £1. Seasonal fresh
juices £2.95. Wine £3 glass,
£11.50-14.50 bottle. Visa,
MC. Children welcome, 2
high chairs.

Swad

Indian Gujarati vegetarian restaurant

850 London Rd, **Thornton Heath**,
Surrey,CR7 7PA

Tel: 020-8683 3344

Open: *Tue–Thu* 10.00–21.00
Fri–Sat 10–22.00
Sun 10.00–21.00
Mon closed

Train: Norbury, West Croydon

Newly refurbished Jan 2007.
Minimum £4.95 to eat. Cobra
and Fosters beer £3.50 large,
£1.50-1.75 small. Children
welcome, high chair. MC,
Visa. Outside catering up to
2,000 people.

Lewisham Market, SE13

Fruit & veg street market

Lewisham High Street, north end
Open: *Mon–Sat* 06.00–16.30

Fantastic value and choice.

Mantanah Thai Cuisine

Thai restaurant

2 Orton Buildings, Portland Rd,
South Norwood, SE25 4UD

Tel: 020-8771 1148

Open: *Tue-Sun* 18.00-23.00
      Mon   closed

Train: Norwood Junction BR
       (Thameslink)

Thai restaurant in deepest south London towards Croydon. Like many Thai restaurants, this one has as many veggie dishes as some vegetarian restaurants.

Starters £3.50-4.70 such as spring roll, golden veg with pepper, sweet potato and plum sauce, deep fried pumpkin, tom yum soup, spicy mushrooms with coconut milk.

Main dishes £3.25-5.45 take-away, add 30p eat in, include the Thai classics of red and green curry £5.25-6.95 plus steamed, coconut or sticky rice £1.65-3.50. Mixed veg £3.75-4.00. You could also try the exotic spicy banana flower with oyster mushrooms and steamed sweet potato. Choice of salads. Wine £2.75 glass, £8.95 bottle. Beers include Thai Singha. Delivery over £15, 10% discount if you collect.

Ambala, Plumstead

Vegetarian sweet shop

62a High Street, **Plumstead**
London SE18 1SL

Tel: 020-8317 0202

Open: *Mon-Sun* 11.30-22.30

Train: Plumstead BR
www.ambalafoods.com

Indian sweets and savouries to take away.

Health Matters

Healthfood shop

47 Lordship Lane, **Dulwich**
London SE22 8EV

Tel: 020-8299 6040
      020-8299 4232 therapies

Open: *Mon-Sat* 9.00-18.30
      Sat   9 00_18.00
      Sun   10.30-16.30

Basic wholefoods including wheat-free, organic, Fair Trade. No take-away.

Bodycare ranges include Dr Hauschka, Organic Pharmacy, Weleda, Lavera, Jäson. BioD and Earth Friendly clearning products.

Supplements, essential fatty acids, herbal remedies, homeopathy. Dulwich Therapy Rooms are in same building by appointment or drop in for masseur, osteopathy and homeopathy.

Provender Wholefoods

Wholefood store, vegetarian cafe and organic bakery

103 Dartmouth Road, **Forest Hill**
London SE23 3HT

Tel: 020-8699-4046

Open: *Mon–Sat* 8.30-18.30
Sun 10.30-16.30

Train: Forest Hill BR
www.provender.org.uk

Friendly wholefood store and café with vegetable bake and pasties, salads and rolls to take away. They make their own organic bread including rye and spelt. Organic fruit and veg arrives Thursdays. Ecover cleaning products, supplements, homeopathic, books. Outside catering. MC, Visa.

Sheel Pharmacy

Health food shop & pharmacy

312-314 Lewisham Road
Lewisham, London SE14

Tel: 020-8297-1551

Open: *Mon–Fri* 9.00-19.00
Sat 9.00-18.00
Sun closed

Not just a pharmacy, they have savoury take-aways and cakes, including vegan and a wide range of vegan foods and cosmetics. Homeopathy. Ecover, BioD and Earth Friendly cleaning products.

10% discounts for Vegetarian and Vegan Society members. Chiropodist and osteopath on by appointment, tattoo removal. Visa, MC.

Well Bean

Organic health food store

9 Old Dover Road, **Blackheath**, London SE3

Tel: 020-8858 6854

Open: *Mon–Fri* 9.00-18.00
Sat–Sun 9-17.00

Vegan manager so plenty of vegan grub including icre-cream cheeses, yogurts; meat substitutes such as Redwood, Frys, Biona, Taifun; Clearspot and Cauldron tofu; sprouts. Gluten-free range. No take-away.

Bodycare ranges include Green People, Faith in Nature, Pitrok, Weleda, Savakan, Zambesia, Botanica. Supplements include A Vogel, Nature's Plus, Viridian, Nature's Own, Nature's Aid, Weleda, Solaray, Lifeplan and others.

Ecover, BioD and Ecolino cleaning products and Veggiewash.

10% Vegetarian & Vegan Society discount with card. Visa, MC.

Well Being Foods

Wholefoods and organic shop

19 **Sydenham Road**
London SE26 5EX

Tel: 020-8659-2003

Open: *Mon–Sat* 9.00-18.00
Sun closed

Complete selection of whole foods and organic fruit and veg. Also take-away pies, pasties, salads, fresh breads and some cakes including vegan slices. Good freezer selection. Body care and household products range. Natural remedies, homeopathy, vitamins.

GNC, Bromley

Health food shop

Unit 254, The Glades, **Bromley**, Kent BR1 1DN

Tel: 020-8290 5938

Open: *Mon–Sat* 9.00-18.00
Thu till 21.00
Sun 10.00-17.00

Specialise in bodybuilding.

Lush

Cruelty-free cosmetics

The Glades Shopping Centre, **Bromley**, BR1 1DN

Tel: 020-84661836

Bluewater, Unit LO51
Bluewater Park, Hedge End Rd
Kent DA9 9SG

Tel: 01322-427 951

Hand-made cosmetics, most of them vegan, see p.69.

Neal's Yard Remedies

Herbs and organic bodycare

32 **Blackheath** Village, SE3 9SY

Tel: 020-8318 6655

Open: *Mon–Sat* 10.00-18.00
Thu till 19.00
Sun 10.00-18.00

8 East St, **Bromley** BR1 1QX

Tel: 8313 9898

Open: *Mon–Wed* 10.00-18.00
Thu 9.00-20.00
Fri–Sat 9.00-18.00
Sun 11.00-17.00

www.nealsyardremedies.com

See page 86. The Bromley store has therapy rooms offering many treatments.

Holland & Barrett

Health food shop

31 Tranquil Vale,
Blackheath, London SE3
Tel: 020-8318 0448
Open: *Mon–Sat* 9.00–18.00
          Sun   10.00–16.00
www.hollandandbarrett.com
Vegetarian sausage rolls, pasties. Swedish Glace vegan ice-cream.

---

56 High Street, **Bromley**
Kent BR1 1EG
Tel: 020-8460 3883

---

33 Winslade Way, **Catford**
London SE6 4JU
Tel: 020-8690–3903
Open: *Mon–Sat* 9.00–17.30
          Sun   10.00–16.00
This branch has sos rolls, pasties, porkless pies, Swedish Glace non-dairy ice-cream.

---

198 Eltham High St, **Eltham**
London SE9 1TS
Tel: 020-8859 7075
Open: *Mon–Sat:* 9.00–17.30
          Sun   closed
No fridge or freezer so no take-aways, though plenty of snacks.

---

67 Riverdale Court, **Lewisham**
London SE13 7ER
Tel: 020-8297 9559
Open: *Mon–Sat:* 9.00–17.30
          Sun: 11.00–17.00
Fridge with pasties, freezer with vegan ice-cream.

Unit 19, The Aylesham Centre
Rye Lane, **Peckham** SE15 5EW
Tel: 020-7639 3354
Open: *Mon–Sat* 9.00–17.30
          Sun   10.00–16.00
Health food shop with lots of veggie snack food.

Unit 6, **Surrey Quays** Shopping
Ctr, Redriff Road, SE16 1LL
Tel: 020-7231 1043
Open: *Mon–Sat* 9.30–18.00
          Thur   until 20.00
          Sun   11.00–17.00
Some veggie sos rolls, pasties, porkless pies. Freezer.

---

81 Powis St, **Woolwich** SE18 8LQ
Tel: 020-8316 5490
Open: *Mon–Sat* 9.00–17.30,
          Sun   10–16.00

This branch has a fridge with pasties and freezer with vegan ice-cream.

Ambala Sweets, Croydon

Indian vegetarian sweet shop

250 London Road, **Croydon**
Surrey CR0 2TH
Tel: 020-8688 0707
Train: West Croydon BR
www.ambalafoods.com

Indian sweets and savouries.

Holland & Barrett

Health food shop

Unit 44, Ashley Centre, **Epsom**
Tel: 01372-728520
Open: Mon-Sat 9.00-17.30
          Sun   11.00-17.00
The frozen and chilled section has pastries, sosage rolls, but no sandwiches.

1098-99 The Mall, Whitgift Centre, **Croydon** CR0 1UU
Tel: 020-8681 5174
Open: *Mon,Sat*   9.00-18.00
          Tue   till 18.30
          Wed,Fri till 19.00
          Thu   till 20.00
          Sun   11.00-17.00
One of the larger stores with fresh take-away snacks such as pies and sos rolls, a big chilled and frozen section. Shampoos, aloe vera bubble bath, natural deodorant. Supplements.

Holland & Barrett

Health food shop

213 High Street, **Sutton** SN1 1LB
Tel: 020-8642 5435
Open: *Mon-Sat* 9.00-17.30,
          Sun   10.00-17.00
Limited fresh take-away delivered Wednesday and sells fast, like pies and pasties, some vegan. Also frozen/chilled section.

Lush, Croydon

Cruelty-free cosmetics

58 North End,
Croydon CR0 1UG
Tel: 020-8681 7332

Hand-made cosmetics, most of them vegan, see Soho for details.

GNC, Sutton

Health food shop

Unit 1-20 St. Nicholas Centre,
Sutton SM1 1AW
Tel: 020-8770 0073
Open: *Mon-Sat* 9.00-17.30
          Sun   11.00-16.30

Specialise in bodybuilding.

The Good Life

Health food shop

1 Waterloo Rd, **Epsom**,KT19 8AY

Tel: 01372-742095

Open: *Mon–Sat* 9-5.30
        Sun   closed

No take-away.

Julian Graves

Health food shop

2 Ashley Centre, **Epsom**,
Surrey KT18 5DA

Tel: 01372 729763

Open: *Mon–Sat* 9-17.30
        Thu   till 19.00
        Sun   10.30-16.30

Lots of dried fruit, nuts, snacks and sweets.

Noah's Health Foods

Health food shop

4 South Parade, Stafford Road,
Wallington, Sutton SM6 9AJ

Tel: 020-8647 1724

Open: *Mon–Sat* 9.00-17.30
        Wed   close 13.00
        Sun   closed

Tube:

Some take-away food. Freezer too.

Sloane Zone 320
(Victoria to Fulham)
Bayswater 332
Chiswick 336
Ealing 338
* Edgware 342
* Hammersmith incl 347
Shepherds Bush, Olympia 353
Harrow & Kenton 356
ounslow & Heathrow 362
Kilburn & Willesden 364
* Kingsbury 368
Notting Hill 371
Southall 375
Twickenham 376
* Wembley 378
Rest of Middlesex 388

WEST LONDON

Portobello Market page 373

Sloane Zone

The area between Hyde Park and the river Thames, from Victoria and Knightsbridge in the east to Kensington and Fulham in the west, is posh London. There are stacks of fashion stores, embassies, million pound apartments, Sloane Ranger "It" girls (think Tara or Tamara), the Royal Albert Hall, Science Museum, Victoria & Albert Museum, Natural History Museum (dinosaurs!), but not a single vegetarian restaurant. Fortunately there are lots of lovely wholefood stores with cafes or take-away food, and mainstream restaurants that offer excellent veggie possibilities.

Rainforest Creations

Raw food stall in market

Chelsea Market, Duke of York Square, **Sloane Square** SW3

Open: *Sat* 10–16.00

Tube: Sloane Square

www.rainforestcreations.co.uk

Vegan raw food heaven with a big box of salad and savouries for £5, cakes £3. See Spitalfields (East London) for more info, or their website.

Organic Café

Vegetarian English and Thai Cafe

The Auction Rooms
71 Lots Road, **Chelsea** SW10

Tel: 020-7351 7771

Open: *Sun only* 12.30–17.00

Tube: Fulham Broadway

Veggie cafe at the back of an auction room offering a very different Sunday out. It's inside the auction rooms where antiques are being sold, and it cannot be seen from the street. English and Thai dishes prepared by the vegan Thai proprietor Vip. Most food is wheat free.

Main course £4, salad £3, main course and salad £6. Try Thai stir-fry rice noodles (pad Thai), or Thai rice and veg curry. Organic teas, coffee and alternatives and flapjacks.

Children welcome. No credit cards.

Luscious Organic

Organic food store, cafe & juice bar, clinic

Open:

Mon–Fri	08.30–20.30
Sat	09.00–21.00
Sun	10.00–21.00

www.lusciousorganic.co.uk shop
www.chienergy.co.uk clinic

240-242 Kensington High St
London W8 6NE
(opposite Odeon cinema)

Tel: 020-7371 6987

Tube: Earls Court,
High Strett Kensington

See map on page 349

Big organic food store with cafe and juice bar at the Earls Court Road end of Kensington High Street. Predominantly vegetarian apart from some baby foods. Lots of Fair Trade stuff especially tea, coffee and chocolate.

The cafe has Laura's Idea breakfasts. 4 soups £2.79–4.49, 4 hot dishes £5.99 for big plate with steamed brown rice and a big salad, such as Moroccan, Thai lentil curry, aduki bean casserole. Muffins, cakes, brownies, slices, cookies 79p–£2.49, some sugar- and gluten-free or vegan.

Lots of juices £2.29-3.49, wheatgrass shot 2oz £1.49. Thick smoothies £2.79. Lots of teas £1.69. Coffees or latte/cappuccino £1.69–2.89, soya or rice milk available. Huge range of sandwiches and salads including Laura's Idea, Taste Matters, Fresh, Just, £1.99-4.29.

The shop has some fruit and veg and lots of organic bread including All Natural Bakery, Artesan, Stamp Collection gluten-free, South London Bakery, Halls. Plenty of tofu, seitan, cutlets, veggie sausages including Paul's, Clearspot, Taifun, Demeter, Dragonfly organic deep-fried, Topas. Swedish Gace vegan ice-cream.

Organic and vegan wines.

Cleaning products include Natural Clean (great new brand), Ecolino, Earth Friendly, BioD.

Bodycare includes the whole range of Dr Hauschka, Weleda, Jäson, Faith in Nature, Skincare Cafe, Avalon, Lavera, Urtekram, Green People.

The whole range of Viridian supplements. Essential oils.

Clinic offering shiatsu, face reading, feng shui, macrobiotic nutrition advice etc.

Planet Organic, SW6

Natural and organic super-market and vegetarian cafe

Open:

Mon–Fri	08.30–20.30
Sat	10.00–19.00
Sun	11.00–17.00

Children welcome, high chairs and toys. MC, Visa, Amex

25 Effey Road, **Fulham,** London SW6

Tel: 020-7731 7222

Tube: Fulham Broadway

The third Planet Organic opened in 2004, just a minute from Fulham Broadway, with a juice bar and café. Most dishes, snacks and cakes have ingredients displayed and if they're gluten-, sugar-free or vegan.

The groceries section has all organic fruit and veg and just about everything for veggies including many kinds of tofu and tempeh, fake meat, pastas including spelt, quinoa and amaranth, macrobiotic Japanese foods, vegan ice-creams, vegan and vegetarian wines and beers.

The vegetarian café section is open throughout the day and all ingredients come from the shop. Eat in or out, hot and cold and salad, mix what you want. Small box £3.25, medium £5, large £6. All organic cakes, sugar and gluten-free muffins, vegan chocolate cake

Juice bar with smoothies

£2.85–£4.50. Cappuccino £1.75, and three kinds of soya milk including vanilla, or rice milk.

Health and bodycare has qualified staff to advise you in nutrition, homeopathy, herbs etc. Vitamins, herbs, tinctures, homeopathy, floral essences and aromatherapy. Suncream, shampoos and conditioners, makeup such as Dr Hauschka, Living Nature, Elysambre, Lavera, Weleda, Green People, Barefoot Botanicals, Urtekram, Jäson.

Magazines and books including Vegetarian Guides, fitness, pilates, yoga products and dvd's.

A great place for presents such as pretty candles and incense. Chocolate and other treats.

If you like this you'll probably like their other stores in Westbourne Grove (West London) and Bloomsbury (Centre).

Sloane Zone **WEST**

Whole Foods Market

Organic wholefood supermarket

Open:

Mon-Sat	08.00-22.00
Sun	12.00-18.00
	Sunday brunch upstairs from 10.00

Children welcome. MC, Visa
www.wholefoods.com

in the old Barkers Dept Store
63-97 **High Street Kensington**
London W8 5FE

Tel: 020-7368 6100
Tube: Kensington High Street

Free parking if spending
over £100

Opened summer 2007, this first UK branch of the US chain is ten times the size of any other UK wholefood store at 75,000 sqare feet. There is a staggering range of healthy foods and a vast cafe area, but a lot more animal produce than you're probably usd to, particularly in the cafes. No artificial preservatives, colours, flavours, sweeteners or hydrogenated fats.

Some items are pricey like cups of chopped fruit in the fridge at £5-£8, but as at Fresh & Wild there are bargain self-serve grains and pulses such as organic lentils at 69p/pound.

The ground floor Provision Hall has a bakery, olives, take-away, flowers and 28 checkouts. The bakery makes artisan breads and has biscuits, tarts, muffins, cookies, pies, cakes and pastries. Look out for vegan sushi £3.75 in the chiller by the take-away section.

Upstairs are several cafes with juices, smoothies, coffees, Middle Eastern mezze, pizzas, salads, vegan sushi, tapas, puddings and cakes. Excellent soya cappuccino/ latte £1.89 (cheaper than Starbucks!) Biodegradable unbleached containers for take-away

The lower level Market Hall has a vast range of organic fruit, veg and herbs, much of it delivered from small local producers or sourced in London markets. Groceries include anything you could buy at Fresh & WIld and a whole lot more. Bulk foods, frozen foods, body care, enviro-cleaning products, cookbooks and housewares, eco-clothing, even hand-baked organic treats for pets.

Also treatment and community rooms.

If you like this you'll probably like the Fresh & Wild stores around London that are also now owned by Wholefoods Market.

WEST Sloane Zone

Amaya SW1

Omnivorous Indian grill restaurant

15 Halkin Arcade, Motcomb Street, **Knightsbridge** SW1X 8JT
Tel: 020-7823 1166

Open: Mon-Sat 12.30-14.15
18.30-23.15
Sun 18.30-22.00

Tube: Knightsbridge

Sister restaurant to the well-known Chutney Mary and Veeraswamy, this is an unusual and very upmarket Indian with grilled vegetarian dishes, so without all the ghee in other Indian restaurants.

Vegetarian tasting menu £22 lunch, £35.50 dinner, with green mango and raw papaya salad, corn kebab, sweet potato chaat, stuffed peppers, spinach fig tikki, spiced vegetables, veg biryani, grilled mango and dhal. A la carte £10 per dish, £5.25 small dishes.

Wine from £19.50 bottle, £5.10 glass. Children should come at 18.30 in order to finish by 20.15, no high chairs. MC, Visa, Amex.

Giraffe, Kensington

Omnivorous global restaurant

7 **Kensington High Street**, London W8 5NP

Tel: 020-7938 1221

Open: Mon-Fri 08.00-23.00
Sat 09.00-23.00
Sun 09.00-22.30
Bank hols 09.00-22.30

Tube: Kensington High Street
Children welcome, kids' menu
www.giraffe.net

Good selection of vegetarian dishes. See Bloombsury branch (central London) for menu.

Hare & Tortoise, Kensington

Noodle and sushi restaurant

373 High St, **Kensington** W14 8QZ (between Warwick Gardens & Warwick Rd, near Olympia)

Tel: 020-7603 8887

Open: Sun-Thu 12.00-23.00
Fri-Sat 12.00-23.30

Tube: Olympia
w3.hareandtortoise-restaurants.co.uk

Huge portions and low prices. Starters £2.90-4.20 include green salad, tofu "duck" pancakes, spring rolls, Chinese greens, edamame steamed soy beans. Miso soup £1.60. Veggie mains £4.75-5.75

include deep-fried tofu and vegetable ramen in soup (like the massive bowls at Wagamama only cheaper); chow mein with tofu and Chinese veg; satay mixed veg and tofu with noodles and sesame.

Freshly pressed juices £1.90-2.10. Wine from £10 bottle, £2.50-3.40 glass. Sake or plum wine £3. Oriental beer from £1.60. Tea £1, coffee £1.20.

No cheques, only cash or card (surcharge of 30p if under £10). Optional 10% service charge for groups of 6+.

Jacob's

Mediterranean omnivorous restaurant

20 **Gloucester Rd**, SW7 4RB (between Cromwell Rd and Kensington Rd)

Tel: 020-7581 9292

Open: *Mon-Sun* 08.00-23.00

Tube: Gloucester Road

A selection of most vegetarian Persian, Armenian and Mediterranean dishes, around 65-70% organic.

Choose your food at the counter from 25 salads, 3 choices on a small plate £7, 6 choices large £10.

Organic home-made cakes and toast for breakfast.

Desserts around £3 include fruit salad and dairy-free cakes, some without eggs.

Organic wine and beer. Wine from £13 bottle, £3.50 glass. Children welcome, high chair. MC, Visa, Amex. Pay and display parking, free after 18.30. Outside catering.

Leon

Omnivorous cafe & take-away

136 Brompton Road, **Knightsbridge** SW3 1HY

Tel: 020-7589 7330

Open: *Mon-Fri* 08.00-23.00
         Sat 09.00-23.00
         Sun 10.00-22.00

Tube: Knightsbridge

www.leonrestaurants.co.uk

New fast food bar with lots of great value veggie food. See Soho branch (page 67) for details or check their website for the full menu.

Le Pain Quotidien

Omnivorous French cafe and bakery

9 Young St, **Kensington** W8 5EH

Tel: 020-7486 6154

Open: *Mon-Fri* 07.00-22.00
Sat-Sun 08.00-22.00
Band hol 08.00-21.00

Tube: High Street Kensington
www.lepainquotidien.com

Next to Wholefoods Market and sister to the original branch in Marylebone, this cafe-style restaurant is an exception to the rule that French and veggie do not go together. Tofu salad £6.95 comes with plenty of tofu with various sauces and hefty wedges of filling bread. Two veggie/vegan soups £2.55 small, £4.95 large. Finish with vegan blueberry muffins or mint tea.

Le Pain Quotidien

Omnivorous French cafe and bakery

201-203 **Kings Rd**, SW3 5ED
(corner Oakley St, opp Fire stn)

Tel: 020-7486 6154

Open: *Mon-Fri* 07.00-22.00
Sat 08.00-22.00
Sun/*BH* 08.00-19.00

Tube: South Kensington,
Sloane Square
www.lepainquotidien.com

As above.

Le Pain Quotidien

Omnivorous cafe and bakery

15-17 Exhibition Road
South Kensington SW7 2HE

Tel: 020-7486 6154

Open: *Mon-Fri* 07.00-22.00
Sat 08.00-22.00
Sun 08.00-19.00

Tube: South Kensington
www.lepainquotidien.com

As above.

Wagamama Kensington

Omnivorous Japanese

Lower Ground Floor, Harvey Nichols, 109-125 **Knightsbridge**
London SW1X 7RJ

Tel: 020-7201 8000

Open: *Mon-Sat* 12.00-23.00
Sun 12-22.00

Tube: Knightsbridge

26 High St, **Kensington**, W8 4PF

Tel: 020-7376 1717

Open: *Mon-Sat* 12.00-23.00
Sun 12-22.00

Tube: Knightsbridge

Omnivorous fast food Japanese noodle bar with over nine veggie and vegan dishes. For menu see Bloomsbury, Central London.

Greens Foods

Health food shop & take-away

11–13 Strutton Ground
off Victoria Street, **Victoria** SW1P

Tel: 020-7222 4588 / 5902

Open: Mon-Fri 08.00–18.00
Sat-Sun closed

Tube: St James's Park

One of the largest health food stores in London, with lots of take-away food, situated midway between Victoria Station & the House of Commons. Nearby are Buckingham Palace and St James's Park, where you could take some food for a picnic.

Wholesome and tasty foods covering a broad range of special diets. Take-away or heat up there £1–£4.50, including sandwiches, ready made meals such as salads, pasta dishes, Thai and Middle Eastern. Vegan cakes.

Extensive range of gluten and wheat-free products. Lots of supplements, herbals, homeopathic, sports and nutrition, essential oils and flower remedies. In store homeopath/herbalist/nutritionist/aromatherapist for consultation or advice on special diets. Toiletries, books, Ecover cleaning products.

Health Craze SW5

Health food shop

115 **Earls Court Road**, SW5

Tel: 020-7244-7784

Open: *Mon-Fri* 11.00–23.00
Sat 11–23.00
Sun 14.00–23.00

Tube: Earls Court

Health food shop that has similar range to their sister shop in Old Brompton Road but no take-away.

Health Craze SW7

Health food shop & take-away

24 Old Brompton Road
South Kensington, London SW7

Tel: 020-7589-5870

Open: *Mon-Fri* 8.45–19.45
Sat 9.30–18.00
Sun closed

Plenty of take-away food such as sandwiches, pasties and samosas, also dried fruit, nuts and seeds. Ready meals and meat substitutes. Swedish Glace and Tofutti vegan ice-cream. Supplements. Good selection of cruelty-free cosmetics including Weleda and Dead Sea Magik.

Health Foods

Health food shop & take away

767 **Fulham Road**, London SW6
Tel: 020-7736 8848
Open: *Mon-Sat* 9.00-17.30
Sun closed

Health food since 1966 with take-away snacks, some vegan. They have a freezer section with vegan ice-cream. Cruelty free toiletries like Dead Sea Magik. Also books.

Vegetarian (but not vegan) sandwiches and meals £1.29-2.50 such as couscous with lentils.

Gluten-free and yeast-free and organic breads from different bakers. Big mother and baby section. Ecover and Biogreen clearning products. A few books.

Lots of vitamins including A Vogel, Lambert's, Solaray, Nature's Own, Biocare, Nature's Gold Algae. Homeopathy, Tisserand aromatherapy.

They have always been big on helping people to help themselves with natural healing and lifestyle since 1966. Top yoga teacher and homeopathic practitioner available by appointment, also relexologist/aromatherapist, aromatherapist/yoga, kinesiologist. Inner Potential Centre, with courses for personal development, spiritual healing and counselling.

10% discount to senior citizens Thursday and Friday, and for everyone every day 9-10a.m.

Holland & Barrett, Victoria

Health food shop

Unit 15, Victoria Place Shopping Ctr, Buckingham Palace Rd
Victoria, SW1W 9SA
Tel: 020-7828-5480
Open: *Mon-Fri* 08.00-20.00
Sat 9.00-19.00
Sun 11.00-18.00
Tube: Victoria

Health food store at the back of Victoria rail station upstairs in the shopping centre where you can stock up on the way to the National Express and Eurolines coach station. There is a Sainsbury's supermarket opposite and a branch of Books Etc nearby for your travel guides.

73 Kings Rd, **Chelsea** SW3 4NX
Tel: 020-7352 4130
Open: *Mon-Sat:* 9.00-19.00
Sun: 11.00-18.00

As well as the usual foods,

this store also offers monthly allergy testing, call ahead. No take-away.

---

192 **Earls Court Rd**, SW5 9QF

Tel: 020-7370 6868

Open: *Mon-Sat* 9.00-19.00
      Sun   11-17.00

Health food store with lots of veggie snacks and fridge with sos rolls.

---

220 **Fulham Rd**, SW10 9NB

Tel: 020-7352 9939

Open: *Mon-Fri* 9.00-18.00
      Sat   9.00-17.30
      Sun   10.30-16.40

Health food store with lots of supplements and snacks. No take-away.

2-10 Jerdan Place, **Fulham**
London SW6 1BW

Tel: 020-7386 5568

Open: *Mon-Sat* 9-18.30
      Sun   11.00-18.00

Formerly a GNC. Fridge and freezer but no take-away.

---

167 **Kensington High St** W8 6NA

Tel: 020-7603 2751

Tube: High St. Kensington

Open: *Mon-Fri* 9.00-19.00
      Sat   10.00-19.00
      Sun   12.00-18.00

Handy for the park, a small store with fridge with drinks, take-away pasties, yogurt, tofu.

94a Brompton Road
Knightsbridge SW3 1ER

Tel: 020-7581 3324

Open: *Mon-Sat:* 9.00-20.00
      Sun: 11.00-18.00

Freezer and fridge with pasties and sosage rolls.

---

10 Warwick Way, **Pimlico**
London SW1V 1QT

Tel: 020-7834-4796

Open: *Mon-Sat* 9.00-18.0
      Sun   11.00-16.00

Take-away sos rolls and pasties. Wide range of supplements.

Neal's Yard Remedies, W11

Herbs and complementary health

121 Sydney Street,
Chelsea SW3 6NR

Tel: 020-7351 6380

Open: *Mon-Sat* 10.00-18.00
      Sun   11.00-17.00

Tube: South Kensington,
      Sloane Square

www.nealsyardremedies.com

Herbs and spices by weight, organic toiletries, natural remedies. Also therapy rooms offering over 20 kinds of healing treatments from acupuncture to yoga.

Lush

Cruelty-free cosmetics

Victoria Rail Station,
by base of escalators and
platforms 15-19,
Unit 42, Lower Concourse,
115 Buckingham Palace Rd
London SW1V 9SJ

Tel: 020-7630 9927

Open: *Mon-Thu* 8.00-20.00
Fri 08.00-21.00
Sat 10.00-19.00
Sun 12.00-19.00

Tube: Victoria

123 **Kings Road**, SW3 4PL
(opposite Burnsall Street)

Tel: 020-7376 8348

Open: *Mon-Sat* 10.00-19.00
Sun 11.00-18.00

Tube: Sloane Square

Hand-made cosmetics, most
of them vegan, see Soho for
details.

Montignac Boutique

Wholefood shop and café

160 Old Brompton Rd
South Kensington SW5

Tel: 020-73702010

Open: *Mon-Fri* 8.30-21.00
Sat 8.30-18.00
Sun 10.00-18.00

Wholefood shop and café
since 1994, with nothing
refined, no sugar, adhering
to the 'Montignac method',
the original low glycaemic
(GI) destination long before
Gillian McKeith.

Freshly cooked daily hot and
cold take-away with some
choices for veggies and
vegans such as eban dishes
for £3.95 including lentils,
canneloni and chickpeas;
flageolot beans; asparagus
or 3-bean soup. It's not all
veggie.

North End Road Market

Street market

South end of North End Road
below Lillie Road, **Fulham**

Open: *Mon-Sat* 7.00-17.00
Thu 7.00-13.00
Sun 11.00-17.00

Tube: Fulham Broadway

Lots of fruit and veg stalls
along the side of the road
which is not pedestrianised,
though the traffic can move
slowly towards the Fulham
Broadway roundabout. Just
past there is the third Planet
Organic store, with a brilliant
cafe area to tank up after
doing the market.

Queens Health Shop

Health food shop

64 **Gloucester Road** SW7 4QT

Tel: 020-7584-4815

Open: *Mon-fri*   9.30-19.00
        Sat   9.00-17.30
        Sun   12.00-16.00

Organic ranges and pre-packed veggie/vegan food to take away such as muesli, flapjacks and chocolate, but no fresh food available.

Large selection of vitamins, skin and body care. Ecover cleaning products.

Revital Health Place

Health food shop

3a The Colonnades, 123/151 Buckingham Palace Rd, **Victoria** SW1W 9SH
(entrance on Belgrave Rd, behind Victoria train station at entrance to Megabus & Green Line)

Tel: 020-7976-6615

Open: Mon-Fri   9.00-19.00
        Sat   9.00-18.00
        Sun   closed

Tube: Victoria

www.revital.co.uk

A great place to stock up before a coach or train journey. Fresh food counter wiht pasties, pizza and cakes. In-store juice and smoothie bar.

Gluten and dairy-free ranges, organic and vegan foods, organic chocolates, carob bars, sugar-free sweets. Macrobiotic foods and a large range of sea vegetables. This branch has organic beers, wines, ales and spirits.

Organic bodycare including Dr Hauschka. Nelsons aromatherapy products.

Food and herbal supplements. Sports nutrition. Trained staff can advise on products and you can book a free consultation with their qualified nutritionist. Lots of books. Healthnotes touch-screen information kiosk.

OTHER OPTIONS:

Randa Lebanese restaurant, 23 **Kensington Church Street**, W8. 020-7937 5363. Every day 12.00-24.00. Set lunch £12.

Rotana Lounge Lebanese restaurant, 3 Beauchamp Place, **Knightsbridge** SW3 1NG. Tel: 020-7581 3619. Mon-Sat 11.30-01.30, Sun 11.30- 23.30. Handy for the museums if you're on a Sloane budget. Mixed mezze plus main course £16, available till 6pm. Dinner £32. Menus on website.

www.rotanalounge.co.uk

Bayswater

Bayswater, on the north side of Hyde Park, does not have a vegetarian restaurant, but does have lots of hotels. It is convenient for **Paddington** Station for trains to the West of England and the 15-minute Heathrow Express. Here are some omnivorous places recommended by readers that offer a good choice of vegetarian dishes.

Bombay Palace

Indian omnivorous restaurant

50 Connaught Street
Paddington W2 2AA

Tel: 020 7723 8855
020 7258 3507

Open: *Mon-Sat* 12.30–15.00
18.00–23.30
Sun 12.30–15.30
18.00–23.00

Tube: Paddington, Marble Arch
Lancaster Gate

www.bombay-palace.co.uk

Ultra smart restaurant. Starters £5.40 such as onion bhajee, Punjabi samosa. 17 vegetarian mains £6.90–8.90 include tarka dal, Punjabi style chickpeas and potato, aloo gobi, okra, bitter gourd,

musroom and green peas, smoked aubergine, baby aubergine with raw mango. Rice £3.50–£4. Biryani £10.80. Tandoori naan or roti £2.50–2.80. Green salad £4.20. Discretionary 15% service charge. GM free.

Business lunch Mon–Fri. Sunday brunch. Private dining suite for up to 30. Cocktail lounge. Patio. Evening home delivery £2.50. MC, Visa.

Connoisseurs

Indian omnivorous restaurant

8 Norfolk Place, London W2
(nr Paddington station, between Praed St and Sussex Gardens)

Tel: 020-7402 3299

Open: *Every day* 12.00–24.00
Lunch 12.00–14.30
Dinner 17.30–24.00
Open bank holidays

Tube: Paddington

There's nothing vegetarian by Paddington station, but at least here there are all the usual Indian vegetable side dishes for £2.95 including chickpeas, spinach, spicy

Planet Organic, W2

Natural and organic supermarket and cafe

Open:

Mon–Sat 08.30–20.30
Sun 12.00–18.00
Children welcome
MC, Visa

42 Westbourne Grove, W2 5SH
(Queensway end)
Tel: 020-7727 2227
Tube: Bayswater,
Queensway

Organic wholefood supermarket, the only one in this street now the nearby Fresh & Wild has closed, with a juice bar and café. Most dishes, snacks and cakes have ingredients displayed and if they're gluten-, sugar-free or vegan. It's not all vegetarian, but the meat/fish counter is right at the back out of sight. No artificial additives in anything, no hydrogenated fat and no refined sugar.

Picnic heaven. Load up here with every kind of veggie food and heaps you never even knew existed. 15 aisles makes this one of the largest retailers of gorgeous organic foods, alcoholic and non-alcoholic drinks.

Juice and coffee bar. Hot food bar (no longer only veggie) and salads, eat in or take-away, box £2.80, medium £4.50, large £5.50, platter £7.50. Juices £2.75–£4.

Huge section devoted to health and body care, including vitamins, herbs, tinctures, floral essences, homeopathy, aromatherapy oils, suncream, makeup, shampoos and conditioners, including Barefoot Botanicals, Dr Hauschka, John Masters, Lavera, Living Nature, Green People, Jäson, Neal's Yard Remedies, Urtekram, Weleda.

Staff are very friendly and well-trained to deal with customer queries, many being practitioners or in training. Homeopath has a treatment room a couple of days a week.

Household goods including Ecover. Organic baby section. Yoga mats, bounce balls.

A great place for presents like pretty candles and incense, chocolate and other treats. Books section includes cookery, dietary, mother and baby and Veggie Guides. Their carrier bags are no longer plastic but GM-free compostable corn starch.

If you like this you'll probably like their other branches in Fulham (Sloane) and off Tottenham Court Rd (Centre).

potato or mushrooms. Rice £1.70-2.95. Veg biriani £5.95. Thali £8.95 with three veg of your choice, onion bhaji, samosa, rice and nan. Set lunch £6.95.

Licensed. Babies and children welcome. Air conditioning. Take-away service, free delivery within 3 miles. Visa, MC, Diners, Amex.

Durbar Tandoori

Indian omnivorous restaurant

24 Hereford Road
Bayswater W2 4AA

Tel: 020-7727 1947/5995

Open: *Sat-Thu* 12.00-14.30
Every day 17.30-23.30
Closed Fri lunchtime

Tube: Notting Hill Gate, Bayswater, Royal Oak

www.durbartandoori.co.uk

Open since 1956 and offering dishes from all over India. Starters £2.75 include bhajias, samosa, dal soup. Parsee vegetable dhansak with pilau rice £6.95. Mushroom or veg biryani £6.25. Veg curry, butternut squash bhajia, aubergine jalfrezi, hot veg jalfrezi all £4.15. Usual Indian veg side dishes £3.25. Rice £1.95-3.45. Tandoori stuffed naan or paratha £1.95. Desserts are all made with dairy

except seasonal fresh fruit salad £3.65.

Tea or coffee £1.45, mint tea £1.95, coffee with spirits £4.75. Freshly squezed orange or carrot juice £2.95. Soft drinks £1.95. Indian beers £2.95-4.45. House wine £3.15 glass, £10.95 bottle. MC, Visa.

Fresco

Omni Lebanese restaurant/

25 **Westbourne Grove**, W2 4UA

Tel: 020-7221 2355

Open: *Mon-Sat* 08.00-23.00
Sun   09.00-23.00

Tube: Queensway, Bayswater Royal Oak

2nd Floor, **Whiteleys**
ShoppingCentre, Queensway W2 4YN
(Juice bar only, no food)

Tel: 020 7243 4084

Open: *Mon-Sat* 10.00-20.00
Sun   09.00-23.00

Tube: Queensway, Bayswater

93 **Praed St**, Paddington W2

Tel: 020-7402 0006

Open: *Mon-Sat* 08.00-17.00
Sat-Sun closed

Tube: Paddington

A cross between a fresh juice bar and a small Lebanese

restaurant, Fresco serves a variety of juices, smoothies and milkshakes (unfortunately no soya milk – yet!), alongside a selection of sandwiches with Middle Eastern fillings and cold mezze dishes. They also have a number of hot main dishes, about half of which are vegetarian.

Kalamaras Restaurant

Greek omnivorous taverna

66 Inverness Mews
Bayswater, W2 3JQ

Tel: 020-7727 5082

Open:
Every day   12.00–15.00
                 17.00–23.30
          (last order 23.00)

Tube: Bayswater, Queensway

MC,Visa, Amex. Sofas.
Children welcome, no high chair.

Mediterranean taverna in a veggieless area on the north side of Hyde Park, close to Paddington Station. Lots of starters £3–3.70 such as scordalia potatoes with lemon juice and garlic, aubergine dip, or fresh artichoke hearts casseroled with broad beans and dill. Or concoct a good meal of starters. Vegetarian moussaka £9.80, made with layers of sautéed potatoes, aubergines, courgettes and mushrooms topped with bechamel sauce which can be omitted for vegans for a bit less money.

Holland & Barrett

Healthfood shop

32 Queensway, W2 4QW

Tel: 020-7727 6449

Open: *Mon–Fri* 9.00–20.00
      Sat   10.00–20.00
      Sun   11.30–20.00

Tube: Queensway

Some take-aways like pasties, but no sandwiches. Frozen foods including dairy-free ice-cream.

MORE IN BAYSWATER: Three Italian restaurant chains on Queensway recommended by a vegan reader:

There is an **ASK** pizza/pasta restaurant in Whiteleys Shopping Centre on Queensway that can serve veggie/vegan pizza and pasta. Tel: 020-7792 1977.

www.askrestaurants.com

Pizza Express at 26 Porchester Road W2 at the corner with Bishop's Bridge Road. Tel: 020-7229 7784.

www.pizzaexpress.com

Bella Italia at 55 and 108 Queensway and in the Whiteleys shopping centre.

www.bellaitalia.co.uk

Chiswick

Woodlands Chiswick

South Indian vegetarian

12–14 Chiswick High Road
London W4 1TH
Tel: 020-8994 9333
Open: *Tue–Sun* 12-15.00
　　　　　18-23.00
　　Mon closed
Tube: Stamford Brook
MC, Visa, Amex
Children welcome, high chairs
www.woodlandsrestaurant.co.uk

One of four branches of this excellent chain with chefs from India. Lunch set meal £7.50. Take-away lunch box £4.50. For menu see Marylebone (Central London).

Giraffe, Chiswick

Omnivorous global restaurant

270 Chiswick High Road
London W4 1PD
Tel: 020-8995 2100
Open: *Mon–Fri* 08.00-23.00
　　Sat 09.00-23.00
　　Sun 09.00-22.30
　　Bank hols 09.00-22.30
Tube: Turnham Green
　　Chiswick Park
www.giraffe.net

Good selection of vegetarian dishes. See Bloombsbury branch (central London) for menu.

Chidren welcome, kids' menu. MC, Visa.

As Nature Intended

Organic & health food shop

201 Chiswick High Road
Chiswick, London W4
Tel: 020-8742-8838
Open: *Mon–Fri* 9.00-20.00
　　Sat 9.00-19.00
　　Sun 10.30-18.30
Tube: Turnham Green
www.asnatureintended.uk.com

95% organic store that aims to combine the variety of a supermarket (over 5,000 products) with the product range found in traditional health food shops. Many items are suitable for those with food allergies such as sugar-, gluten-, salt- or yeast-free. Not completely vegetarian.

Bread and gluten-free muffins. Wide range of sandwiches and pies to take away. Many Japanese and tofu-based foods and tempeh.

Vegan and veggie wines are clearly labelled and there is a leaflet in case you're unsure what constitutes a vegan wine.

Herbal and homeopathic remedies, aromatherapy oils, beauty and skincare products. Vitamins and minerals. Lots of books.

Everyone in the remedies section is a practitioner or has had training. Certain days therapists offer treatments. Lots of information on recommended treatments for various conditions on their website.

Pay and display car park at front.

near Turnham Green underground, packed to the ceiling with hand-picked organic and natural products avoiding synthetic preservatives, and which the staff use themselves, including Dr Hauschka, Burt's Bees, Solgar, Biocare, Weleda, Barefoot Botanicals.

Wide range of organic breads, dairy-free cheese, cream cheese and ice-cream. Lots of Fair Trade products including Palestinian olive oil. A whole wall of teas. Organic herbs and spices. Spirulina and green superfoods. Truly Scrumptious frozen baby food.

Natural remedies including Nature's Plus, Bioforce tinctures, Potters.

Ecover cleaning products.

The Natural Food Store
– Health My God Given Wealth

Wholefood shop

41 Turnham Green Terrace
London W4 1RG

Tel: 020-8995-4906

Open: *Mon-Fri* 9.30-18.00
Sat 9.30-17.30
Sun closed

Tube: Turnham Green

Friendly wholefood shop

Holland & Barrett

Healthfood shop

416 Chiswick High Rd
London W4 5TF

Tel: 020-8994-1683

Open: *Mon-Sat* 9.00-17.30
Sun 11.00-16.00

Small take-away section and some frozen food available at this store.

Ealing

Bella Italia, Ealing

Omnivorous Italian restaurants

36 New Broadway, W5 5AH
Tel: 020-8579 7089
Open: *Mon–Thu* 08.00–23.00
Fri–Sat 08.00–23.30
Sun 09.00–22.30
Tube: Ealing Broadway

---

45 The Mall, Ealing W5 3TJ
Tel: 020-8840 5888
Open: *Sun–Thu* 09.30–23.00
Fri–Sat 09.30–23.30
Tube: Ealing Broadway (closest)
Ealing Common
www.bellaitalia.co.uk

As Ealing is bereft of veggie restaurants, these are a possibility when you're out with a gang of carnivores.

Toasted focaccia topped with veggies £4.10, soup of the day £3.75, garlic bread for 2 or 3 to share £4.95, marinated olives £1.95, pasta and pizzas £5.75–7.95. Lots of desserts but we couldn't see any vegan ones.

Wine from £11.75 bottle, £3.25–4.25 glass. Beer and cider £2.95–3.55. Pot of tea £1.70. Coffees, hot choc £1.55–1.95.

Butler's Thai Cafe

Omnivorous Thai restaurant

14 St Mary Road, Ealing Green
London W5 5ES
Tel: 020-8579 8803
020-8840 7893
Open: *Mon–Sun* 17.30–23.00
Tube: South Ealing

18 veggie dishes on the back page of the menu, £3.95–4.50, such as deep fried beancurd or mixed veg, soups, salads, red or green curry, sweet & sour veg, rice noodles with mixed veg. Fully licensed. Free delivery within 2 miles (then £1/mile) 18.30–22.00, minimum £15.

Hare & Tortoise, Ealing

Noodle and sushi restaurant

38 Haven Green, Ealing W5 2NX
Tel: 020-8810 7066
Open: *Mon–Sun* 12.00–23.00
Tube: Ealing Broadway
w3.hareandtortoise-restaurants.co.uk

Huge portions and good prices. Starters £2.90–4.20 include green salad, tofu "duck" pancakes, spring rolls, Chinese greens, edamame steamed soy beans. Miso soup £1.60. Veggie mains £4.75-5.75 include deep-fried tofu and vegetable ramen in soup (like the massive bowls at Wagamama only cheaper); chow mein with tofu and Chinese veg; satay mixed veg and tofu with noodles and sesame.

Freshly pressed juices £1.90-2.10. Wine from £10 bottle, £2.50-3.40 glass. Sake or plum wine £3. Oriental beer from £1.60. Tea £1, coffee £1.20. No cheques, only cash or card (surcharge of 30p if under £10). Optional 10% service charge for groups of 6+.

Pizza Express

Omnivorous Italian restaurant

23 Bond Street, Ealing W5 5AS

Tel: 020-8567 7690

Open: *Mon-Sun* 11.30-24.00

Tube: Ealing Broadway 6 mins
www.pizzaexpress.com (menu)

Unusual nibbles £1.75-1.95 are roasted nuts and seeds with chilli, rock salt and rosemary £1.95, or marinated Italian tomatoes £1.85. Bruschetta £3.50, broad bean salad £3.85, pasta or pizza £6.95-8.95.

Lots of desserts, but nothing looks vegan and some including the sorbet aren't even labelled vegetarian.

Wine from £11.75 bottle, £6.25 half bottle, £3.20-4.10 glass. Beer or low alcohol beer £2.25-3.10. Soft drinks and juices £1.35-1.95. Teas £1.25-1.45, coffees and liqueurs £1.50-3.35.

As Nature Intended

Organic & health food shop

17-21 High Street, Ealing
London W5 5DB

Tel: 020-8840 1404

Open: *Mon-Fri* 08.30-20.00
Sat-Sun 09.00-19.00
Sun/ 10.30-18.30
Bank Hols

Tube: Ealing Broadway
www.asnatureintended.uk.com

Sister to the Chiswick store with the same gigantic range, this one opened in 2005.

Holland & Barrett, Ealing

Health food shop

6 Ealing Broadway, W5 2XA
Tel: 020-8840 1070
Open: *Mon–Fri* 08.00–19.00
Sat 9.00–18.00
Sun 11.00–17.00
Tube: Ealing Broadway

Freezer and fridge with take-away pasties.

Holland & Barrett, E. Bwy

Health food shop

61 The Broadway
West Ealing W13 9BP
Tel: 020-8840 7558
Open: *Mon–Sat* 9.00–17.30
Sun 11.00–16.00
Tube: West Ealing

Freezer and fridge with take-away pastries.

Millenium Healthfoods

Health food shop

Unit 50b Ealing Broadway Centre
Ealing, London W5
Tel: 020-8840-6949
Open: *Mon–Sat* 9.00–18.00
Sun 11.00–17.00

No fresh take away, but has a freezer counter. Also household goods, Ecover, body care products, supplements, homeopathic remedies and aromatherapy oils.

10% discount over £10 for Vegetarian Society members.

Stockwell Healthy Living

Health food shop

42 High Street, Ealing W5 5DB
Tel: 020-8840 4888
Open: *Mon–Thu* 9.00–20.00
Fri–Sat 9.00–19.00
Sun 10.00–18.00
Tube: Ealing Broadway

Veggie and vegan foodstuffs including organic fruit & veg. Take–away such as vegan pasties, jacket potatoes, fresh juice, tea, coffee. 2 seats and a table. No freezer.

Body and skin care. Supplements and sports

nutrition. Herbal remedies. Baby stuff. Some cleaning products.

There is an attached yoga and pilates studio and gym. Resident acupuncturist in this store, and a naturopath at their other store nearby, Stockwell Pharmacy.

MC, Visa. Loyalty card for regular customers.

Woodfield Organics

Organic fruit & veg box scheme

36 Woodfield Avenue, Ealing, London W5 1PA

Tel: 07847 450358
020 8998 1170

Open: *Mon–Sat* 9.00–17.30
Sun 11.00–16.00

Tube: West Ealing
www.woodfieldorganics.com
anne@woodfieldorganics.co.uk

Delivering fruit & veg to your door in Ealing and surrounding areas, from small organic suppliers who pick to order whenever posible. Lots of vegetable recipes on their website.

ALSO IN EALING: There are many restaurants in Ealing. These ones offer vegetarian dishes with vegan options and have been recommended by a local vegan reader.

Cafe Uno at 24 New Broadway, Ealing W5 2XA. Tel: 020-8567 9093.

The Thai Restaurant at 57 New Broadway, Ealing, W5 5AH.

Monty's Tandoori at 1 The Mall, Ealing Broadway, W5 2PJ.

Edgware

Celebrations

Vegetarian tapas bar & restaurant

100 High St, Edgware HA8 7HF

Tel: 020-8905 6167

Open: *Mon* closed
Tue–Sun 12.00–15.00
18.00–22.30
(last orders 21.30)

Tube: Edgware

Totally vegetarian Indian tapas and a dance floor for special occasions. Most food is cooked to order. Vegans beware some dishes contain Quorn made with eggs. Separate bar.

Hot or cold tapas from £1.50 such as bhel poori mix, masala papad £1.50, spicy peanuts or olives £2.50, corn chaat £3.95. Hot samosas, masala mogo, garlic chips, masala chips, bhajias.

Main courses £3.95–5.95 include mock veg chicken tikka or tandoori, sauteed sausages or jeera chicken. Mixed veg, veg keema, jalfrezi, dhansak. Rice from £2.50 to £5.95 for a biryani.

Lunch special thalis £6.95 and £9.95, evening £10.95.

Desserts all contain milk except carrot halva £2.95.

House wine £3.20 small bottle (a bit more than a glass), full bottle £9.95.

Children welcome, high chairs. Visa, MC.

You can hire the whole restaurant for minimum 60 to 100 people. They can cater for Jains (no onion or garlic).

Mayura Restaurant

Vegetarian Indian restaurant

38 South Parade, Mollison Way Edgware, Middlesex HA8 5QL

Tel: 020-8951 1093

Open: *Mon–Sun* 12.00–22.00
Fri–Sat till 22.30

Tube: Queensbury

Incredibly good value with prices that are amazingly low and a big menu of 100 items including tiffin and chaat. Big portions and tasty. Although there are a lot of lacto-vegetarian products on the menu, there is a decent

Mr Man

Open:

Mon–Fri   12–14.30 & 18–22.30
Sat–Sun   12.00–22.30

Visa, MC over £10. No alcohol.
Children welcome, one high chair.
10% service charge.
(Formerly called Chai)

236 Station Road
Edgware, Middlesex HA8 7AU
Tel: 020-8905 3033

Tube: Edgware
www.vegmrman.com menu
Free delivery within 3 miles,
minimum £12.

Almost entirely vegan, they specialize in an astonishing range of fake meats and lots of other dishes. The ideal night out for both reluctant and avid vegetarians, with 90 items on the menu. Hot dishes are labelled with 1, 2 and one with 3 red warning chillis.

Lunch buffet Mon–Sat (12–2.30pm) £4.50 with soft drink or tea, Sun and bank holidays (12–3pm) £5.50 with fruit salad too. Buffet take-out box £3 large, £2.50 small.

12 appetizers £2.50 to £4 including 8 soups, tempura deep fried veg, satay veg chicken on skewers, crispy tofu, crispy seaweed or tofu, dumplings, spring rolls, veg sesame prawn toast,dim sum, or a platter for £5.50 for minimum two people.

You will be spoilt for choice with over 40 main courses £5.50–6.00. Meat substitutes include crispy vegetarian beancurd duck with pancakes; veg lamb wrap; veg fish and veg chicken dishes; hot chilli veg chicken (that's the 3 chillis dish, if you fink you is 'ard enough); veg steak; sweet & sour veg pork. Vegetables include monk's veg in clay pot; spicy aubergine hotpot. Tofu dishes include with mixed veg and mushrooms; with veg and cashew; braised with mushroom and veg in black bean sauce. Indian hot masala mushrooms or curry mixed veg £4.50.

21 noodle and rice dishes £1.50–4.80 such as udon Shanghai style, or stir-fried greens and tofu with noodles.

Two set meals for two or more people: £8.50 with 4 starters, veg chicken with cashew, spicy aubergine, veg fried rice, mandarin toffee banana; £9.95 spicy (one chilli) Szechuan style with hot & sour soup, veg crispy duck, tofu, veg meat with chilli and garlic, veg chicken, fried rice, lychees.

choice for vegans and the manager/owner is very helpful.

14 Indian starters 30p–£1.20 include methu vadai, sambhar vadai, or try a Tandoori or Chinese style one £2.50 such as mixed tikka or Szechwan spicy mogo. 20 kinds of dosa and uttapam £1.25–2.25 and 20 more curry side dishes £1.25–2.99. 20 Indian and Chinese flavours of rice and biryani £1.25–2.99. 12 kinds of tandoori bread 75p–£1.99.

Tea 50p, coffee 60p.

Outside catering.

Satyam Restaurant

Vegetarian Indian restaurant

23 Queensbury Station Parade
Edgware, Middlesex HA8 5NR

Tel: 020-8732 4469

Open: *Tue–Thu* 12.00–22.00
Fri–Sat 12.00–23.00
Sun 10.00–23.00
(*breakfast* 10.00–12.30)
Mon closed

Tube: Queensbury

Sunday breakfast £3.99 eat as much as you like, potato curry, masala poori, jelabi, with chili, chutneys, dosa, idli sambhar, juices and masala tea.

A la carte usual starters £2.50–3.50 or try something different such as corn bhajiya or cassava with herbs, spices, peppers, garlic and Chinese sauces. Soups £2.75 include vegetable Manchurian, hot and sour, sweetcorn, mushroom, or tomato and vegetable.

Dosas 8 dosas £3.50–5.50 or king-size for a family £9.99. Gujarati thali £4.99, unlimited £6.99. Over 35 curries, side dishes, idli, uttappam, and Chinese dishes £2.99–5.50. Chinese platter £7.99. Pizzas made to order £4.99–8.50. Veg biryani £4.99. Rice £2–£2.50. Bombay style vegetable sandwich £2.50.

Freshly prepared juices £2.75–3.99 or a jug for £9.99. Water £1. Teas £1.25, Indian coffee £1.50.

Kids welcome, high chairs. Kids like their potato chips. Under 3 years no charge. Last orders 15 mins before closing. No alcohol. Some items without onion or garlic. Visa, MC.

Satyam Sweet Mart

Vegetarian Indian sweet shop

24 Queensbury Station Parade
Edgware, Middlesex HA8 5NR

Tel: 020-8952 3947

Open: Tue-Fri 10.30-19.00
Sat 09.30-19.00
Sun 08.00-18.00
Mon closed

Tube: Queensbury

www.satyamsweetmart.com

Next to Satyam vegetarian restaurant. Indian savouries and sweets including some vegan ones. Everything made fresh on site.

Vegetarian Guarati style outside catering, minimum 50 people, call for quote. www.laxmicatering.co.uk

Shay Naiy Sweet Mart

Vegetarian Indian take-away

11 North Parade, Mollison Way
Edgware, Middlesex HA8 5QH

Tel: 020-8905 6677

Open: Tue-Sat 10.00-19.00
Sun 09.00-16.00
Mon closed

Tube: Queensbury

Set meal deal £2.99 with choice of veg curry of the day, daal and rice with 2 chapatis or theplas.

Savouries are all vegan 40p-£1.75 including bhajias, rotis, kachori, khichi, mogo, samosas, spring rolls. Lots of Indian sweets sold by weight but none vegan.

Drinks 50p-£2.50. Outside catering.

Tamu Tamu

Vegetarian Indian Kenyan take-away

40 South Parade, Mollison Way
Edgware, Middlesex HA8 5QL

Tel: 020-8951 4322

Open: Mon-Sat 10.00-19.00
Sun 08.30-16.00

Tube: Queensbury

Chaluka Kenyan style food. Indian sweets, savouries, curries, snacks and take-aways, nothing over £3, including maize flour cakes with greens, beans and maize, some unusual bhajias, (such as banana, green chilli and spinach), toasted masala veg sandwich with chips, puris, samosas, spring rolls, masala mogo (cassava), falafel with chutney, idlis.

You can call in advance to place your order and collect within 25 minutes. Diwali and Christmas hampers. Catering for 10 to 1,000.

Diet & Health Centre

Health food shop

28 Watling Avenue, Burnt Oak
Edgware,.Middlesex HA8

Tel: 020-8952-9629

Open: *Mon–Sat* 9.00–17.30
Sun closed

Tube: Burnt Oak

No fresh take-away here but
they do have a good freezer
section with frozen meals
and vegan ice-cream.

Range of cruelty-free
toiletries. Ecover cleaning
products. Homeopaty, herbal
remedies, aromatherapy.

*The Gate, Hammersmith,
crème de la crème of veggie restaurants*

HAMMERSMITH
Shepherds Bush & Olympia

Hammersmith might at first glance seem like a huge round-about under a giant flyover. However as well as being an important conference and business centre, there are fabulous walks by the peaceful Thames, some great British pubs, and the Riverside Studios for arty cinema and theatre. A little to the north, **Shepherds Bush Green** has the Bush Theatre where many top music acts perform.

There are terrific vegetarian dining possibilities. **The Gate** and **Blah Blah Blah** are two of London's longest established vegetarian restaurants, the former up-market and popular with celebs, the latter very popular and now doing vegan desserts. **Sagar** is a great value Indian restaurant. Vegans flock from all over London to gourmet vegan restaurant **222** for its great value lunchtime buffet, 7 days a week. If you long for the much missed Country Life, whose lease ran out,

*222, West Kensington, crème de
la soya crème of vegan restaurants*

HAMMERSMITH
Shepherds Bush & Olympia

SHEPHERDS BUSH

NOTTING HILL (SEE P.371)

Wok p.355

Blah Blah Blah p.354

GOLDHAWK ROAD

Bush Garden p.354

GOLDHAWK ROAD

SHEPHERDS BUSH RD

EALING (SEE P.338)

SHEPHERDS BUSH RD

HAMMERSMITH

BEADON RD

Rainforest Creations p.352

Bushwacker p.352

Kings Mall Lyric Theatre

HAMMERSMITH

KING STREET

HAMMERSMITH

CHISWICK (SEE P.336)

DOWN P

Sagar p.352

The Gate p.350 Temple Lodge p.390

QUEEN CAROLINE ST

FLYOVER

RICHMOND (SEE P.289)

HAMMERSMITH

Holland & Barrett p.353

S.W.A. The Way to Stay p.397

then know that chef Ben Asamani hails from there, but his new restaurant is also open Friday night and Saturday and has wine.

Raw food fans can now get their fix from the **Rainforest Creations** stall on Thursdsay lunchtimes and some Saturdays. Look out for amazing salads and cakes.

The new **Bush Garden Cafe** in Shepherds Bush started out vegetarian but made concessions because of customer demand, so the more of us go there the more they can keep it veggie. This is a common problem for new places and a good reason to always support your local veggiepreneur.

If you're coming to a trade show at **Olympia** or **Earls Court**, most of the catering there is staggeringly awful, even at health trade shows, especially if you are a vegan. If you're lucky they might have some hummus salad sandwiches. Don't panic, as well as the new **Crussh** soup and salad bars, we've listed a few possibilities nearby such as the Lebanese shops, and there are restaurants in Kensington (see Sloane Zone).

KENSINGTON OLYMPIA

Olympia

Hare & Tortoise p.324

Luscious Organic p.321

SLOANE ZONE (SEE P320)

RD

NORTH END ROAD

222 restaurant p.351

Chef Ben Asamani at 222

The Gate

International vegetarian restaurant

Open:

Mon–Fri 12.00–15.00 (not Sat)
Mon–Sat 18.00–23.00
(last orders)
Sun closed
Visa, MC, Amex. Book at least 2 days ahead at the weekend:
hammersmith@gateveg.co.uk

51 Queen Caroline St
Hammersmith, London W6 9QL
Tel: 020-8748 6932
Tube: Hammersmith
Kids welcome, high chairs.
Menus at www.gateveg.co.uk
See map on page 348

Top class international vegetarian restaurant. A finalist for the Vegetarian Society's best gourmet UK vegetarian restaurant of 2004 and popular with famous veggies. Unique setting in an artist's studio with modernist leanings. Many vegan and gluten-free options, cleared marked on the menu, which changes frequently with the seasons. Beautiful courtyard tables in summer.

Nine starters £5, most vegan or can be, such as marinated Greek olives, soup of the day, beetroot and horseradish potato cake, sweetcorn fritters, warm root vegetable salad, Indian pancake. Mezze platter £14.50 (serves 2) with a selection of all starters.

5 mains, 4 vegan or vegan option, £8.50–13.75, such as wild mushroom rosti, a celeriac and potato rosti served on a bed of pan-fried Savoy cabbage, topped with sauteed girolles, pied blue, oyster and horse mushrooms, finished with a whiskey cep sauce; mussamen curry with pumpkin, baby onions, baby corn, mange-tout and pineapple cooked in a richly spiced coconut sauce, served with wild and basmati rice and a paw-paw salsa; aubergin teriyaki; tortillas. Pasta of the day. Side orders like rocket salad, French beans or roast potatos £2.95–3.50.

Seasonal specials such as the May 6-course wild food festival £40. 7 desserts, 2 or 3 vegan or vegan options, £4.50–£6, such as apple and blackberry charlotte and ice-cream.

Extensive wine menu, 3/4 vegan. House wine £12.75 bottle, £3.50 glass. Dessert wine £2.50–4.50.

Coffees, teas and herb teas £1.50–1.95, can do decaffeinated or with soya milk.

Open:
Every day 12–15.30 buffet only
        17.30–22.30 a la carte
Children welcome, high chairs
www.222veggievegan.com

222 North End Road, West
Kensington, London W14 9NU
Tel: 020-7381 2322
Tube: West Brompton, West
Kensington, Fulham Broadway
See map on page 349.

See map on page 349.

Head Chef Ben Asamani previously ran the kitchens at Country Life and Plant and now offers outstandingly tasty and healthy (organic where possible) cuisine with vegan desserts to die for 7 days a week. Lunchtime buffet £7.50, evening a la carte. Organic where possible.

Lunch buffet £7.50, with a selection of hot dishes and salad. Take-away box £4.95.

Starters £3.25-4.50 include soup; avocado with tomato sauce and vegan cream; black eye bean and tofu pate pancake with tomato chunks and cream sauce; pitta with dips; baked mushroooms in extra virgin olive oil with special oatmeal on a bed of salad with tartar sauce.

Main courses £7.50-10.50 such as marinated organic tofu baked in oat crumbs on tomato wholemeal spaghetti; vegan burger; chickpea curry; 222 Gardens, eastern meets Afro-Carib with plantain, okra, falafels, tomato salsa, baked aubergines, courgettes and crispy garlic bread; Seitan Stroganoff; Broccolini di Parma pancakes with tofu cottage cheese and pimento sauce; pasta with leek and wild mushrooms, in lime and garlic with cashew cream; tofu and mince burger; salad; chickpea curry; Ben's Special West Indian stir-fry.

Side dishes £1.50-2.20 include garlic bread, yam, baked plantain. Salads £1.95-4.75 include mixed leaf; broccoli and mushroom; Jerusalem artichokes and sundried tomatoes; tomato, tofu and cucumber; roast courgettes and aubergines.

Desserts £3.70-4.50 include vegan ice-cream, tofu cheesecake with warm vanilla soya dessert or ice-cream, cakes, pancake with vanilla-chocolate sauce.

House wine £2.50 glass, £10.50 bottle. Service at your discretion. 10% discount for Vegetarian/Vegan Society . Outside catering. Visa, MC.

WEST

Hammersmith

Rainforest Creations

Raw food stall

Lyric Square, King Street
Hammersmith W6

Open: Thur   10.00–15.00
       also 1st & 3rd Saturday

Tube: Hammersmith
www.rainforestcreations.co.uk

Vegan raw food heaven with a big box of salad and savouries for £5, cakes £3. See Spitalfields (East London) for more info.

Sagar

Indian vegetarian restaurant

157 King St, Hammersmith W6
Tel: 020-8741 8563

Open: Mon–Fri   12–14.45
               17.30–22.45
               (Fri – 23.30)
       Sat   12–23.30
       Sun   12–22.45

Tube: Hammersmith
Visa, MC, Amex.
Children welcome, 1 baby chair

South Indian vegetarian restaurant near the Town Hall. Starters from £3. Main courses £4.95–6.75 such as dosas. Thali set meal £9.95–12.45 with starters, curries and dessert.

Some vegan food as they use both vegetable or butter ghee in different dishes, and they have vegan mango sorbet dessert.

Wine £2.85 glass, £10.95 bottle.

There are new branches in Twickenham and Tottenham Court Road, see the latter (Centre) full page entry for more examples of dishes.

Bushwacker Wholefoods

Wholefood shop

132 King Street,
Hammersmith, London W6 0QU
Tel: 020-8748-2061

Open: Mon–Sat 9.30–18.00
Sun & bank holidays closed

Tube: Hammersmith

Vegetarian wholefood shop, completely GM free, with plenty for vegans. Organic fruit and veg. Good range of take-away ready-to-eat meals and salads, pasties, samosas. Speciality ranges include macrobiotic, gluten-free and Fair Trade. Non-dairy cheese, ice-cream.

Skin and body-care, books, natural remedies and aromatherapy oils. Vitamins include Solgar, Biocare, Vogel (Bioforce). Household cleaning products include Ecover, Ecolino and Earth Friendly.

Curent campaigning issues in the window such as the supplements directive.

Holland & Barrett

Health food store

Unit 5, Kings Mall, King St Hammersmith, London W6 0DP

Tel: 020-8748 9792

Open: *Mon-Sat* 9.00-17.30
Sun 10.00-16.00

Tube: Hammersmith

A few take-aways such as soya sausage rolls. Non-dairy ice-cream.

Crussh, Earls Court/Olympia

Omnivorous juice bar and cafe

Earls Court 1 Exhibition Centre Warwick Road SW5 9TA

Tel: 020-020-7370 8354

Tube: Earls Court

Earls Court 2 Exhibition Centre Warwick Rd SW5 9TA

Tel: 020-7370 8351

Tube: Earls Court

Olympia Exhibition Centre Hammersmith Road W14 8UX

Tel: 020-020-7598 2758

Tube: Kensington Olympia
www.crussh.com

Conference centres and exhibitions are generally rubbish for veggies and even worse for vegans. You might find a hummous sandwich if you're lucky and they haven't sold out. But at Crussh they make juices in front of you, have vegan soup, salads and sandwiches to eat in or take away.

There are Middle Eastern shops opposite Olympia where you can pick up nuts, pitta or flat bread and hummous, and fruit. Or walk a couple of minutes to Hare & Tortoise (see page 324).

For a fabulous buffet lunch take an hour out to walk to 222 vegan restaurant on North End Road and stuff yourself silly, or get a bus down to Hammersmith and eat at Sagar. In the evening it's easy to take a bus or tube to Soho where you'll be spoilt for choice for veggie venues, pubs, cafes and cinemas.

Blah Blah Blah

Vegetarian restaurant

78 Goldhawk Road
Shepherds Bush, W12 8HA

Tel: 020 8746 1337

Open: *Mon-Sat* 12.30-14.30
18.30-22.30
Sun closed

Tube: Shepherds Bush
Cash or cheque.with ID.
Bring your own alcohol.
Menu www.gonumber.com/2524

Long-established vegetarian restaurant on two floors near Shepherds Bush Green. International menu changes every 4 to 6 weeks. Now much more vegan-friendly with vegan-option dishes marked on the online menu and always a vegan dessert.

At least two hot or cold starters £5.45 such as rolled aubergine kofta, mushroom and aubergine timbali, salads, soup of the day.

Five main courses £9.95 – 12.95such as Thai green curry with basmati rice and fruit salsa; vegetable pie and chips with onion gravy .

Four desserts £5.45, always at least one vegan such as summer pudding or poached pears with vanilla ice-cream and chocolate sauce.

No booze so bring your own and pay £1.45 corkage per person. Fresh organge juice £1.50. NB: no credit cards.

Bush Garden Cafe

90% vegetarian cafe/deli and organic food shop

59 Goldhawk Road,
Shepherds Bush, W12 8EG

Tel: 020-8743 6372

Open: *Mon-Fri* 08.00-19.00
Sat 9.00-17.00
Sun closed

Tube: Goldhawk Road 1 min
Shepherds Bush

Newish almost veggie cafe and deli with lots of organic food and a garden. They started out 100% veggie but had to add a couple of non-veggie dishes to keep the customer numbers up, so please spread the word to your veggie friends.

Breakfast served till midday (Saturday till 14.30) from £3.10 such as home-made muesli, granola, builder's full English cooked veggie breakfast £4.80.

They specialise in salads £5-£7. Point to what you want in the deli counter such as pasta, butternut squash with sundried tomatoes, roasted peppers, beetroot with apple and cucumber, superfood salad with green beans and alfalfa. Soups £3.50 eat-in, £2.75 take-away. Hot dishes £3.50, though mostly with cheese.

Wheat-free and gluten-free cakes £2.50 in, £2.10 take-away. Freshly squeezed juices and smoothies £2.80 in, £2.50 out. Cappu/soyaccino or hot choc £1.85, industrial strength cappuccino £2.20. Tea £1.45.

Garden with play area for kids and toys. High chairs. Kids' menu.

The organic shop is GM free and has organic bread, granola, rice cakes, crisps, olive oil, coffee, soya milk, wine etc. Visa, MC.

Holland & Barrett

Health food store

112 Shepherds Bush Centre
Shepherds Bush, W12 5PP

Tel: 020-8743 1045

Open: *Mon-Fri* 9.30-19.00
Sat 9.30-18.00
Sun 11.00-16.00

Tube: Shepherds Bush

Opposite the Central Line tube station with some take-away savouries such as soya sausage rolls. Vegan ice-cream.

Wok

Omnivorous Chinese restaurant

167 The Vale, Acton. London W3

Tel: 020-8740 0888

Open: *Mon-Fri* 12.00-22.00
Sat-Sun 13.00-23.00

Tube: Shepherds Bush

Omnivorous Chinese buffet restaurant west of Shepherds Bush where you can eat as much as you like for just £5. Take-away box £3 or £4 large. It used to be called Vegan Thai Buffet and is still half vegetarian with stir-fried rice, spring rolls, tofu, stir-fry veg, soya meats and noodles.

Market Place

Vegetarian health food shop

8 Market Place
Acton, London W3 6QS

Tel: 020-8993-3848

Open: *Mon-Sat* 9.00-17.45
Sun closed

Tube: Acton Town

Fridge and freezer with veggie-burgers, sausages, vegan ice-cream. No take-away.Lots of sports nutrition stuff. Big range of vitamins, especially Solgar and children's. Cosmetics, especially Avalon. Aromatherapy supplies. MC, Visa.

Harrow

Man Chui

Chinese omnivorous restaurant

190 Kenton Rd, Middx HA3 8BL
(on corner of Villa Court Ave)

Tel: 020-8909 9888

Open: Mon-Sun 12-14.30,
18-23.30

Tube: Kenton

Chinese restaurant with extensive and tasty vegan section on the menu. Apart from the tofu and veggie dishes, there are many fake meat items, around £4.90 each. Wine £2.70 glass, £9.90 bottle. Children welcome, high chairs. MC, Visa, Amex.

Natraj

Vegetarian Indian take-away

341 Northolt Road, South Harrow, Middlesex HA2 8JB

Tel: 020-8426 8903

Open: Mon-Tue,
Thu-Sat 10.00-19.30
Sun 10.00-16.30
Wed closed

Tube: South Harrow

Indian vegetarian take-away with plenty for vegans.

Starters/snacks such as bhajias, sweets, samosas etc.

6 curries every day are vegan such as spinach and chickpea, okra and potato, cabbage and potato, soya bean, kidney bean and butterbean mix. A regular take-away box of curry is £2.50, large £3.50. Box of rice £1.50 and £2.50. Or get a box of half curry, half rice for £2 or £3, ideal for lunch.

Omshree Sweet Mart

Vegetarian Indian take-away

446 Rayners Lane, Pinner HA5 5DX (just north of tube)

Tel: 020-8868 9885

Open: Mon-Sat 10.00-20.30
Sun 10.00-17.00

Tube: Rayners Lane

A handy stop-off if you are changing between Piccadilly and Metropolitan lines or on your way to Uxbridge. (Don't forget to swipe your Oyster card in and out so it knows you did not go via central London.) Indian sweets and savouries such as samosas, rice and curry. A reader says the behl poori is good.

Pradip

Indian vegetarian restaurant & shop

154 Kenton Road, Kenton,
Harrow, Middlesex HA3 8AZ

Tel: 020-8909 2232
Shop: 020-8907 8399

Restaurant open:
      Tue–Sun 12–16.00
            18–22.00
Shop: *Tue–Sat* 10–19.00
      Sun   9–17.00
      Mon   closed

Tube: Kenton Road

www.pradipsweet.co.uk menus

Indian vegetarian restaurant with sweet shop next door. They specialise in Gujarati food from the west of India. You can eat well here for under £10.

All day buffet Fri–Sun £7.90 includes starter, main course and dessert, children up to 10 £5.90, no sharing. Also thalis £4.90, add £1 for a starter or dessert.

Being next to a sweet shop they're good at desserts, including Lebanese baklava, date rolls, vegan ladhu and coconut sweets.

Soft drinks, juices and hot drinks £1–2, have a jug of juice £4.50–5.50.

They use vegetable ghee in cooking and butter ghee in sweets. No alcohol. Visa, MC. Children welcome, 2 high chairs. Outside catering service. The restaurant takes party bookings of up to 110 people outside normal opening times.

Ram's Gujarati

Indian Surti vegetarian restaurant

203 Kenton Road, Kenton,
Harrow, Middlesex

Tel: 020-8907 2022
Open:
Every day 12–15.00 & 18–23.00
Tube: Kenton Rd 5 mins

Indian Gujarati vegetarian cuisine from the city of Surat. Around £8.99 for a thali with starter such as bhajias, papodoms, two curries or dahl from the menu, three djipatis, dahl and dessert.

They use butter ghee, but vegetable ghee is available.

Desserts include vegan halva. Milkshakes can be made with soya milk.

Wine £3.10 glass, £9.60 bottle. Beer 330ml £2.50, 660ml £3.80.

Wheelchair access and toilet. Visa, MC. Very child friendly, high chairs.

Sakonis

Vegetarian Indo-Chinese restaurant

5-8 Dominion Parade
Station Road, Harrow HA1 2TR

Tel: 020-8863-3399

Open: *Sun-Thu* 12.00-21.30
(last entry to restaurant)
Fri-Sat 12.00-22.00
Mon closed
(except bank holiday)

Same menu as Wembley branch with Indian and Chinese dishes. Buffet 12-3pm £7.99, 6.30-9.30pm £10.99. The buffet is a combination of the whole menu with 30+ items including starters and 3 desserts (which are not vegan). Or eat a la carte, average £9 for 2 courses.

Children welcome, 7 high chairs. No alcohol. MC, Visa.

Saravana Bhavan

Vegetarian South Indian restaurant

403, Alexandra Avenue, Rayners Lane, Harrow HA2 9SG

Tel: 020-8866 8350
Mobile: 0795 687 7077

Open: see website

Tube: Rayners Lane

www.saravanabhavan.co.uk

Opening after this book goes to press, a new branch of the East Ham restaurant. See East London for details or the website to find out if it's open.

Shayona

Vegetarian sweet shop

168 Pinner Road, Harrow
Middlesex HA1 4JP

Tel: 020-8427 5650

Open: *Mon-Fri* 10.00-19.00
Sat-Sun 10.00-18.00

Tube: Pinner
www.sayacaterers.com

Sweets and savouries such as samosas, kachori, spring rolls to take-away. Some of the sweets are dairy-free such rassgulla and rasso-malai.

Sri Rathiga

Vegetarian South Indian restaurant

57 Station Rd, Harrow HA1 2TY

Tel: 020-8863 8822

Open: *Mon-Sun* 11.00-23.00

Tube: Harrow & Wealdstone,
         Harrow-on-the-Hill

www.srirathiga.co.uk

Rasam soup £1.25. Starters from sambar vada £1.35-to cashewnut pakoda £3.95. 15 dosas and uttapam £2.50-3.95, family dosa £6.99. Rice and Indian breads £1.50-2.25, biryani £3.25. Thali 12-4pm £5.25, mini tiffin any time £4.99 with drink, mini masala dosa, mini uttampam, idly, vada, upma and sweet. Desserts £1.50-1.95.

Soft drinks and juices £1-1.95.

Outdoor catering with South Indian dishes prepared "at your doorstep."

Swadisht

Vegetarian Indian restaurant

195 Streatfield Road, Kenton, Harrow, Middlesex HA3 9DA (Honeypot Lane, by Woolworths)

Tel: 020 8905 0202

Open: Every day 12.30-23.00
         (last orders 22.30,
         close earlier if not busy)

Tube: Kenton Road

South, North, Gujarati Indian and Chinese dishes. A la carte, four people can have two courses for £30.

Starters and snacks £1.95-4.95 include samosas, bhajias, kachori, mogo or chilli chips, crispy coated mushrooms, Indian falafel with nan, many kinds of chaat. Dosas, idli or uttappam £3.95-5.25. Over 20 Indo-Chinese dishes £2.95-4.95 such as soups, spring rolls, sweet & sour veg, stir-fry aubergine, plus 20 kinds of rice and noodles. They even have Mexican tortilla chips, nacho or fajitas.

Desserts £1-2.50, they told us gulab jamun is vegan but it turned out not to be.

Fresh juices from £2.75. No alcohol. Two high chairs. MC, Visa over £10.

Veggie Inn

Vegetarian Chinese restaurant

123 Headstone Road
Harrow HA1 1PG

Tel: 020-8863 6144

Open:
Mon, Wed–Sat 12.00–14.30
Mon, Wed–Sun 18.00–23.00
Tue closed all day
Sun closed lunchtime

Tube: Harrow-on-the-Hill

Menu www.veggieinn.com

Really nice restaurant with almost 100 items on the menu including lots of vegan fake meat dishes. Desserts include vegan ice-cream and banana fritters.

No alcohol, bring your own £1 per person corkage. Children welcome, one high chair. Visa, MC. Themed evenings, e.g. Valentine's. Free local delivery over £15.

Bodywise Health Foods

Health food shop

249 Station Road, Harrow, Middlesex HA1 2TB

Tel: 020-8861 3336

Open: *Mon–Sat* 9.00–18.00
Sun closed

Tube: Harrow-on-the-Hill

Health food shop with focus on complete nutrition and complementary therapies. Health foods, chilled foods, gluten-free including bread. Full range of vitamins, minerals, supplements and sports nutrition. Lots of herbal and homeopathic remedies. Natural cosmetics include their own brand Eco Cosmetics. Books.

There is an in-house complementary therapy clinic with different practitioners visiting daily for reflexology, kinesiology, homeopathy, amatsu, Reiki, Thai and Swedish massage.

Bodywise Health Foods

Health food shop

65 Bridge Street, Pinner,
Middlesex HA5 3HZ

Tel: 020-8429 1336

Open: *Mon-Sat* 9.00-18.00
          Sun   closed

Tube: Pinner

See Harrow branch for details, also an in-house complementary therapies clinic.

Holland & Barrett

Health food shop

22-24 College Road
Harrow, Middlesex HA1 1BE

Tel: 020-8427 4794

Open: *Mon-Sat* 9.00-17.30
          Sun   11-17.00

Tube: Harrow-on-the-Hill

Health food shop with a few take-aways like pasties. No freezer.

Hounslow

Indian Deli

Vegetarian South & North Indian cafe

6 Cavendish Parade, off Bath Rd
Hounslow, Middlesex TW4 7DJ
(opposite Hounslow West tube)

Tel: 020-8570 2333

Open: Buffet lunch
   Mon–Sun 12.00–16.00
         18.00–21.30
   (doors close 21.00)

Tube: Hounslow West
(36 mins from Piccadilly Circus)

www.indiandeli.co.uk menus

If you like the bargain basic Indian Veg buffet in Islington, you'll like this friendly cafe even more with its more varied all-you-can-eat buffet. It may not take any longer to get to as there's no walk from the tube. Buffet £4.50, thali £4.

A la carte starters 50p–£1.50. Curries £3.50. Rice £1.50–2.50, biryani £3.50. Dosas £2.50–3.00. Salad £2. Plenty of vegan choices (some are hot!) often including a TVP dish and possibly a sweet.

Outside catering. MC, Visa over £10.

Sukhsagar Sweet Mart

Vegetarian take-away

171 Staines Road, Hounslow
Middlesex TW3 3JB
(due south of Hounslow West
tube at end of Martindale Rd)

Tel: 020-8572 4547

Open: *Tue–Sun* 10.00–19.00
    Mon   closed

Tube: Hounslow West

Bhel poori £1.75. Samosas, kachori 35p or 3 for £1, fried in veg oil. Hot meails such as rice and veg, thali, best to phone order.

Ambala

Vegetarian Indian sweet shop

123 Kingsley Road, Hounslow
Middlesex TW3 4AJ
(junction Taunton Ave)

Tel: 020-8569 6578

Open: *Mon–Sun* 10.00–19.45

Tube: Hounslow East

www.ambalafoods.com

Indian sweets and savouries.

Holland & Barrett

Health food shop

183–185 High Street, Hounslow
Middlesex TW3 1BL

Tel: 020-8572 6066

Open: *Mon–Sat* 9.00–17.30
          Sun   10.00–17.00

Tube: Hounslow Central

There are a freezer and
fridge with take-away food.

Unit 9a The Longford Centre
High Street, Feltham TW13 4BH

Tel: 020-8751 4474

Open: *Mon–Sat* 9.00–17.30
          Sun   11.00–17.00

Freezer and fridge with
vegan jumbo sos rolls.

Revital Health Store

Wholefood shop

154 High Street, Hounslow
Middlesex TW3 1LR

Tel: 020-8572-0310

Open: *Mon–Sat* 9.00–17.30
      Sun   11.00–16.00

Tube: Hounslow Central
www.revital.co.uk

Lots of organic food, a wide
range of toiletries and
cruelty-free cosmetics. They
have a take-away section
with pies, sos rolls, cutlets,
salads and burgers, some of
which are vegan.

Bodycare including Dr
Hauschka, cleaning
products, vitamins and
minerals, lots of sports
nutrition, herbal and homeopathy, aromatherapy.
Healthnotes touch-screen
information kiosk which you
can browswe and ask them
to print out any pages.

Giraffe, Heathrow 1

Omnivorous global restaurant

Terminal 1 Airside, Heathrow
Airport, Hounslow TW6 1QE

Tel: 020-8607 5980

Open: *Mon–Sun* 05.15–21.30
          *Bank hols*09.00–22.30

Tube: Heathrow 1–3
Children welcome, kids' menu
www.giraffe.net

Good selection of vegetarian
dishes. See Bloomsbury
branch (page 95) for menu.

Wagamama, Heathrow 5

Omnivorous Japanese restaurant

After security, departures level,
HeathrowTerminal 5, TW6 2GA

Open: *Mon–Sun* 05.30–23.00

www.wagamama.com

Opened March 2008. Enjoy
very filling veggie dishes
while your bags are sent to
Milan. See page 93 for menu.

Kilburn & Willesden

Bhavna Sweet Mart

Indian veggie & vegan take-away

237 High Road, Willesden NW10
Tel: 020-8459 2516
Open: *Every day* 10.00-20.00
Tube: Willesden Grn, Dollis Hill

Indian vegetarian and vegan take-away with 7 seats. Large portions of curry with rice £2, with naan £2.60. Parathas, bhajias and sweets.

Everything is made with sunflower oil except the sweets which use butter ghee.

Don't get there too late in the day in case all the best stuff's been scoffed, or pre-order your food by phone. They are even open on Christmas Day and New Year's Day if you feel like something different!

Saravanas

South Indian vegetarian restaurant

77-81 Dudden Hill Lane
Willesden NW10 1BD
(just up the road from Sabras)
Tel: 020-8459 4900
Open: *Every day* 12.00-22.30
 last orders
Tube: Dollis Hill

Buffet lunch every day till 3.30pm £4.25 including soft drink, coffee or tea. House wine £2.45 glass, £3.25 large, £11.95 bottle.

Children welcome, high chairs. Visa, MC.

Hugo's Restaurant

Omnivorous organic restaurant

25 Lonsdale Road
Queens Park NW6 6RA
Tel: 020-7372 1232
Open: *Mon-Sun* 9.30-22.30
Tube: Queen's Park

Organic omnivorous restaurant with vegetarian dishes marked on the global menu. They don't use any animal fat in cooking or preparation. Some veggie options may be vegan, but we advise vegans to phone first as the menu differs every day.

All-day brunch menu (till 4pm) includes a full English veggie (can be vegan) breakfast for £6.50, or pancake with maple syrup and/or fruit salad. Croissants and toast £3.50.

Lunch from 12.30-16.00 with daily special on the board, £2-£12, e.g. pasta £7.50, veg stir fry with brown rice £7.80, herb risotto £8.50, big soup £4.50.

Evening main courses £10.80-12.20 might include wild mushroom risotto with truffle oil, pasta, squash ragout, or white musrooms, lentils and tomato casserole. Side dishes at £3.80.

Desserts £5.50 but none vegan.

House wine £3.50 glass, £12.80 bottle. Children welcome, high chairs. 12.5% service charge. MC, Visa.

Human Nature

Health food store & take-away

25 Malvern Road, London NW6

Tel: 020-7328 5452

Open: *Mon-Fri* 9.00-18.15
      Sat   9.00-17.30
      Sun/bank holiday closed

Quite a lot of take-away food including pies of all kinds and sausage rolls, falafel, pastries.

They stock most veggie foods. Household products include Ecover and refills for the all-purpose clearner. Toiletries. Supplements include Now, Vtarite, Nature's Own.

The manager, Mr Nari Sadhuram, sells veggie remedies for various maladies such as jet-lag and hangovers, and is also a trained masseur so you can have a Swedish or an Indian head massage or make an appointment for a home visit.

Meeras Health Food Ctr.

Health food shop

2 High Street, Harlesden
London NW10 4LX

Tel: 020-8965 7610

Open: *Mon-Sat* 10.00-18.00
Sun closed

No fresh take-away but they have dried fruits, nuts and seeds, flapjacks. Freezer with soya ice-cream.

Vitamins and supplements. include Sogar, Now, Health Aid. Free advice on products. Bodycare. Ecover.

Mistry

Health food shop and pharmacy

16-20 Station Parade
Willesden Green, NW2 4NH

Tel: 020-8450 7002

Open: *Mon-Sat* 9.30-19.00
Sun closed

Tube: Willesden Green

Take-away food includes veggie and vegan sandwiches £1.79. Pharmacy and homeopath next door, sometimes acupuncture..

Olive Tree

Vegetarian wholefood shop

152 Willesden Lane NW6 7TH

Tel: 020-7328 9078

Open: Mon-Sat 10.00-18.30
(Sat -18.00)
Wed 13.00-19.00
Sun closed

Large take-away selection inc-ludes rolls and sandwiches and some meals such as Laura's Idea.

Large selection of fresh organic fruit and veg.

Flower remedies, vitamins and supplements. Bodycare. Ecover and refills for some. All displayed in a charming old worldly style wooden interior.

Revital Health Shop

Health food shop

35 High Road, Willesden NW10
(near Walm Lane)

Tel: 020-8459-3382

Open: *Mon-Sat* 9.30-19.00
Sun 11.00-16.00

Tube: Willesden Green
www.revital.co.uk

Lots of organic and special diet foods. Fridge and freezer section, take-away food includes pies and pasties, many of them vegan. Green & Blacks chocolate. Echinacea lolly pops!

Lots of vitamins and minerals and the nutritionist on site gives free advice on supplements. Sports nutrition. Book section. Health Notes software for customers to browse. Aromatherapy oils, homeopathy, Bach flower and herbal remedies.

Bodycare including Dr Hauschka. Cleaning products: Ecover, Enviroclean, Earth Friendly.

Mail order with freephone number 0800-252875.

Holland & Barrett

Health food shop

42 Kilburn High Road
Kilburn, NW6 4HJ

Tel: 020-7624 9297

Open: *Mon-Sat* 9.00-18.00
Sun 11.00-17.00

Tube:

Fridge and freezer.

Kingsbury

Rose

Indian vegetarian restaurant

532-534 Kingsbury Road
London NW9 9HH (near HSBC)
Tel: 0800-583 8905
Open: *Every day* 12-22.30
Tube: Kingsbury

North and South Indian and Chinese vegetarian restaurant and take-away. Gigantic menu, over 100 dishes. Excellent value. Buffet lunch Mon-Fri 12-15.00, £5.99. No alcohol. Children welcome, high chairs. MC, Visa.

Chhappan Bhog, Kingsbury

Indian vegetarian sweet shop

560 Kingsbury Road, Kingsbury
NW9 9HJ (opposite Barclays)
Tel: 020-8204 7009
Open: *Mon-Sun* 9.00-20.00
Tube: Kinsbury
www.chhappanbhog.co.uk

Mainly a sweet mart, but also sell some take-away snacks and a few seats to eat in. £2.50 for rice and curry. Cash only.

Gayatri Sweet Mart

Vegetarian Indian take away

467 Kingsbury Road
Kingsbury, London NW9 9DY
Tel: 020-8206 1677
Open: *Mon-Fri* 10.30-18.30
  Sat 10.00-18.30
  Sun 9.00-16.00
Tube: Kingsbury

46 dishes, snacks and mixes £7-£8 per kilo. Savouries such as samosa 45p, bhajias, dhokra, kachori. Sweets (not vegan) include barfis, pendas, ladoos, chevda (Bombay mix).

Supreme Sweets

Indian vegetarian take-away / cafe

706 Kenton Road, Kenton,
Harrow, Middlesex HA3 9QX
Tel: 020-8206 2212
Open: *Mon-Fri* 10.00-19.00
  Sat 9.30-19.00
  Sun 8.30-17.00
Tube: Kingsbury

Sweets and savouries such as bhajias £7 per kilo, samosas and pakoras from 40p. Also frozen products like

Jays Pure

Open:
365 days a year, 12.30–23.00
Visa, MC.
No alcohol but they have a licence so may start.
Children welcome, 2 high chairs.

547 Kingsbury Road
London NW9 9EL

Tel: 020-8204 1555
Tube: Kingsbury

Vegetarian restaurant, take-away & juice bar with a great menu and so much choice. Fast food but healthy with Indian, Chinese, Mexican and Thai menus. They use sunflower oil in cooking so many dishes are suitable for vegans.

Snacks or starters from £1.25 up to £6.50 including the usual Indian favourites and others, such as kachori (three piece turnover filled with dhal), corn bhaji, mogo chips, chilli mushroom, stir-fried aubergine or King Pow corn. There are also Thai dishes such as Thai green curry, or Thai noodles priced at £3–£5.

Indian mains are all under £6 and include vegetable biriyani and Hyderabad masala dosa.

Chinese curries such as baby corn with mushroom Szechuan style, aubergine black bean sauce, Manchurian cauliflower, all around £5.50–£6.

The Mexican dishes are tortilla chips, tacos with chili bean and salad, burritos with picante sauce, enchilladas, Mexican rice and refried beans. These are £3 up to £6.50.

They also have 2 types of veggie burger and 7 types of noodles.

Indian desserts £3.60-5.00 but nothing vegan.

Fresh orange juice £2.75, passion fruit £3. Smoothies £2.75, but no soya milk. Coffee £1, tea 90p.

samosas, kachoris and spring rolls. 75% of items are vegan, vegetable oil in savouries but butter ghee in sweets. Soft drinks. They have a few seats. MC, Visa.

Catering for weddings and parties, they prepare for you to collect but deliver on orders over 100 people.

Udupi Palace

South Indian vegetarian cafe

Unit 12-13, Kingsbury Arcade, 574-612 Kingsbury Road, NW9 9HL (opposite Kingsbury tube)

Tel: 020-8204 1404

Open: *Mon-Sun* 10-21.00

Tube: Kingsbury

Take-away and small cafe with 10 seats. Lunch special £2.50 for curry, dahl, 2 chapatis, rice and dessert (usually with milk, but they can do without). Masala dosa £3.50, iddli steamed rice cakes, samosas, puris, bhajias. Freshly squeezed orange or carrot juice £2.50. Indian filter coffee £1. They specialise in fried lentil doughnuts (vegan) £2.50 with chutney sambar. Cash only.

Health First

Health food shop

664 Kingsbury High Road, London NW9 9HA

Tel: 020-8238 9336

Open: *Mon-Sat* 9.30-19.00
Sun closed

Tube: Kingbury (opposite)

Wholefoods, frozen and chilled food including vegan cheese and ice-cream. Supplements, body-building. No take-away.

Notting Hill

Garden Café

Omnivorous café

The London Lighthouse
111–117 Lancaster Road, W11

Tel: 020-7313 2900

Open: *Mon–Fri* 9–14.30
Sat–Sun closed
(occasionally open Sat
if events on)

Tube: Ladbroke Grove

Friendly omnivorous café, stylishly decorated, which always has some veggie meals, sometimes vegan. The London Lighthouse is a centre advising on HIV and the cafe is open to the public. On summer days the French windows open out onto a peaceful and relaxing, beautiful garden. Special days such as African when they always cater for veggies and vegans.

Good quality food at very reasonable prices with meals around £4, such as pasta, stuffed peppers or aubergine with rice or bulgur, served with veg. Salad bar with some vegan items at 60p per portion. Baked potatoes every day £2.50 with different fillings such as veggiemince, dairy-free broccoli mornay.

Freshly ground coffee, latte or large cappuccino £1.50, tea, juice, but no soya milk. (Usually when we say no soya milk, by the next edition there is!)

Greek sweets but all with honey.

House wine £10 bottle, £5 small bottle, £2.50 glass. Tea or filter coffee £1.80, no soya milk.

Children welcome but no high chairs. No credit cards.

Lush, Portobello

Cruelty-free cosmetics

202 Portobello Road, W11 1LA
(near Westbourne Park Rd)

Tel: 020-7229 4212

Open: *Mon–Fri* 10.00–18.00
Sat 9.00–18.00
Sun 10.30–17.30

Tube: Ladbroke Grove

www.lush.co.uk

Hand-made cosmetics, most of them vegan. See Soho for details.

The Grain Shop

Vegetarian bakery & take-away only

269a Portobello Road
Notting Hill, W11 (in Portobello
market, opposite Tavistock Rd)

Tel: 020-7229 5571

Open: *Mon-Sat* 9.30-18.00
Sun 10.00-16.30

Tube: Ladbroke Grove

Vegetarian take-away and bakery that uses organic flour. 16 hot dishes, 13 of which are suitable for vegans, such as tofu stir-fry, veg curry or ratatouille, as well as salads all made on the premises. Medium £3.99, large £5.20.

Specialist breads and cakes for allergy free diets, also gluten-free pastries and sugar-free items. MC, Visa.

Holland & Barrett

Health food shop

139 Kensington Church Street
London W8 7EN

Tel: 020-7937 5819

Tube: Notting Hill

Open: *Mon-Sat* 9.00-18.00
closed Sun

Small health food store with no fridge so no take-aways.

Portobello Whole Foods

Vegetarian wholefood shop

266 Portobello Road
Ladbroke Grove, W10 5TY
(Junction with Cambrige Gardens just under the Westway; north end of market)

Tel: 020-8968 9133

Open: *Mon-Sat* 9.30-18.00
Sun 11:00-17.00

Tube: Ladbroke Grove

Excellent large wholefood shop in Portobello market area. They pack all their own dry products like nuts, dried fruit, grains and beans, make their own muesli, and have extended the range of organic fruit and veg. Non-dairy cheeses and ice-cream.

New big fridge with a wide range of organic sandwiches £2.50, tortillas, pies, sushi wraps, salads £2.20. Laura's Idea vegan healthy breakfast granola pots £2.20.

Vitamins and supplements. Large range of toiletries including soaps, toothpastes and moisturisers. Biodegradable cleaning products, Ecover refills.

Clothes market opposite on Sundays on Portobello Green. (see Portobello Market)

Portobello Market

Market

Portobello Road, W11

Open: *Mon–Sat* 8.00–18.30
not Thur afternoon.
Mon–Thu fruit & veg only.
Fri–Sat are the main days.

Tube: Ladbroke Grove,
Notting Hill Gate

Gigantic market, competing with Walthamstow for the title of longest in Britain. Monday to Thursday it's just fruit and veg. Friday and Saturday are the main days, with pricier antiques at the south end, fruit and veg in the middle, and at the north end there's household brick-a-brack on Fridays and that plus clothes on Saturdays.

On Sundays on Portobello Green (opposite Portobello Whole Foods), there is another market with vintage and new clothes, second-hand jewellery, crystals and cards.

NOTTING HILL EXTRA: These have been recommended as good stand-bys by vegan readers.

There's a **Pizza Express** on 137 Notting Hill Gate.

ASK Pizza/Pasta at 145 Notting Hill Gate on the way to Holland Park W11.

Head over to Queensway W2 for **Bella Italia** at 55 and 108 and in the Whiteleys shopping centre.

www.bellaitalia.co.uk

Al Waha (Lebanese) at 75 Westbourne Grove, Notting Hill W2 4UL. Tel: 020-7229 0806.

www.alwaharestaurant.com

The only Indian recommended to us in Notting Hill is **Notting Hill Tandoori** at 23 All Saints Road W11. There are a lot of unusual vegetable dishes.

Finally, there's British grub at the **S & M Cafe** (that's "Sausage and Mash" not something involving fake leather and chains) at 268 Portobello Road W11. They usually have a few different veggie sausages on offer each day, including a vegan sausage and mash option too!

Neal's Yard Remedies, W11

Herbs and complementary health

9 Elgin Crescent, Notting Hill
London W11 2JA

Tel: 020-7727 3998

Open: *Mon–Sat* 9.00–18.30
Sun 11.00–17.00

Tube: Ladbroke Grove,
Notting Hill Gate

www.nealsyardremedies.com

Herbs and spices by weight, organic toiletries, natural remedies, books on homeopathy and remedies. All products tested on human volunteers, not animals. Mostly organic, lots of Fair Trade. They also have therapy rooms offering 30 kinds of healing treatments from acupuncture to shiatsu.

Green Baby, Notting Hill

Organic baby clothing

5 Elgin Crescent, W11

Tel: 020-7792 8140

Open: *Mon–Fri* 9.30–17.30
Sat 9.30–18.00
Sun 11.00–17.00

Tube: Ladbroke Grove,
Notting Hill

www.greenbaby.co.uk

Organic cotton baby and children's clothing, organic nappies.

Southall

You could think you are in India on a cool day, with a Gurudwara Sikh temple, sari shops and lots of great food stores for stocking up in bulk.with rice, pulses and spices.

Shahanshah

Vegetarian North Indian restaurant, take-away and sweet shop

60 North Road, Southall
Middlesex UB1 2JL
Tel: 020-8574-1493
Open: *every day* 10.00-20.00
Train: Southall BR
Children welcome, 2 high chairs

Starters £1-1.25 such as two samosas (take-away 30p each) or pakora (tak-away £4.50/kg). Main meal £5 such as curry and rice. Some food is vegan as they use butter ghee, groundnut and sunflower oil.

Outside seating for 10 people and around 30 inside. No alcohol. No cards. They cater for parties and weddings.

Delhi Wala

Vegetarian Indian restaurant and snack shop

11 King Street, Southall,
Middlesex UB2 4DG
Tel: 020-8574 0873
Open: every day 10.00-22.00
Train: Southall BR
www.delhiwala.co.uk

South of the station away from the Broadway. Punjabi and South Indian dishes from £1.50 starters, main dishes from £3, rice £1.50-1.75. Some of the sweets are dairy-free.

Children welcome, 2 high chairs. No alcohol. MC, Visa.

Ambala, Southall

Vegetarian Indian sweet shop

107 The Broadway, Southall
Middlesex UB1 1RP
Tel: 020-8843 9049
Open: *Mon-Sun* 09.00-21.00
Train: Southall BR
www.ambalafoods.com

Indian sweets and savouries.

WEST Southall

Chhappan Bhog, Southall

Indian vegetarian sweet shop

1 The Broadway, Southall,
Middlesex UB1 1JR

Tel: 020-8574 7607

Open: *Mon–Sun* 9.30-20.30

Train: Southall BR

www.chhappanbhog.co.uk

Sweet shop with two tables and some some take-away snacks such as samosas. Mini-meal £3.50 such as paratha and chickpeas. Canned drinks 60p. Visa, MC minimum £10. Another branch in Kingsbury.

Twickenham

Sagar, Twickenham

Vegetarian Indian restaurant

27 York Street, Twickenham
Middlesex TW1 3JZ

Tel: 020-8744 3868

Open: *Mon–Fri* 12-14.45
18.00-22.45
Fri eve till 23.30
Sat 12.00-23.30
Sun 12.00-22.45
Bank Hol 13.00-22.00

Train: Twickenham 5 mins walk. Bus stop H towards Richmond immediately outside.

New branch with the same menu as Hammersmith and Tottenham Court Road, with Hammersmith and this one being slightly cheaper.

Starters from £3, main courses such as dosa pancakes £4.95-£6.75 Thalis £9.95-12.45. Special lunch fixed menu Mon–Fri £4.95, basically a thali. Lunch box £2.95 available 12.00-14.45 every day with two curries, one rice, one bread, salad and raita or something else if you're vegan.

Desserts from £2.25, vegans can have mango sorbet.

Twickenham

House wine £2.85 glass, £10.95 bottle.

Children welcome, high chair. MC, Visa.

There is one copy of the main menu with vegan items marked up, or ask the knowledgeable waiter. For more examples dishes, see the full page entry for the new Tottenham Court Road branch (Centre).

Gaia Wholefoods

Wholefood shop

123 St Margarets Rd
Twickenham, Middx TW1 2LH
Tel: 020-9892 2262
Open: *Mon-Fri* 9.30-19.00
    Sat 9.30-17.00
    Sun closed

Wholefood shop selling fresh organic fruit and vegetables, Japanese macrobiotics, organic bread, gluten-free products. Also some vegan take-aways such as pastries.

Also body care, eco cleaning products, vitamins, herbal tinctures, dried herbs, flower remedies, homeopathy, aromatherapy.

Healthy Harvest Food Store

Wholefood shop

In Squires Garden Centre car park, 6 Cross Road, Twickenham Middlesex TW2 5PA
Tel: 020-8943 0692
Open: *Mon-Sat* 9.30-17.30
    Sun 10.30-16.30

Get your gardening goodies and tank up on grub at this wholefood shop in a garden centre between Twickenham and Hampton Court. Usual foods plus serve yourself wholefoods. Vegetarian (but not vegan) pasties and flapjacks. (Just as well as the garden centre restaurant just does corpse and 2 veg.)

Holland & Barrett

Healthfood shop

313 King St, Twickenham Middlesex TW1 3SD
Tel: 020-8891-6696
Open: *Mon-Sat* 09.00-17.30
    Sun 11.00-16.00

Fresh veggie take-away snacks like pies, pastries and soyos rolls arrive every Tuesday. Freezer section.

WEMBLEY

West London veggie hotspot

Wembley is home to a large Indian community and you won't be disappointed by the huge selection of food available here, whether you come for the Sunday market, a conference, concert or to support your team in the final.

Head down **Wembley High Road** to **Ealing Road** which has veggie zones at the north and south ends. There are stacks of Gujarati and other Indian vegetarian restaurants, with more opening every year. This could one day be the first vegetarian street in Britain. Huge competition ensures that menus are packed with gastronomic sensations and prices are great value.

Long established favourites include **Chetna's**, **Sakonis** (now serving breakfast, also Chinese dishes), **Jashan** (Gujarati and Chinese) and **Maru's** (Indian and Kenyan Asian). **Tulsi** is a huge place if you're planning a party for over 100 people.

Newer places include **Chennai Dosa** (with its 6 foot long family dosa), **Chowpatty** (great lunch thali), **Dosa Junction** (the closest to Wembley park tube if coming from central London). **Sarashwathy Bavans** and **Sanghamam** (formerly called Saravana Bhavan) are right opposite Wembley Central tube.

Some restaurants have alcohol, some don't, and we tell you how much for a glass or bottle of house wine. They all welcome children.

There are many Indian **sweet shops** where you can pick up a fast lunch on the run or stock up on snacks and savouries.

If you're all curried out, there's even a vegetarian **Pizza Parlour**. On the High Road is **Health First** independent wholefood, while **Holland & Barrett** has a few take-away items in the fridge.

Dosa Junction p.381

Health First p.387

Holland & Barrett p.387

Saraswathy Bavans p.384

Sanghamam p.385

Tulsi p.386

Suraj Sweet Market p.386

Chenna Dosa p.380

Naklank p.382

Jashan p.381

Shayona p.385

WEMBLEY PARK

WEMBLEY STADIUM

WEMBLEY CENTRAL

PARK LANE

HIGH

CHAPLIN ROAD

EALING ROAD

UNION RD

LONDON ROAD

CECIL AVENUE

ST JOHNS RD

LYON PK AVE

DOUGLAS AV

CLAYTON AV

Sakonis p.383

EAGLE ROAD

Pizza Parlour p.383

BOWRONS AV

Adricana p.380

BRAEMAR AV

Maru's p.382

Chowpattyp.380

ST JAMES GDNS

Ambala p.387

Royal Sweets280 p.383

MOUNT PLEASANT

Dosa Corner p.381

ONE TREE HILL RECREATION GROUND

ALPERTON

EALING RD

WEMBLEY STADIUM

Veggie Guides .com

Africana

Gujarati and South Indian restaurant

224 Ealing Road, Wembley
Tel: 020-8795 2455
Open: every day 13–22.00
Tube: Wembley Central

You know it's good when it's full of Indian people! 20 starters £2–2.50. Thalis £5.50–7.50. Curries £3.50–4.00 with rice or paratha. Desserts £2–3. Soft drinks and juices 90p–£3. Also take-away frozen samosas, spring rolls etc.

Chennai Dosa Vegetarian

Vegetarian South Indian restaurant

3 Ealing Rd, Wembley HA0 2AA
Tel: 020-8782 8822
Open: *Mon–Sun* 10.30–22.30
Tube: Wembley Central
www.chennaidosa.com

Rasam tamarind soup 95p. Starters 30p–£2.99. Dosas, uthapam and curries £1.60–2.95. Executive packed lunch Mon–Fri £3.50 with plain rice, veg sambar, porial, pachadi and poppadum. Look out for their 6-foot family dosa. No alcohol. MC, Visa.

Another omnivorous branch at 529 High Road, Wembley.

Chowpatty

Vegetarian Indian restaurant

234 Ealing Road, Wembley
Middlesex HA0 4QL
Tel: 020 8795 0077
Open: *Mon–Sat* 10.00–22.00
Tube: Alperton, Wembley Central

Named after Mumbai's famous beach, this is a new vegetarian restaurant in a road where the pickings for vegetarians were already far from slim (although the newcomers are always welcome). The prices are cheap and the variety good. You can get a lunchtime thali for £3.99 which includes a dal, two vegetable dishes, chappatis, rice and pickle; and you can choose from south, east or north Indian for a main.

Starters, £1.45–£2.95, with chaats, bhel puri and paani puri.

Mains, £2.75–£4.95, such as rajma chawal (red kidney beans with rice) from Punjab in the north, idli and dosas from south India, or Indo-Chinese offerings in the form of noodles or Chinese idli. Lemon or coconut rice, £1.99.

Drinks from £1.25, with delicious sweet or salted lime soda at £1.95. Beers £2.75.

House wine £6.95 for a bottle. Visa, MC.

Dosa Junction

Vegetarian South Indian restaurant

402 High Road, Wembley

Tel: 020-8900 0252

Open: *Mon–Sun* 11.00–24.00

Tube: Wembley Park
Wembley Stadium BR

The closest restaurant to Wembley Park tube for those coming from central London on the Metropolitan line. Bright interior, amazing value, and a bargain £3.95 buffet lunch Mon–Fri 12.00–15.00.

Breakfast dosa or idly set menu £3.95. Usual starters and tandoori veg kebabs £1.20–3.45. Curries, dosas , uttapam £1.95–3.45. 10 kinds of rice £2.50–3.95, and 10 types of breads 60p–£1.75. Thalis £3.95–4.95. Also some Chinese dishes £2.95–3.50 such as baby corn chilli or veg fried rice.

Desserts £1.25–2.50.

Soft drinks, tea and coffee £1–£1.50. House wine £9.95 bottle, £2.50 glass. Beer £2–3. Spirits £1.50–£2.

Outside catering and private parties.

Dosa Corner

Omnivorous South Indian restaurant

6 Sunleigh Parade, Mount Pleasant, off Ealing Road, Alperton HA0 4LP

Tel: 020-8902 2811

Open: *Mon–Sun* 11.00–24.00

Tube: Alperton

Run by the same people as Dosa Junction, this one is down the Alperton end of Wembley. This one isn't veggie but has stacks of the same dishes so we've included it in case you're running with a pack of carnivores who veto a veggie venue.

Jashan

Gujarati Indian restaurant

1–2 Coronet Parade, Ealing Road Wembley, Middlesex HA0 4AY (corner of Union Road)

Tel: 020-8900-9800

Open: *Mon–Fri* 12.00–15.30
18.00–23.00
Sat–Sun 12.00–23.00

Tube: Wembley Central, Alperton
Alcohol free zone.
Children welcome, high chairs.
www.jashanrestaurants.com

Huge menu of North and South Indian and Chinese dishes for around £3–£5.

South Indian dishes include idli, medu wada, uttapam, dosas. Indo Chinese dishes £3.75–5.25 such as aubergine steak with black bean sauce, Szechuan veg with cashews, Thai red kari. They even have spaghettti.

Many cold drinks such as fresh lime juice with soda water. £1–£3. Tea £1, coffee £1.10, hot chocolate £2.25.

Maru's Bhajia House

Vegetarian Indian café

230 Ealing Road, Alperton, Wembley, Middlesex HA0 4QL

Tel: 020 8903 6771

Open: *Mon–Thu* 12.30-20.30
Fri–Sun 12.30-21.30

Tube: Alperton,Wembley Central

Children welcome, high chair
No alcohol.. MC, Visa, Amex.
www.mambhajia.com

Ealing Road has a number of inexpensive Gujarati and south Indian restaurants. Maru's Kenyan Asian cuisine has been a firm favourite since 1976 with bhajias of course, samosas, maize and assorted snacks. Before that the family had a restaurant in East Africa from 1949 to 1972.

The Maru bhajia has always been the main item on the menu, made from potato slices mixed with gram (chickpea) flour fried with spices, with their special tamarind sauce.

Asian film stars fill up here on pani puri, kachori and vada. £3.40 for a portion, £6.80 for a double portion.

Desserts include fruit cocktail. Fresh passion fruit juice £3.

This is a café with seating for 30 to 34 people and gets very busy.

Naklank Sweet Mart

Gujarati Indian café take-away

50b Ealing Road
Wembley, Middlesex HA0 4TQ

Tel: 020-8902 8008

Open: *Mon–Sat* 10.00-19.00
Sun 12.00-19.00

Tube: Wembley Central
Alperton

Alcohol free zone.
Children welcome.

Gujarati vegetarian Indian eat in (5 seats inside) or take-away. Everything made on the premises with 39 different sweets and savouries, samosas, pakoras, 20 kinds of bhajia. Curries from £2.50 and mostly vegan. All traditionally made. Small seating area with two tables inside. Outside catering service.

Pizza Parlour

Vegetarian pizza restaurant

218 Ealing Road, Wembley

Tel: 020-8900 9999

Open: *Tue-Fri* 12.00-15.00
17.00-22.00
Sat-Sun 13.00-22.00
Mon (except bank hol) Closed

Tube: Wembley Central,
Alperton

Vegetarian pizzas from £3.50, side dishes such as potato wedges and masala or chilli chats from £1.50. Eat in or take away.

Wine from £2 for a glass, £12.99 for a bottle. Beers £2.30. MC, Visa.

Royal Sweets

Vegetarian Indian sweet shop

280 Ealing Road, Alperton, Middlesex HA0 4LL

Tel: 020-8903 9359

Open: *Tue-Sun* 10.00-19.00
Mon closed

Tube: Alperton

Indian sweets only, no savouries. Some are without milk though they say all may contain traces of nuts.

Sakonis

Indian restaurant and take-away

127-129 Ealing Road
Wembley, Middlesex HA0 4BP

Tel: 020-8903-9601 / 1058

Open:
Every day breakfast 08.00-11.00
(*weekend* 9-11.00)
Summer
Sun-Thu 12-22.00
Fri-Sat 12-22.30
Winter
Sun-Thu 12-21.30
Fri-Sat 12-22.00

Tube: Wembley Central, Alperton

Vegetarian Indian snack bar, take-away and delivery service with an extensive menu of over 100 Gujarati, North Indian and Chinese dishes.

Buffet south Indian breakfast weekends 9–11am £3.99, with idli, masala dosa, puri potato curry, umpa, jelabi, ghatia, sambaroo and masala tea.

Buffet lunch every day, eat as much as you like for £7.99, dinner £10.99, choose from over 30 items from starters to desserts.

Buffet dinner every day 19–21.30, £7.99 + 10%.

Starters and bites £1.50–£4.25 such as sev puri, pani puri, samosas, toasted sandwiches, spring rolls, mogo chips, khichi (rice flour steamed with spices), Chinese soups. £2.75.

Main dishes £3–£7 such as plain or masala or chutney or Mysore dosa, farari cutlets, vegetable biriyani, corn bhajia, veggie burger and chips, uttapa. 30 Chinese dishes prepared Indian style include aubergine and chilli in hot black bean sauce, mixed Szechuan vegetables, stir-fried veg.

Lots of sweets £2–£3, fruit shakes and fresh juices from £2.75, including fresh coconut water. Teas and hot chocolate £1.30.

Most items can be prepared hot, medium, mild or without onion or garlic. Take-away Indian sweet shop too.

Sarashwathy Bavans

South Indian vegetarian restaurant

549 High Road, Wembley
Middlesex HA0 2DJ

Tel: 020-8902 1515

Open: *Mon–Sun* 12.00–23.00

Tube: Wembley Central

www.sarashwathy.com

Visa, MC (minimum £10).

No alcohol. Children welcome, high chair

South Indian fare and Indo-Chinese choices. This is a new and popular place which offers free delivery within a 3 mile radius (minimum order of £12) and outside catering orders. Starters, £1.75–£5.25, with samosas, soups and vegetable rolls; mains from £3.95 with large selection of dosas, idli and noodles. Fresh juices from £1.95.

Sanghamam

South Indian vegetarian restaurant

531-3 Wembley High Road
Middlesex HA0 2DJ
(corner Ealing Rd opposite HSBC)

Tel: 020-8900 0777

Open: *Mon-Sun* 12.00-23.00

Tube: Wembley Central

www.sanghamam.co.uk menu

Fomerly called Saravanaa Bhavan, now under new ownership. South Indian and Gujarati food and very popular with local Indians. Great for dosas, idlis, chaat.

Starters £2.25-3.95 include golden fried baby corn, mixed bajia. Curry dishes £3.50. Mushroom or veg biryani and various pulaos £3.95. Business lunch £3.95, South Indian thali £4.95, North Indian £5.95, Gujarati £6.95. Dosas and uttappam £2.50-4.25. Some Chinese dishes £3.50-3.95. Rice and noodles £2.50-4.25.

Dessert £1.50-3.00 include fruit salad. Juices £2.25. Tea £1, coffee £1.50.

They can host a wedding, family or corporate event or party with a banquet hall for 100, 2 family rooms and 2 bars. Outdoor, house and corporate catering.

Shayona, Wembley

Vegetarian Indian sweet shop

3B Coronet Parade, Ealing Rd
Wembley, Middlesex HA1 4AY

Tel: 020-8903 5539

Open: *Mon-Sat* 10.00-19.00
Sun 10.00-18.00

Tube: Wembley Central

www.sayacaterers.com

Mainly Gujarati food including sweets and savouries ready to eat. Also frozen samosas to fry at home. Previously called Saya.

Sweets and savouries such as samosas, kachori, spring rolls to take-away. Some of the sweets are dairy-free such as rassgulla and rassomalai.

Shayona, Neasden

Vegetarian Indian restaurant & shop

54–62 Meadow Garth, off
Brentfield Rd, Neasden NW10
8HD
(in the car park of the temple)
Tel: 020-8965 8387
Shop: *Mon–Fri*   10.00–20.00
        Sat   10.00–22.00
        Sun   10.00–21.00
Restaurant closes 1 hour earlier
Tube: Neasden,
        Stonebridge Park

www.sayacaterers.com

www.mandir.org (temple)

This branch also has a
restaurant and snack shop
for eating in or having a
drink.

Set menu £6.50 with two
curries, djipati, samosas,
fried rice. Starters from 80p
for 2 samosas to £2.50 for
puri or syaa chatt. Channa
masala and paratha £3. Fried
rice £2. Falafel £3. Vege
quarter pounder £3.50. You
need to book if you come as
a group.

Children welcome.   No
alcohol. MC, Visa.

There are branches of the
shop in Wembley and Pinner.

Suraj Sweet Mart

Vegetarian Indian sweet shop

44a Ealing Road, Wembley
(corner of Chaplin Road)
Tel: 020-8900 1339
Open: Mon–Sat 9.30–19.00
        Sun   9.00–19.99
Tube: Wembley Central

Sweets, snacks such as
samosas, bhajia, veg cutlets.
Mini lunch available.

Tulsi

Indian vegetarian restaurant

22/22A Ealing Road
Wembley HA0 4TL
Tel: 020-8900 8526
Open: *Tue–Thu* 11.00–15.00
                  18.00–22.30
        Fri–Sun 11.00–23.00
        Mon   10.30–18.00
Tube: Wembley Central
www.tulsirestaurant.co.uk

Big south Indian place with
Indo-Chinese offerings, 120
seats and another 110
upstairs in the private party
hall, and over 200 items on
the menu. Staples such as
idli, uttapam and a huge
range of unusual dosas £3–
£6. 10 soups £2.50–£3.
Vegetable dishes from £3.70
and fried rice, noodles and
chow mein from £4. Fresh

juices and shakes £2–£3 (no soya milk).

Lunch thali £7.50 12.00–15.00, dinner thali £7.90 £19.00–22.00.

House wine £3.50 glass, £12 bottle. Beer £2.50 pint, £1.50 half. Indian beer £2–3.50. Children welcome, high chairs.

Ambala

Vegetarian Indian sweet shop

6 Glenmore Parade, off Ealing Rd
Wembley, Middlesex HA0 4BP

Tel: 020-020 8903 9740
Open: *Mon–Sun* 10.00–20.00
Tube: Alperton

Indian sweets and savouries.

Health First

Health food shop

536 High Rd, Wembley HA9 7BS
(opposite HSBC bank)

Tel: 020-8900 2684
Open: *Mon–Sat* 9.30–18.00
     Sun closed
Tube: Wembley Central

Wholefoods, frozen and chilled food including vegan cheese and ice-cream. Supplements, body-building. No take-away.

Holland & Barrett

Health food shop

Unit 21 Wembley Sq, High Rd, Wembley, Middlesex HA9 7AJ

Tel: 020-8902-6959
Open: *Mon–Sat* 9.00–17.30
     Sun closed
Tube: Wembley Central
     Wembley Stadium

They have a small take-away section with pastries, plus usual health foods, a chiller cabinet and freezer section.

Bodywise Health Foods

Health food shop

22 High Street, **Ruislip**
Middlesex HA4 7AN

Tel: 01895-638187

Open: *Mon–Sat* 9.00–17.30
Sun closed

Tube: Ruislip

See Harrow branch for details. In-house complementary therapies clinic.

GNC, Uxbridge

Health food shop

7 Chequers Square, The Pavilions, **Uxbridge** UB8 1LN

Tel: 01895-254538

Open: *Mon–Sat* 9.00–17.00
Sat 9.00–17.30
Sun 9.00–17.30

Freezer and fridge with some take-away food.

Holland & Barrett

Health food shop

151 Field End Road
Eastcote HA5 1QL

Tel: 020-8866 0919

Open: *Mon–Sat* 9.00–17.30
Sun 11.00–16.00

No fridge or freezer.

Holland & Barrett

Health food shop

17-19 Pantile Walk
Uxbridge, Middx UB8 1LT

Tel: 01895-237841

Open: *Mon–Sat* 9.00–17.30
Thu till 18.00
Sun 10.30–16.30

Fridge and freezer with take-away pasties etc.

Revital Health Centre

Health food shop

78 High Street, **Ruislip** HA4 7AA
(near Ickenham Rd)

Tel: 01895-629959

Open: *Mon–Sat* 9.00–18.00
Sun closed

Tube: Ruislip
www.revital.co.uk

Health foods. Bodycare and natural beauty including Dr Hauschka. Mother and baby products. Supplements. Herbal and ayurvedic. Healthnotes touch-screen information kiosk

You can book a free appointment with their nutritionist. Professional treatments include aromatherapy, Indian head massage, Reiki, kinesiology or facial rejuvenation. To book call 01895-833045 or 07702 322699.

VEGETARIAN LONDON
HOT TIPS

Accommodation

Guest Houses & Hotels 390

Backpacker Hostels 398

Camping in London 399

Moving to London 401

Vegetarian Caterers 402

Local Groups 404

National Organisations 410

100% Veggie places to stay

Stephanie Rothner

Vegetarian Bed & breakfast

44 Grove Road
North Finchley, London N12 9DY

Tel: 020-8446 1604
Mobile: 07956-406446

Tube: Woodside Park then 15 min walk or Finchely bus terminal

Open: All year round

Vegetarian homely bed and breakfast in north London. Single £20. Sole occupancy of the double room is £24 or for two sharing £40. Shared bathroom. TV in the rooms.

Veggie breakfast with soya milk and margarine always available. Children over 12 only. No smoking or pets.

Shops and restaurants with veggie food nearby including Rani Indian vegetarian restaurant.

If the house if full up then you can also stay nearby for the same price at Dora Rothner Vegetarian B&B, 23 The Ridgeway, Finchley N3 2PG, tel 020-8346 0246, tube: Finchley Central then 8 minute walk.

Temple Lodge

Vegetarian bed & breakfast

51 Queen Caroline Street
Hammersmith, London W6 9QL

Tel: 020-8748 8388
Fax: 020-8748 8322

Tube: Hammersmith, 5 mins

Open: All year

templelodgeclub@ btconnect.com

No smoking throughout.

See map page 348

Temple Lodge is a quiet oasis on the west side of central London. There are five single rooms at £40 per night or £260 per week, four small twins at £50 per room per night or £310 per week, three large twins £60 / £380, one double £65/ £415.

A hearty continental breakfast is served. Soya milk and vegan margarine are available on request.

You won't have to walk far for lunch or dinner as The Gate gourmet vegetarian restaurant is on the same premises. (closed Sunday) There is also a cheap and vergy tasty vegetarian Indian

Veggie–friendly places to stay

restaurant Sagar at 157 King Street and the fabulous vegan restaurant 222 at 222 North End Road which does a great lunchtime buffet.

Visitors are invited to join in with activities of the Christian Community and will have the opportunity of joining the Temple Lodge Club for a nominal fee of £1. The house offers many facilities for the use of guests, such as a kitchen, a quiet and secluded garden and a large library.

All major tourist attractions are reached easily by public transport. Pleasant walks along the River Thames are easily accessible. Historic houses, Kew Gardens, the Waterfowl sanctuary of the Wetlands Centre and three theatres are all within walking distance. Close to Olympia and Earls Court Exhibition Centres and the Hammersmith Apollo Theatre.

Washbasins in rooms. No TV.

For more places to eat nearby see Hammersmith page 348.

The Lanesborough

Luxury central hotel

Hyde Park Corner, **Knightsbridge** London SW1X 7TA

Tel: 020-7259 5599

Fax: 020-7259 5606

For reservations in USA call toll free 1–800 999 1828 fax: 1–800 937 8278

Tube: Hyde Park Corner

Open: All year round

www.lanesborough.com

Luxury hotel popular with veggie rock and movie stars and C.E.O.'s. Singles £285, doubles £395 up to the royal suite for £5000, all plus VAT.

If a veggie/vegan breakfast is required you have to give prior notice at the time of booking. Services include 24 hour butler, fitness studio, spa studio, business centre, complimentary internet access in your room with on-demand film.

The in-house restaurant **The Conservatory** features gourmet vegetarian dinners, prepared by top chef Paul Gayler or one of his brigade of 40 chefs. Lunch is £24 for

Veggie–friendly places to stay

(continued)

2 courses or £27.50 for three, dinner prices depend on the day of the week but usually range from £32–£44 per head. The vegetarian a la carte menu often has vegan options but not always so phone ahead. There is live music every night and dancing on Friday and Saturday nights.

For more places to eat nearby see the Sloane Zone section.

Lincoln House Hotel

Central vegetarian-friendly hotel

33 Gloucester Place (junction with George St), **Marble Arch** London W1U 8HY

Tel: 020–7486 7630
Fax: 020–7486 0166

Tube: Marble Arch
Airbus A2, A6 for Stansted and Luton airports. Near Paddington station for Heathrow Express.

Open: All year round

www.lincoln-house-hotel.co.uk

See map page 117

Full English cooked vegetarian or vegan (with prior notice) or continental breakfast available at this independent hotel in an 18th century Georgian building on the north side of Oxford Street, close to Hyde Park.

All rooms are en suite. Prices vary according to time of year and length of stay but start from single £59, double £69, triple £109, family £119. Check website for full details and discounts.

There are traditional English pubs nearby.

Rooms have a small fridge, satellite TV, hairdryer, trouser press, tea and coffee, free wi-fi. Photocopying, faxing, printing available.

Children welcome, high chairs, baby cots. No pets except guide dogs with prior notice. MC, Visa, Amex.

Free parking nearby 6.30pm to 8a.m. and all day Sun and public holidays. Discounted parking at nearby NCP car park.

See Marylebone section (Central London) for where to eat out wholefood shops.

Liz Heavenstone's

Self-catering apartments / B&B

Liz Heavenstone's Guest House
192 Regents Park Road
Primrose Hill, London NW1 8XP

Tel: 020-7722 7139

Fax: 020-7722 6869

Tube: Chalk Farm

Open: All year

london-availability@onetel.com

Cosy, top floor apartment in a Regency terrace in Primrose Hill village, on the edge of Regent's Park. Two double/twin rooms, £60 per room per night, one with own bathroom, one with shower, which become a self contained apartment with living room when both rooms are taken. There's also a futon for an extra bed in one room. Good for self-catering as the kitchen-breakfast room has fridge, dishwasher, cooker, and microwave-cum-oven. Complimentary tea, herbal teas and coffee are included.

Add £5 per person for self-service vegetarian organic breakfast, which can easily be veganized, and they'll happily cater for special diets if you tell them in advance. There are always tea, coffee and herbal drinks, and the breakfast room has a bowl of fruit.

Children welcome but no pets. Discreet smokers tolerated. They have plenty of info on London for guests. Good location, close to the centre but not in the centre. Nearby are Triyoga Centre (www.triyoga.co.uk), which has drop-in classes and a vegetarian cafe, Primrose Hill, Regents Park, Manna vegetarian restaurant, Cafe Seventy-Nine and Sesame wholefood store. Green Note veggie restaurant is also nearby. Camden is a short walk away with the giant Fresh & Wild shop, a big Holland & Barrett health food store, and lots of places to eat out veggie.

Two minutes walk to Chalk Farm underground. Prior telephone booking is essential, do not just turn up.

There is now another self-catering apartment in the same building on the first floor with bay windows, newly refurbished with ecological paint. It has two big rooms, one a living room/kitchen with sofa-bed, and is available for short holiday lets.

See Camden and Primrose Hill sections (North London).

Veggie–friendly places to stay

(continued)

Hampstead Village Guesthouse

Veggie friendly hotel

2 Kemplay Road
Hampstead, London NW3 1SY

Tel: 020-7435 8679
Fax: 020-7794 0254

Tube: Hampstead

Parking can be arranged.

Open: All year round

www.HampsteadGuesthouse.com
info@HampsteadGuesthouse.com

Veggie friendly 1872 Victorian guest house in a peaceful setting close to the heath and tube. In the heart of lively Hampstead Village, a fun area with art cinema, restaurants with veggie food, coffee shops and pubs. The large, very comfortable rooms are full of character with sitting area, writing desk, remote control TV, hairdryer, iron, fridge (brilliant for veggies), kettle, telephone, books and even a hot-waterbottle to cuddle.

En suite double £95, en suite single £75. Double £80, singles £55 and £65. Large studio with kitchen and shower £100 for 1, £125 for 2, £145 for 3, £160 for 4, £175 for 5. Parking £10 per day.

Optional breakfast £7 from 8.00 a.m., 9.00 at weekends until late, can be in the garden in summer and you can invite guests.

Booking requires credit card, pay on arrival in cash, sterling (travellers) cheques or credit card (5% surcharge). No smoking anywhere. No meals except breakfast, but there are veggie restaurants and a wholefood store in the area and veggie dishes in other nearby restaurants.

See Hampstead (North London) for where to eat and shop nearby, or head down the hill to Primrose Hill and Camden.

HAMPSTEAD VILLAGE GUESTHOUSE

2 Kemplay Road, Hampstead
London NW3 1SY

www.hampsteadguesthouse.com
tel: +44 (0)20 7435 8679   **Fax:** +44 (0)20 7794 0254
e-mail: info@hampsteadguesthouse.com

- Peaceful setting, close to Hampstead Heath, yet in the heart of lively Hampstead Village.

- Close to underground and bus. Centre of London in 10 minutes.

- Large rooms full of character, plus modern amenities: TV, kettle and direct-dial telephone.

- breakfast in the garden, weather permitting.

- Accomodation from £55.

- No smoking.

"If you're looking for something a little different, make a beeline for Annemarie van der Meer's Hampstead home."
Chosen as one of the "Hotels of the Year". The Which? Hotel Guide 2000.

Veggie–friendly places to stay

(continued)

Mount View

Vegetarian friendly guest house

31 Mount View Road
London N4 4SS

Tel: 020-8340 9222
Fax: 020-8342 8494

Tube: Finsbury Park & W7 bus

Open: All year round

www.mountviewguesthouse.com
MountViewBB@aol.com

Smart Victorian house with garden in a quieter area of North London, combining tranquility and the gentle pace of village life but within easy reach of central London. A quiet haven after a busy day sightseeing. Rooms decorated using natural materials.

Double en suite with sofa in bay window and antique furniture £35 per person. Double £25 per person. Twin with shower £27.50. Single £40–45. 10% discount for 7+ nights.

Vegetarian breakfast available. Vegan and other diets on request.

No evening meal, but Haelan Centre health food store is nearby and Jai Krishna vegetarian restaurant. There are plenty more vegetarian restaurant on the Victoria and Piccadilly underground lines which go right through central London.

15 minutes walking from Finsbury Park tube and rail station, luggage can be collected when you arrive.

Near Highgate cemetery, Hampstead Heath with Kenwood House, Alexandra Palace.

All rooms with tv, hairdryer, washbasin, tea and coffee making facilities. Washing machine and dryer and internet access available on request. Payphone.

Unrestricted parking in street. No smoking throughout. No pets. Children welcome but no high chair. Dutch and French spoken. MC, Visa

AA 5 diamonds.

For places to eat out and shop nearby see North London: FInsbury Park & Archway, Muswell Hill & Crouch End, Highgate.

S.W.A. The Way to Stay

Vegetarian-friendly guest house

67 Rannoch Road, **Hammersmith**
London W6 9SS

Tel: 020-7385 4904
Fax: 020-7610 3235
Tube: Hammersmith
Open: All year round
www.thewaytostay.co.uk
See map page 348

Quiet Edwardian family home in Hammersmith close to the river, traditional pubs, antique shops and some vegetarian restaurants.

3 rooms, £25 per person double/twin/triple, £36 single, reductions for children if sharing with 2 adults.

Continental breakfast. Tea, coffee, hot chocolate. Cereals, muesli (not vegan) and toast, or rice or oat cakes. Soya milk available. Vegans tell them what you'd like when booking.

Central heating and TV in all rooms. Smoking only in the garden. Parking in the street £1.60 per hour Mon-Fri 9-5pm, no time limit. No pets.

Deposit by cheque required, or overseas by bank transfer or Western Union, balance in cash.

They also act as agent for other nearby B&B's at the same price in Chiswick, Earls Court, Hammersmith, Fulham, Kensington and Putney.

Mrs M Draper

Vegetarian-friendly bed & breakfast

31 The Ridgeway, **Finchley**,
London N3 2PG
(off Ballards Lane)

Tel: 020-8346 7985
Tube: Finchley Central 10 mins
82 bus or night bus
Open: All year round

Originally completely vegetarian and still doing a great self-serve (uncooked) breakfast when you want it with fruit, wholemeal bread, cereal, soya milk available, just ask for what you need.

2 doubles £50, 1 single £40, and you also have your own sitting room and a separate kitchen to prepare your own meals. Garden with patio and chairs for breakfast.

Children welcome, cot, high chair. Small well-behaved dogs welcome.

See Finchley, page 208.

Backpacker Hostels

Generator Hostel

The king of hostels, fab location

Compton Place,
behind 37 Tavistock Place,
London WC1H 9SD

Tel: 020-7388 7666

Fax: 020-7388 7666

Tube: Russell Square,
Kings Cross, Euston

Open: All year, 24 hours

info@the-generator.co.uk
www.the-generator.co.uk

See map page 89

International 837 bed hostel in Bloomsbury. The cheapest dorms you have to wait for, so you'll probably pay £17 for a 4-bed room. Nearby are Vegetarian Paradise restaurant and Alara Wholefoods (where vegans can buy breakfast). Age 18-35, but older young-at-hearts welcome. Busy bar. Bring earplugs and a padlock for your locker. Towels provided.

Other Hostels

Rock bottom accommodation

www.piccadillyhotel.net
www.astorhostels.com
www.st-christophers.co.uk
www.wakeuplondon.co.uk
www.yhalondon.org.uk
www.ukhostels.com
www.totalhostels.com

Our favourite guidebooks for budget places are *Lonely Planet, Rough Guides* or *Let's Go London, England, Britain* or *Europe.* Off season you can often just turn up, but at weekends and in summer you absolutely must reserve ahead for your first night.

If you've just got off a coach or airport train at Victoria station, there are some accommodation agencies that can sort out your first night's stay for a small commission.

Camping in London

Crystal Palace Campsite

Camping in south-east London

Crystal Palace Parade,
London SE19

Tel: 020-8778 7155

Train: Crystal Palace BR or bus 3
(24 hours) to Trafalgar Square.

Open: All year round

www.caravanclub.co.uk then
search on Crystal Palace.

This is a caravan park so electricity is available but no shop or cooking facilities, though they sell camping gas and there is a Sainsbury's supermarket . They do have laundry and washing facilities though. Tent field open Easter to Sept, weather permitting. Pitch £4.90-8.30 depending on time of year, each adult £5-6.50, non-members of the Caravan Club add £7. No charge for car.

There's great veggie eating nearby at Spirited Palace organic vegan cafe and Domali cafe-bar, and a green shop that sells nifty camping gadgets and wholefoods. See the Crystal Palace section of South London

Lee Valley Camping, Edmonton

Camping in north-east London

Meridan Way, Edmonton
London N9 0AS

Tel: 020-8803 6900

Tube: Tottenham Hale,
Edmonton BR

Open: All year except most of
Dec and New Year

www.leevalleypark.org.uk

Huge well equipped camping and caravan park set in 6 acres with sports centre and leisure complex with 12 screen cinema, swimming pool, 18-hole golf course, kids' play area, 3 pubs and pizza restaurant. Acts as bus terminal for those going into town.

There is a minimum £6.40 adult, £2.90 under-16, minimum charge for one person and tent £9.60. Electricity is £2.70, dogs and awnings £1.65. Disabled-friendly. Maximum 14 nights.

On site shop open 09.00-20.00.

Camping in London

Lee Valley Campsite, Sewardstone

Camping in north-east London

Sewardstone Road, Chingford, London E4 7RA

Tel: 020-8529 5689

Tube: bus service to Walthamstow underground (Victoria line)

Open: March–October

www.leevalleypark.org.uk

Near Epping Forest and handy for central London. Shop and children's play area. Supervised pets permitted. Disabled access.

£6.45 adult, £2.90 under-16, minimum charge for one person £9.35. Electricity £2.70. Day visitors £2 adult, £1 child. Disabled-friendly.

Abbey Wood Campsite

Camping in south-east London

Federation Rd, Abbey Wood London SE2 0LS (east of Greenwich)

Tel: 020-8311 7708

Train: Abbey Wood 5 mins, frequent trains to central London

Open: All year

www.caravanclub.co.uk

Caravan club site with a rural feel. Pitch £4.90–8.30 depending on time of year, each adult £5–6.50, non-members of the Caravan Club add £7. Wireless internet.

Moving to London

If you're moving to London for at least six months, then an apartment (flat) with friends can be cheaper than a hostel and much quieter. And much nicer too if you share a kitchen with veggies. Finding an apartment is a full time job for a few days but it can be done if you're persistent.

A single or double room in a houseshare will be £70–120 per week, a studio flat £100 per week and up. You'll need a month's deposit, a month's rent up front, and the contract will normally be a six months assured shorthold tenancy. Staying in a hostel for the first weeks is a lot less hassle while you find a job and you can get some mates there, or go to vegetarian and vegan events to find new friends. (page 405)

A word of warning: London is expensive. The majority of people work hard so they can afford to enjoy it to the full, but live in a small space, probably just one or maybe two rooms. People who turn up wanting to move in with them without paying rent create awkwardness and embarrassment all round. So before coming, make sure you have plenty of money to tide you over for a few weeks while you find a job.

LOOT
London's free ads newspaper

www.loot.com

If you want to rent a whole apartment, this is the place. Browse to get a feel for areas and prices. You can place an ad yourself and let the landlords come to you. Search on "veg" to find veggie houseshares. A printed version of LOOT can be bought in newsagents.

VegCom
Veggie accommodation adverts

www.vegcom.org.uk and click on VegCom

Vegans and veggies looking for flatmates, free.

Gumtree
Free adverts

www.gumtree.com

Like Loot only easier to use.

Vegetarian Caterers

Many restaurants in this book do outside catering, and this is indicated in the text. Here are a few suggestions that are particularly good. If you want a wicked **vegan cake** for an office or birthday party, call Beatroot (Soho), Pogo Cafe (East London), or try Bea's cafe at 44 Theobalds Rd, WC1.

Barty's Creative Catering

Vegetarian & vegan catering service

83 Stanley Gardenens,
Teddington,
Middlesex TW 11 8SY
Tel: 020-8977 9064

Vegetarian and vegan catering service who will cater for any event, weddings parties, and especially charity events and confer-ences.

Leon's Vegetarian Catering

Vegetarian and vegan catering

www.leonlewis.co.uk
leonsveg@aol.com
132b London Rd, Brentwood,
Essex CM14 4NS
Tel: 01277-218661

Mouthwatering vegetarian and vegan catering, buffets, cookery demonstrations, any event nationwide. Amazing fungus forays in the woods in autumn and late spring, followed by cooking the booty and quaffing from Leon's extensive wine cellar.

Naklank

Vegetarian Indian catering

50b Ealing Road, Wembley,
Middlesex HAO 4TQ
Tel: 020-8902 8008

Indian sweet shop and restaurant catering for parties and weddings.

Organic Delivery Company

Vegetarian grocery delivery service

www.organicdelivery.co.uk
Tel: 020-7739 8181

Not exactly a caterer, but for people with no time to shop they will deliver organic vegetarian groceries, household products, baby food and booze, to your home or office, daytime and evening. Regular orders or one-off deliveries.

Rootmaster

Vegan catering

www.root-master.co.uk
Tel: 07912 389314

Gourmet vegan catering from the red double decker bus restaurant off Brick Lane. You pick up, they can deliver, or just hire the 28-seat top deck for your party.

Shambhu's

Vegan caterers

Tel: 020-8931 0030
www.shambhus.co.uk
email: mail@shambhus.co.uk

Reasonably-priced quality vegan meals delivered to individuals or groups.

Shayona Caterers

Vegetarian Indian catering

Saya Enterprises Ltd, Unit 21, Abbey Ind Estate, Mount Pleasant, Wembley HA0 1NR

Tel: 020-8900 0314
Fax: 020-8900 2058

www.sayacaterers.com
admin@sayaltd.co.uk

Previously called Saya. They also have 3 shops and a restaurant, see West London.

Veggies Catering Campaign

Vegan catering cooperative

The Sumac Centre,
245 Gladstone Street
Nottingham NG7 6HX
Tel: 0845-458 9595
www.veggies.org.uk

Part of a large resource centre, Veggies do low cost veggie and vegan catering nationwide for events, organisations and charities with burgers, salads and, cakes. Awarded best vegan caterer by the Vegan Society.

Wild Cherry

Vegetarian Buddhist catering

241 Globe Road, Bethnal Green
London E2 0JD
Tel: 020-8980 6678

Vegetarian Buddhist group that runs a café and does outside catering.

The Window

Vegetarian conference centre

13 Windsor St, Islington N1 8QG
Tel: 020-7288 7008. Map p.229
www.thewindow.org.uk

London's only meeting, conference and wedding venue with exclusively vegetarian in-house catering.

Local Groups

Some of these are campaigning groups – these usually have the word "animal". Others are mainly social – look for the word "vegan" or "vegetarian". Check with the websites of the Vegan Society or Vegetarian Society for new groups, e.g. www.vegsoc.org/network

Bromley Animal Rights

16 Parkside Avenue,
Bromley BR1 2EJ
Tel: 020-8464 6035

Bromley and Environs Vegetarian Group

For the latest newsletter send A5 sae to Kathy Silk, BEVEG, c/o Bronwen Humphreys, The Vegetarian Society, Parkdale, Dunham Rd, Altrincham, Cheshire WA14 4QG.

Or email messages clearly headed BEVEG to bron@vegsoc.org

Meet last Tuesday morning of the month (except December) 10.30-12 noon at the URG Church, Widmore Road, Bromley (next door to Boots). Bring a friend on your first visit if you wish. We are a friendly crowd and we look forward to meeting you. Admission/refreshments 75p. Vegans welcome.

Bromley Eating Experience

Diana Elvin: Tel: 020-8777 1680

Events: Meetings on the second Saturday of alternate months from March, 12-3pm. Usually with speaker or video. Bring non-flesh food and soft drinks to share, buffet style. All welcome. Parking on site. Friends MeetingHouse,Ravensbourne Road, Bromley.

Ealing Veggie Group

Neena Panesar.
ealingveg@yahoo.co.uk

London Vegan Festival

c/o CALF, BM Box 8889, London WC1N 3XX. www.vegancampaigns.org.uk/festival robandal55@googlemail.com

The annual London Vegan Festival is a huge event with over 100 stalls and lots of speakers and entertainers.

The 2008 one is on Sunday 7th September, 11am–8pm at Kensington Town Hall, Hornton Street W8 (underground High Street Kensington), £1 entry, under 16 free. Food, stalls, speakers, entertainment, workshops and good vibes!

Croydon Vegans

61 Warren Road,
Croydon CR0 6PF.
Tel: 020-8655 3797.
tandj@moosenet.
free-online.co.uk

Campaigning and social events. Fundraising for Animal Aid and other organisations. Regular newsletter.

Croydon Vegetarian Group

Helen Buckland
Tel: 020-8688 6325

Group promoting vegetarianism, with information stalls and events. Offers of help always welcome. No media calls please.

Vegan Harlow

info@veganharlow.co.uk
www.veganharlow.co.uk

Harrow Vegetarian Society

Mr K Joshi
Tel: 020 8907 1235
Email:kjoshi@pradipsweet.co.uk

Hertsveg

www.hertsveg.makessense.co.uk
Amanda Bryant 07979 735169

Hertsveg is the new local vegan group for the East Herts area. We welcome anyone to join us with a genuine interest in veganism as a dietry path and a compassionate way of life. We meet once a month for an evening vegan meal.

HUNT SABOTEURS

www.huntsabs.org.uk
info@huntsabs.org.uk
BM HSA, London WC1N 3XX
Telephone 0845 450 0727 (24hr answering machine)

Hunt saboteurs? But hunting has been banned hasn't it?! Tell that to some of the hunts, some of which are still intent on hounding our wildlife to death.

Hunt sabs are active in and around London, and throughout the UK, as there is much still to be done to stop bloodsports. Join the national Hunt Saboteurs Association and/or become an active sab out in the fields – see website for full details.

Kingston and Richmond Vegetarians

Martin 020-8541 3437
John 020-8977 9648

walker@martinlake.plus.com

Vegetarians, vegans and those interested in vegetarianism are welcome to join our small but friendly group. Monthly restaurant visit as well as campaigning and other events.

Lesbian Vegan Group

http://groups.yahoo.com/group/lvegangroup

japope_1982@hotmail.co.uk

London-based social group for lesbian and bisexual vegans. Vegetarians are welcome, but eat vegan food when with the group. The group meets at restaurants and members' houses for potluck meals where everyone brings a different dish. Picnics in summer. Members from many countries.

London Animal Rights

www.londonanimalrights.org.uk
info@londonanimalrights.org.uk
Tel: 07899 775493

Helps to co-ordinate various animal rights campaigns in the London area. There is an email, phone and text list to inform about forthcoming events and demos in the London area. LAR also organise transport to demos in other parts of the country. There are also bi-monthly meetings in Central London.

Muslim Vegan and Vegetarian Society

Rafeeque Ahmed
59 Brey Towers, 136 Adelaide Rd, London NW3 3JU.
Tel: 020-7483 1742.

Publishes Islam and Vegetarianism book, for £1 post free. Main emphasis is on the vegan side, also raw food, combining, timing and additive free.

Young Jains

www.youngjains.org.uk

Occasional vegetarian educational events.

London Vegans

www.londonvegans.org.uk
020-8931 1904

London Vegans exists to promote veganism in the London area. Various social events, such as monthly meetings, restaurant visits and walks. Also information stalls at a variety of events throughout the year, ranging from small bazaars to large festivals. Details of these and other events in The London Vegans Diary, which is updated frequently. For information on the next London Vegans events see the website or telephone the Info Line on (020) 8931 1904 (24 hours) for updates.

Meetings: 6.30pm, last Wednesday of each month (not December) at Millman Street Community Rooms, Millman Street, London WC1 (entrance through security door adjacent to 38a – press the bell marked Community Centre). Doors open at 6.30pm, but the speaker usually commences just after 7pm. Nearest tube: Russell Square

Telephone enquiries (about London Vegans, or veganism in general):

Julie / Brian: 020-8446 3480

E-mail: Brian and Julie at information@londonvegans.org.uk, type "enquiry" in the subject line.

Paul Halford on 01206-861846

Postal enquiries:
7 Deansbrook Road, Edgware, Middlesex HA8 9BE.

Subscriptions (or a request to be e-mailed full diary) subsscriptions@londonvegans.org.uk

Or leave message on infoline 020 8931 1904

Press and media *only*
020-32398433or media@londonvegans.org.uk or call the Vegan Society on 0121 523 1730.

Also don't miss Julie and Brian's website: www.veganlondon.co.uk

North West Vegetarian Group

Jayjit & Chetna Shah, 3 St David Close, Cowley, UB8 3SE.
Tel: 01895 441 881
chetna_jayjit@yahoo.com

Vegetarian Society affiliated group.

Raw Food Party

Tel: 020-7624 4531
Swiss Cottage, London
www.rawfoodparty.com
moonlight@rawfoodparty.com

Classes and events to help you improve your health by switching to raw food veganism. They also host occasional raw gourmet dinner parties and sell a variety of snack foods mail order.

SEAR

www.se-ar.org.uk
BM Sear,.London WC1N 3XX
Tel: 07810 024098

South-East Animal Rights campaigning group, meetings in Croydon.

South West London Veg Info Centre

K Brown, Flat 424, Brandenburgh House, 116 Fulham Palace Road, London W6 9HH
Tel: 020-8741 6793
swveg1@yahoo.co.uk

Vegetarian Society affiliated group.

Twickenham & Surrey Vegetarian & Vegan Group

Lesley Dove 020-8941 8075
email: lesley@vegan4life.org.uk

Events will include pot luck parties at members' homes, pub meets, picnics in the summer, and possibly some joint events with other vegetarian/vegan groups. Families very welcome to most gatherings. This group has a young families section which includes an e-group.

Vegan Campaigns

www.vegancampaigns.org.uk
Subscribe to email list:
vegancampaigns@lists.rbgi.net

Vegan Campaigns, BM 2300,
London WC1N 3XX
General enquiries: 07960
036044. Media enquiries ONLY:
020-32398433

Very active group formed in
April 2005 to promote
veganism, primarily in the
London area. Activities
include vegan food fairs,
veggie burger give-aways,
street stalls and helping to
organise the London Vegan
Festival.

Occasional meetings in
Central London and an email
list to inform about events
and campaigns planned:

The impressive website has
reasons for going vegan, a
guide to going and staying
vegan, stacks of recipes, and
a guide to running a vegan
stall. For more details fill out
the form on the website.

Vegetarian & Vegan Essex

www.essex.veginfo.org.uk

Social events and a website
full of tips and a directory of
places to eat out in Essex.

Founder Karin runs a PR and
events company for people
who make a difference called
www.mad-promotions.com
and started the veggie
internet TV station
www.veggievision.co.uk with
cookery, celebs etc. (page 9)

Vegetarian Cycling and Athletic Club

www.vcac.vegfolk.co.uk

Veggie Socials

www.veggiesocials.co.uk

Free social group for veggies
who can attend events in
London and surrounding
areas.

Young Indian Vegetarians

Nitin Mehta, M.B.E.,
226 London Rd, West Croydon,
Surrey CR0 2TE
Tel: 020-8681 8884

www.
youngindianvegetarians.co.uk
animalahimsa@yahoo.co.uk

Active, campaigning group.
Welcomes opportunity to
give talks, presentations.
Various big events around
London.

National Organisations

If there's no vegetarian or animal rights group listed near you, contact any of these for the address of your local contact or group. If you want to go veggie or vegan, or know someone who might be interested, they have stacks of literature to help you and can answer questions. If you want to help spread the word and get active for animal rights, they would love to hear from you. And they all have brilliant websites. Always enclose a stamped addressed envelope or a donation.

Animal Aid

www.animalaid.org.uk
The Old Chapel, Bradford St,
Tonbridge, Kent TN9 1AW.

Tel: 01732-364 546
Fax: 01732-366 533

£18 waged, £10 unwaged, £20 joint, £7 youth (16 or under), £22 overseas, £25 joint, £300 life. The experts on U-18 campaigns for all areas of animal rights. Campaigns from factory farming, vivisection and promoting vegetarianism to horse racing, pheasant shooting and wildlife culls. On-line shop for all vegan goodies, including chocolates, wine, shoes, toiletries and cosmetics.

See advert page 24.

Animal Rights Coalition

www.arcnews.org.uk
PO Box 339,
Wolverhampton WV10 7BZ

Tel: 0845-458 0146

Network of local animal groups and campaigners. Online magazine.

People for the Ethical Treatment of Animals

www.peta.org.uk

Huge website includes a vegetarian starter kit, lists of charities that do and don't test on animals, info sheets

See page 13.

Realfood

PO Box 339,
Wolverhampton WV10 7BZ
Tel: 0845-458 0146
www.realfood.org.uk

Campaigning vegan group making it easier for people to follow a vegan diet.

Vegan Buddies

www.veganbuddies.org.uk

If you want to go vegan but find it hard, sign up and get a local buddy to help you make the transition. New and aspiring vegans can advertise for help, while isolated vegans can find out more easily who is in their area. They also need people to give advice, and to advertise the fact that they exist. You can also post specific questions and requests for advice.

Check out London Vegans and Vegan Campaigns too. (see previous section)

The Vegan Society

www.vegansociety.com
See advert page 14.

The Vegetarian Society

www.vegsoc.org

Vegetarian and Vegan Foundation

www.vegetarian.org.uk
See advert page 21.

Veggies, Nottingham

www.veggies.org.uk
Tel: 0845-458 9595

Publishes the Animal Rights Calendar and Animal Contacts Directory, available on line, which lists every veggie and vegan business and animal rights group in the country.

Viva! (Vegetarians International Voice for Animals)

www.viva.org.uk
See advert page 21.

Campaign Against Cruelty

an activist's handbook

by Alex Bourke and Ronny Worsey

We tell you how to:

launch a local campaigning **group**
*run different kinds of **street stalls***
arrange a meeting or video showing
***speak in public** or to groups*
produce **leaflets, posters and newsletters**
raise money
promote veggie and vegan food in your area
organise a demonstration
utilise the **press, radio and tv**
*understand how **the law** affects your right to protest*
192 pages

£4.99 from **www.vegetarianguides.co.uk**

Plus a huge **directory of books, magazines, websites and groups** that can provide you with info on all aspects of campaigning.

Relied on by group founders throughout the country and written by two dedicated, effective and inspiring campaigners, with contributions from frontline activists throughout Britain and overseas, this book contains all the advice you need to start saving animals' lives now.

So, what are you waiting for?

The entire book online at **www.vegetarianguides.co.uk/campaign**

To get active in London visit **www.vegancampaigns.org.uk**

VEGETARIAN LONDON
INDEXES

WHERE TO EAT

Vegan   414

Organic   415

Cheap   416

Posh   417

Drink Alcohol   418

Have Coffee & Tea   420

Veggie Breakfast   422

With the Kids   424

A–Z INDEX   426

For a free, printable list of new openings and closures since this guide was printed visit:

www.vegetarianguides.co.uk

Eat Vegan	Eat organic	Eat cheap	Eat posh
Drink & Eat veggie	Have coffee & tea	Have a veggie breakfast	Take kids

Care and feeding of your vegan: he or she will purr with delight at superb buffets, vegan cakes, desserts and soya ice-cream.

Central

Beatroot, Soho	56
* Buddha Café, Soho	63
* Buffet V, New Oxford St	94
* Chi, Covent Garden	80
Food for Thought, Covent Gdn	74
Foyles Café, Soho	66
* Gi Gi Hut, Euston	113
Health Food Centre, Warren St	100
* Joi, Tottenham Court Rd	103
Maoz, Soho	59
Neal's Yard Salad Bar, Covent Gdn	76
Red Veg, Soho	61
* Saf, Shoreditch	134
* Tai, Greek Street	63
* Tai Buffet, Euston	113
* Tai Buffet, Piccadilly	63
* Tai Express, Old Compton St	64
* Tai Veg, Greatt Chapel St	64
* Veg, Theobald's Rd	94
* VitaOrganic, Soho	54
* Wai, Goodge Street	103
* Zen Garden, Leather Lane	137

East

Gossip Café, Broadway Market	164
Hornbeam Café, Walthamstow	191
* Pogo Café, Hackney	181
* Rainforest Creations, Spitalfields	161
* Rootmaster, Brick Lane	156
Spital Felafel	160
* Vegan Stall, Broadway Market	166

* 100% vegan

North

* CTV, Golders Green	215
Falafel Queen, Camden	199
Friendly Falafels, Hampstead	218
Ha Ha Veggie Bar, Camden	199
InSpiral Lounge, Camden	198
Madder Rose, Primrose Hill	248
* Peking Palace, Archway	214
* Rainforest Creations, N22	259
* Tai Buffet, Camden	204
* Tai Buffet, Islington	233
* Tony's, Kings Cross	239

South

Bonnington Cafe, Vauxhall	304
* Burger Stall, Borough Market	287
Lorentson's, Brixton Market	266
Pepperton UK, Croydon	311
Pulse, London Bridge	284
Riverside Vegetaria	283
* Spirited Palace, Crystal Palace	278
* Vegan Stall, Borough Market	287

West

* 222, West Kensington	351
Gate, The, Hammersmith	350
Grain Shop, Portobello	372
Indian Deli, Hounslow	362
Luscious Organic, Kensington	321
Man Chui, Kenton	356
Mr Man, Edgware	343
Organic Café, Chelsea (Sunday)	320
Planet Organic, Westbourne Grove	333
* Rainforest Creations, Chelsea	320
* Rainforest Creations, Hammersmith	352

| Eat posh | Eat cheap | **Eat organic** | Eat vegan |
| Take kids | Have a veggie breakfast | Have coffee & tea | Drink & Eat veggie |

Where to ?

Specialists in organic meals, snacks, provisions, fruit and vegetables.

Farmaround organic deliveries	21
Organic box schemes	15

Central

Fresh & Wild, Soho	62
Greens & Beans, Drummond St	108
Peppercorn's, Goodge St	104
Planet Organic, Tottenham Ct Rd	102
Quiet Revolution, Marylebone	123
Saf, Shoreditch	134
Total Organics, Marylebone	125
VitaOrganic, Soho	54

East

Broadway Organic Foods	166
Chegworth Valley, Broadway Market	162
Eostre, Walthamstow	191
The Grocery, Shoreditch	188
mOrganics shop, Hoxton	187
Pogo Café, Hackney	181
Rainforest Creations, Spitalfields	161
Spitalfields Organics	160
Wholsum, Dalston	182

North

Bumblebee	241
Eostre Organics Co-op, N7	224
Fresh & Wild, Camden	202
Fresh and Wild, Stoke Newington	253
Green Note, Camden	201
Haelan Centre, Crouch End	245
InSpiral Lounge, Camden	198
Just Natural, Crouch End	244
Madder Rose Cafe, Primrose Hill	248
Manna, Primrose Hill	247

Mother Earth, Highbury	225
Mother Earth, Stoke Newington	257
OHFS Natural Foods, Archway	213
Paradise Foods, Kentish Town	240
Peppercorn's, West Hampstead	220
Rainforest Creations, N22	259
Tony's, Kings Cross	239
Planet Organic, Islington	236

South

As Nature Intended, Balham	300
Borough Market	287
Dandelion, Clapham	276
Esme, Brixton	269
FareShares, Walworth	307
Fresh & Wild, Clapham	273
Greenbag, Clapham	274
It's A Green Thing, Crystal Palace	279
Spirited Palace, Crystal Palace	278
Tide Tables, Richmond	291
Total Organics, Borough Market	287
Well Bean, Blackheath	314

West

As Nature Intended, Chiswick	336
As Nature Intended, Ealing	339
Bush Garden Café, Shepherds Bush	354
Hugo's Restaurant, Queens Park	364
Jacob's, Gloucester Road	325
Luscious Organic, Kensington	321
Organic Café, Chelsea (Sunday)	320
Planet Organic, Fulham	322
Planet Organic, Westbourne Grove	333
Rainforest Creations, Hammersmith	352
Whole Foods Market, Kensington	323

Eat Vegan	Eat organic	Eat cheap	Eat posh
Drink & Eat veggie	Have coffee & tea	Have a veggie breakfast	Take kids

All-you-can-eat bargain buffets, student favourites, big portions at low low prices.

Central

Alara, Bloomsbury	90
Beatroot, Soho	56
Buddha Café, Soho	63
Buffet V, New Oxford Street	94
Chi, Covent Garden	80
Chutneys, Drummond Street	109
Diwana, Drummond Street	109
Gi Gi Hut, Euston Road	113
Govinda's, Soho	57
The Greenery, Farringdon	135
Gujarati Rasoi, Exmouth Market	138
Hare & Tortoise, Bloomsbury	96
Health Food Centre, Warren Street	100
Joi, Tottenham Court Road	103
Konditor & Cook, South Bank	149
LSE Café, Aldwych	81
Maoz, Soho	59
Mary Ward Café, Bloomsbury	91
Meze Café, Great Portland Street	114
Rasa Express, Euston	113
Rasa Express, Rathbone St	103
Ravi Shankar, Drummond Street	110
Rye Wholefoods, Clerkenwell	136
Sagar, Tottenham Court Road	101
Tai, Greek Street	63
Tai Buffet, Euston Road	113
Tai Buffet, Piccadilly	63
Tai Express, Old Compton St	64
Tai Veg, Gt Chapel St	64
Troia, South Bank	151
Veg, Theobald's Rd	94
Vegetarian Paradise, Bloomsbury	94
Wai, Goodge Street	103
Wheatley's, Clerkenwell	136
Yumnation, Holborn	92
Zen Garden, Leather Lane	137

East

Broadway Market stalls	166
Chennai, East Ham x2	170
Gallery Café, Bethnal Green	177
Hookah Lounge, Brick Lane	158
Hornbeam Café, Walthamstow	191
Lennie's, Shoreditch x2	185
Spital Felafel	160
Swaad, Leytonstone	189
Saravana Bhavan, East Ham	170

North

Camden Market	199
CTV, Golders Green	215
Friendly Falafels, Hampstead	218
Gallery Cafe, Holloway Road	212
Greenhouse, Wood Green	259
Indian Veg Bhelpuri, Islington	231
Phoenicia, Kentish Town	240
St Gabriel Cafe, Finsbury Park	211
Tai Buffet, Camden	204
Tai Buffet, Islington	233
Tony's Natural Foods	239

South

Bonnington Cafe, Vauxhall	304
Greenbag, Clapham	274
Hare & Tortoise, Putney	288
Honest Foods, Brixton	268
Pulse, London Bridge	284
Santok Maa's, Thornton Heath	309
Shahee Bhelpoori, Streatham	294
Spring Gardens Café, Vauxhall	305
St Gabriel Cafe, Kennington	306

West

Bhavna Sweet Mart, Willesden	364
Chhappan Bhog, Kingsbury	368
Chhappan Bhog, Southall	376
Chowpatty, Wembley	380
Indian Deli, Hounslow	362
Leon, Knightsbridge	325
Mayura, Edgware	342
Mr Man, Edgware	343
Natraj, South Harrow	356
Organic Café, Chelsea (Sunday)	320
Saravanas, Willesden	364
Shay Naiy Sweet Mar, Edgware	345

Elegance, gourmet grub and perhaps candles for a romantic soiree or important client.

Central

Carnevale, Old Street	130
Chor Bizarre, Mayfair	126
The Conservatory, Knightsbridge	391
Eat & Two Veg, Marylebone	119
John Lewis Coffee Shop	122
Levant, Marylebone	122
Neal's Yard Salad Bar, Covent Gdn	76
OXO Tower Restaurant, South Bank	150
The Place Below, Cheapside	131
Rasa, Bond Street	120
Saf, Shoreditch	134
Sofra, Mayfair	126
Stella McCartney, Mayfair (shoes)	127
Tas, The Cut SE1	146
Tas, Farringdon	139
Woodlands, Marylebone	118

East

Rasa, Stoke Newington	252
Saf, Shoreditch	134

North

Daniel Field hairdresser, New Barnet	263
Equa Boutique, Islington	237
Ottolenghi, Islington	234
Hampstead Cuisine School	221
Manna, Primrose Hill	247
Muang Thai, Camden	207
Peking Palace, Archway	214
Rani, Finchley	209
Rasa, Stoke Newington	252
Thai Square, Islington	235
Woodlands, Hampstead	218

South

Riverside Vegetaria, Kingston	283

West

222, West Kensington	351
Amaya, Knightsbridge	324
Bombay Palace, Paddington	332
Conservatory, The, Knightsbridge	391
The Gate, Hammersmith	350
Randa, Kensington Church St	331
Rotana Lounge, Knightsbridge	331
Whole Foods Market, Kensington	323
Woodlands, Chiswick	336

Eat Vegan	Eat organic	Eat cheap	Eat posh
Drink & Eat veggie	Have coffee & tea	Have a veggie breakfast	Take kids

Quaff while you scoff at these licensed eateries, or bring your own (BYO) from the nearby offie.

Central

Adonis, Goodge Street	104
African Gallery Kitchen, Euston	110
Azzurro, South Bank	147
Carnevale, Old Street	130
Carrie Awaze, Covent Garden	79
Carthage, Covent Garden	80
Chor Bizarre, Mayfair	126
Chutneys, Euston	109
Cubana, South Bank	147
Diwana, Euston	109
Eat & Two Veg, Marylebone	119
Ev, South Bank	148
First Out, Covent Gdn	78
Gaby's, Leicester Square	66
Giraffe, Bloomsbury	95
Giraffe, Marylebone	121
Giraffe, South Bank	149
Hare & Tortoise, Bloomsbury	96
Inshoku, South Bank	149
Just Falafs, Covent Gdn	75
Just Falafs, Soho	58
Leon, Cannon St	139
Leon, Carnaby St	67
Leon, Ludgate Circus	139
Leon, Regent St	122
Leon, Strand	81
Levant, Marylebone	122
Meson Don Felipe, South Bank	150
Mildred's, Soho	60
Neal's Yard Salad Bar, Covent Gdn	76
OXO Tower, South Bank	150
Paradiso, South Bank	151
Rasa, Bond Street	120
Ravi Shankar, Euston	110
Saf, Shoreditch	134
Sagar, Tottenham Court Rd	101
Sofra, Mayfair	126
Sofra, St Christopher's Place	126
Tai, Greek Street	63
Tas, The Cut	146
Tas, British Museum	96
Tas, Farringdon Rd	139
Tiffin Bites, City x3	139
Troia, South Bank	151
Wagamama, Bloomsbury (menu)	93
Wagamama, Covent Gdn	82
Wagamama, City x 5	140
Wagamama, Soho x 3	68
Wagamama, South Bank	152
Wagamama, Wigmore St	124
Woodlands Piccadilly	64
Woodlands, Marylebone	118
Zen Garden, Leather Lane	137

East

Amita, Green Street	173
Giraffe, Spitalfields	159
Hookah Lounge, Brick Lane	158
Leon, Canary Wharf	169
Leon, Spitalfields	159
Pembury Tavern, Hackney	179
Pogo Café, Hackney	181
Ronak Restaurant, Forest Gate	172
Rootmaster, Brick Lane	156
Saf, Shoreditch	134
Solché Cilician, Broadway Market	163
Swaad, Leytonstone	189
Thai Garden, Bethnal Green	178
Viet Hoa, Shoreditch	188
Wagamama, Canary Wharf	169

North

Candid Café, Angel	233
Clicia, Stoke Newington	255
CTV, Golders Green	215
The Dervish, Stoke Newington	254
Gallipoli (3 branches), Islington	234
Giraffe, Hampstead	219
Giraffe, Islington	234
Giraffe, Muswell Hill	243
Green Note, Camden (veggie pub)	201
Grittz, High Barnet	262
InSpiral Lounge, Camden	198
Jai Krishna, Finsbury Park	211

Le Mignon, Camden — 203
Lemon Grass, Camden — 205
Man Chui III. Finchley — 208
Manna, Primrose Hill — 247
Max Orient Buffet, Camden — 204
Mercado Cantina, Stoke Newington — 255
Muang Thai, Camden — 207
Ottolenghi, Islington — 234
The Ottomans, Finchley — 208
Pavilion Café, Highgate Wood — 227
Rajen's Thali Hut, West Hendon — 222
Rani, Finchley — 209
Rasa, Stoke Newington — 252
Shamsudeen, Stoke Newington — 256
Tai Buffet, Camden — 204
Tai Buffet, Islington — 233
Thai Square, Islington — 235
Tupelo Honey, Camden — 203
Wagamama, Brent Cross — 223
Wagamama, Camden — 204
Wagamama, Islington — 235
Woodlands, Hampstead — 218
Yum Yum, Stoke Newington — 256
Zigni House, Essex Road — 235

South

Bonnington Cafe, Vauxhall — 304
Carmen, Clapham (tapas bar) — 272
Courtyard Cafe, Vauxhall — 302
David Wong, Tooting — 296
Domali, Crystal Palace — 280
Eco, Clapham — 274
Giraffe, Battersea — 274
Giraffe, Richmond — 290
Giraffe, Wimbledon — 308
Hare & Tortoise, Putney — 288
Hing Loong, Borough — 285
Hive Bar & Restaurant, Brixton — 268
Jasmin, Clapham — 275
Kastoori, Tooting — 298
Leon, Bankside — 285
Lounge Bar, Brixton — 267
Mantanah Thai Cuisine, Peckham — 313
Pepperton UK, Croydon — 311
Pili Pili, Welling — 312
Riverside Vegetaria, Kingston — 283
Santok Maa's, Thornton Heath — 309

Shahee Bhelpoori, Streatham — 294
Swad, Thornton Heath — 312
Tas Café, South Bank x3 — 286
Wagamama, Kingston — 282
Wagamama, Putney — 288
Wagamama, London Bridge — 286
Wagamama, Richmond — 290
Wholemeal Café, Streatham — 293
Yum Yum, Clapham — 276

West

222, West Kensington — 351
Amaya, Knightsbridge — 324
Bella Italia, Ealing x2 — 338
Blah Blah Blah, Shepherds Bush — 354
Bombay Palace, Paddington — 332
Butler's Thai Cafe, Ealing — 338
Celebrations, Edgware — 342
Chowpatty, Wembley — 380
Connoisseurs, Paddington — 332
The Conservatory, Knightsbridge — 391
Dosa Junction, Wembley — 381
Durbar Tandoori, Bayswater — 334
Garden Café, Ladbroke Grove — 371
The Gate, Hammersmith — 350
Giraffe, Chiswick — 336
Giraffe, Heathrow 1 — 363
Giraffe, Kensington — 324
Hare & Tortoise, Ealing — 338
Hare & Tortoise, Kensington — 324
Hugo's Restaurant, Queens Park — 364
Jacob's, Gloucester Rd SW7 — 325
Kalamaras, Bayswater — 335
Leon, Knightsbridge — 325
Luscious Organic, Kensington — 321
Man Chui, Kenton — 356
Pizza Express, Ealing — 339
Pizza Parlour, Wembley — 383
Ram's Gujarati Restaurant, Kenton — 357
Sagar, Hammersmith — 352
Sagar, Twickenham — 376
Saravanas, Willesden — 364
Tulsi, Wembley — 386
Veggie Inn, Harrow — 360
Wagamama Kensington — 326
Wagamama, Heathrow 5 — 363
Woodlands Chiswick — 336

eat Vegan	Eat organic	Eat cheap	Eat posh
Drink & Eat veggie	Have coffee & tea	Have a veggie breakfast	Take kids

Favourite chill out spots for sipping tea, (soya) cappuccino, latte, nibbling cake.

Central

Alara, Bloomsbury	90
Bean Juice, St Christopher's Place	121
Beatroot, Soho	56
Carrie Awaze, Covent Garden	79
Casse-Croute, South Bank	147
Coffee@Goswell Road	138
Coffee@Whitecross St	138
Coopers, South Bank	145
First Out, Covent Garden	78
Food for Thought, Covent Garden	74
Foyles Café, Soho	66
Fresco, Marylebone	121
Fresh & Wild, Soho	62
Gaby's, Leicester Square	66
Govinda's, Soho	57
The Greenery, Farringdon	135
Greens & Beans, Euston	108
Hummus Bros, Soho	67
John Lewis Coffee Shop	122
Just Falafs, Covent Garden	75
Just Falafs, Soho	58
Le Pain Quotidien, Covent Garden	82
Le Pain Quotidien, Marylebone	123
Le Pain Quotidien, South Bank	151
Lebanese cafes, Edgware Road	124
Leon, Carnaby Street	67
Leon, Regent Street	122
Leon, Strand	81
LSE Café	81
Maoz, Soho	59
Mary Ward Café, Bloomsbury	91
Meze Café, Great Portland St	114
Neal's Yard Salad Bar, Covent Gdn	76
The Place Below, Cheapside	131
Planet Organic, Tottenham Ct Rd	102
Quiet Revolution, Marylebone	123
Red Veg, Soho	61
Rye Wholefoods, Clerkenwell	136
Total Organics, Marylebone	125
Wheatley's, Clerkenwell	136
Woolley's, Theobalds Road	96
World Food Café, Covent Garden	77
Yumnation, Holborn	92

East

Bagel Factory, Canary Wharf	168
Coffee@157, Brick Lane	155
Coffee@Brick Lane	158
Crussh, Canary Wharf Jubilee Place	168
Crussh, Canary W Tower Concourse	168
Frizzante @ City Farm, Hackney	167
Gallery Café, Bethnal Green	177
Gossip Café, Broadway Market	164
Hookah Lounge, Brick Lane	158
Hornbeam Café, Walthamstow	191
Lennie's Snack Bar, Shoreditch	186
Leon, Canary Wharf	169
Leon, Spitalfields	159
mOrganics Café, Hoxton	187
Pogo Café, Hackney	181
Spitalfields Market	160
Spital Felafel	160
Wild Cherry, Bethnal Green	176

North

Bliss Patisserie, Angel	234
Cafe Seventy-Nine, Primrose Hill	249
Candid Café, Angel	233
Clicia, Stoke Newington	255
Coby's, Golders Green	215
The Dervish, Stoke Newington	254
Fresh & Wild, Camden	202
Fresh and Wild, Stoke Newington	253
Giraffe, Islington	234
Green Note, Camden	201
Greenhouse, Wood Green	259
Higher Taste, Newington Green	258
InSpiral Lounge, Camden	198
Le Pain Quotidien, St Pancras	238
Madder Rose Cafe, Primrose Hill	248
Marrakech, Camden	200
Mother Earth, Newington Green	258
My Village, Camden	206
Pavilion Café, Highgate Wood	227
Phoenicia, Kentish Town	240
Pita, Golders Green	216
Queens Wood Cafe	227
The Red Hedgehog, Highgate	228
St Gabriel Cafe, Finsbury Park	211
Straw Bale Café, Highury	224
Taboon Bakery, Golders Green	217
Tony's, Kings Cross	239
Tupelo Honey, Camden	203

South

Arlington Cafe, Southwark	284
Bonnington Cafe, Vauxhall	304
Coffee@ Bermondsey St	285
Coffee@ Tower Bridge Rrd	285
Courtyard Cafe, Vauxhall	302
Café Crema, New Cross	310
Fresh & Wild, Clapham	273
Green Cafe, Richmond	289
Greenbag, Clapham	274
Hive Bar & Restaurant, Brixton	268
Hollyhock Café, Richmond	289
Honest Foods, Brixton	268
Leon, Bankside	285
Pepperton UK, Croydon	311
Provender Wholefoods, Forest Hill	314
Royal Teas, Greenwich	281
Spirited Palace, Crystal Palace	278
Spring Gardens Cafe, Vauxhall	305
Synergy Centre, Oval	302
Tide Tables, Richmnod	291
Wholemeal Café, Streatham	293

West

Bush Garden Café, Shepherds Bush	354
Garden Café, Ladbroke Grove	371
Jays Pure, Kingsbury	369
Le Pain Quotidien, S. Kensington	326
Le Pain Quotidien, High St Ken	326
Le Pain Quotidien, Kings Road	326
Leon, Knightsbridge	325
Luscious Organic, Kensington	321
Maru's Bhajia House, Wembley	382
Montignac Boutique, S. Kensington	330
Naklank Sweet Mart	382
Organic Café, Chelsea (Sunday)	320
Planet Organic, Fulham	322
Planet Organic, Westbourne Grove	333
Udupi Palace, Kingsbury	370
Whole Foods Market	323

Where to ?

| Eat Vegan | Eat organic | Eat cheap | Eat posh |
| Drink & Eat veggie | Have coffee & tea | **Have a veggie breakfast** | Take kids |

Open early for a bowl of muesli, full English cooked veggie breakfast, or Sunday brunch.

Central

Bean Juice, St Christopher's Place	121
Beatroot, Soho	56
Eat & Two Veg, Marylebone	119
Fresh & Wild, Soho	62
Futures VTA, the City	137
Gaby's, Leicester Square	66
Giraffe, Bloomsbury	95
Giraffe, Marylebone	121
Giraffe, South Bank	149
The Greenery, Farringdon	135
Greens & Beans Café, Euston	108
Just Falafs, Covent Garden	75
Just Falafs, Soho	58
Le Pain Quotidien, Marylebone	123
Leon, Cannon St	139
Leon, Carnaby St	67
Leon, Ludgate Circus	139
Leon, Regent St	122
Leon, Strand	81
Mary Ward Café, Bloomsbury	91
Meze Café, Great Portland St	114
Neal's Yard Salad Bar, Covent Gdn	76
The Place Below, Cheapside	131
Pure, Moregate	133
The Souk, Trafalgar Square	82
Tiffin Bites, Liverpool St	139
Tiffin Bites, Moorgate	139
Tiffin Bites, St Pauls	139
Woolley's, Theobalds Rd	96
Yumnation, Holborn	92

East

Coffee@157, Brick Lane	155
Crussh, Canary Wharf Jubilee Place	168
Crussh, Canary W Tower Concourse	168
Gallery Café, Globe Town E2	177
Giraffe, Spitalfields	159
Gossip Café, Broadway Market	164
Lennie's Snack Bar, Shoreditch	186
Leon, Canary Wharf	169
Leon, Spitalfields	159
mOrganics Café, Hoxton	187
Pogo Café, Hackney E8	181
Solché Cilician, Broadway Market	163
Wild Cherry, Globe Town	176

North

Cafe Seventy-Nine, Primrose Hill	249
Clicia, Stoke Newington	255
Giraffe, Hampstead	219
Giraffe, Islington	234
Giraffe, Muswell Hill	243
Madder Rose Cafe, Primrose Hill	248

South

Café Crema, New Cross	310
Coffee@Bermondsey St	285
Coffee@ Tower Bbidge Rd	285
Domali, Crystal Palace	280
Lorentson's, Brixton Market	266
Giraffe, Battersea	274
Giraffe, Wimbledon	308
Green Cafe, Richmond	289
Greenbag, Clapham	274
Hollyhock Café, Richmond	289
Pulse, London Bridge	284
Spring Gardens Cafe, Vauxhall	305
Tide Tables, Richmond	291

West

Bush Garden Café, Shepherds Bush	354
Giraffe, Chiswick	336
Giraffe, Heathrow 1	363
Giraffe, Kensington	324
Hugo's Restaurant, Queens Park	364
Le Pain Quotidien, High St Ken	326
Le Pain Quotidien, Kings Road	326
Le Pain Quotidien, South Ken	326
Leon, Knightsbridge	325
Luscious Organic, Kensington	321
Planet Organic, Fulham	322
Planet Organic, Westbourne Grove	333
Sakonis, Wembley	383
Satyam Restaurant, Edgware	344
Wagamama, Heathrow 5	363

| Eat vegan | Eat organic | Eat cheap | Eat posh |
| Drink & Eat veggie | Have coffee & tea | Have a veggie breakfast | Take kids |

These places welcome the little darlings with high chairs, children's portions or special menus.

| Mishel, children's entertainer | 19 |
| Rubber Ritchie, contortionist | 19 |

Central

Carthage, Covent Garden	80
Giraffe, Bloomsbury	95
Giraffe, Marylebone	121
Giraffe, South Bank	149
Govinda's, Soho	57
Just Falafs, Soho	58
Le Pain Quotidien, South Bank	151
Paradiso, South Bank	151
Red Veg, Soho	61
Sagar, Tottenham Court Rd	101
Sofra, Mayfair	126
Sofra, St Christopher's Place	126
Tai Buffet, Euston	113
Tas, The Cut	146
Troia, South Bank	151
Yumnation, Holborn	92
Tiffin Bites, Liverpool St	139
Tiffin Bites, Moorgate	139
Tiffin Bites, St Pauls	139

East

Amita, Green Street E7	173
Chawalla, Green Street E7	172
Chennai, East Ham E12	170
Frizzante @ City Farm, Hackney	167
Gallery Café, Globe Town E2	177
Giraffe, Spitalfields	159
Lennie's Snack Bar, Shoreditch	186
Pogo Café, Hackney	181
Ronak Restaurant, Forest Gate	172

Saravana Bhavan, East Ham	170
Solché Cilician, Broadway Market	163
Spice Green, Green Street E7	173
Swaad, Leytonstone E11	189
Thai Garden, Globe Town E2	178
Viet Hoa, Hoxton E2	188
Wild Cherry, Globe Town E2	176

North

Bliss Patisserie, Angel	234
Cafe Seventy-Nine, Primrose Hill	249
Candid Café, Angel	233
Dervish, Stoke Newington	254
Gallery Cafe, Holloway Rd N7	212
Giraffe, Hampstead	219
Giraffe, Islington	234
Giraffe, Muswell Hill	243
Green Baby, Angel	237
Grittz, High Barnet	262
Lemon Grass, Camden	205
Madder Rose Cafe	248
Man Chui III, Finchley	208
Manna, Primrose Hill	247
Max Orient Buffet, Camden	204
Muang Thai, Camden	207
My Village, Camden	206
Pavilion Café, Highgate Wood	227
Peking Palace, Archway	214
Queens Wood Cafe	227
Rajen's Thali Hut, West Hendon	222
Straw Bale Café, Highury	224
Woodlands, Hampstead	218
Yum Yum, Stoke Newington	256

South

Café Crema, New Cross	310
Carmen, Clapham	272
Lorentson's, Brixton Market	266
Giraffe, Battersea	274
Giraffe, Richmond	290
Giraffe, Wimbledon	308
Green Baby, Greenwich	281
Green Baby, Richmond	292
Green Cafe, Richmond	289
Greenbag, Clapham	274
Hollyhock Café, Richmond	289
It's A Green Thing, Crystal Palace	279
Kastoori, Tooting	298
Lounge Bar, Brixton	267
Pili Pili, Welling	312
Riverside Vegetaria, Kingston	283
Santok Maa's, Thornton Heath	309
Sarashwathy Bavans, Tooting	299
Shahee Bhelpoori, Streatham	294
Swad, Thornton Heath	312
Tide Tables, Richmond	291
Wholemeal Café, Streatham	293
Yum Yum, Clapham	276

West

Bush Garden Café, Shepherds Bush	354
Celebrations, Edgware	342
Connoisseurs, Paddington	332
Delhi Wala, Hounslow	375
Garden Café, Ladbroke Grove	371
The Gate, Hammersmith	350
Giraffe, Chiswick	336
Giraffe, Heathrow 1	363
Giraffe, Kensington	324
Green Baby, Notting Hill	374
Hugo's Restaurant, Queens Park	364
Jacob's, Gloucester Rd SW7	325
Jashan, Wembley	381
Jays Pure, Kingsbury	369
Kalamaras, Bayswater	335
Man Chui, Kenton	356
Maru's Bhajia House, Wembley	382
Mr Man, Edgware	343
Pradip, Kenton	357
Ram's Gujarati Restaurant, Kenton	357
Rose, Kingsbury	368
Sagar, Hammersmith	352
Sagar, Twickenham	376
Sakonis, Harrow	358
Sarashwathy Bavans, Wembley	384
Saravanas, Willesden	364
Satyam Restaurant, Edgware	344
Shahanshah , Southall	375
Shayona, Neasden	386
Swadisht, Kenton	359
Tulsi, Wembley	386
Veggie Inn, Harrow	360

Index A–Z

A

222, West Kensington	351
2 Figs, Newington Green	258
Abbey Wood Campsite	400
Accommodation	390
Accountants	15
Adonis, Goodge Street W1	104
African Gallery Kitchen, Euston	110
Africana, Wembley	380
Ah Mirage, Tooting	297
Al Waha, Notting Hill	373
Alara, Bloomsbury	90
Ale, vegetarian	42
Alicer's Veggies	10
Alternative Health Store, Whetstone	260
Amaya, Knightsbridge	324
Ambala, overview	46
Croydon	317
Brick Lane	155
Euston	112
Green St E7	173
Hounslow	362
Ilford	193
Leyton E10	189
Plumstead	313
Southall	375
Tooting	296
Walthamstow E17	191
Wembley	387
Wood Green	260
Amita, Green Street E7	173
Animal Aid	24, 410
Animal Rights	15
Animal Rights Coalition	410
Animals Count	21, 26
Antimony Balance, Farringdon	132
Applejacks, StratfordE15	190
Arabica Food & Spice	
Borough Market	287
Broadway Market	166
ARC	410
Archway	213
Arlington Café, Soho	65
Arlington Cafe, Southwark	284
As Nature Intended, Balham	300
As Nature Intended Chiswick	336
As Nature Intended, Ealing	339

Asamani, Ben	349, 351
Ask Pizza	46
Notting Hill	373
Whiteleys	335
Astor Hostels	398
Athletic Club, Vegetarian	409
Azzurro, South Bank	147

B

B Green Health Food Plus, N3	210
B never too busy to be beautiful	
Carnaby St W1	70
Covent Garden WC2	84
Back to Eden, Clapton E5	182
Backpacker Hostels	398
Bagel Factory, Canary Wharf	168
Baldwin's Health Food, Walworth	306
Balham	300
Balham Wholefood	300
Barty's Creative Catering	402
Basic Wholefoods, Camberwell	303
Battersea	271
Bayswater	332
Beach Burrito Café, Soho	65
Bean Juice, Marylebone	121
Beanie's	10
Bea's Café, WC1 (vegan cakes)	402
Beatroot, Soho	56
Bed & Breakfast, veggie-friendly	390
Beer, vegetarian	42
Bella Italia	46
108 Queensway	335
55 Queensway	335
Ealing New Broadway	338
Ealing The Mall	338
Whiteleys	335
Berwick Street Market, Soho	68
Best, Sarah	29, 35
Bethnal Green	174
BEVEG	404
Beyond Skin women's shoes	38
Bhavna Sweet Mart, Willesden	364
Bhel Poori House, Euston	111
Big Van Company	27
Birkenstock, Covent Garden	85
Bishop-Weston, Johannes	12
Bishop-Weston, Yvonne	22, 23

Blackheath 314
Blah Blah Blah, Shepherds Bush 354
Bliss Patisserie, Angel 234
Bloomsbury 88
B'Nice rice-cream 10
Bodybuilding, Vegan 19
Bodywise Health Foods, Harrow 360
Bodywise Health Foods, Pinner 361
Bodywise Health Foods, Ruislip 388
Bombay Palace, Paddington 332
Bonnington Cafe, Vauxhall 304
Borough Market, London Bridge 287
Bourgeois Boheme 39
Bourke, Alex 6
Box Schemes 15
Breakfast, Hackney 184
Brent Cross 223
Brick Lane 154
Brindisi tapas bar, Borough 287
Bristol Vegan Fayre 44
British Museum 88
Brixton 266
Brixton Market 269
Brixton Wholefoods 269
Broadway Books 162
Broadway Market 162
Broadway Organic Foods 166
Bromley 315
Bromley Animal Rights 404
Bromley Eating Experience 404
Bromley Vegetarian Group 404
Brydon, Nadia, herbalist/raw guru 22, 35
Buddha Café, Soho 63
Buffet V, New Oxford Street 94
Bumblebee, Brecknock Rd N7 241
Burger Stall, Borough Market 287
Bush Garden Café, Shepherds Bush 354
Bushwacker Wholefoods, W6 352
Butler's Thai Cafe, Ealing 338
Bygrave, Liz, raw food teacher 35

C

Café Crema, New Cross 310
Cafe Seventy-Nine, Primrose Hill 249
Cake, Top 5 places for 53
Cakes, where to get a big vegan one 402
Camden 196
Camden Market 196
Camping 399
Canary Wharf 168
Candid Café, Angel 233

Carmen, Clapham 272
Carnevale, the City 130
Carrie Awaze, Covent Garden 79
Carthage, Covent Garden 80
Casse-Croute, South Bank 147
Cat Food, veggie 5, 19
Caterers, veggie 15, 402
Catering, vegan 25
Celebrations, Edgware 342
Central London 49
Centre Point Food Store, Tott Ct Rd 84
Chain restaurants overview 46
Chandni Sweet Mart, West Hendon 223
Chapel Market, Islington 236
Charing Cross 72
Charities that don't send cows 16
Chawalla, Green Street E7 7, 172
Cheese, non-dairy 22
Chegworth Valley, Broadway Market 162
Chelsea 320
Chennai Dosa, Tooting 296
Chennai Dosa Vegetarian, Wembley 380
Chennai Dosa, East Ham E12 170
Chennai Dosa, Wembley 380
Chennai Restaurant, East Ham E12 170
Chhappan Bhog, Kingsbury 368
Chhappan Bhog, Southall 376
Chi, Covent Garden 80
Chingford 192
Chiswick 336
Chor Bizarre, Mayfair 126
Chowpatty, Wembley 380
Chutneys, Euston 109
Cider, veggie scrumpy 42
City Sweet Centre, Stratford E7 173
City, the 128
Clapham 271
Clean Bean Tofu Factory 160
Clicia, Stoke Newington 255
Coby's, Golders Green 215
Coe, Alison 12
Coffee@157 Brick Lane 155
Coffee@Bermondsey St 285
Coffee@Brick Lane 158
Coffee@Goswell Road 138
Coffee@tower bridge rd 285
Coffee@Whitecross St 138
Connoisseurs, Paddington 332
Conservative Party 25
The Conservatory, Knightsbridge 391
Contact Centre, dating 17
Contortionist, vegan 19
Cook, Liz 22

Index A–Z

Coopers, South Bank 145
Cosmetics & Bodycare 16
Cosmetics, Top 5 places for 53
Country Life, W1 51
County Hall, South Bank 143
Courtyard Cafe, Vauxhall 302
Covent Garden 72
Crema Café, New Cross 310
Crocs shoes, Covent Garden 85
Crouch End 244
Croydon 311
Croydon Vegans 405
Croydon Vegetarian Group 405
Crush, Olympia 353
   overview 46
   Canary Wharf Jubilee Place 168
   Canary Wharf Tower Concourse 168
   Earls Court 1 353
   Earls Court 2 353
Crystal Palace 278
Crystal Palace Campsite 399
CTV, Golders Green 215
Cubana, South Bank 147
Cut, the, SE1 143
Cycling Club, Vegetarian 409

D

Dali Universe, SE1 143
Dandelion, Clapham 276
Daniel Field hairdresser, New Barnet 263
Dating agencies, veggie 16
David Wong, Tooting 296
Davis, Andrew, raw food teacher 35
de Boo, Jasmijn, Animals Count 12
Delhi Wala, Hounslow 375
Dentist, vegetarian 19
Dervish, Stoke Newington 254
Diet & Health Centre, Edgware 346
Diwana, Euston 109
Dog Food, veggie 5, 19
Domali, Crystal Palace 280
Dora Rothner veggie B&B 390
Dosa Corner, Wembley 381
Dosa Junction, Wembley 381
Draper, Mrs M, b&b 397
Drummond Street 107
Dulwich 312
Durbar Tandoori, Bayswater 334

E

Ealing 338
Ealing Veggie Group 404
Earls Court 353
Earth Natural Foods, Kentish Town 242
East End emergencies 161
East Ham 170
Eat & Two Veg, Marylebone 119
Eco People, Broadway Market 167
Eco People, Spitalfields 160
Eco, Brixton 266
Eco, Clapham 274
Ecover 43
Edgware 342
Edgware Road 116
Elephant & Castle 306
Embankment 72
Entertainers, veggie 19
Eostre Organics Higbury N7 224
Eostre Organics, Walthamstow E17 191
Equa Boutique, Islington 237
Esme, Brixton 269
Essex 193
Ethical Wares 38
Ethnic restaurants 46
Euphoria @Lorentson's, Brixton 266
Euston 106
Ev, South Bank 148
Events, veggie 45
Evolution gift shop, Bethnal Green 175

F

Falafel cafes, Leicester Square 65
Falafel Queen, Camden 199
Falafels, West End guide 52
FareShares Food Co-op, Walworth 307
Farmaround organic delivery 21
Farmers Market, Stoke Newington 257
Feng Sushi, Borough SE1 287
Feng Sushi, South Bank 152
Festivals Calendar 44
Festival of Life 33
Festival Wines 42
Festivals, Vegan 44
Finchley 208, 390, 397
Finchley Health Food 210
Finsbury Park 211

Indexes

Fiori Corner Cafe, Leicester Square 65
First Out, Covent Garden 78
Fish 25
Fitness & Bodybuilding, Vegan 19
Five Boys, Highbury 226
Food & Fitness, South Chingford E4 192
Food For All, Stoke Newington 257
Food for Thought, Covent Garden 74
Food For Thought, Kingston 282
Forest Gate 172
Foyles Café, Soho 66
Freerangers 38
Fresco, Marylebone 121
Fresco, Paddington 334
Fresco, Westbourne Grove 334
Fresco, Whiteleys 334
Fresh & Wild, Camden 202
Fresh & Wild, Clapham 273
Fresh & Wild, Soho 62
Fresh and Wild, Stoke Newington 253
Fresh Network 28, 35
Friendly Falafels, Hampstead 218
Friends Organic, Roman Road E2 175
Frizzante @ City Farm, Hackney 167
Fruit and Veg stall, Liverpool St 142
Fruit Garden, Marylebone 126
Fry's 10
Fulham 320
Fungus Forays, Hampstead 219
Futures VTA, the City 137

G

Gabriel's Wharf, South Bank 143
Gaby's, Leicester Square 66
Gaia Wholefoods, Twickenham 377
Gallery Café, Bethnal Green E2 153, 177
Gallery Cafe, Holloway Road N7 212
Gallipoli (3 branches), Islington 234
Garden Café, Ladbroke Grove W11 371
Gardener, Jem, Vinceremos 42
Gardening, vegan organic 19
The Gate, Hammersmith 350
Gayatri Sweet Mart, Kingsbury 368
Generator Hostel 398
Get Fresh! Magazine 30
Gi Gi Hut, Euston 113
Giraffe, overview 46
 Battersea 274
 Bloomsbury 95
 Chiswick 336
 Hampstead 219
 Heathrow 1 363
 Islington 234

 Kensington 324
 Marylebone 121
 Muswell Hill 243
 Richmond 290
 South Bank 149
 Spitalfields 159
 Wimbledon 308
Globe Town 174
GNC
 Putney 289
 Wimbledon 308
 Bond St 127
 Bromley 315
 Covent Garden 83
 Muswell Hill 243
 Plaza 68
 Romford 193
 Sutton 317
 Uxbridge 388
Going Veggie or Vegan 27
Golders Green 215
Good Life, Epsom 318
Gossip Café, Broadway Market 164
Govinda's, Soho 57
Grain Shop, Portobello 372
Granard House Fruit & Veg, E9 184
Greasy Spoon cafes, East End 161
Green Baby, Greenwich 281
Green Baby, Islington 237
Green Baby, Notting Hill 374
Green Baby, Richmond 292
Green Cafe, Richmond 289
Green Events magazine 45
Green Note, Camden 201
Green Party 25
Green Street, E7 7, 172
Greenbag, Clapham 274
The Greenery Cafe, Farringdon 135
Greenhouse, Wood Green 259
Greenlands Health, Greenwich 281
Greens & Beans Café, Euston 108
Greens & Beans shop, Euston 112
Greens Foods, Victoria 327
Greenwich 281
Gritts, High Barnet 262
The Grocery, Shoreditch E2 188
Guest Houses 390
Gujarati Rasoi, Broadway Market 166
Gujarati Rasoi, Exmouth Market 138
Gumtree 401
Gupta Sweet Centre, Euston 112
Gupta Sweet Centre, Hendon 223

Index A–Z

H

H&T Accountancy   14, 15
Ha Ha Veggie Bar, Camden   199
Hackney   179
Haelan Centre, Crouch End   245
Haggerston Store, E8   183
Hairdressers, veggie   20
Hammersmith   347, 390, 397
Hampstead   218, 394
Hampstead Cuisine School   221
Hampstead Health Food   219
Hampstead Village Guest House   394
Hare & Tortoise, overview   46
    Bloomsbury   96
    Ealing   338
    Kensington   324
    Putney   288
Harlow, Vegan   405
Harrow   356
Harrow Vegetarian Society   405
HSA (Hunt Saboteurs Association)   405
Health Craze, Earls Court   327
Health Craze, South Kensington   327
Health First, Kingsbury   370
Health First, Wembley   387
Health Food Centre, Warren Street   100
Health Food Centre, Balham   301
Health Foods, Fulham   328
Health Matters, Dulwich   313
Health My God Given Wealth   337
Health Store, Tooting   297
Health Zone Ltd, Wimbledon   308
Healthy Harvest Food Store   377
Healthy Image, West Hampstead   222
Heathrow – where to eat   363
Heavenstone, Liz, apartments   393
Helios, Covent Garden   86
Hendon   223
Herbalism, Medical   22
Hertsveg   405
Highbury   224
Higher Taste, Newington Green   258
Highgate   227
Hing Loong, Borough   285
Hive Bar & Restaurant, Brixton   268
Holidays, veggie   18, 20
Holloway Road   212, 224

Hollyhock Café, Richmond   289
Honest Foods, Brixton   268
Hookah Lounge, Brick Lane   158
Hooper, Dr Mike, vegan GP   11
Hornbeam Café, Walthamstow E17   191
Hostels   398
Hotels   390
Hounslow   362
Hoxton   185
Hoxton Fruit & Veg, N1   186
Hugo's Restaurant, Queens Park   364
Human Nature, NW6   365
Hummus Bros, Soho   67
Hunt Saboteurs Association   405
Hypnotherapy   20
Hypnotherapy training   43

Holland & Barrett

Overview   46
Barking   193
Baker St W1   125
Barnet   262
Blackheath   316
Bloomsbury WC1   97
Bond St W1   127
Brent Cross   223
Bromley   316
Camden   205
Catford   316
Charing Cross Rd   69
Cheapside   141
Chelsea   328
Chiswick   337
Clapham, Northcote Rd   277
Clapham, St Johns Rd   277
Covent Garden   83
Dalston   183
Ealing Broadway   340
Earls Court   329
Eastcote   388
East Ham   171
Edmonton N9   261
Eltham   316
Embankment, Villiers Street   84
Enfield   262
Epsom   318
Fulham Road   329

Golders Green   217
Hammersmith   353
Hampstead   219
Harrow   361
High Holborn   141
Holloway Road N7   212
Hounslow   363
Ilford   193
Islington, 212 Upper St N1   236
Islington, 31 Upper St N1   236
Jerdan Place, Fulham   329
Kensington Church St   372
Kensington High St   329
Kilburn   367
Kingston   282
Knightsbridge   329
Leadenhall St   141
Lewisham   316
Loughton   194
Ludgate Circus   141
Mare St, Hackney E8   183
Marylebone High St   124
Muswell Hill   243
Norbury   295
Oxford St   69
Palmers Green N13   261
Peckham   316
Pimlico   329
Putney   288
Queensway   335
Richmond   290
Romford   194
Shepherds Bush   355
St Johns Wood NW8   246
Stratford E15   190
Surrey Quays   316
Sutton   318
Swiss Cottage   222
Tooting   297
Twickenham   377
Uxbridge   388
Victoria   328
Walthamstow E17   191
Wembley   387
West Ealing   340
Whitechapel   159
Whitgift Croydon   318
Wimbledon   308
Wood Green   260
Woolwich   316

I

Ice-cream (dairy-free)   20
Los Iguanas, South Bank   152
IMAX cinema, South Bank   143
Incredible Edibles, Kings Cross   238
Indian Deli, Hounslow   362
Indian Veg Bhelpuri   195, 231
Indian Vegetarians, Young   409
Inshoku, South Bank   149
InSpiral Lounge, Camden   198
Inverness Street Market, Camden   200
Islington   229
Islington Farmers' Market   237
It's A Green Thing, Crystal Palace   279
Ital and Vital Takeaway, Seven Sisters 260
Italian restaurants, overview   46

J

Jackson & Jackson, accountants   15
Jacob's, Glouocester Rd SW7   325
Jacobs, Brian, hypnotherapist   20, 43
Jai Krishna, Finsbury Park   211
Jains, Young   406
Jashan, Wembley   381
Jasmin, Clapham   275
Jays Pure, Kingsbury   369
John Lewis Coffee Shop   122
Joi, Tottenham Court Rd   103
Julian Graves, Epsom   318
Julian Graves, Oxford St   69
Just Falafs, Covent Garden   75
Just Falafs, Soho   58
Just Natural, Crouch End   244

K

Kalamaras, Bayswater   335
Karnaphuli, Stoke Newington   255
Kastoori, Tooting   298
Kennington   306
Kensington   320
Kentish Town   240
Kenton   357
Kilburn   364
Kings Cross   229, 238
Kingsbury   368
Kingsland High St, E8   184
Kingsland Road, E8   184
Kingston & Richmond Vegetarians   406
Kingston-upon-Thames   282

Index A–Z

Klein, Christine 143
Knight, Andrew, the ethical vet 11
Knightsbridge 320
Konditor & Cook, South Bank 149

L

Landfield Fruit & Veg, E5 183
Lane, Robin 12
Lanesborough Hotel 391
Late night munchies, East 184
Late night West End 53
Le Mignon, Camden 203
Le Pain Quotidien, overview 46
  Covent Garden 82
  Kensington High Street W8 326
  Kings Road SW3 326
  Marylebone 123
  South Bank 151
  South Kensington SW7 326
  St Pancras 238
Leather 13, 37
Leather Lane Market 142
Lebanese cafes, Edgware Rd 124
Lebanese restaurants, overview 46
Lee Valley Camping 399
Lee Valley Campsite 400
Lemon Grass, Camden 205
Lennie's Larder, Shoreditch E2 185
Lennie's Snack Bar, Shoreditch E2 186
Leon, overview 46
  Bankside 285
  Canary Wharf 169
  Cannon St 139
  Carnaby St 67
  Knightsbridge 325
  Ludgate Circus 139
  Regent St 122
  Spitalfields 159
  Strand 81
Leon's Catering 402
Lesbian Vegan Group 406
Levant, Marylebone 122
Lewisham 312, 314
Lewisham Market, SE13 312
Leyton 189, 192
Leytonstone 189
Liberal Democrats 25

Lifescape magazine 20
Lincoln House Hotel 392
Little Miss Tree 35
Liz Heavenstone apartments 393
Local Groups 404
London Animal Rights 406
London Bridge 284
London Buddhist Centre, E2 175
London Eye 143
London Fields park 162
London Vegan Festival 44, 404
London Vegans 407
Loot 401
Lorentson's, Brixton Market 266
Los Iguanas, South Bank 152
Lounge Bar, Brixton 267
Lower Marsh, Waterloo 143
Lower Marsh Market, Waterloo 152
LSE Café, Aldwych 81
Luscious Organic, Kensington 321
Lush
  Bromley 315
  Covent Garden 84
  Carnaby St 69
  Croydon 317
  Kingston 282
  Liverpool Street Station 142
  Portobello 371
  Regent St 69
  Romford 194
  South Molton St 127
  Victoria 330
  Wimbledon 309

M

Macrobiotics 22
Madder Rose Cafe, Primrose Hill 248
Magazines 20
Malaysian vegan 54
Man Chui III. Finchley 208
Man Chui, Kenton 356
Manna, Primrose Hill 247
Manor Park 170
Mantanah Thai Cuisine, Peckham 313
Maoz, Soho 59
Marchmont Street, WC1 88
Market Place, Acton 355

Marks & Spencer, Covent Garden	87
Marrakech, Camden	200
Maru's Bhajia House, Wembley	382
Mary Ward Café, Bloomsbury	91
Marylebone	116
Max Orient Buffet, Camden	204
Mayfair	126
Mayura, Edgware	342
McCartney, Stella, Mayfair shop	127
Meat substitutes	22
Medical Herbalism	22
Meeras Health Food Ctr, Willesden	366
Mehta, Nitin, M.B.E.	409
Mercado Cantina, Stoke Newington	255
Meson Don Felipe, South Bank	150
Meze Café, Great Portland Street	114
Middlesex	388
Mildred's, Soho	60
Milk 'n' Honey, Golders Green	216
Milk, soya	26
Millenium Healthfoods, Ealing	340
Mirch Masala, Tooting	297
Mishel, children's entertainer	19
Mistry, House of, Hampstead	220
Mistry, Willesden	366
Moggy Fodder, vegan	19
Montignac Boutique, S. Kensington	330
Monty's Tandoori, Ealing	341
mOrganics Café, Hoxton E2	187
mOrganics shop, Hoxton E2	187
Mother Earth, Highbury	225
Mother Earth, Newington Green	258
Mother Earth, Stoke Newington	257
Mount View Guest House	396
Moving to London	401
Mr Man, Edgware	343
Muang Thai, Camden	207
Muslim Veg Society	406
Muswell Hill	243
My Village, Camden	206

N

Naklank Catering	402
Naklank Sweet Mart, Wembley	382
National Organisations	410
National Theatre, South Bank	143
Natraj, South Harrow	356
Natural Food Store, Turnham Green	337
Natural Health, N12	210
Natural Shoe Store	85
Nature's Choice, Leytonstone E11	189

Nature's Way, Streatham	295
Neal's Yard	73
Neal's Yard Remedies	
Blackheath	315
Borough	287
Camden	207
Carnaby St	70
Chelsea	329
Clapham	277
Covent Garden	86
Kingston	282
Marylebone	126
Notting Hill	374
Richmond	292
St Pancras	238
Neal's Yard Salad Bar, Covent Gdn	76
Neale, Graham	26
New Cross	310
Newington Green	250
Noah's Health Foods, Wallington	318
North End Road Market, Fulham	330
North West Vegetarian Group	408
Northcote Road Market, Clapham	277
Norwood	313
Notting Hill	371
Notting Hill Tandoori	373
Novellino, Golders Green	217
Nutri Centre, Great Portland St W1	114
Nutrition	22
Nutritionists	22

O

OHFS Natural Foods, Archway	213
Old Vic Theatre	143
Olive Tree, Willesden	366
Oliver's Wholefood, Kew	290
Olympia	353
Omegas	25
Omshree Sweet Mart, Pinner	356
Organic & Natural, Clapton E5	182
Organic Café, Chelsea	320
Organic Delivery Company	402
Ottolenghi, Islington N1	234
The Ottomans, Finchley	208
OXO Tower Restaurant, South Bank	150

Index A–Z

P

Pain Quotidien, see Le Pain Quotidien
Paradise Foods, Kentish Town 240
Paradiso, South Bank 151
Parker, Catherine, raw teacher 33, 35
Pavilion Café, Highgate Wood 227
Peking Palace, Archway 214
Pembury Fruit & Veg, Lower Clapton 184
Pembury Tavern, Hackney E8 179
People for the Ethical Treatment
   of Animals 13, 410
Peppercorn's, Goodge Street W1 104
Peppercorn's, West Hampstead 220
Pepperton UK, Croydon 311
PETA 13, 410
Phoenicia, Kentish Town 240
Phoenix Palace, Marylebone NW1 123
Piccadilly Hostel 398
Picnic, Bloomsbury 88
Picnic, West End 53
Pilgrims, Newington Green 258
Pili Pili, Welling 312
Ping Pong, South Bank 152
Pinner 356
Pita, Golders Green 216
Pitfield Brewery 42
Pizza Express, overview 46
   Ealing 339
   Porchester Rd W2 335
Pizza Parlour, Wembley 383
Place Below, The, Cheapside 131
Planet Organic, Fulham 322
Planet Organic, Islington 236
Planet Organic, Tottenham Ct Rd 102
Planet Organic, Westbourne Grove 333
Plant Based Nutrition 22, 25
Plumstead 313
Pogo Café, Hackney E8 181
Political Parties 25
Pooja, Tooting 297
Portobello Market 373
Portobello Whole Foods 372
Pradip, Kenton 357
Prelabito, Broadway Market 162
Pret-à-Manger 46
Primrose Hill 246, 393
Prince Charles Cinema 71

Protecting Animals in Democracy 26
Provender Wholefoods, SE23 314
Pub on the Park, London Fields 184
Pulse, London Bridge 284
Pure, Moregate 133
Pure Health, Southgate N14 261
Pure, Peter, Raw Food Party 35
Putney 288

Q

Queens Health Shop, SW7 331
Queens Wood Cafe 227
Quiet Revolution, Marylebone 123

R

Rainforest Creations
   overview, Spitalfields 161
   Chelsea 320
   Hammersmith 352
   Alexandra Palace N22 259
Rajen's Thali Hut, West Hendon 222
Ram's Gujarati Restaurant, Kenton 357
Ram's Gujarati Sweet Shop, Kenton 357
Randa, Kensington Church St 331
Rani, Finchley 209
Ranyard, Claire 174
Rasa Express, Euston 113
Rasa Express, Rathbone St W1 103
Rasa, Mayfair 120
Rasa, Stoke Newington 252
Ravi Shankar, Euston 110
Raw Fairies 35
Raw Food 29
Raw Food Party 408
Raw Food School, the 35
Raw restaurants 34
Realfood 411
The Red Hedgehog, Highgate 228
Red Veg, Soho 61
Removals 26

Revital Health Shop
   Belsize Park 221
   Hounslow 363
   Marylebone 125
   Richmond 292

Ruislip 388
Victoria 331
Willesden 366
Rice Cream 10
Richmond & Kingston Vegetarians 406
Richmond-upon-Thames 289
Ridley Road Market, Dalston E8 184
Rimini Café, Leicester Square 65
Riverside Vegetaria, Kingston 283
Roman Road Market, E2 175
Romford 193
Ronak Restaurant, Forest Gate E7 172
Ronny, vegan chef & author 41, 42
Rootmaster, Brick Lane 156
Rootmaster Catering 403
Rose, Kingsbury 368
Rotana Lounge, Knightsbridge 331
Rother, Dora B&B 390
Rother, Stephanie B&B 390
Royal Festival Hall, South Bank 143
Royal Sweets, Alperton 383
Royal Teas, Greenwich 281
Rubber Ritchie, vegan contortionist 19
Ruislip 388
Rye Wholefoods, Clerkenwell 136

S

S&M Café, Portobello 373
S.G. Manning, Brixton Hill 270
S.W.A. The Way to Stay 397
Saf, Shoreditch 134
Sagar, Tottenham Court Road 101
Sagar, Hammersmith 352
Sagar, Twickenham 376
Sakonis, Forest Gate E7 173
Sakonis, Harrow 358
Sakonis, Wembley 383
Sanghamam, Wembley 385
Santok Maa's, Thornton Heath 309
Sarashwathy Bavans, Tooting 299
Sarashwathy Bavans, Wembley 384
Saravana Bhavan, East Ham E12 170
Saravana Bhavan, Rayners Lane 358
Saravanaa Bhavan, Wembley 385
Saravanas, Willesden 364
Satyam Restaurant, Edgware 344
Satyam Sweet Mart 345
SEAR (South-East Animal Rights) 408
Second Nature, Walthamstow E17 192
Sedlescombe Wines 42, 160
Sesame Health Foods, Primrose Hill 246

Seven Sisters Rail Station 261
Sewardstone Campsite 400
Shahanshah , Southall 375
Shahee Bhelpoori, Streatham 294
Shambu's Catering 403
Shamsudeen, Stoke Newington 256
Shay Naiy Sweet Mart, Edgware 345
Shayona Caterers 403
Shayona, Neasden 386
Shayona, Pinner 358
Shayona, Wembley 385
Sheel Pharmacy, Lewisham 314
Shepherds Bush 347
Shiv Darshan Sweets, Tooting 297
Shivalanka, Lakshmi, Herbalist 22
Shoe repairs 38
Shoes & accessories 26
Shoes, vegetarian 37, 86
Shoreditch 185
Simply Natural, Wanstead E11 190
Singapore Sam, Canary Wharf 169
Skiing, Veggie 18
Sloane Zone 320
Sofra, Mayfair 126
Sofra, St Christopher's Place 126
Soho 50
Solché Cilician, Broadway Market 163
Souk, The, Trafalgar Square 82
Soup + Salad, E1 159
Soups & Salads, Canary Wharf 169
South Bank 143
South West London Veg Info Centre 408
Southall 375
South-East Animal Rights 408
Soya Milk 26
Spice Green, Forest Gate E7 173
Spirited Palace, Crystal Palace 278
Spital Felafel 160
Spitalfields Market 155, 160
Spitalfields Organics 160
Spizzico, High Barnet 262
Spring Gardens Cafe, Vauxhall 305
Sri Rathiga, Harrow 359
St Christoper's Hostels 398
St Gabriel Cafe, Finsbury Park N4 211
St Gabriel Cafe, Kennington SE11 306
Stachowska, Dominika 11
Stella McCartney, Mayfair shop 127
Stephanie Rothner B&B 390
Stockwell Healthy Living, Ealing 340
Stoke Newington 250
Stratford, E15 190
Straw Bale Café, Highury 224

Index A–Z

Streatham 293
Sukhsagar Sweet Mart, Hounslow 362
Supreme Sweets, Kingsbury 368
Suraj Sweet Mart, Wembley 386
Surrey & Twickenham Veg Group 408
Sushi, Canary Wharf 169
Swaad, Leytonstone E11 189
Swad, Thornton Heath 312
Swadisht, Kenton 359
Sweet Sensations, raw food classes 35
Synergy Centre, Oval 302

T

Taboon Bakery, Golders Green 217
Tai Buffet, Camden 204
Tai Buffet, Euston 113
Tai Buffet, Islington 233
Tai Buffet, Piccadilly 63
Tai Express, Old Compton St 64
Tai Veg, Gt Chapel St 64
Tai, Greek Street 63
Tamu Tamu, Edgware 345
Tas, Borough SE1 286
Tas, British Museum 96
Tas, The Cut 146
Tas, Farringdon Rd 139
Tas Café, Borough SE1 286
Tas Firin, Bethnal Green E2 158
Tas Pide, London Bridge 286
Temple Health Foods, NW11 217
Temple Lodge 390
Tesco, Covent Garden 87
Thai Garden, Bethnal Green E2 178
Thai Restaurant, Ealing 341
Thai Square, Islington 235
Thornton Heath, Surrey 312
Tide Tables, Richmond 291
Tiffin Bites, Canary Wharf 169
Tiffin Bites, Liverpool St 139
Tiffin Bites, Moorgate 139
Tiffin Bites, St Pauls 139
TLC Dental Surgery, Plaistow E13 171
Today's Living, Clapham 276
Tony's, Kings Cross 239
Tooting 296
Top 5 53
Total Organics, Marylebone 125

Total Organics, Borough Market 287
Tottenham Court Road 98
Travel, veggie 47
Travel guides 26
Troia, South Bank 151
Tulsi, Wembley 386
Tupelo Honey, Camden 203
Turkish restaurants, overview 46
TV on the internet 26
Twickenham 376
Twickenham & Surey Veg Group 408
Two Figs, Newington Green 258
Two Two Two, West Kensington 351

U

Udupi Palace, Kingsbury 370
Union News, South Bank 286
Uno, Café, overview 46
    Ealing 341
Unpackaged, Exmouth Market EC1 238
Updates to this book 6, 47

V

Vauxhall 302
Veg Essex 409
Veg, Theobald's Rd 94
Vegan Buddies 27, 411
Vegan Campaigns 409
Vegan Cobbler 38
Vegan Harlow 405
The Vegan magazine 20
Vegan Organic Network 19
Vegan Society 14, 15, 16
Vegan Stall, Borough Market 287
Vegan Stall, Broadway Market 166
Vegan Views magazine 20
Vegan, going 27
VegCom 401
Vegepets.info 14
Vegetarian & Vegan Foundation 21
Vegetarian Cycling & Athletic Club 409
Vegetarian Guides 47
Vegetarian Paradise, Bloomsbury 94
Vegetarian Shoes 36–37
Vegetarian Society 411
Vegetarians International Voice

for Animals (Viva!)	21
Vegfam charity	17
Veggie Inn, Harrow	360
Veggie Matchmakers	17
Veggie Roadshows	44
Veggie Snow	18
Veggie Vision	9
Veggie, going	27
Veggiepets.com	5
Veggies Catering Campaign	403, 411
Vegi Ventures	18
Victoria Health Foods, Muswell Hill	244
Victoria Park	174
Viet Hoa, Hoxton E2	188
Vinceremos	40
Vintage Roots	40
Vita Health, Leyton E10	192
VitaOrganic, Soho	54
Viva!	21, 44
VVF	21

W

Wagamama, overview	46
Bloomsbury (menu)	93
Brent Cross	223
Camden	204
Canary Wharf	169
Covent Garden	82
Fleet Street	140
Haymarket	68
Heathrow 5	363
Islington	235
Kensington	326
Kingston	282
Leicester Square	68
Liverpool St	140
London Bridge	286
Mansion House	140
Moorgate	140
Putney	288
Richmond	290
Soho	68
South Bank	152
Tower Hill	140
Wigmore St	124
Wai, Goodge Street W1	103
Walthamstow	191
Walthamstow Market	192
Walworth	306
Wanstead, E11	190
Wanted for next edition	27
Wasabi Sushi, Embankment	83

Waterloo	143
Well Bean, Blackheath	314
Well Being Foods, SE26	315
Welling, Kent	312
Wembley	378
West End	50
West End dinner, top 5	53
West End lunch, top 5	53
West Hampstead	221
West Hendon	222
What's On Listings	27
Wheatley's, Clerkenwell	136
Whole Foods Market, Kensington	323
Wholemeal Café, Streatham	293
Wholemeal Shop, Well Street E9	167
Wholsum, Dalston E8	182
Wild Cherry Catering	403
Wild Cherry, Bethnal Green E2	176
Willesden	364
Wimbledon	308
Window, the, Islington	403
Wine and Beer, veggie	26
Wine, vegetarian	41
Wok, Acton	355
Wombledon	308
Woodfield Organics, Ealing	341
Woodlands, Chiswick	336
Woodlands, Hampstead	218
Woodlands, Piccadilly	64
Woodlands, Marylebone	118
Woolley's, Theobalds Road	96
World Food Café, Covent Garden	77

Y

Yagga	7
YHA hostels	398
Young Indian Vegetarians	409
Young Jains	406
Young Vic Theatre	143
Youth Hostels Association	398
Yum Yum, Clapham SW11	276
Yum Yum, Stoke Newington N16	256
Yumnation, Holborn	92

Z

Zelda's Pod, N1	232
Zen Garden, Leather Lane	137
Zephaniah, Benjamin	7
Zero, Hoxton	161
Zigni House, Essex Road	235

VEGAN PASSPORT

edited by George Rodger of the Vegan Society

The passport-sized travelling companion for vegans has 56 languages, covering 93% of the world's population, with a page for each saying what vegans do and don't eat in great detail. Let the waiter show it to the cook and you'll be sure of a totally vegan, animal-free feast in restaurants anywhere even if no one speaks a word of your language.

Includes English, Afrikaans, Albanian, Arabic, Basque, Bengali, Bulgarian, Catalan, Chinese, Croatian, Czech, Danish, Dutch, Finnish, French, German, Goan, Greek, Gujurati, Hebrew, Hindi, Hungarian, Indonesian, Italian, Japanese, Kannada, Korean, Malagasay, Malay, Maltese, Marathi, Mongolian, Nepali, Norwegian, Persian, Polish, Portuguese, Romanian, Russian, Serbian, Shona, Sinhalese, Slovak, Somali, Spanish, Swahili, Swedish, Tagalog, Tamil, Thai, Turkish, Ukrainian, Urdu, Vietnamese, Yoruba, Esperanto... Plus a page of pictures of what we do and don't eat if all else fails.

The essential companion to *Vegetarian Europe*.

Available from Vegetarian Guides

VEGETARIAN
EUROPE

by Alex Bourke

"This travel guide covers the top 48 destinations in Europe - where to stay and where to eat - and is an ideal springboard for that European holiday you always wanted to take, but were unsure about the food." - **The Vegetarian Society**

"A wacky guide to the best vegetarian eateries. If eating in, take some tips on urban foraging for ingredients. Veggie Vocab lists phrases to help you shop." - **The Times**

The Euroveggie comprehensive guide
300 scrumptious vegetarian restaurants, cafes and take-aways in 48 cities in 23 countries.

Top weekend destinations + tourist hotspots
Amsterdam, Athens, Barcelona, Brussels, Copenhagen, Dublin, London, Prague.... Big Paris section.

In depth reviews
by researchers who live in the cities.

Totally independent
no restaurant pays to be in the guide.

Vegetarian Guides

from www.vegetarianguides.co.uk

VEGETARIAN
BRITAIN

edited by Alex Bourke

170 vegetarian, vegan and veg-friendly hotels and guest houses, 600 restaurants and cafes, 500 health food stores.

Features in-depth coverage of holiday hotspots Brighton, Cornwall, Devon, Edinburgh, Lake District, London, Scottish Highlands and Wales. A full page for guest houses tells you what's in the area so you don't need to send off for brochures, room prices per person, directions, what's on the menu for vegans.

Perfect for weekends away, holidays and dining out in a new town. Includes maps and indexes for vegan, dog-friendly and children welcome.

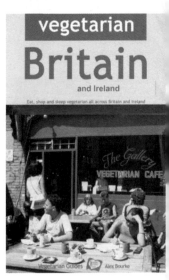

Read extracts and purchase at

www.vegetarianguides.co.uk